D1520653

Critical Essays on

EMILY BRONTË

CRITICAL ESSAYS
ON
BRITISH LITERATURE

Zack Bowen, General Editor
University of Miami

Critical Essays on
EMILY BRONTË

edited by

THOMAS JOHN WINNIFRITH

G. K. Hall & Co.
An Imprint of Simon & Schuster Macmillan
New York

Prentice Hall International
London   Mexico City   New Delhi   Singapore   Sydney   Toronto

G. K. Hall & Co.
An Imprint of Simon & Schuster Macmillan
1633 Broadway
New York, NY 10019

Library of Congress Cataloging-in-Publication Data

Critical essays on Emily Brontë / edited by Thomas John Winnifrith.
    p. cm.—(Critical essays on British literature)
  Includes bibliographical references and index.
  ISBN 0-7838-0008-8 (alk. paper)
  1. Brontë, Emily, 1818–1848—Criticism and interpretation.
  2. Women and literature—England—History—19th century
I. Winnifrith, Tom. II. Series.
PR4173.C75 1997
823′.8—dc20   96-30937
                                       CIP

10 9 8 7 6 5 4 3 2 1

Printed in the United States of America

Contents

Acknowledgments	ix
General Editor's Note	xi
Publisher's Note	xiii
Introduction	1
THOMAS JOHN WINNIFRITH	

BIOGRAPHY

Introduction	5
THOMAS JOHN WINNIFRITH	
Brontë's Religion	8
THOMAS JOHN WINNIFRITH	
Brontë's Reading and Education	19
JOHN HEWISH	
The Themes of *Wuthering Heights*	33
EDWARD CHITHAM	
Brontë in 1845	48
JULIET BARKER	
The Hidden Ghost	52
WINIFRED GERIN	
The Shattered Prison	55
KATHLEEN FRANK	

POETRY

Introduction	59
THOMAS JOHN WINNIFRITH	

A Reconstruction of Gondal   61
    FANNY RATCHFORD

The Gondal Saga   62
    MARY VISICK

Emily Brontë: The Latitude of Interpretation   77
    DENIS DONOGHUE

The Lyricism of Emily Brontë   90
    BARBARA HARDY

Brontë as Heretic   109
    STEVIE DAVIES

WUTHERING HEIGHTS: THE FIRST HUNDRED YEARS

Introduction   115
    THOMAS JOHN WINNIFRITH

Wuthering Heights   119
    MARY WARD

Jane Eyre and Wuthering Heights   130
    VIRGINIA WOOLF

The Structure of Wuthering Heights   132
    C. P. SANGER

Emily Brontë and Wuthering Heights   144
    DAVID CECIL

Tempest in the Soul: The Theme and Structure
of Wuthering Heights   151
    MELVIN WATSON

Emily Brontë: Wuthering Heights   161
    ARNOLD KETTLE

CRITICISM 1950–1975

Introduction   177
    THOMAS JOHN WINNIFRITH

Nelly Dean and the Power of Wuthering Heights   180
    JOHN MATHISON

The Rejection of Heathcliff?   198
    MIRIAM ALLOTT

A Fresh Approach to *Wuthering Heights*   205
   QUEENIE LEAVIS

Wuthering Heights   216
   FRANK KERMODE

Wuthering Heights   223
   TERRY EAGLETON

CRITICISM 1975–1995

Decoding *Wuthering Heights*   243
   GILLIAN FRITH

Select Bibliography   263
Index   269

Acknowledgments

◆

The editor would like to acknowledge the permission granted to print the essays in this volume from the following sources. The Macmillan Press is thanked for allowing extracts from T. J. Winnifrith, *The Brontës and Their Background*, J. Hewish, *Emily Brontë*, and T. Eagleton, *Myths of Power*. Blackwells is thanked for allowing an extract from E. Chitham, *A Life of Emily Brontë*. Weidenfeld and Nicholson is thanked for allowing an extract from J. Barker, *The Brontës*. Oxford University Press is thanked for allowing an extract from W. Gerin, *Emily Brontë*. Houghton Mifflin is thanked for allowing an extract from K. Frank, *A Chainless Soul*. The University of Texas Press is thanked for allowing an extract from F. Ratchford, *Gondal's Queen*. M. Visick is thanked for allowing an extract from her book *The Genesis of Wuthering Heights*, and B. Hardy for allowing an extract from her essay "The Lyricism of Emily Brontë." Harvard University Press is thanked for allowing an extract from D. Donoghue's essay "Emily Brontë: The Latitude of Interpretation." Prentice Hall is thanked for allowing an extract from S. Davies, *Emily Brontë*. Harcourt Brace is thanked for allowing an extract from V. Woolf's essay "*Jane Eyre* and *Wuthering Heights*." Chatto and Windus is thanked for allowing an extract from C. P. Sanger's essay "The Structure of *Wuthering Heights*" and Q. D. Leavis, *Lectures in America*. Constable Publishers is thanked for allowing an extract from D. Cecil, *Early Victorian Novelists*. The University of California Press is thanked for allowing extracts from M. Watson's essay "Tempest in the Soul" and J. Mathison's essay "Nelly Dean and the Power of *Wuthering Heights*." Unwin Hyman is thanked for allowing an extract from A. Kettle's *An Introduction to the English Novel*. The editors of *Essays in Criticism* are thanked for allowing an extract from M. Allott's essay "The Rejection of Heathcliff." Peters, Fraser, and Dunlop is thanked for allowing an extract from F. Kermode, *The Classic*. G. Frith is thanked for allowing the inclusion of her essay on modern criticism of *Wuthering Heights*.

General Editor's Note

◆

The Critical Essays on British Literature series provides a variety of approaches to both classical and contemporary writers of Britain and Ireland. The formats of the volumes in the series vary with the thematic designs of individual editors and with the amount and nature of existing reviews and criticism, augmented, where appropriate, by original essays by recognized authorities. It is hoped that each volume will be unique in developing a new overall perspective on its particular subject.

In the introductory biography, Winnifrith sketches in the salient undisputed facts of Brontë's life before proceeding on to his first series of essays, including his own study of Brontë's religion. The volume is divided into sections of essays on biography, Brontë's poetry, and three separate critical eras: 1848-1951, 1952-75, and 1975-95. Winnifrith provides brief individual introductions to the first four sections, while the voluminous criticism of the last two decades is summarized and discussed in an independent essay by Gillian Frith, especially written for this book. There is a similarly divided bibliography at the end of the book. The selection reflects the recent attention given to Brontë's life in relation to her work and attempts to rectify the comparative dearth of critical attention to her poetry.

ZACK BOWEN
University of Miami

Publisher's Note

◆

Producing a volume that contains both newly commissioned and reprinted material presents the publisher with the challenge of balancing the desire to achieve stylistic consistency with the need to preserve the integrity of works first published elsewhere. In the Critical Essays series, essays commissioned especially for a particular volume are edited to be consistent with G. K. Hall's house style; reprinted essays appear in the style in which they were first published, with only typographical errors corrected. Consequently, shifts in style from one essay to another are the result of our efforts to be faithful to each text as it was originally published.

Introduction

◆

THOMAS JOHN WINNIFRITH

There are a number of obstacles in the way of anyone trying to assemble a collection of critical essays on Emily Brontë. First, there are already many similar collections, listed in the bibliography. Most of these have focused their attention on *Wuthering Heights,* and some have concentrated on modern critics. The number of such collections is an indication of the vast quantity of articles that *Wuthering Heights* has attracted, and this brings us to the second difficulty. A summary of critical opinion without some damaging omissions seems almost impossible, and this is particularly worrying in view of the diversity of opinion. For *Wuthering Heights* is a book that asks difficult questions but does not give easy answers, and indeed the same may be said of Brontë's poetry and life. Is Heathcliff hero or villain? Should we look at him or at the elder Catherine for the key to the story? Are the narrators fools or knaves, both or neither? Does the second generation add to the book or subtract from it? Modern critical trends placing emphasis on the response of the reader rather than the intentions of the writer have found *Wuthering Heights* an unusually rich field for different readings, and no collection of articles can do full justice to this richness.

My solution to these difficulties is as follows. In an effort to add something new to this particular collection, I have devoted more space than is usual to biography. In spite of the unpopularity of biography in certain critical circles and the danger inherent in approaching the novels of the Brontës through a study of their lives, there has been a spate of recent books about the Brontës in general and Emily in particular. Such books seem worthy of some notice. Of course, the dearth of primary material about Emily's early life and the absence of correspondence apart from a few short letters and pathetic diary notes makes any such biography difficult to write, and there has been too much conjecture in many biographies. Nevertheless, it is possible to gain some information about Emily's religious background, her reading, and the circumstances surrounding the writing of *Wuthering Heights,* although there are still various interpretations of Emily's apparent collapse as a writer in the two years before her baffling death.

The poetry of all the Brontës has been unduly neglected, being inadequately edited and used as a kind of adjunct to a study of the novels or as a biographical aid. Emily's superiority as a poet over her sisters is generally recognized, although the rather pedestrian efforts of Charlotte and Anne may have reduced interest in Brontë poetry. There are indeed comparatively few discussions of Emily's poems, and there is therefore nothing of the difficulty that faces the student of *Wuthering Heights* criticism in making a representative choice. There are of course difficulties of interpretation, some of which are connected to the fact that some but not all of the poems are linked to the saga in prose by Emily and Anne about the mysterious land of Gondal. This saga, unlike Charlotte's and Branwell's tales about Angria, has entirely disappeared. In spite of this problem, it seemed right to give reasonable space to some of the articles that show a proper appreciation of Emily's poetic genius.

In trying to tackle the immense number of critical articles on *Wuthering Heights* and their diversity, I have concentrated on a few major analyses written between the years 1900 and 1975. Articles in the last twenty years, of which there is a good selection in P. Stoneman's *New Casebook* on *Wuthering Heights* (London: Macmillan, 1994), are summarized by G. Frith. Contemporary reviews and nineteenth-century opinion can be found in M. Allott's book on *The Brontës* in the *Critical Heritage* series (London: Routledge and Kegan Paul, 1974), but I have included a brief synopsis of this period if only to dispel the popular opinion that nineteenth-century criticism was uniformly hostile and uniformly worthless. Modern criticism is almost entirely favorable but tends to leave the average reader a little bemused, and it is to be hoped that Frith's article will help such readers.

Selections from articles and books have been presented without omissions or alterations except in the case of footnotes, which have been omitted in the case of Mathisons's, Donoghue's, and Kermode's contributions and shortened and altered for the sake of uniformity in other cases. There have been a few other omissions in Donoghue's article. Comment on each critic's presentation is confined to the introduction of each section. References to *Wuthering Heights* are given by chapter in view of the multiplicity of editions. References to poems are given by the page number of the edition by C. W. Hatfield, *The Complete Poems of Emily Jane Brontë* (New York; Columbia University Press, 1941), and to letters by the page, volume, and number of the edition by T. J. Wise and J. A. Symington, *The Brontës: Their Lives, Friendships and Correspondence* (Oxford: Basil Blackwell, 1932).

BIOGRAPHY

Introduction

THOMAS JOHN WINNIFRITH

Unlike Charlotte Brontë, who died a famous woman, whose letters were preserved, and whose novels contain obvious if somewhat misleading links with her life, Emily offers little help to the biographer. We can trace the bare bones of her life usually through association with Charlotte. There are few clues in *Wuthering Heights* and the poetry, although this has not deterred speculation and conjecture. Early biographers, such as Mary Robinson and Charles Simpson, were appreciative but hardly scholarly. Of the biographical commentators selected, John Hewish and Edward Chitham are the best, but even some of their conclusions are open to doubt.

Emily was born on July 30, 1818, in Thornton, Yorkshire. The family moved to Haworth in April 1820, but Mrs. Brontë died 18 months later. Emily attended Cowan Bridge School in 1824 and 1825, but the death of her two elder sisters, Maria and Elizabeth, caused her to be removed. She spent most of the rest of her life at home, receiving some kind of education from her mother's sister, Elizabeth Branwell. The Brontës had few friends but amused themselves with reading and writing. Emily and her younger sister Anne invented an imaginary land called Gondal and wrote poetry and prose stories about it. In 1835 Emily was sent to school at Roe Head, where Charlotte was a teacher, but she did not stay for long, apparently suffering from homesickness. In 1838 and 1839 she was a schoolteacher at Law Hill near Halifax. Chitham was the first to discover the correct date of this stay, and he speculates whether Law Hill and the nearby house of High Sunderland Hall provided some inspiration for *Wuthering Heights*.

At home in 1839 Emily lived with her brother, father, and aunt. Charlotte and Anne were trying to earn their livings as governesses. The Brontës were a religious family, but they did not agree with each other on all points of religious doctrine. In particular the younger Brontës appear to have rejected the orthodox doctrine of such clergymen as their father on eternal punishment for the wicked, and in the first essay I examine ways in which Emily's early poetry points to this rejection. In 1842 Emily and Charlotte went to Belgium where they were taught French by M. Heger, principally and unfairly known as the man with whom Charlotte fell in love and who became the model for her heroes, who are married men or Belgians or schoolmasters or a combination of these. But M. Heger was also a teacher of genius, and it is the great virtue of Hewish's argument in the second extract that he is able to show ways in which the year in Belgium, although providing no material for *Wuthering Heights,* developed Emily as a writer of bold, original, and deep philosophical ideas.

Emily returned home at the end of 1842 and remained at Haworth for the rest of her life. Elizabeth Branwell had died shortly before the sisters reached home, and it seems that it fell to Emily to take on the burden of housekeeping for her father. Charlotte returned to Belgium, and Anne was employed as a governess at the Robinson household, where she was joined by her brother Branwell. Eighteen forty-three and 1844 were years of low poetic output for Emily. It has been suggested that she became proficient in German, and even Latin and Greek, but this is largely conjecture. We do not know when *Wuthering Heights* was started. There is speculation but no certain evidence about Emily's relations with her brother, father, and her two sisters during these years.

In June 1845 Branwell was dismissed from his post. Shortly afterward Anne and Emily wrote the fourth and last of the diary papers, which they had composed at four-year intervals. Extracts from these papers can be found in the selection from Juliet Barker's important book on the Brontës. Barker, the latest but not the last of a long line of Brontë biographers, shows a healthy iconoclasm in questioning a number of Brontë legends. The gloomy but inspiring Emily of most biographers is replaced by a surprisingly cheerful figure, insensitively lost in a world of her own and blind to the troubles of her family. It has to be said that the diary paper rather supports this picture, although subsequent evidence may point in the other direction.

In the autumn of 1845, Charlotte discovered a volume of poems written by her sister. She was impressed by the power of these poems but said that Emily was angry at the discovery. Eventually it was decided to publish a selection from each sister's poetry, and such a selection appeared in May 1846. Already the Brontës had started on their novels, and by July 1846 they were announcing to publishers that they had completed three one-volume novels. It was not until the end of 1847, however, that *Wuthering Heights* was published, and it appeared then as a two-volume novel.

Most of Emily's greatest poems were written during 1845, with the most famous, "No Coward Soul," dated January 2, 1846. Chitham's account of the themes of *Wuthering Heights* is quite right to take account of her poetry, although he perhaps goes too far in trying to draw in other strands of Emily's life in his chapter on her novel. He also has to contend, as do all Brontë biographers, with the apparent collapse of creativity on Emily's part, since we have only the manuscript of one not very good Gondal poem after "No Coward Soul." There is no certain solution to this puzzle. It has been suggested, and Chitham goes along with this possibility, that Emily was busy in 1847 expanding *Wuthering Heights* to make a two-volume novel. It has also been pointed out that Emily may have been writing a second novel, and Barker, without much evidence, thinks that Charlotte destroyed it.

Winifred Gerin raises this possibility and the alternative possibility that Emily may have destroyed the manuscript herself in her discussion of why Emily not only declined as a writer but declined as a person in the last year of her life. The eager death of Emily Brontë has fascinated biographers, perhaps partly because it seems to parallel that of the elder Catherine, summed up rather insensitively by her doctor as a stout, hearty lass, and of Heathcliff, apparently at the height of his powers just before his strange death. Gerin attributes Emily's decline in health and creativity to the shock of having her works published and adversely criticized, whereas Kathleen Frank, whose moving if slightly sentimental account of Emily's death concludes this biographical section, suggests that Catherine, Heathcliff, and Emily were suffering from the fashionable anorexia nervosa. It has to be said that there is little evidence for either hypothesis; the more pragmatic Barker even doubts the well-known story that Emily died on the downstairs sofa still displayed at Haworth parsonage, although it is clear that Emily was still writing after it had been decided to publish her poetry and that criticism of her novel was not as harsh as has sometimes been made out. But the extracts from Frank and Gerin have been included because they do bring out the baffling mixture of weakness and strength, pathos and brutality, even pity and fear that characterize Emily Brontë and many of her creations.

Brontë's Religion

God is the God of justice and mercy; then, assuredly, each pain that he inflicts on his creatures, be they human or animal, rational or irrational, each suffering of our unhappy nature is only a seed for that divine harvest which will be gathered when sin having spent its last drop of poison, death having thrown its last dart, both will expire on the funeral pyre of a universe in flame, and will leave their former victims to an eternal realm of happiness and glory.[1]

For other evidence of Emily's religious position apart from *Wuthering Heights* there are only the poems to consult, since the one piece of biographical information on this subject is singularly unhelpful. In the words of Charlotte,

> *One time I mentioned that someone had asked me what religion I was of (with a view to getting me for a partisan), and that I had said that was between God and me. Emily (who was lying on the hearthrug) exclaimed, "That's right." This was all I ever heard Emily say on religious subjects.* (1, p. 137)

Even the poems have been discounted as evidence by the thesis of Miss Ratchford that they are all part of an immense Gondal Saga. This thesis is difficult to uphold since so many of the poems cannot be fitted into the saga, and there are also inconsistent pieces of evidence such as Emily's annoyance at the discovery of her poems and her division of her poems into two notebooks, only one of which was entitled *Gondal Poems.*[2] In any case we could not ignore the subjective element in the poems, even if they were all part of an immense Gondal saga.

In fact the Gondal element can be used to explain contradictions that do appear in the poems, since it is obvious that not all characters will hold the same theological views. The poems are also written over a period of ten years,[3] during which it would be only natural for the author to modify her views. In spite of these two reservations there is in the poems a considerable body of evidence to support the view that Emily held the following consistent and connecting set of axioms: (1) Hell exists only on earth, and no souls suffer

*Reprinted from T. Winnifrith, *The Brontës and Their Background* (London: Macmillan, 1973), 63–75.

torment after death. (2) A soul that has suffered sufficiently on earth attains its heaven. (3) A soul that has not suffered is in limbo for a time, but is redeemed by others' sufferings if not by its own, after enduring the *poena damni*, deprivation of the desired heaven.

In poems written before 1840 there are plenty of references to stoical suffering (pp. 36, 59), a childhood heaven similar to that described in *Wuthering Heights* (pp. 39, 40, 121–22, 135), and a general sympathy with sinners.

> *Do I despise the timid deer*
> *Because his limbs are fleet with fear?*
> *Or would I mock the wolf's death-howl*
> *Because his form is gaunt and foul?*
> *Or hear with joy the leveret's cry*
> *Because it cannot bravely die?* (pp. 132–33)

There are also traces of a rather Wagnerian doctrine of redemption, not through suffering, but through love. Such a doctrine does draw attention to a difficulty of orthodox believers in hell. If one was virtuous and loved someone who was not, then after death, not only did the wicked suffer the hell, but the righteous suffered in heaven deprived of the presence of the loved one and tortured by thoughts of his torture. The problem may seem an artificial one, relying as it does on a rather literal view of the after-life. But it was not thought artificial in the nineteenth century, finding expression in poems like *Festus* and *The Blessed Damozel*.[4] Emily Brontë saw the problem and was to find a solution to it, although not perhaps in this early period, in which the poems contain plenty of references to heaven and hell but no very convincing exposition of the three axioms and some contradictions of them.

> *Shut from his Maker's smile*
> *The accursed man shall be:*
> *Compassion reigns a little while,*
> *Revenge eternally.* (p. 121)

In the next four years Emily wrote poems that did much to clear away the cobwebs of a conventional heaven and hell. Eternal punishment is clearly rejected,

> *No; that I feel can never be;*
> *A God of hate could hardly bear*
> *To watch through all eternity*
> *His own creation's dread despair! . . .,*

and suffering brings salvation,

> *If I have sinned, long, long ago*
> *That sin was purified by woe.* (p. 138)

The first two axioms are also supported in other poems (pp. 138–45), but the third is only hinted at in the idea of atonement,

> *There let thy bleeding branch atone*
> *For every torturing tear . . .* (p. 150)

and the idea that the souls of the wicked do have some hope from the help of the good,

> *And in all space, and in all time,*
> *And through Eternity,*
> *To aid a Spirit lost in crime,*
> *I have no hope but thee.* (pp. 151–52)

On the other hand the latter passage comes from a poem which contains lines like,

> *The guiltless blood upon my hands*
> *Will shut me out from Heaven . . .,* (p. 151)

which appear to re-assert the orthodox beliefs, and it is very difficult to formulate a coherent philosophy from poems of which the interpretation is so obscure.

In the last period of her life from 1844 onwards, Emily Brontë worked her way towards a clear picture of how heaven was won and what it was like, as she herself worked her own grim way to salvation. It is harder to find contradiction of the axioms, and there is an abundance of references to support them. The lines,

> *No promised Heaven, these wild Desires*
> *Could all or half fulfil;*
> *No threatened Hell, with quenchless fires,*
> *Subdue this quenchless will! . . .,* (p. 220)

suggest a rejection of the conventional heaven and hell; indeed conventional religion is condemned in,

> *Vain are the thousand creeds*
> *That move men's hearts, unutterably vain*
> *Worthless as withered weeds,*
> *Or idlest froth amid the boundless main.* (p. 243)

It is also satisfying to find the sinful A.G.A. apparently winning a quiet grave. The intensely moving lines,

> *I would lose no sting, would wish no torture less;*
> *The more that anguish racks the earlier it will bless;*

> *And robed in fires of Hell, or bright with heavenly shine,*
> *If it but herald Death, the vision is divine . . ., (p. 239)*

contain a clear statement of the second axiom.

What is less certain is the third axiom. This is a pity, because without it the doctrine is sinisterly masochistic. The more we suffer in this world, the quicker we get what we want in the next, Emily may have reflected as she tottered down to feed the animals on the day of her death, but such an attitude is selfish and short-sighted if it leads, as it did in Heathcliff's case, to the misery of others. There are traces of asceticism in Emily's life and lines like,

> *So stood I, in Heaven's glorious sun*
> *And in the glare of Hell*
> *My spirit drank a mingled tone*
> *Of seraph's song and demon's moan . . ., (p. 196)*

and the doctrine, found in the essay on *The Butterfly,* that we do not and should not suffer for our own salvation but for the sake of others, sometimes finds it hard to make its way against this *Schadenfreude.* The doctrine is best suggested in the lines,

> *Yet thou a future peace shall win*
> *Because thy soul is clear;*
> *And I who had the heart to sin*
> *Will find a heart to bear.*
> *Till far beyond earth's frenzied strife*
> *That makes destruction joy,*
> *Thy perished faith shall spring to life*
> *And my remorse shall die. (p. 198)*

The words,

> *Strike it down, that other boughs may flourish*
> *Where that perished sapling used to be . . ., (p. 225)*

give the necessary idea of sacrifice, though much of the sacrifice and despair of the poems seems purposeless, just as much of the grimness and the brutality of *Wuthering Heights* seem to have no message of hope.

The composition of *Wuthering Heights* is usually dated to the last period of Emily's life, although this is not certain.[5] The novel gives a fairly definite, though cryptic, account of salvation won by suffering; there are references to more orthodox heavens and hells, but these are by implication criticised. The only satisfactory guide to Emily's beliefs in *Wuthering Heights* is an analysis of all references to heaven and hell; we can eliminate merely the conventional uses of heaven as a synonym for God, hell for death, and both heaven and hell in oaths. Even these conventional uses are perhaps indicative of the way in which Emily Brontë's mind was concerned with salvation.

Of greater significance than these conventional uses are the passages where Emily Brontë uses these words and their synonyms as images to refer to earthly joy and discontent. Thus Lockwood greets with delight "a perfect misanthropist's heaven," Hindley sits with Frances in his "paradise on the hearth," while Joseph finds his elysium sitting "alone, beside a roaring fire; a quart of ale on the table near him, bristling with large pieces of toasted oatcake; and his black short pipe in his mouth" (i, iii, xxiii). Emily does not pass moral judgement on her characters, being usually reckoned to be above morality, but it is difficult to escape the conclusion that she thought, as we think, Lockwood, Hindley, and Joseph characters of extraordinary selfishness, especially on the occasions in which their elysium is being described. It looks as if by enjoying the pleasures of this world they are missing the full joys of heaven which they would have obtained had they been prepared to endure a little suffering. There is more to heaven than toasted oatcakes.

That heaven can be different for different people is made abundantly clear in the passage where Linton and Cathy compare their differing ideas of the pleasantest way of spending a hot July day.

> *He wanted all to lie in an ecstasy of peace; I wanted all to sparkle and dance in a glorious jubilee. I said his heaven would be only half alive; and he said mine would be drunk: I said I should fall asleep in his; and he said he could not breathe in mine.* (xxiv)

This discussion is used principally to show that Linton and Cathy are unsuited to each other in this world, but it does raise interesting questions about Linton's future fate. Lacking the heroic qualities of his father without any redeeming conventional virtues,[6] Linton might seem an unlikely candidate for salvation; yet this passage suggests he has a vision and a hope of heaven. On the other hand it is a heaven which Cathy is right to call half alive, and since it involves lying on a bank of heath with the larks singing high up overhead it does look suspiciously like Socinian annihilation.

A third passage where heaven is used principally as an image of earthly happiness, but with undertones of real heaven, comes when Heathcliff and Catherine see Isabella and Edgar quarrelling over a dog, alone in Thrushcross Grange, and say that they would have thought themselves in heaven in such a situation (vi). This passage is indicative of Catherine's and Heathcliff's idea of an earthly heaven, the paradise of childhood innocence, to which there are many references in the poems. But it is Catherine rather than Heathcliff who says that she imagines the pampered existence in Thrushcross Grange to be heavenly, and this warns us of Catherine's future marriage to Edgar Linton, a marriage which is as wrong for Catherine as the heaven of which she dreamt and which did not seem to be her home. This reference to heaven and others made by Catherine and Heathcliff must be reserved for later discussion, as they are not to be taken as images, but taken literally as referring to a better world beyond this one.

With hell the distinction between the image use and the literal use is less easy to make, as if we do believe that Emily thought hell was on earth, any reference to earthly suffering as hellish can be taken literally. Perhaps we could say that Heathcliff was not really in hell until Catherine's death. When he says that he will be in hell until Nelly has carried his message to Catherine (x) he is speaking figuratively, as he is also when he says that Catherine is in hell isolated from him (xiv). These passages are different from the one where he says, "Two words would comprehend my future—*death* and *hell:* existence after losing her would be hell" (xiv). Or again a key passage for showing the earthly hell of Heathcliff and the purgatory suffered by Catherine as a ghost is this:

> *"Is it not sufficient for your infernal selfishness that while you are at peace I shall writhe in the torments of hell?" "I shall not be at peace," moaned Catherine . . . "I'm not wishing you greater torment than I have, Heathcliff. I only wish us never to be parted: and should a word of mine distress you hereafter, think I feel the same distress underground, and for my own sake, forgive me."* (xv)

Catherine suffers as she would suffer in an orthodox hell or purgatory, but, since her life was so clearly connected with Heathcliff's, she would have suffered just as much in an orthodox heaven. In fact Catherine appears to suffer in a kind of ghostly limbo from which she tries to gain access through Lockwood's window to the real world. Ghosts seem to have no very clear defined place in an orthodox theological framework, their sufferings being neither substantial nor severe enough for hell, and their restlessness not making them very good candidates for heaven. But Catherine's ghost shows the way in which salvation is won by suffering. Catherine is not the only person to suffer. Heathcliff prays that Catherine may wake in torment to haunt him as long as he is living. His prayer is granted. "She showed herself, as she often was in life, a devil to me. And, since then, sometimes more and sometimes less, I've been the sport of that intolerable torture!" (xxix). This is the earthly hell in which Emily Brontë believes, but it leads to heaven. "Last night I was on the threshold of hell. To-day, I am within sight of my heaven" (xxxiv).

Before coming on to the mystical heaven of Catherine and Heathcliff it is necessary to eliminate the views on heaven and hell of Joseph and Nelly Dean. We need not quote extensively to show the views of Joseph who condemns even Nelly Dean to perdition for her attempts to show a little life. Joseph is a Calvinist, although his belief in predestination is not important, and indeed is only once mentioned by him. "All warks together for gooid to them as is chozzen, and piked out fro'th' rubbidge" (ix). The important thing for Joseph is that many were damned and few were saved. Such a view is explicitly condemned in the poems, and Nelly Dean criticises Joseph for his pharisaical outlook. And yet, though she rejected eternal damnation, we feel a certain affinity between Emily and Joseph; both seem to believe that gloom is good for the soul, and there are traces of determinism in Emily's outlook.

Indeed it is a feature of Emily Brontë's art and her morality that she extends the net of her sympathy so widely. In concentrating on the heroic struggles of Heathcliff we should not lose sight of the more elegiac pathos of Edgar or the robust common sense of Nelly Dean. Nelly Dean, however, though more of an amiable character than Joseph, does not, as far as theology is concerned, have as much affinity with Emily Brontë. She may be held to represent the orthodox Anglican attitude in the same way that Joseph represents the outlook of the extreme Dissenter.[7] We learn a great deal about her conventional morality, but not a great deal about her theology. She urges Heathcliff to read a Bible before his death, and says that it is God's job to punish sinners, but we do not obtain any information about her idea of hell. Conventional Christians are rarely clear on this point, especially if they belong to the school of thought which emphasises the tranquillity of heaven.

> *I don't know if it be a peculiarity in me, but I am seldom otherwise than happy while watching in the chamber of death, should no frenzied or despairing mourner share the duty with me. I see a repose that neither earth nor hell can break, and I feel an assurance of the endless and shadowless hereafter—the Eternity they have entered—where life is boundless in its duration, and love in its sympathy, and joy in its fulness.* (xvi)

Nelly shares Emily's views about the importance of heaven, but is wrong in thinking Catherine has attained it. Her conventional morality is shown throughout the book to be a series of half truths, although in this particular passage she seems more full of doubt than usual. She is interested in making frequent comparisons between Heathcliff and the devil. Sometimes the references to Heathcliff's diabolical nature and fiendish appearance are merely figurative, but, as we have seen before in the case of hell, it is difficult to distinguish image from reality. Sometimes, moreover, Nelly expressly drops the image, as when she says, "and, truly, it appeared as if the lad *were* possessed of something diabolical at that period" (viii). Other characters apart from Heathcliff are described as being possessed by a devil, but it is Heathcliff who is generally compared with the devil. Cathy makes the most appropriate comparison when she says, "You *are* miserable, are you not? Lonely, like the devil, and envious like him? *Nobody* loves you—*nobody* will cry for you when you die! I wouldn't be you!" (xxix). Orthodox Christians have often been worried by the exact status of the devil. Is he an independent monarch, God's viceroy in hell, or a prisoner suffering the most damnable tortures, merely consoling himself by finding fellow-sufferers? Like Marlowe's Mephistophilis, Emily Brontë seems to favour the devil's being the chief prisoner and like Marlowe too she places hell on earth.

> *Within the bowels of these elements,*
> *Where we are tortured and remain for ever.*
> *Hell hath no limits, nor is circumscribed*
> *In one self place, but where we are is hell,*
> *And where hell is, there must we ever be:*
> *And to be short, when all the world dissolves*
> *And every creature shall be purified,*
> *All places shall be hell that are not heaven.*[8]

And so to heaven, to which the references in *Wuthering Heights* are few but important. Firstly we have the passage where Nelly Dean comments on the behaviour of Heathcliff and Catherine after Mr Earnshaw's death.

> *The little souls were comforting each other with better thoughts than I could have hit on: no parson in the world ever pictured heaven so beautifully as they did, in their innocent talk; and while I sobbed and listened, I could not help wishing we were all there safe together.* (v)

This is further evidence, if we need it, of Nelly's conventional piety, but it also suggests a childhood heaven to which we find other references in the poems. The asexual nature of Heathcliff's and Catherine's love is another link with the childhood heaven.[9]

A more revealing passage comes when Catherine dreams that she has been in heaven and disliked it.

> *I was only going to say that heaven did not seem to be my home; and I broke my heart with weeping to come back to earth; and the angels were so angry that they flung me out in the middle of the heath on the top of Wuthering Heights; where I woke sobbing for joy . . . I've no more business to marry Edgar Linton than I have to be in heaven.* (ix)

Catherine neither desires nor deserves heaven, and, if we take the reference to her ghost literally, she does not obtain it for some time. Does she obtain it with Heathcliff in the end? This is not clearly stated. We get what in Lockwood's eyes are contradictory thoughts on the subject, the notion that Catherine and Heathcliff are to be seen walking, and his own view that no one could imagine unquiet slumbers in that quiet earth (xxxiv). Lockwood's conventional ideas of contradiction are not to be taken seriously. For Catherine and Heathcliff to be united would be heaven, even if it were not a tranquil heaven.

There is one further negative piece of evidence to support the thesis that suffering brings salvation. Suicide is twice mentioned in the book. Catherine, with typical selfishness, talks of killing herself to spite Edgar (xii), and Heathcliff, when he comes back after his absence, says that he intended to kill himself after killing Hindley and catching a glimpse of Catherine (x). After the death of Catherine, Heathcliff does not raise the subject; it could be argued that Heathcliff does, like Emily Brontë, virtually kill himself through neglect, but he does not do this for some time. If heaven was to be with Catherine, why did he not make haste to join her? Pride may have detained him, zeal for revenge may have added strength to his resolve, but he had achieved his revenge and soothed his pride before the book begins, and yet lives on. Heaven was not so easy for him to gain, either for himself or for Catherine.

It so happens that in *Wuthering Heights* we begin with Cathy and Hareton in the depths of misery and end with them living in comparative happiness; in between we have the story of Heathcliff's protracted agony. Their happiness, however, is only a pale shadow of the happiness in heaven of Heathcliff and Catherine, the main characters of the book. In *Jane Eyre* and *The Tenant of Wildfell Hall* it is the main characters who win earthly happiness after much suffering, and thus the message that earthly tribulation brings heavenly salvation for others as well as for oneself is blurred, although Arthur Huntingdon and St John Rivers in their different ways suggest the message. There are other differences between the three books. Anne and Charlotte still have hankerings after the conventional heaven and hell, in which characters like Helen Huntingdon's aunt and St John Rivers, who are not all that wrong-headed, believe. Against this we have the theology of Joseph who believes that all songs are the signs of the devil, of Nelly Dean who believes that Edgar Linton is an ideal specimen of manhood, and of Mr Lockwood who thinks that young Cathy is married to Heathcliff and that a pile of dead rabbits constitute her pets. In *The Tenant of Wildfell Hall* and *Jane Eyre* it is easy to make a conventional division of good and bad characters; this is impossible in *Wuthering Heights,* as can be seen from an examination of the articles making heroes and villains out of the most unlikely people;[10] *Wuthering Heights* has the sincerity of original thought, whereas *The Tenant of Wildfell Hall* and to a lesser extent *Jane Eyre* are derivative. Anne's and Charlotte's theological teaching is not integrated into the body of the novel, and the shift from the novelist to the preacher is obvious; with Emily there is no such shift, and, though the whole novel seems full of the doctrine of salvation through suffering, the existence of this doctrine has escaped many readers.

We shall find these same differences between the three sisters in spheres other than the theological. In the case of Anne Brontë it is easy to extract the theological, sexual, and social doctrines, and to comment on them separately; contemporary reviewers did this, and though we may not agree with the unfavourable comments on the unorthodoxy of the doctrines, it is not unfair to consider her novels in this way, because they have so little else to offer. Charlotte's views are a little more difficult to disentangle because she appears to have made some effort to modify them in the light of contemporary opinion which she was so much more successful in satisfying. Nor is it wholly fair to Charlotte Brontë to consider her novels merely by an objective appraisal of the views expressed in them. To do so is to leave out of account the force of what Matthew Arnold, a perceptive though hostile critic, has called the "hunger, rebellion and rage,"[11] which raises Charlotte Brontë out of the ruck of English novelists. Yet we can ascribe definite views to Charlotte and comment on the coherence and confidence with which these views are expressed. But, although we have shown Emily Brontë to be more bold and more consistent than her sisters in her theological teaching, it still seems almost insulting to her novel to dissect it in such a way that we only consider it from one point of view. As Matthew Arnold, an early admirer of Emily,[12] said of Shakespeare, "Others abide our question; thou art free."[13] Or again, as Virginia Woolf fittingly, if despairingly, summed up *Wuthering Heights,*

That gigantic ambition is to be felt throughout the novel—a struggle half thwarted but of superb conviction, to say something through the mouths of her characters which is not merely "I love" or "I hate," but "we, the whole human race" and "you, the eternal powers . . ." the sentence remains unfinished.[14]

Notes

1. Emily Brontë, *Five Essays Written in French,* trans. L. W. Nagel (Austin: University of Texas Press, 1948).
2. F. Ratchford, in *Gondal's Queen* (Austin: University of Texas Press, 1955), 31, tries to get round these objections by arguing that many of the poems in the untitled notebook are definitely of Gondal, but this has hardly been established.
3. Although there is still the possibility of doubt about the authorship of some of Emily's poems, we can, thanks to the existence of C. Hatfield, *The Complete Poems of Emily Jane Brontë* (New York: Columbia University Press, 1941), be confident about their date and text.
4. Christina Rossetti was also worried by this problem. Although eventually coming down on the side of orthodoxy, and perhaps refusing various suitors because of her orthodox views, she shows traces of unorthodoxy in the notebooks found in the Bodleian Library that contain unpublished poems and the first drafts of poems later revised for publication.
5. D. du Maurier, in *The Infernal Genius of Branwell Brontë* (London: Gollancz, 1958), dates the occasion on which Branwell is alleged to have read *Wuthering Heights* to 1842 and gives persuasive, if not convincing, parallels between *Wuthering Heights* and poems and letters of Branwell (91, 104); we can accept the force of these parallels without swallowing the story that Branwell wrote *Wuthering Heights.*
6. See D. Cecil, *Early Victorian Novelists* (London: Constable, 1934), 166; in spite of his warning that Emily does away with the ordinary antithesis of good and evil (154), Cecil appears to be able to find plenty of "bad" characteristics in Linton, and it is not difficult to do so. What is difficult to justify is Cecil's contention that these bad characteristics are a result of Linton's combining the bad qualities of both storm and calm. On the evidence of this passage, it would be a great deal easier to say that Linton is all calm and that Emily Brontë disapproved of calm.
7. The religious loyalties of the two are clearly indicated in the passage in which Nelly Dean says that in the absence of any church she usually goes to the chapel attended by Joseph. This chapel is either Methodist or Baptist, but she is not sure which.
8. C. Marlowe, *Dr Faustus,* ed. J. Greg (Oxford: Clarendon Press, 1950), 11, 117–24.
9. The nature of Heathcliff's and Catherine's love remains unchanged by the onset of puberty and the approach of death.

10. See, for example, James Hafley, "The Villain in *Wuthering Heights*," *Nineteenth Century Fiction* 13 (1958):199–215, where the villain is Nelly Dean.

11. M. Arnold, *The Letters of Matthew Arnold,* ed. G. Russell (London: Macmillan, 1895), 1,29.

12. M. Arnold, *The Poems of Matthew Arnold,* ed. K. Allott (London: Longman, 1965), 395.

13. Ibid., 48.

14. V. Woolf, *The English Common Reader* (London: The Hogarth Press, 1925), 202.

Brontë's Reading and Education

JOHN HEWISH*

Emily Brontë returned from her Halifax post to three years of austere seclusion at home. By the middle of 1839 the correspondence shows that she was there to undertake some domestic commissions for Charlotte, who was away working as a governess with the Sidgwick family.

> Dearest Lavinia [This may have been an allusion to some long-lost character in a silver-fork novel]—I am most exceedingly obliged to you for all the trouble you have taken in seeking up my things and sending them all right. The box and its contents were most acceptable. I only wish I had asked you to send me some letter-paper. This is my last sheet but two. When you can send the other articles of raiment now manufacturing, I shall be right down glad of them. (1, p. 178)

Emily had evidently been able to force herself to endure a teacher's life this once for a substantial period, but the desired pattern of her existence was unchanged. (As mentioned, she had at Halifax surroundings similar to those of Haworth.) In 1848 Charlotte described her sister's temperament to Dr Epps, calling it "highly nervous." Spiritual response to place is closely connected with health and that, in turn, with a particular way of life.

So her sister Anne's comment is the only appropriate summary of her external life during 1839 to 1842, during which all the rest of the Brontë children took situations of one kind or another. "We are all doing something for our livelihood except Emily, who is, however, as busy as any of us, and earns her food and raiment as much as we do." (1, p. 239)

"The Gondals still flourish bright as ever," she wrote in 1845, but before Brussels there is a tendency towards more direct expression of her ideas and experience, indicating intellectual development. Lockwood, it will be remembered, misguidedly visited Wuthering Heights for company, and in her private poems his creator did not always suppress her loneliness, that recurrent Brontë theme. In early April 1839 Anne, like her heroine *Agnes Grey*, went as governess to a family near Mirfield. Emily's poem "By R. Gleneden" (p. 102)

*Reprinted from J. Hewish, *Emily Brontë: A Critical Biographical Study* (London: Macmillan, 1964), 54–72.

seems to reflect the event, whereas "Fair sinks the summer evening now" is a more open poem of solitude written when Charlotte also was away.

> Then why is all so sad and lone?
> No merry foot-step on the stair—
> No laugh—no heart-awaking tone,
> But voiceless silence everywhere. (p. 125)

Another element of Lockwood appears to derive from this period. The attractive young curate William Weightman was at Haworth from August 1839 until his death in 1842. His private life came in for a good deal of comment from Charlotte: "I am afraid," she wrote to Ellen Nussey, "he is very fickle—not to you in particular, but to half a dozen other ladies, he has just cut his enamorata at Swansea, and sent her back all her letters . . ." (I, p. 209) Lockwood's retreat from an affair at the seaside (*Wuthering Heights,* ch. 1) emphasises his timidity, and throws into relief the huge commitment of the protagonists.

The world is not entirely excluded from the Gondal poems of this period. With its wars, exiled heroes and revolutionary students, Gondal was coloured by the mood of the nineteenth century.

> *Their* feet shall never waken more
> The echoes in these galleries wide,
> Nor dare the snow on the mountain's brow,
> Nor skim the river's frozen flow,
>
> Nor wander down its side.
> They who have been our life—our soul—
> Through summer-youth, from childhood's spring—
> Who bound us in one vigorous whole
> To stand 'gainst Tyranny's control
> For ever triumphing— (p. 111)

The evidence as to whether this was a people's or a monarchical tyranny is contradictory. According to the voice of busy common sense much of Emily Brontë's poetry represents an escape from an intolerably narrow existence. One's response to the passions of creatures whose world is partly shut-off from the modern reader is inevitably limited; as it also is to the rather solipsistic response to nature—a generalised nature—of the more personal poems. Yet the wise and evidently hard-won detachment that enabled her to realise the presence of nature, briefly,

> I watch this cloudy evening fall,
> After a day of rain:
> Blue mists, *sweet* mists of summer pall

> The horizon's mountain-chain.
> The damp stands in the long, green grass
> As thick as morning's tears . . . (p. 122)

> I've seen the purple heather-bell
> Look out by many a storm-worn stone . . . (p. 114)

as well as her own "uncertainties, difficulties, doubts," is admirable. (But stones in her poetry are all too rarely individual and actual, like this one.) In her 1845 note the struggle to come to terms with her existence, and perhaps with her longing for transcendence, shows briefly: "Having learnt to make the most of the present, and long for the future with [less?] fidgetiness . . ." (II, p. 51)

"An imagination feeding quite wantonly on extremes of passion" is revealed in the Gondal poems, according to David Daiches. They are passionate, certainly, but not wanton or erotic. The cosmos of the Gondal love poems reveals not abandon, but a continual state of tension, an irresistible passion encounters an immovable morality. Passion can be indulged only at another's expense, and remorse and love are permanent and inescapable. Intensity of feeling must be paid for.

> Sweeter far than placid pleasure,
> Purer, higher, beyond measure,
> Yet alas the sooner turning
> Into hopeless, endless mourning. (p. 121)

If the emotions felt in this world are so painful, to have to suffer retribution in the next is harsh indeed.

> Shall these long, agonising years
> Be punished by eternal tears?

> No; *that* I feel can never be;
> A God of *hate* could hardly bear
> To watch through all eternity
> His own creations dread despair! (p. 138)

The tortuosity of some of Emily Brontë's poetry does, in an abstract way, embody the involvement of sin and retribution.

> Yet could I with past pleasures
> Past woe's oblivion buy,
> That by the death of my dearest treasures
> My deadliest pains might die . . . (p. 130)

This is a world in which nothing is forgotten; an emotion, once experienced, remains dominant.

There let thy bleeding branch atone
For every torturing tear:
Shall my young sins, my sins alone,
Be everlasting here?

Who bade thee keep that cursed name
A pledge for memory?
As if Oblivion ever came
To breathe its bliss on me;

As if, through all the 'wildering maze
Of mad hours left behind,
I once forgot the early days
That thou wouldst call to mind. (p. 150)

The now-emergent, later dominant, theme is the sense of the incongruity of pain and evil with the splendour of nature. A state of semi-permanent rebellion against the inadequacy of the Christian eschatology to provide any adequate answer to this situation results. The abstraction of Christian bliss is no substitute for the joy of earth. (Emily Brontë remained virtually silent in public on the question of religion. Not in itself surprising, in this age it was unusual.) Nevertheless the Christian cosmos continually shapes the thought of the poems. These attitudes appear in a group of poems significantly copied into her non-Gondal manuscript book in 1844, but dated early in 1841. Most important, because most direct, is "I see around me tombstones grey." There is too much woe on earth to forget in heaven: the angels are happy, but see how inexperienced they are!

Sweet land of light! thy children fair
Know nought akin to our despair;
Nor have they felt, nor can they tell
What tenants haunt each mortal cell,
What gloomy guests we hold within—
Torments and madness, tears and sin!
Well, may they live in extasy
Their long eternity of joy;
At least we would not bring them down
With us to weep, with us to groan.

In this, in view of her background, rather daring poem, heaven is a cheat, seducing us from our rightful allegiance to earth.

We would not leave our native home
For *any* world beyond the Tomb.
No—rather on thy kindly breast
Let us be laid in lasting rest;

> Or waken but to share with thee
> A mutual immortality. (p. 166)

The idea is, of course, repeated by Catherine Earnshaw in *Wuthering Heights* ("Heaven did not seem to be my home") and is an essential part of Emily Brontë's outlook. (This naturalism may be the legacy of a major poet to a less important one. The Preface to *Prometheus Unbound* states that "one great poet is a masterpiece of nature which another not only ought to study, but must study," and the poem itself, that uneven but central statement of romanticism, contains the same characterisation of Earth as "I see around me tombstones grey.") A few days before the date on the poem, Emily wrote a kind of "Ode to the West Wind," "Aye, there it is! It wakes to-night" (p. 165)

> Yes, I could swear that glorious wind
> Has swept the world aside,
> Has dashed its memory from thy mind
> Like foam-bells from the tide—
>
> And thou art now a spirit pouring
> Thy presence into all—
> The essence of the Tempest's roaring
> And of the Tempest's fall—
>
> A universal influence
> From Thine own influence free;
> A principle of life, intense,
> Lost to mortality.

The response to Shelley, tempered with her own consciousness of the Christian world-picture, suggests that this most important influence dates from this time. It is, I think, manifest in later poems, and indirectly—but very revealingly—in *Wuthering Heights*. Emily Brontë's poetry is thus an uncensored record of the growth of her mind. The side that her sister was allowed to see is apparent in the 1841 "birthday note," written in parallel with another by Anne. They evidently agreed to write them at four-yearly intervals and to open them together. The four papers were recovered by Shorter from the material kept by Mr Nicholls,[1] tightly folded like messages from secret agents. Emily's shows her putting a good face on the project to run a school of their own—part of the reason for their forthcoming studies on the Continent. The real reason, in Charlotte's case, was to a great extent the desire to escape to a fuller existence.

Emily's prose notes are evidence of a more compartmented mind than that of Emily Dickinson, for instance, whose poems and letters clearly come from the same region of their author's mind. The conflict between her ideas as revealed by, say, "I see around me tombstones grey" and the orthodox family atmosphere may have had something to do with it, but reserve was also part of her nature. (She was, inconsistently, to drop it to some extent when writing for M. Heger.)

> A scheme is at present in agitation for setting us up in a school of our own; as yet nothing is determined, but I hope and trust it may go on and prosper, and answer our highest expectations. This day four years I wonder whether we shall still be dragging on in our present condition, or established to our heart's content. Time will show.
>
> I guess that at the time appointed for the opening of this paper, we, Charlotte, Anne and I, shall be all merrily seated in our own sitting room in some pleasant and flourishing seminary, having just gathered in for the midsummer ladyday. Our debts will be paid off, and we shall have cash in hand to a considerable amount. Papa aunt and Branwell will either have been or be coming to visit us. It will be a fine warm summer evening, very different from this bleak look-out, and Anne and I will perchance slip out into the garden for a few minutes to peruse our papers. (II, p. 51)

"Dragging on in our present condition"—the Tennysonian accents of lassitude are less predictable in Emily than in her sisters, who were both enduring situations away from home. In her parallel note Anne Brontë recorded: "This is Emily's birthday. She has now completed her 23rd year, and is, I believe, at home." (Her being at home seems not to have been such an accepted state of affairs.) Anne's reference to Law Hill solves no problems. "Emily has been a teacher at Miss Patchet's [*sic*] school, and left it."

Whether they took over Miss Wooler's school, which had been offered, or ran their own at the parsonage, they would need languages. Their friends the Taylors were already at a Brussels finishing school, and the city was noted for a low cost of living and good teachers. To Charlotte, the guiding spirit, Brussels meant much more than diplomas in languages—it meant freedom and culture.

It seems that Emily would have preferred that they take over the Wooler school. No prospect, evidently, could have been less welcome than a Catholic school in the Low Countries. She had, as might be expected, to be persuaded to accompany her sister, rather than Anne, who, as governess, deserved the education more, and whose claims Emily advocated (1, pp. 245–47). The reasons for Charlotte's insistence that the prior claim was Emily's and her readiness to take her to continental exile after the Roe Head "failure" and her anxiety about her at Law Hill can only be conjectural. It may not be indulging in undue partisanship to suggest that she needed Emily's mature companionship and good sense. But when summarising this period in the Preface already discussed, Charlotte described her sister undergoing another crisis. "Once more she seemed sinking, but this time she rallied through the mere force of resolution: with inward remorse and shame she looked back on her former failure, and resolved to conquer in this second ordeal."[2] Perhaps, but there is nothing about this in Charlotte's letters at the time. The pattern of contradictions in the evidence about Emily Brontë in Brussels seems partly a result of afterthoughts by various witnesses. Another contradiction is Mary Taylor's comment to Mrs Gaskell (reported in *The Life of Charlotte Brontë*), that in London, where they stayed on their way to Brussels in February 1842, the reserved Emily seemed well informed, like her sister, and "certainly never took her opinion, but always had one to offer."

"Little gained, at vast expense," she wrote in a poem shortly before leaving the pensionnat. At this time she was not much concerned with worldly or cultural accomplishments. Like Novalis, with whom she has been compared, she created for herself in the visible world an invisible one. Her seriousness, to judge from the poems already mentioned, had long since eliminated any merely facile Byronism. Her reflective and fundamentally religious cast of mind was tinged with world-weariness and nihilism, contending with traditional faith.

> Look on the grave where thou must sleep,
> Thy last and strongest foe;
> 'Twill be endurance not to weep
> If that repose be woe.

Almost from the first, Emily Brontë's preoccupation with death is absolutely fundamental to her artistic character. It may have originated in Evangelicalism, but its outcome was very un-Evangelical. Her sense of life, and of the importance of intense feeling, "Sweeter far than placid pleasures," was also strong. She went to Brussels at a time when romanticism was in flood in the French-speaking countries, when de Nerval, on the banks of the Rhine, could exclaim, "le pays d'Hoffmann!" Unfortunately her conversations with her teachers must remain largely imaginary, apart from the few facts reported by Mrs Gaskell. Yet a singular aspect of her work, or one that would be more singular in another writer, is the exclusion of any direct trace of the Brussels months.

The background is familiar (and has recently been re-created in great detail by Miss W. Gerin[3]). Much, nevertheless, remains unclear concerning the characters of the Hegers, those respected Brussels figures, and their exact relations with the two Brontës.

It was an ironic encounter between a teacher with a more than average interest in writing and the sisters who had been writing for most of their lives. Heger's instruction combined the enlightened and the dryly pedantic. He taught French direct and seems to have known little English. Emily's struggle to overcome her weakness in languages is evident, though according to Mrs Gaskell they could both read it fluently. (Emily wrote fewer poems than at any comparable period of her life during these months.)

Emily and he don't draw well together at all. When he is very ferocious with me I cry; that sets all things straight. Emily works like a horse, and she has had great difficulties to contend with, far greater than I have had. (I, pp. 260–61)

His relationship with female pupils was very personal, perhaps mildly flirtatious,[4] and *a priori* Emily Brontë must have refused any relationship of the kind that affected her sister so deeply. She openly disagreed with his academic instruction in writing—mainly by copying stylistic gems. But there was another side to his teaching: his contemporaries left many tributes to his brilliance and sympathy, his talent for arousing his pupils' interest. It was no commonplace mind that appealed to Charlotte so strongly.[5] He was interested in the strategy of creative work, telling students "not to fight with a difficult sentence, but to take it for a walk with one, or sleep with it present in one's mind."[6] In addition to the sympathy of the artist *manqué,* M. Heger manifested a devout Catholicism[7] in a school in which the basis of the curriculum was religion (1, p. 252).[8] It is tempting to read something of his clash with Emily in the passage in *Villette* where Paul Emanuel, the French instructor, exclaims against English women, "their slovenly dress, their pedantic education, their impious scepticism, their insufferable pride" (xxviii). (Emily was careless about her dress, according to their co-pupils in Brussels the Wheelwright sisters.[9])

Her surviving devoirs reveal her outlook on man as, approximately, a social, political and religious being; they show Emily Brontë the "Philosopher" and the woman. The classroom forced her ideas into the open. (Emily's fine, regular spiky longhand suggests a temperament of great precision: the essays are set out like ledger entries.) Trenchant and well shaped, "Le Chat" has a characteristically sardonic quality; it is the first statement in prose of her romantic misanthropy, pessimism, and dislike of convention. Hervey's *Meditations* and Wesley's *Compendium of Natural Philosophy,*[10] the seventeenth-century "character" and the French *physiologie* are possible models.

le chat, encore qu'il differe en quelque points physiques, est extrêment semblable à nous en disposition.

Il peut-être des gens, en vérité, qui diraient que cette ressemblance ne lui approche qu'aux hommes les plus méchants; qu'elle est bornée a son exces de hypocrisie, de cruauté et d'ingratitude, vices détestables dans notre race et également odieux en celle des chats . . . je reponds, que si l'hypocrisie, le cruauté et l'ingratitude sont exclusivement la propriété des méchants, cette classe renferme tout le monde. . . .

(the cat, although he differs in some physical traits, is extremely like us in disposition.

In truth, there may be people who would say that the resemblance is close only in the meanest human beings, that it is limited to their excessive hypocrisy, cruelty and ingratitude—detestable vices in our species and equally odious in the cat's . . . I answer that if hypocrisy, cruelty and ingratitude are the characteristics exclusively of mean people, this class includes everyone . . .)

notre education [she wrote, tactlessly] développe une de ces qualites en grande perfection, les autres fleurissent sans soin, et loin de les condamner nous regardons tous les trois avec beaucoup de complaisance.

(our education develops one of these qualities in great perfection, the others thrive without cultivation, and we, far from condemning them, look upon all three with great complacency.)

(Translations of Emily Brontë's French, which was written after three months' formal instruction, tend to flatter it. M. Bellour, who is preparing a French edition of the Brontës' works, has called it "plus qu'hésitant.")

After selecting these Victorian domestic vices of hypocrisy and cruelty she concentrates on the latter. A sensitive lady "who has murdered half a dozen lap-dogs in pure affection" would accuse the cat of cruelty, but her husband hunts bagged foxes, and though she dare not be in at the death herself, she encourages cruelty in her children.

J'ai vous vue embrasser avec transport votre enfant quand il [?] vous montrer un beau papillon écrasé entre ses cruels petits doigts; at à ce moment, j'ai voulu bien avoir un chat avec la queue d'un rat demi englouti, pendant de sa bouche, à presenter comme l'image, la vraie copie de votre ange; vous ne pourriez refuser de le baiser, et s'il vous égratignait tous deux en revanche, tant mieux, les petits garçons sont assez liables à reconnaître ainsi les caresses de leur amis, et la ressemblance serait plus parfaite.[11]

(I have seen you enthusiastically hug your child when he [ran?] to show you a beautiful butterfly crushed between his cruel little fingers; then I would very much like to have had a cat with the tail of a half-swallowed rat hanging from his mouth to show you, as the exact image of your little angel; you could not help but kiss him, and if he scratched you both in revenge, so much the better, little boys are quite likely thus to greet the caresses of their friends, and the resemblance would be so much the better.)

It suggests a savage parody of John Earle's sentimental "character" of the child. She concludes:

The ingratitude of cats is another word for penetration. They know how to value our favours, because they know the motives behind them. And if these are sometimes good, they undoubtedly remember that they owe all their good and bad qualities to the great ancestor of the human race, for certainly the cat was not bad in Paradise.

The actual workings of a poetic imagination may contradict its direct statement of its ideas, but these devoirs throw light on the nature of *Wuthering*

Heights. They show that, as with Breughel or Bosch, Emily's images of cruelty are placed in a religious or cosmological frame; they arise in speculation about the nature of man and reality.

"Whenever the Brontës could be national, they were so," wrote Mrs Gaskell.[12] Emily's "Portrait du roi Harold avant la bataille" was written after Heger had read them Hugo's portrait of Mirabeau, and analysed its design and (one can hear him) "ce qu'on pourrait appeler la charpente."[13] Harold was much admired in the early nineteenth century. His portrait here lacks the bite of "The Cat." It shows a stereotyped hero freed from the falsities of the court to face the ultimate reality of death.

> He has an inner conviction that no mortal power can defeat him. Only the hand of death can gain the victory over his arms, and Harold is ready to cede to him, because to the hero the touch of that hand is like the stroke that liberates the slave.[14]

Heger's pencilled criticism of the aptness of the final simile can still be deciphered. It is a clue to their failure to "draw well together."

"Le Papillon" was written later in the summer of 1842. Whereas "Le Chat" is a recognisable if "sick" and inverted piece from the bestiary, in "Le Papillon" the treatment is quite different. It opens on a deeply personal note. The author is meditating on the cruelty of nature and is in one of those moods "lorsque le monde de l'imagination souffre un hiver," the metaphor is terse and beautiful as if from the pen of a Benjamin Constant. The essay makes an unsuccessful attempt to reconcile a *mondo cane* with Christian belief. (To Emily the human species enjoyed no special category of suffering.)

> l'univers me paraissait une vaste machine construit seulement pour produire le mal: je doutais presque de la bonté de Dieu, dans ce qu'il n'anéantit pas l'homme sur le jour du premier peche. "Le monde aussi dû étre detruit," je dis "écrasé comme j'écrase ce reptile qui n'a fait rien pendant sa vie que de rendre tout ce qu'il touche aussi dégoùtant que lui meme."[15]
>
> (the universe seemed to me a vast machine made solely to produce evil: I doubted even the goodness of God for not destroying man on the day of his first sin. "The world too, should be destroyed," I said, "wiped out as I wipe out this reptile that has done nothing in its life but to make everything it touches as disgusting as itself.")

Her rose, destroyed by the caterpillar, is sick, and it is difficult to see how the sudden appearance of the butterfly, a moment of beauty that rebukes the thinker as a symbol of the world to come—"an inner voice reminded me that the creature should not judge his creator"—is an adequate answer to the universe of cruelty already evoked, in which pain and beauty exist side by side. The forceful *Weltschmerz* of the opening is telling enough to make one wonder whether the pious coda was written for M. Heger, and the "cours d'instruction basé sur la religion" of the pensionnat. But the essay contains two poles of her reflection, which veers between heterodox extremes and near-orthodoxy. Its thought, in "the saint leaves enough misery here below to sadden him even before the throne of God," is identical to that of "I see around me tombstones grey," but the conclusion is different. Here, too, the comparison with *Wuthering Heights* is interesting. The essay provides a statement of the element of nineteenth-century rationalism implicit in the novel, and its imagery recurs in the famous closing paragraph ("watched the moths fluttering among the heath and hare-bells") in a context of which the meaning is more equivocal and more satisfying.

In July 1842 Charlotte was hoping that they would be able to stay on in Brussels after the autumn: "Mme Heger has made a proposal for both me and Emily to stay another half-year—offering to dismiss her English master and take me as teacher—also to employ Emily some part of each day as in [*sic*] teaching music . . ." (I, p. 267). The Hegers were "beginning to recognise the valuable parts of her nature under her singularities." But, as with a recent moral extremist such as Simone Weil, reactions varied. "I simply disliked her from the first," wrote one of their co-pupils, Laetitia Wheelwright.

> Her tallish, ungainly, ill-dressed figure contrasting so strongly with Charlotte's trim, neat person, although their dresses were alike, always answering our jokes with: "I wish to be as God made me." She taught my three youngest sisters music for four months, to my annoyance, as she would only take them in play hours, naturally causing many tears to small children, the eldest ten, the youngest seven. Fortunately she was summoned home in November, and did not return to Brussels. Charlotte was so devotedly attached to her, and thought so highly of her talents.[16]

Another English family found her throughout "as impenetrable to friendly advances as at the beginning," but for Mlle Bassompierre, a Belgian pupil, "Mlle Emilie was much less brilliant, but much more sympathetic than her sister. She was working hard at drawing, and had become very skilled. She gave me an attractive signed landscape, which I have carefully kept . . ."[17]

There has been so much speculation about her knowledge of German that Charlotte's reference to her rapid progress is interesting, as the only evidence. (The vignette of Diana Rivers, in *Jane Eyre* reading German is suggestive, but inconclusive.) The extent of her knowledge of German literature in the original is unknown. The indications in *Wuthering Heights,* considered below, point to possible familiarity with translations. The compounds in her poems, "overfly," "undergloom," "seablue," "seadeep" are suggestive, but probably Tennysonian, if not entirely her own.

At moments she evidently sought "another clime, another sky" during the Low Countries' summer. Her poetic landscape had never been more northern than in "Written in Aspin Castle" (p. 176), dated 20 August 1842 and 6 February 1843 and evidently finished after her return.

How do I love to hear the flow
Of Aspin's water murmuring low;
And hours long listen to the breeze
That sighs in Rockden's waving trees.

To-night, there is no wind to wake
One ripple on the lonely lake;
To-night, the clouds subdued and grey
Starlight and moonlight shut away.

Her "Palace of Death" essay, begun in the new school half in October, is
not necessarily connected with a series of deaths in the Brontës' limited circle
during the last months of 1842. (The curate William Weightman died of
cholera at Haworth in September, and their fellow-pupil in Brussels, Martha
Taylor, also in October, while Miss Branwell's death was imminent.) The subject was evidently set for them, since Charlotte produced a very similar essay.
The immediate example or source is not known, but it has been shown to be
the type of *fable* so dear to the classicising French mind. Emily's "Palais de la
Mort" is a *danse macabre,* with some touches worthy of Bunyan; it shows how
well she could bring the allegorical form to life. Intemperance, the mysterious
stranger before whom all the contestants for the office of Death's Prime Min-
ister must give way, "avait une figure qui paraissait rayonner de joie et de
santé," and even Death is uneasy at her approach. But she is there simply to
herald the approach of Civilisation, "before whom this whole assembly will be
forced to yield." The presence of Civilisation in such company is compromising and it would be interesting to know whether Emily departed from her
source in order to be ironical at the expense of Victorian meliorism. Intemperance and civilisation are similarly associated with death in one of Florian's
Fables published in 1792.[18]

M. Heger's appreciation of the devoirs is apparent in his tribute to
Emily, as reported by Mrs Gaskell.

He seems to have rated Emily's genius as something even higher than Charlotte's; and her estimation of their relative powers was the same. Emily had a
head for logic and a capability of argument, unusual in a man and rare indeed
in a woman, according to M. Heger. Impairing the force of this gift was a stub-
born tenacity of will which rendered her obtuse to all reasoning where her own
wishes, or her own sense of right was concerned. "She should have been a
man—a great navigator," said M. Heger, in speaking of her. "Her powerful
reason would have deduced new spheres of discovery from the knowledge of
the old; and her strong imperious will would never have been daunted by
opposition or difficulty; never have given way but with life." And yet, moreover, her faculty of imagination was such that, if she had written a history, her
view of scenes and characters would have been so vivid and so powerfully
expressed and supported by such a show of argument, that it would have dom-
inated over the reader, whatever might have been his cooler perceptions of its

truth. But she appeared egotistical and exacting compared with Charlotte, who was always unselfish [this is M. Heger's testimony]; and in the anxiety of the elder to make her younger sister contented, she allowed her to exercise a kind of unconscious tyranny over her.[19]

The sombre autobiographical poem "The evening passes fast away" (p. 179), the last dated in Brussels (though it was finished in Haworth according to its second date), is unillumined even by the delight in nature she was to recover sometimes at home. In part it is a recapitulation of the themes of the devoirs, a dialogue between world-weariness, a flickering sense of life, and some form of religious promise.

> The evening passes fast away,
> 'Tis almost time to rest;
> What thoughts has left the vanished day?
> What feelings in thy breast?
>
> "The vanished day? It leaves a sense
> Of labour hardly done;
> Of little gained with vast expense—
> A sense of grief alone!
>
> "Time stands before the door of Death,
> Upbraiding bitterly;
> And Conscience, with exhaustless breath,
> Pours black reproach on me:
>
> "And though I think that Conscience lies,
> And Time should Fate condemn;
> Still, weak Repentance clouds my eyes,
> And makes me yield to them!"

It is a partial denial of the repentance of the "Butterfly" essay, and though the poem closes piously, it does so without the force of these first stanzas. (Her poetic strength, in her "late" poems, is largely the ability to do without orthodox reassurance. As belief narrows, the artistic integrity of the poems increases.)

Mary Taylor's letters to Ellen Nussey during and after this period show that any alleviation of Emily's usual *terribiltá* was a matter of comment. She recorded her impressions of her taciturnity during an evening following a visit to her sister Martha's grave near Brussels (an occasion reproduced in *Shirley*) and found Miss Nussey's report—that she had become more accessible—difficult to square with them (I, pp. 274–75, 292). M. Heger's letter to Mr Brontë, when their aunt's death caused their sudden return, could be taken as confirming Miss Nussey: "Mlle Emily was learning the piano, and having lessons from the best teacher in Belgium; already she had her own pupils;

hence she was losing both the rest of her ignorance and, of what was worse, her shyness" (1, p. 292).

But this coolness in 1842, compared with the warmth reported by Mrs Gaskell above, indicates that by then a legend was in being, after the publication of *Wuthering Heights* and its author's death.

Notes

1.   C. Shorter, *The Brontës and Their Circle* (London: Hodder and Stoughton, 1896).
2.   Charlotte Brontë, "Biographical Notice of Ellis and Acton Bell," preface to the 1850 edition of *Wuthering Heights*.
3.   W. Gerin, *Charlotte Brontë: The Evolution of Genius* (Oxford: Clarendon Press, 1967), 181–255.
4.   E. Weir, "New Brontë Material Comes to Light," *Brontë Society Transactions* 59 (1949): 249–56.
5.   L. Quievreux, *Bruxelles, les Brontës et la famille Heger* (Brussels: Editions de DM services, 1953). See also Heger obituary in *L'Indépendance Belge,* May 1896, quoted in Chadwick, *In the Footsteps of the Brontës* (London: Pitman, 1914) 219–222, and Gerin, 194.
6.   F. Macdonald, *The Secret of Charlotte Brontë* (London: T., C., and E. C. Jack, 1914), 221.
7.   Gaskell, *The Gift of Charlotte Brontë* (London: Dent, 1971), 145–67. See also Quievreux and *L'Indépendance Belge,* May 1896.
8.   Heger Prospectus.
9.   Draft letter from C. Wheelwright to C. Shorter, quoted by J. Green, "The Brontë-Wheelright friendship," typescript in Brontë Parsonage Museum, published in *Friends' Quarterly Examiner* 50 (1916): 140–63, 220–40.
10.   Suggested in J. Hillis Miller, *The Disappearance of God* (Cambridge, Mass.: Harvard University Press. 1963), 163.
11.   Berg Collection, New York Public Library (author's translation).
12.   Gaskell, 145–67.
13.   Ibid.
14.   Bonnell Collection at Brontë Parsonage Museum (author's translation).
15.   Berg Collection.
16.   Draft letter from C. Wheelwright to C. Shorter, quoted by J. Green, "The Brontë-Wheelright friendship," typescript in Brontë Parsonage Museum, published in *Friends' Quarterly Examiner* 50 (1916): 140–63, 220–40.
17.   W. Field, *Brontë Society Transactions* 23 (1913): 25–29.
18.   J. Maxwell, "Emily Brontë's The Palace of Death," *Brontë Society Transactions* 77 (1967): 139–40.
19.   Gaskell, 145–67.

The Themes of *Wuthering Heights*

EDWARD CHITHAM*

About the third week in August 1846, *Agnes Grey* and *Wuthering Heights* (as a one-volume novel) were presumably returned to Haworth with *The Professor.* Charlotte told Mrs Gaskell that her rejected novel reached her in Manchester "on the very day that her father was to submit to his operation" for cataract.[1] We may suppose that Emily or Anne unwrapped the parcel of manuscripts and re-directed *The Professor.* The eye operation was a success, and when Charlotte returned, decisions would have to be made about the three novels. Mrs Gaskell is our earliest source for this:

> The three tales had each tried their fate in vain together, at length they were sent forth separately, and for many months with still-continued ill success. . . . Not only did *The Professor* return again to try his chance among the London publishers, but she began, in this time of care and depressing inquietude . . . *Jane Eyre.*[2]

There follows an interesting account of Charlotte's methods of composition, which we cannot pursue. Then Mrs Gaskell enlarges on Charlotte's account in the "Preface" of the sisters' workshop sessions in the evenings.

> The sisters retained their old habit, which was begun in their aunt's lifetime, of putting away their work at nine o'clock, and beginning their study, pacing up and down the sitting room. At this time, they talked over the stories they were engaged upon, and described their plots. Once or twice a week, each read to the others what she had written, and heard what they had to say about it. Charlotte told me, that the remarks made had seldom any effect in inducing her to alter her work, so possessed was she with the feeling that she had described reality; but the readings were of great and stirring interest to all, taking them out of the gnawing pressure of daily-recurring cares, and setting them in a free place. It was on one of these occasions that Charlotte determined to make her heroine plain, small and unattractive, in defiance of the accepted canon.[3]

If Mrs Gaskell's story is true, we may reasonably ask what the other sisters were reading aloud in reply to Charlotte's first passages from *Jane Eyre*

*Reprinted from E. Chitham, *A Life of Emily Brontë* (Oxford: Basil Blackwell, 1987), 196–214.

(that the occasion described followed September 1846 is implied by the final sentence: the early stages of *Jane Eyre* are being discussed). Anne was contributing the first outline of chapters of *Wildfell Hall,* probably. What else could Emily have been reading but a new version of *Wuthering Heights?*

There are problems in accepting this thesis. If Mrs Gaskell's earlier statement is right, the three first novels were still going the rounds of the publishers, in separate packets. Charlotte had moved on from *The Professor,* Anne from *Agnes Grey;* Emily might have nothing to read unless she left *The Life of the Emperor Julius* (in a Yorkshire setting), or whatever *Wuthering Heights* was called, and began again from memory or notes. Could she have done this? Possibly the two novels of the younger sisters were not being sent out until Emily had revised her contribution to fill the gap the third novel had left. Possibly some publisher had been attracted to *Agnes Grey* and suggested an expansion of *Wuthering Heights,* so that the two novels were both at Haworth, and Anne had no need to recast hers. Of course, these are only plausible suggestions: certainty is unattainable.

In any case, it looks as if the decision to persevere with the novels was not immediate. Almost as soon as the novels returned from London, both girls went back to working on Gondal. Anne's poem of 14 September 1846 may be considered to refer obliquely to Branwell. It is an interesting fiction, the full title of which has not been deciphered, but which deals with a man whose heart has grown bitter as he thinks back to his childhood. An incident in it is drawn from an incident in Branwell's youth. Emily's poem, begun the same day, is a thoughtful and complex ballad in which the name Gondal is not mentioned: "Why ask to know the date: the clime?" She seems to have written about 150 lines of it before putting it on one side. When Charlotte returned from Manchester, the three girls must have made a decision about their novels, as we have suggested. As for the poem, we shall come back to it.

I have suggested that *Wuthering Heights* now began to be recast and expanded. It seems quite impossible to say what this revision added. We may speculate that the 1845–6 version of the novel, which was sent off to the publishers with *Agnes Grey* and *The Professor,* told the story of Heathcliff (who had been Julius in mid-1845), possibly through Lockwood's eyes. Catherine had been developed from Geraldine, Edgar from Alfred. Isabella, romantic and spoilt, takes a name that had been used in Gondal. It may be pure coincidence that an Isabella Linton is found in Glascar (Co. Down) meeting house registers, but perhaps Emily's long memory had recalled a name mentioned by her father when talking about his youthful exploits. The geography of Thrushcross and the Heights, drawn from North Halifax, must have been early in the novel. But it could possibly have been written without Nelly. The "Chinese box" style of narrative is common to *Wuthering Heights* and *Wildfell Hall.* The two books have a complex relationship, but it may be that this structure was discussed by Emily and Anne during late 1846 in one of the workshop sessions mentioned. Nelly is not closely paralleled by any Gondal figure. She could be the inspired addition of 1846–7 who enabled the novel to seem acceptable to Newby. Verbally, she is an adaptation, descending from Eilís ("Alice"), Emily's grandmother. Nelly is Ellen and is obviously related to Ellis (Emily's pseudonym), and her Christian name. Like many of the parts donned by this actress, Nelly is a part of Emily, the well-read housekeeper at Haworth parsonage.

We may now be in a better position to see how *Wuthering Heights* emerges from the life experience of its author and the poetry she has written. That the burning intensity of the book mirrors an almost self-consuming intensity in Emily we have clearly seen. The many themes of the novel, crystallizing about the demonic Heathcliff, all cast their shadows before, in earlier work or anecdotes about Emily. As Mary Visick shows, the book was in unconscious process as far back as the 1830s, though it could not have been guessed how it would look when complete. The themes, like Heathcliff, were "always, always" in Emily's mind. Though planning of the actual book on paper may have begun in 1845, and been renewed in an 1846 revision, events and characters had been circling round Emily's imagination almost all her life. It is hard to see how she might write a second book without duplication, for *Wuthering Heights* is a chart of the inner country of her dreams. In this section, I propose to disentangle some of the threads of the tapestry to show the origin of each, as near as may be in chronological order.

Firstly, the fabric of the novel is *oral*. Though narrative techniques owe something, clearly, to Scott, Lord Lytton and other novelists, the story is heard, aloud, whether the speaker is Lockwood, Nelly, Joseph, or Catherine. From her earliest days, Emily heard stories told, as well as read. At the lowest, deepest level of her unconscious mind lies the layer formed when a fascinated little girl heard the magical and arresting tales told by her Irish father, who (despite eccentricity) loved to be with children, yarning to them. These tales formed patterns in her mind: she heard them over and over again and learnt them. Miss Robinson reports that even at fifteen Emily "wore a strange expression, gratified, pleased, as though she had gained something which seemed to complete a picture in her mind" when her father told "fearful stories of superstitious Ireland" in the parsonage at breakfast.[4] "This was the same Emily who at five years of age used to startle the nursery with her fantastic fairy stories," comments Miss Robinson. Two topics dealt with by Mr Brontë were the stirring days of the 1798 rebellion and the ancestral legend of the foundling, Welsh. This was family history. Emily was half a little Irish girl, with a voracious appetite for such history, and living an intense and troubling inner life. She looked for clues to her own personality; in her ancestry, she found them.

Mr Brontë seems to have transferred to the family some of his own inheritance of ballads. He is credited with composing some in far-distant Ballynaskeagh.[5] J. F. Goodridge suggests that "Fair Annie" is the ballad mentioned in *Wuthering Heights,* Chapter 32, and we are throughout reminded of such ballads as "Cold blows the wind," in which a mourning lover is apparently the cause of his sweetheart's inability to rest in the grave.[6] Ballad forms and ballad speech seem to underlie *Wuthering Heights*. The rapid movement of many ballads seems to influence the arbitrary way in which Emily Brontë treats time. As John Hewish points out, the childhood of the younger Catherine lasts only a paragraph or two. She reaches the age of thirteen without leaving Thrushcross Park (as Hewish wryly remarks, "She has not had time!").[7]

At this level the live and dead meet and intermingle. We have seen examples of Emily Brontë's closeness to the dead, greater sometimes than her closeness to the living. Ballads such as "Cold blows the wind" and "The Grey Cock" combine the sense of the dead as decomposing body and as disembodied spirit in exactly the same manner as *Wuthering Heights*. For example, in "The Grey Cock," the dead lover comes to his love's window at the dead of night. After they have kissed, shaken hands and embraced, "Mary" asks,

> *"O Willie, dear, O dearest Willie,*
> *Where is that colour you'd some time ago?"*
> *"O Mary dear, the clay has changed me;*
> *I am but the ghost of your Willie O."*[8]

In such a stanza, the ballad-maker has it both ways. The dead man is a corpse and can be changed by the "clay" in his grave; but he is also a ghost, who can fly to the loved one's window at night. The ambiguity is not resolved either here or in *Wuthering Heights*.

A number of writers have examined Emily's use of dialect in the character of Joseph, though there is evidence that this was changed by the printers even in the 1847 edition, and the whole was considerably modified by Charlotte in 1850. K. M. Petyt of Reading University concludes that "she is surprisingly good—better than either of her sisters."[9] He shows that she has consistent principles of transcription and generally holds to them. Branwell and Charlotte made attempts at Haworth dialect in the juvenilia, and of course there are dialect speakers in *Jane Eyre* and *Wildfell Hall,* but it looks as if Emily's superior ear and memory are responsible for her greater accuracy. The evidence underlines the oral nature of the novel, which is clearly meant to be spoken and heard rather than read silently.

Secondly, written literary exemplars played some part in the creation of Emily's novel, but the solid evidence, despite enormous labours, is hard to come by. So much is this so that there is still an occasional disposition to take Charlotte's view as the correct one. She presents her sister as a "naive" artist.

> [*Wuthering Heights*] is rustic all through. . . . Had she but lived, her mind would of itself have grown like a strong tree, loftier, straighter, wider-spreading, and its matured fruits would have attained a mellow ripeness and sunnier bloom; but on that mind time and experience alone could work; to the influence of other intellects, it was not amenable.[10]

Charlotte is doubtless thinking of her own attempts to wrestle with Emily's intellect, and we understand why she considers her sister impossible to influence. However, the traces in her work of Wordsworth, Coleridge and Shelley, as well as of Byron and Shakespeare show that Charlotte misunderstood her sister's thought processes.

At one time Byron was considered the major influence on the work of all the Brontës and there can be no doubt that he is there quite strongly. Mention has already been made of Moore's *Life of Byron,* and John Hewish showed that the diary papers were inspired by Byron's example. From his life the name Augusta may have been picked up, and "The Prisoner of Chillon" seems to have been an influence on such poems as "The Prisoner." Byron's personality seems also to have struck a deep chord in Emily. Winifred Gerin points to a similarity between Heathcliff's shock at his rejection by Catherine—so it seems to him at the time—and the occasion when Mary Chaworth, loved by Byron as a young man, said to a maid, "Do you think I could care for that lame boy?" and was overheard by him.[11] Byron ran out of the house and vanished into the night. The parallel between this incident and Heathcliff's departure is not likely to be coincidence. But the incident had certainly been fully integrated into Emily's subconscious; there is no feel in the story of this being inconsistent or inappropriate.

Scott had been well known to the Brontës since childhood. Similarities between *The Black Dwarf* and *Wuthering Heights* have many times been remarked, and John Hewish notes the influence of *Old Mortality.*[12] Scott's wide moorland scenes and emphasis on adventure fed into Gondal; he was one of the sources of the Brontës' absorption with things Scottish. The Gothic horror novel also leaves traces on *Wuthering Heights,* and their avid reading of *Blackwood's* did not cease when the Brontës grew up. Hewish notes parallels between Emily's novel and *The Bridegroom of Barna,* by Bartholomew Simmonds, published in *Blackwood's* in November 1840.[13] If such stories were used deliberately in the construction of *Wuthering Heights,* we have to think of Emily either re-reading back numbers of the magazine in 1845, or casting back in her long memory. But there is no suggestion that they were used deliberately; only that Emily had a much more receptive attitude to other intellects than Charlotte realized.

The evidence that Emily was interested in German literature is circumstantial. It was German she learnt in the parsonage kitchen during 1843–4, but it is not clear what she hoped to do with her knowledge. We cannot possibly know how far she had been able to progress with the subject during her stay on the continent or whether she had ever read a novel in that language. This was perhaps unnecessary. There were frequent articles on German literature in the magazines such as *Blackwood's* and *Fraser's.* Her account of Heathcliff's revenge, through the acquisition of the Earnshaw property, suggested to early commentators that she had read E. T. A. Hoffmann's *Das Majorat,* reviewed in *Blackwood's* in December 1826. Another Hoffmann story, *The*

Devil's Elixir, had been reviewed two years earlier. An excellent account of the influence on *Wuthering Heights* of these and other literary sources can be found in Hewish's book.[14]

Thirdly, there is *the theme of duality.* In his book, *The Mind of Emily Brontë,* Herbert Dingle notes what he calls her "positive" character.[15] He points out that there are few similes, few comparisons, either in the poems or the novel. Emily *states,* she does not compare. What is more, she states contradictory thoughts or feelings in adjacent poems, as we have observed. We have noted a similar duality, or ambiguity, in her attitude to life after death. But sometimes her dualities constitute poles of mythic intensity. Such duality sometimes seems to be a constituent of the human mind: so at any rate a host of philosophers have thought. Plainly, Emily sees these dualities as cosmic.

For many people the primal duality is that of father and mother. In some ways there is not a strong opposition in the Brontës' works between male and female. One could parallel Charlotte's observation in other contexts:

> . . . for an example of constancy and tenderness, remark that of Edgar Linton. (Some people will think these qualities do not shine so well incarnate in a man as they would do in a woman, but Ellis Bell could never be brought to comprehend this notion: nothing moved her more than any insinuation that the faithfulness and clemency, the long-suffering and loving-kindness which are esteemed virtues in the daughters of Eve, become foibles in the sons of Adam.)[16]

What echo of past arguments lurks in this comment? The only men who are on record as being "kind" to Emily, except for her father and brother, are Robert Heaton and William Weightman. The comment does, however, square with a general tendency in the Brontës to play down sex-differences, as in their choice of neutral pseudonyms, or Anne's insistence in *Wildfell Hall* that boys and girls should have the same education.

Emily's father was strong, kindly, short-tempered, scholarly, fond of children, romantic and dutiful. Her mother was kindly and intelligent, but died too soon for Emily to know her well. If she recalled her, it may have been as a fretful invalid. The "good" characters in *Wuthering Heights* have a peevish, feeble side to their constancy.

The next duality was that of Maria and Elizabeth. As I have tried to show, the two sisters differed quite markedly. Maria was apparently thought of as an intellectual. She was very much her father's daughter, striving hard to fulfil his loving ideal for her. She had great determination, but was rather unworldly, and she may have courted disaster stubbornly. She knew her role, and she played it to death. Elizabeth was patient too, but not an intellectual. Where Maria could not be bothered with the feminine arts such as sewing, Elizabeth (who, however, also sewed badly) may have provided a less self-confidently intellectual leadership. These two alternative mothers may have provided differing models, and even when they died alternative allies were presented to Emily by her two remaining sisters, Charlotte and Anne. We have seen how in fact she fluctuated between the two, collaborating with Anne in Gondal, but going to Belgium with Charlotte.

It is sure that Emily began to see things in terms of pairs, which might contrast. This is so in Gondal. In May 1845, when perhaps *Wuthering Heights* was already beginning, she wrote two contrasting poems called later "The two children." The two are "A. E." and "R. C.," who might be anyone. It is symbolic that the two poems have sometimes been thought to be one only, with contrasting parts. In a sense the two children are one child: the boy and his "guardian angel." Early in the poem, we hear that

> *Never has a blue streak*
> *Cleft the clouds since morn—*
> *Never has his grim Fate*
> *Smiled since he was born*

But as the metre changes and we reach the second half (or second poem) we meet a seraph, a "Child of Delight! with sunbright hair . . ." This spirit denies that she comes from heaven, but

> *I, the image of light and gladness*
> *Saw and pitied that mournful boy,*
> *And I swore to take his gloomy sadness,*
> *And give to him my beamy joy. . . .*
>
> *Guardian angel, he lacks no longer;*
> *Evil fortune he need not fear:*
> *Fate is strong, but Love is stronger;*
> *And more unsleeping than angel's care.* (p. 228)

The two children are two sides of the same being, just as Catherine and Heathcliff are two parts of a whole. Even more, this reminds us of the two second-generation protagonists, Hareton and the second Catherine. We must be right in concluding that Emily saw herself thus divided: these two children are two sides of Emily's own nature.

Elsewhere in the poetry, Emily does not compromise. She embraces *both* alternatives. "Yet my heart loves December's smile/As much as July's beam." To some extent, the opposition and reconciliation of extremes appears to be a commonplace of philosophy and sub-philosophic thought. It is certainly a strong feature of Emily Brontë's work, strongest of all in the novel.

Fourthly, and linked to this, is the emphasis on separation and reunion. Separation from the beloved was a recurrent experience in Emily's childhood. The loss of her mother must have remained as a subconscious trauma. Such a loss is sometimes perceived as incurring guilt, and any such guilt feeling would have been accentuated by the loss of the two sisters in circumstances where Emily could perhaps have palliated matters. We have seen that bad temper caused discord between Emily and her surviving sisters. As Anne says in "Self-communion": "there was cruel bitterness/When jarring discords rose between."[17] But Anne was as patient as Elizabeth, and reconciliation was possible. The lines which follow in "Self-Communion" tell us that the relationship between Emily and Anne was not all peace. It is possible that Emily was compelled to play tricks on her "twin" sometimes, just as she played tricks on Charlotte.

Still, for significant periods Emily and Anne did achieve a close and joyous affection. We have seen Ellen's picture of them physically intertwined, and we have Anne's strong "Oh, I have known a wondrous joy / In early friendship's pure delight." We have seen the two sharing the moors and the dining room table, and the glorious secret of a "Tin Box" with Gondal magic in it. We have Anne's bright poem about Alexander and Zenobia, who cannot be forever parted. These two are in a sense "lovers," but they are very young, sharing a romantic and sentimental attachment. The attachment between Emily and Anne may well have been sentimental, and when they played at Gondal lovers, it was probably romantic. Heathcliff and Catherine, similarly, are soul-mates; it is Edgar who marries Catherine for the normal satisfactions of family life, as Mary Visick notes.

The fifth point to be considered is that many Gondal themes, worked and reworked, found their ultimate place in *Wuthering Heights*. The most obvious is infidelity. "A. G. A." seems to work her way through three lovers in the Gondal poems: there is Alexander, Lord of Elbë, who appears in such poems as "Lord of Elbë, on Elbë hill"; Lord Alfred, who becomes Edgar; and Julius Brenzaida. Infidelity was of great interest to the little Brontës as they played in their nursery. To Charlotte and Branwell the theme appears to have been eternally attractive, and Branwell may have dabbled with the practice in real life. Anne encountered infidelity at Thorp Green, surely in more cases than just that of her brother: the topic became a major element in *Wildfell Hall*. There was a great deal of infidelity among the four children, not of course in love, but in taking sides and playing one off against the other. Translating this into the sphere of marital love, Anne seems to imply that in heaven such problems will be ironed out by the introduction and encouragement of plural affections. Emily allows Catherine to see no problem at all in retaining and monopolizing the love of both Edgar and Heathcliff. The arguments propounded by Shelley seem to have been an influence.

There are a number of mysterious children in Gondal. Some are "unblessed, unfriended," like Alexandria, who is abandoned in "I've seen this dell in July's shine," possibly by A. G. A. There is the venom-spitting girl of the final Gondal poem, involved in civil war; pretty Blanche, who turned into a gipsy; "A. A.," the subject of "This shall be thy lullaby," and many more. They are all isolated, appearing from nowhere, and unloved: the relevance to

Heathcliff is obvious. That they are all *children* is also important: we shall soon turn to examine Emily's view of childhood.

Wuthering Heights is set in a haunted landscape. If Heathcliff walks, as they say he does, he is the successor to the ghost of Aspin Castle:

> *Yet of the native shepherds none*
> *In open day and cheerful sun,*
> *Will tread its labyrinths alone;*
> *Far less when evening's pensive hour*
> *Hushes the bird and shuts the flower,*
> *And gives to Fancy magic power*
> *O'er each familiar tone.*

> *For round their hearths they'll tell the tale,*
> *And every listener swears it true,*
> *How wanders there a phantom pale*
> *With spirit-eyes of dreamy blue.* (p. 176)

A Gothic ghost, whom Emily is half dismissing here with her use of the word "Fancy." But he is the lighter part of a much deeper theme, which arises from Emily's deep feeling that the dead do not leave the earth.

We recall her two contradictory views on death. The dead body itself remains important:

> *Beneath the turf my footsteps tread*
> *Lie low and lone the silent dead;*
> *Beneath the turf, beneath the mould—*
> *Forever dark, forever cold.*

This is acceptable, because "Heaven itself, so pure and blest, / Could never give my spirit rest." (p. 166) We have Catherine's account of her dream ringing in our ears. On the other hand, in "Aye, there it is," we have the Platonic and Shelleyan

> *Thus truly when that breast is cold*
> *Thy prisoned soul shall rise,*
> *The dungeon mingle with the mould—*
> *The captive with the skies.* (p. 165)

Emily does not reconcile these two views of death, and however many times we read and re-read the closing pages of the novel, we cannot be sure what her final conclusion was as none is reached. She could not reconcile opposing views, as "Enough of thought, philosopher" tells us. That the dead live perpetually in the sense that they are always pervading our thoughts is a view that Emily constantly portrays, in the poems as much as in *Wuthering Heights*.

The sixth, and final point, is that Nature is a Gondal theme too, in a way. Emily's absorption in it is the chief cause of her moving her fictional world to a Yorkshire climate. In fact, her close geographical knowledge of the "lone green lane" suggests that she transfers Yorkshire features lock, stock and barrel to Gondal, though this should not be taken to mean that the lane is necessarily the path from Haworth to the moors, as is often suggested.

Charlotte made Emily's love of the moors a main plank in her apologia for her sister. Emily did indeed adore (in a real sense) the world of nature, but in an interesting way. It is not correct to think of her as a nature poet in the manner of John Clare, for instance. She does not produce the minute descriptions of the plant and animal kingdoms which we have from the Shropshire writer, Mary Webb. On the other hand, weather, times of day, seasons, clouds, winds, sunlight, grey stones, masses of heather, the wheeling lapwing, imbue a great deal of her work. They are not described in set pieces. Emily's technique is almost "dead-pan." For example, when in Chapter 21 the young Cathy drags Nelly across the moor on 20 March for an hour's "ramble," the following words help us to visualize the wild, open scenery:

> I found plenty of entertainment in listening to the larks singing *far and near,* and enjoying the *sweet, warm sunshine . . . moor-game,* so many hillocks to *climb* and pass . . . *cloudless* pleasure . . . a *great way off* . . . I began to be weary. (xxi)

In this passage, and many others, Emily conveys the feel of a bright spring day in the Pennines, but she does not particularize. Ellen Nussey testified to the way in which Emily lost her inhibitions in these wide open spaces, far from human habitation. But her love of nature goes further than simply "escaping from the palaces of instruction" to be with the lapwings and moor-game. In the last analysis Emily is truly a Stoic in valuing nature in every form. *Secundum naturam vivere,* the Stoic motto, might well be hers. You must not interfere with me, she seems to say; "I wish to be as God made me." This needs to be taken into account when we watch her dying, as she might consider, *"secundum naturam."*

This view of nature is often called nature mysticism, or pantheism. The Romantics taught something like it to a whole generation, and Mr Brontë was not untouched by it. The question is often posed, "Was Emily Brontë a mystic?" It is not always clear what kind of answer can be given to such a question, but it cannot be evaded. In the passage from *Shirley,* originally in French, where "Eva" has an ecstatic experience before the world is properly formed, we have Charlotte's view of what Emily might possibly have felt, and a second clue is generally thought to be found in the central passage of "The Prisoner," in which the captive speaks of her nocturnal visitant, that takes away her normal human senses.

As an aside, however, it must be said that we have to be very careful in commenting on the latter passage. At least one well-known Brontë commentator quotes Charlotte's 1850 additions to explain the nature of the visitant:

What I love shall come like visitant of air,
Safe in secret power from lurking human snare;
Who loves me, no word of mine shall e'er betray,
Though for faith unstained my life must forfeit pay.

Burn then, little lamp; glimmer straight and clear—
Hush, a rustling wing stirs, methinks, the air;
He for whom I wait, thus ever comes to me;
Strange Power! I trust thy might; trust thou my constancy.

These well-known lines are *not* by Emily Brontë. They show, once again, what Charlotte thought Emily might be feeling; and once again they are apologetic: we shall return to them.

It seems likely that when people ask "Was Emily Brontë a mystic," they are seeking to understand her personal attitude to religion and love. They are also trying to probe the nature of the ecstatic moments she seems to have experienced, and which seem to be evidenced both in her poetry and in Charlotte's accounts of her sister. The subjective evidence for these experiences is strong in the poetry, and objective evidence is not lacking. We do have to be most careful, however, in extracting evidence from poems, some of which are intended to be fictional. All the same, no one would doubt that the experiences Wordsworth dwells on in "Tintern Abbey" and "The Prelude" are not fictive, and Emily Brontë is entitled to a careful reading of her poetic accounts of similar experiences, especially since the principal actors in *Wuthering Heights* feel similar emotions.

I have already suggested that the first trace of these feelings occurred when Emily was six, perhaps at Cowan Bridge. Romer Wilson, indeed, links the onset of the "visions" with a fit Emily is supposed to have suffered. I should not exclude this possibility, though it seems more likely that Emily's account of a lonely child withdrawing from cheerful, lively society betokens an emotional rather than a physical crisis. We must always bear in mind the volatility of Emily's emotions, shown in her childhood tempers. The deprivation of her mother could not be glossed over in her mind, and perhaps a joyous moment would soon turn to sorrow even while the nursling is being petted. She writes of a "voice," and the characters in *Wuthering Heights* often seem to act as though interior but separate forces are motivating them. The impression is ambivalent: in "I saw thee, child, one summer's day," dated July 1837, the child of the poem is struck by the passionate desire to know the future, but is overcome instead by an almost physical presence. The description foreshadows Heathcliff's intuition in the presence of Catherine:[18]

A fearful anguish in his eyes
Fixed strainedly on the vacant air;
Heavily bursts in long-drawn sighs
His panting breath, enchained by fear. (p. 40)

Such a description would be hard to write for anyone who had not experienced something like it. It seems that Emily's mind visualized an unknown, unspecified entity which could terrorize her. How near this feeling was to epilepsy or hysteria we cannot know. Terror was not the only emotion it might convey; when the visitant appears in other poems, it is benign, and of course Heathcliff welcomes it.

The intellectual force in *Wuthering Heights* is gigantic. As we see Emily Brontë now in 1846 struggling with the form of the novel we may recall M. Heger's opinion of her as a supreme intelligence. We may be inclined to place more emphasis on her emotional power, but in the novel she succeeds in channelling this through rational construction to a masterpiece. Once she had endured these moments of intense and surprising emotion, she needed to wrestle with them and try to formulate some theories which would satisfy her own questioning. One possible explanation she toys with is ghosts; we have seen how Aspin Castle has its ghost, and the final pages of *Wuthering Heights* repeat this solution rather wistfully. The literary convention of the ghost was a little overworked; Emily could not always take it quite seriously. She is equally unconvinced by Charlotte's orthodoxy and Anne's universalism.

"How clear she shines!" of 13 April 1843 showed us how Emily worked herself into this kind of vision, just as Heathcliff tries to induce a vision of Catherine. Emily invokes "Fancy," who is bending "my lonely couch above." The metaphor is from the goodnight kiss of a mother (or elder sister) for her child. "Fancy" is seen as a sort of latter-night Maria or Elizabeth, who can comfort and placate the wounded spirit of the wakeful Emily. She gazes fixedly out of the window, at the stars that glow "Above me in that stormless sea," and allows herself a waking "dream," under the patronage of Fancy. A year later, Emily is more inclined to call her faculty "Imagination" and to set it against "Reason," which will "tell the suffering heart how vain / Its cherished dreams must always be. . . ." Imagination is

> *ever there to bring*
> *The hovering visions back and breathe*
> *New glories o'er the blighted spring*
> *And call a lovelier life from death,*
> *And whisper with a voice divine*
> *Of real worlds as bright as thine.* (p. 206)

At this point Emily seems to consider "heaven" or some such further dimension a "real" world. She does not, however, "trust" to Imagination's "phantom bliss," but at evening, she finds it a solace.

All these poems lead to *Wuthering Heights,* because they speak of a deliberate attempt by Emily Brontë to cultivate methods of approaching the once-spontaneous experience. As a Wordsworthian, she realizes that "the glory and the dream" is fitful, but a semblance of it can be restored. "O thy bright eyes" of 14 October 1844 is more intense. She calls the faculty "God of Visions" and says she had chosen it beyond Wealth, Power, Glory and Pleasure. It is "ever present, phantom thing" and has become a "King" to her. The account of imagination here is much more intense and emotional. The vision is "My slave, my comrade, and my King" and even more emotionally

> *My Darling Pain that wounds and sears*
> *And wrings a blessing out from tears*
> *By deadening me to real cares.* (p. 209)

Emily is writing of a mentally induced vision, willed as an intense pleasure, but surprisingly also an intense pain. Heathcliff shares this pain and pleasure; for Emily in 1846 it may be that he came to represent them.

Sometimes the description of these visions is most distanced and sceptical, as though Emily would withdraw from the title of "mystic" or cannot in honesty attain it. In "A day dream" of 5 March 1844, a Shelleyan cosmic dream is recorded, but in slightly mocking terms. Sometimes, the vision is apparently in human shape. In "My comforter" of 10 February 1844, a writer is being described whose printed words "heard" by the person whose audial memory and visualization had once enabled her to read "very prettily" seem to become a vision of that person. Gradually, it may be, the envisioned poet became the envisioned hero of *Wuthering Heights*.

Whether such an intense imaginative life, sometimes willed and sometimes spontaneous, can be called mystic is for the reader to decide. Certainly the novel could not be the same without this bodily withdrawal and emotional dynamism, which became focused on Heathcliff and Catherine. Judging by the dates of poems which express the same compressed feeling, Heathcliff was already potent in the version of *Wuthering Heights* sent to Colburn in 1846. Emily was at her "mystical" height in "The Prisoner," already mentioned as the poem she may have been copying into her B manuscript on the day Charlotte discovered it. "Rochelle" (earlier "Geraldine," later Catherine) is specific about a wild visionary experience:

> *He comes with western winds, with evening's wandering airs,*
> *With that clear dusk of heaven that brings the thickest stars;*
> *Winds take a pensive tone, and stars a tender fire,*
> *And visions rise and change which kill me with desire—*

But will Emily be precise about these "visions"? What does she mean by saying that they "rise and change"?

There may be some clue in the next stanza, which continues

> *Desire for nothing known in my maturer years*
> *When joy grew mad with awe at counting future tears;*

When, if my spirit's sky was full of flashes warm,
I knew not whence they came, from sun or thunderstorm. (p. 238)

David Cecil considers that the family at the Heights are "children of storm," and Heathcliff the most so.[19] Here Rochelle-Emily says that emotional heat constitutes the greatest value, whether the heat is sunny or stormy. One effect of *Wuthering Heights* is to leave the reader believing in the moral value of emotion as such, whether it issues in conventionally good or bad acts. "Rochelle" recalls the most powerful instances of this heightened feeling as taking place in childhood, as Catherine and Heathcliff yearn to return to their free days of rambling on the moor. "Mysticism" involves a stormy communion with the self of the past, and the natural world where it lived. In adulthood, "Rochelle" works herself up to a point where she is beyond humanity. The frantic passion of Heathcliff also takes him beyond humanity, to a point where he is sure that his lost love is situated "within two yards' distance"; he gazes at her while the vision "communicated, apparently, both pleasure and pain, in exquisite extremes" (xxxiv).

Mysticism perhaps also implies intense love; we commonly use the word of a religious communicant who expresses his or her love of God. As we have seen earlier, Emily expressly says she has not been involved with any earthly love. As a violently emotional child, she was nursed by Maria and Elizabeth, petted by Miss Evans, cuddled in bed by Charlotte while they made up their very special plays, then transferred her affection to Anne, with whom she is found intertwined as a young teenager. A voracious reader and dweller in the land of poetry, she takes to Byron and develops a passion for Shelleyan ideas so intense as to bring the writer before her eyes. I have suggested elsewhere that *Epipsychidion* may have been a special favourite, as it seems to address Emily directly. She loves her animals, but is so extremely shy that she hardly stops to nod to any curate she sees. The persona she adopts is so dense that only children can penetrate it. In writing *Wuthering Heights* she can elude all communication difficulties, and become legitimately absorbed in frenzied, heart-warming creativity.

We should not leave *Wuthering Heights* without re-emphasizing the recurrent images of childhood in it. Deep in the poetry we have found many references to lonely, imprisoned, emotional children. One vital element in the novel is the terrible yearning for lost childhood, Wordsworth's idea of the extension of heaven. "The child is father of the man" could be Emily's theme song. Stevie Davies points out the centrality of the image of the lapwings, abandoned in their nest to become winter skeletons, remembered and contemplated by Catherine as she nears her own end, in a state of dementia and mystic vision.[20]

This nest destroyed is a metaphor for the Brontë family itself, with one parent dead and leaving two of her children to become tiny skeletons. Stevie Davies goes further, and points to the emphasis on motherhood in the centre of *Wuthering Heights;* at the central axis of the novel Catherine, erstwhile child, who, with Heathcliff, "pictured Heaven so beautifully . . . in their innocent talk," suffers, dies and gives birth to a regenerated new Catherine. So, too, Emily Brontë, at one time busy pairing off fictional characters in a Gondal plan, does not attain motherhood except through building her novel on the skeletons of past pain, and brings to birth her resurrected A. G. A.

The biographer cannot explain *Wuthering Heights.* The process of using the novel to understand the life, and the life to understand the novel, can easily become circular. I have tried to remain aware of the trap. What is clear, surely, is that *Wuthering Heights* is in all ways consistent with Emily's life as we know it and in particular with her inner life, as that emerges before us in her rare oracular statements, and especially in her poetry.

Notes

1.   E. Gaskell, *The Life of Charlotte Brontë* (London: Dent, 1971), 213.
2.   Ibid.
3.   Ibid., 215.
4.   A. Robinson, *Emily Brontë* (London: W. H. Allen, 1883), 50–51.
5.   E. Chitham, *The Brontës' Irish Background* (London: Macmillan, 1986), 171.
6.   J. Goodridge, "A New Heaven and a New Earth," in *The Art of Emily Brontë*, ed. A. Smith (London: Orion Press, 1976), 170–71.
7.   J. Hewish, *Emily Brontë* (London: Macmillan, 1969), 116.
8.   Sung by Mrs. C. Costello. In R. Vaughan Williams and A. Lloyd, *The Penguin Book of English Folk Songs* (Harmondsworth: Penguin, 1950), 52.
9.   K. Petyt, *Emily Brontë and the Haworth Dialect* (Yorkshire Dialect Society, 1970).
10.   Charlotte Brontë, "Biographical Notice of Ellis and Acton Bell," preface to the 1850 edition of *Wuthering Heights*.
11.   W. Gerin, *Emily Brontë* (Oxford: Clarendon Press, 1971), 45.
12.   Hewish, 121.
13.   Ibid., 122–23.
14.   Ibid., 124ff.
15.   H. Dingle, *The Mind of Emily Brontë* (London: Martin, Brown and O Keefe, 1974), 33. But cf. M. Schorer, "Fiction and the Matrix of Analogy," *The Kenyon Review* 9 (1949): 539–60, where some examples of comparison and analogy are given. These do not, I think, invalidate Dingle's point.
16.   Charlotte Brontë, "Biographical Notice."
17.   Anne Brontë, *The Poems of Anne Brontë*, ed. E. Chitham (London: Macmillan, 1979), 155.
18.   *Wuthering Heights*, xxxiv. "Now, I perceived he was not looking at the wall, for when I regarded him alone it seemed, exactly, that he gazed at something within two yards' distance. And, whatever it was, it communicated, apparently, both pleasure and pain, in exquisite extremes; at least, the anguished, yet raptured expression of his countenance suggested that idea."
19.   D. Cecil, *Early Victorian Novelists* (London: Constable, 1934), 173ff.
20.   S. Davies, *Emily Brontë* (Hemel Hempstead: Harvester, 1988).

Brontë in 1845

Juliet Barker*

Emily's cheerfulness reflected both her contentment in her role as house-keeper and, more importantly, her fulfillment as a writer. From the volume of her poetry one can deduce that she had been working steadily since the new year, producing a number of poems, including five which she herself judged worthy of publication the following year.[1] This is confirmed by her diary paper, written for her twenty-seventh birthday, 30 July 1845:

> The Gondals still flo[u]rish bright as ever I am at present writing a work on the First Wars—Anne has been writing some articles on this and a book by Henry Sophona—We intend sticking firm by the rascals as long as they delight us which I am glad to say they do at present—(II, p. 90)

Emily seems to have been completely unaware that Anne no longer shared her own unabated enthusiasm for Gondal. In her last half year at Thorp Green Anne's poetry had grown progressively more autobiographical and more unhappy in tone, even when it retained its Gondal context.[2] She had still been able to find some solace in the imaginary world as a retreat from reality when she wrote this poem on 24 January:

> Call me away; there's nothing here,
>   That wins my soul to stay;
> Then let me leave this prospect drear;
>   And hasten far away.
>
> To our belovèd land I'll flee,
>   Our land of thought and soul,
> Where I have roved so oft with thee,
>   Beyond the Worlds controll.[3]

Though it may be reading too much into what may be written in Gondal character, by 1 June she had moved into a state of depression and self-loathing which only piety could cure.

*Reprinted from J. Barker, *The Brontës* (London: Weidenfeld and Nicholson, 1994), 453–56.

Oppressed with sin and wo,
A burdened heart I bear,
Opposed by many a mighty foe:
But I will not despair.

With this polluted heart,
I dare to come to Thee,
"Devine" Holy and Mighty as Thou art:
For Thou wilt pardon me.[4]

In her diary paper, which she wrote on Thursday, 31 July, "sitting in the Dining Room in the Rocking Chair before the fire with my feet on the fender," Anne's disillusionment with Gondal is quite clearly spelt out.

Emily is engaged in writing <the> Emperor Julius's life She has read some of it and I very much want to hear the rest—She is writing some poetry too I wonder what it is about—I <am writing> have begun the third volume of passages in the life of an Individual, I wish I had <finnish> finished it— . . . We have not yet finished our Gondal chronicles that we began three years and a half ago when will they be done?—The Gondals are at present in a sad state the Republicans are uppermost but the Royalists are not quite overcome—the young sovereigns with their brothers and sisters are still at the palace of Instruction—The Unique Society <we> above half a year ago were wrecked on a dezart Island <du> as they were returning from Garldin—they are still there but we have not played at them much yet—The Gondals in general are not in first rate playing condition—will they improve? (II, p. 52)

The railway trip to York with Emily a month earlier had obviously done little to stimulate Anne's interest in Gondal, even though she had joined in playing at the characters.

Anne's diary paper, in sharp contrast to Emily's, reveals a depression that extends beyond the disappointment with Gondal. This was perhaps inevitable given the uncertainty of her future, now that she had finally resigned her post at Thorp Green; it is likely, too, that she was worried about what had already happened there and apprehensive about what might happen in her absence.

Yesterday was Emily's birthday and the time when we should have opened our 1845 [sic: should be 1841] paper but by mistake we opened it to day instead—How many things have happened since it was written—some pleasant some far otherwise—Yet I was then at Thorp Green and now I am only just escaped from it—I was wishing to leave [?it] then and if I had known that I had four years longer to stay how wretched I should have been—<then too. I was writing the fourth volume of Sophala—> but during my stay I have had some very unpleasant and undreamt of experience of human <nature> nature— . . . I wonder how we shall all be and where and how situated <when

we open this pap> on the thirtyeth of July 1848 When if we are all alive
Emily will be just <thirty> 30 I shall be in my 29th year Charlotte in her
33rd and Branwell in his 32nd and what changes shall we have seen and
known and shall we be much changed ourselves? I hope not—for the worse at
least—I for my part cannot well be *flatter* or older in mind than I am now—
(II, p. 53)

Despite their closeness, Emily seems to have had little sympathy with Anne's
low spirits. Indeed, it is curious that Emily should ever have gained the reputation of being the most sympathetic of the Brontës, particularly in her dealings with Branwell,⁵ as all the evidence points to the fact that she was so
absorbed in herself and her literary creations that she had little time for the
genuine suffering of her family. Her attitude at this time seems to have been
brusque to the point of heartlessness. This is understandable where Charlotte
was concerned, since her problems were largely self-inflicted, but it is surprising to find Emily equally unsympathetic towards Anne, who was the victim
of circumstances beyond her control. Her impatience with her siblings is evident in her diary paper.

> I should have mentioned that last summer the school scheme was revived in
> full vigor—we had prospectuses printed despatched letters to all acquaintances
> imparting our plans and did our little all—but it was found no go—now I
> dont desire a school at all and none of us have any great longing for it—we
> have cash enough for our present wants with a prospect of accumulation—we
> are all in decent health—only that papa has a complaint in his eyes and with
> the exception of B[ranwell] who I hope will be better and do better, hereafter. I
> am quite contented for myself—not as idle as formerly, altogether as hearty
> and having learnt to make the most of the present and hope for the future with
> less fidgetiness that I cannot do all I wish—seldom or [n]ever troubled with
> nothing to do <illegible> and merely desiring that every body could be as
> comfortable as myself and as undesponding and then we should have a very
> tolerable world of it—

It was all very well for Emily to feel irritation at the rest of her family's
despondency, but her place was secure and she was no longer expected to go
out into the world to earn her living like them. Her preoccupations are neatly
summed up at the end of her paper.

> Tabby has just been teasing me to turn as formerly to "pilloputate"—Anne and
> I should have picked the black currants if it had been fine and sunshiny—I
> must hurry off now to my turning and ironing I have plenty of work on hands
> and writing and am altogether full of business with best wishes for the whole
> house till 1848—July 30th and as much longer as may be I conclude EJ
> Brontë

The diary papers are as interesting for what they omit as for what they
include. The one subject which must have been foremost in every member of

the Brontë family's mind was barely touched upon. Emily's entry was cryptic in its brevity.

Anne left her situation at Thorp Green of her own accord—June 1845 Branwell left—July 1845[6]

Notes

1. The five poems published in *Poems,* were "Enough of Thought, Philosopher," February 3, 1845 (p. 220); "Cold in the earth and the deep snow piled above thee!," March 3, 1845 (p. 222); "Death, that struck when I was most confiding," April 10, 1845 (p. 224); "Ah! why, because the dazzling sun," April 14, 1845 (p. 225); and "How beautiful the Earth is still," June 2, 1845 (p. 231).

2. I think it is dangerous to argue that all Anne's religious poems, particularly those written during the spring and early summer of 1845, are autobiographical. There are many parallels in both story line and mood between the poems written by Anne and Emily at this time. We also know from Emily's 1845 diary that they were then both writing about the First Wars between the Royalists and Republicans. The subject matter naturally lent itself to the contemplation of blighted hopes and expressions of despair at the separation of families and lovers by the political divide. Anne's poem "I love the silent hour of night," which is usually regarded as a personal lamentation for William Weightman, is closely paralleled by Emily's "Cold in the earth and the deep snow piled above thee!," also written at this time. Similarly, Anne's "Oppressed with sin and wo" and "When sinks my heart in hopeless gloom" find strong echoes in Emily's "How beautiful the Earth is still," the first and last poems being written on consecutive days in June. The fact that Anne's heroes and heroines look to God rather than hope or imagination for comfort is simply a reflection of her character. If, as I suspect, most of Anne's poems of this period belong in a Gondal setting, then the depth of her despair at Thorp Green may have been unduly exaggerated.

3. "Call me away, there's nothing here," January 14, 1845, in E. Chitham, *The poems of Anne Brontë* (Oxford: Macmillan, 1979), 107. I cannot agree with Chitham that this poem reflects the Branwell-Mrs. Robinson situation. The lovers are clearly a Gondal Romeo and Juliet, and as we know from Emily's diary paper that both she and Anne were writing about the First Wars, it seems likely that one came from a Royalist family, the other from a Republican family.

4. "Oppressed with sin and wo," June 1, 1845, in Chitham, 114.

5. The myth of Emily's sympathy and secret support to a beleaguered Branwell relies on two principal sources: Emily's poem "Well, some may hate and some may scorn," which expresses pity for a man of "ruined hopes" and "blighted fame" who has died unlamented, and the tradition that Emily used to put a lighted lamp in the parsonage window to guide the drunken Branwell home from the Black Bull. The poem belongs to 1839, and there is no contemporary source for the tradition, which, if true, would have meant that Emily was encouraging Branwell's vices, a scenario that is inherently unlikely.

6. The printed text (II, p. 49) omits the phrase about Branwell. Emily's apparent lack of concern about the situation is even more striking because in the original manuscript, which may have been copied out from rough drafts, she transposed the first sentence of the next paragraph into her statement about Branwell. What she actually wrote was, "Branwell <went our first long Jo> left- July 1845."

The Hidden Ghost

WINIFRED GERIN*

It might be argued that by 1848 Emily had nothing further to say, that her explorations into the life of the spirit had ended with *Wuthering Heights* and the preserved poems. Perhaps the truth must be faced that there were no further voyages to make; M. Heger's navigator had crossed her last sea.

Most inhibiting of all perhaps had been the act of publication itself. For in a girl of such singular reticence, to be exposed to the world, even to the sympathetic eyes of Mr. Smith and Mr. Williams, was an appalling experience. Emily's conduct, as related by Charlotte, was one of untamed indifferent incivility, noticeably different from her former obliging and considerate conduct towards her sisters when the school plan was debated. Fear of exposure might well be strong enough to frustrate the will to write; such a reaction on the part of an intensely shy girl would not be unnatural. The evidence of Charlotte's numerous excuses for Ellis Bell's unsociable conduct partially corroborates this. But even such a rejection of human contacts would not account for what appears to have been the complete cessation of the poetic experience. Emily had written, during the last ten years at least, for herself alone; one would have thought that, had the inspiration been there, nothing could have broken her of the habit.

Fragments of two versions of the same poem—"Why Ask to know the Date, the Clime"—remain as her total poetic output for the period from September 1846 to May 1848. In a similar period of eighteen months, September 1843 to May 1845, she had written twenty-one poems, which included some of her best. The solitude she enjoyed during the simultaneous absence from home of Charlotte, Anne, and Branwell during 1843 and 1844, was no doubt conducive to the writing of poetry, but all of *Wuthering Heights* was probably written while the whole family was at home, between October 1845 and June 1846. Material conditions, such as want of space in which to write, seem not to have affected her; her own drawing of herself writing in her little room with her desk on her knees, is confirmed by the evidence of the servants who noticed her and Anne taking their desks into the garden during the summer of 1847 and early settling under the currant bushes to write.[1] No mater-

*Reprinted from W. Gerin, *Emily Brontë* (Oxford: Clarendon Press, 1971), 246–49.

ial difficulties would have prevented her writing—if the will to write had remained. Emily's absolute refusal to co-operate further in the publishing projects of the Bells must be seen as part of a general withdrawal into herself that marked the periods immediately preceding and following the death of Branwell. When the reprint of the *Poems* came out late in October, the reviews were as unsatisfactory as those for the first edition, and Charlotte's wounded comments show how deeply she felt the fresh insult to Ellis's genius. Acknowledging the *Standard of Freedom* and the *Morning Herald* sent by Smith, Elder on 2 November, she wrote: "As critiques, I should have thought more of them had they more fully recognized Ellis Bell's merits; but the lovers of abstract poetry are few in number" (II, p. 269). "Blind is he as a bat, insensate as any stone, to the merits of Ellis," she cried over the reviewer in the *Spectator* (II, p. 271). Ellis, if she glanced through such notices, could only have felt justified in turning her back on them all.

Barely a month after Branwell's death she did not even answer when spoken to. Uncommunicative she had always been, as though afraid "of revealing herself," as Ellen Nussey had early noted. Even when pleased, her utmost expression of thanks had often been no more than a smile (one of those rare smiles that Ellen Nussey again thought were "something to remember through life"). But whereas formerly Charlotte had spoken and written freely on behalf of Anne and Emily, an increasing scrupulousness is observable in her reports on Emily as though she really feared to "exceed her commission." Thanking Ellen for the box of gifts for the household sent on her last return from Brookroyd in September 1847, she wrote: "Emily is just now sitting on the floor of the bedroom where I am writing, looking at her apples. She smiled when I gave them and the collar to her as your presents, with an expression at once well pleased and slightly surprised" (II, p. 143). When George Smith suggested sending down to Haworth parcels of books from Cornhill—not as gifts but as loans—Charlotte thankfully accepted them on behalf of all the family, and added: "the loan of the books is indeed well-timed; no more acceptable benefit could have been conferred on my dear sister Emily, who is at present too ill to occupy herself . . . with anything but reading. She smiled when I told her Mr. Smith was going to send some more books—she was pleased" (II, p. 271).

By then, the final and alarming stage of Emily's withdrawal into herself had been reached. The severe cold and cough had, to the horror of the family, been recognized as "inflammation of the lungs" by 2 November. Her illness, its relentless progress, the emaciation, the fever, the shortness of breath, the pain in the side, all confirmed the family's terrors of worse to come. In the face of this physical reality they were naturally less inclined than posterity is to reflect upon her spiritual condition.

In the great poem written in October 1845—published in 1846 as "The Prisoner"—Emily gave to the jailor those haunting lines:

> And I am rough and rude, yet not more rough to see
> Than is the hidden ghost which has its home in me! . . . (p. 237)

The sense of the separateness of the spirit immured inside the body here becomes a visual reality, an inescapable condition of human nature from which the sensitive and the insensitive have to suffer alike.

The subject treated was not a new one for Emily; she had invented stories about prisoners immured in dungeons all her life, ever since the time of the children's games in the parsonage cellars; it was one of her favourite symbols, a regular Gondal theme. In this very poem the rescuing party strays in the crypts, and only after long and idle wandering through the vaults, comes on the prisoner confined behind triple walls. The prisoner had reached a condition of near-silence; counting on her weakness, her jailor expected no resistance, and was incredulous to hear her speak. And when she spoke it was with defiance, to reveal her certainty of deliverance, through the nightly visitations of a "messenger of Hope," who came to her "with western winds, with evening's wandering airs, / With that clear dusk of heaven that brings the thickest stars"—the condition, in short, that had always been the most propitious to Emily's own spiritual release.

To the modern reader seeking to discover what happened to Emily Brontë in her last months, such a state of imprisonment appears to have become her own condition. The way out was lost, and her cell was inaccessible to would-be rescuers. Her almost total silence and unresponsiveness to outside contacts completed her isolation. Seeking to penetrate that isolation, all that her family could do was to repeat, as Charlotte did in letter after letter: "I *do* wish I knew her state of mind . . . I wish I knew her feelings more clearly . . . but she will not give an explanation of her feelings" (II, p. 289).

What explanation could Emily give, except that she was immured and could not get out? that she was waiting for her "messenger of Hope," and that he had ceased to come?

Note

1.   E. Chadwick, *In the Footsteps of the Brontës* (London: Pitman, 1914), 311.

The Shattered Prison

KATHLEEN FRANK*

On Monday, 18 December, Emily was even worse, but still she would allow no one to interfere when she went to feed the dogs after tea. She prepared their meal of meat and bread scraps in the kitchen and then walked into the cold passageway with the food. She staggered on the uneven flagstones and fell back, gasping, against the wall, but she refused to let Charlotte or Anne help her. She somehow managed to muster hidden reserves of strength and fed the dogs herself. Then she joined Charlotte and Anne in the dining room. They sat near the fire with their needlework; Emily was too weak to sew and Charlotte tried to interest her by reading from a volume of Emerson's essays which Williams had sent. Charlotte read on aloud, the ticking of the clock in the hallway punctuating the gaps of silence when she looked up from the page to see if Emily was following, or even listening. Emily didn't appear to be, and after a while Charlotte laid the book aside, planning to continue the next day. They all went to bed early, shortly after their father.

It took long, dark hours and hours for the dawn to come, and when its wan, grey light filled the uncurtained parsonage windows it brought no hope with it. Charlotte had lain awake throughout the night, listening for Emily's cough, waiting for day, as if a revolution of the earth could touch or change the course of an individual life. By 7 a.m., at her usual time, Emily had managed to get up, dress, and come down to the kitchen unaided. At breakfast, Patrick Brontë and Charlotte and Anne all read in Emily's face what would befall her—befall them all—before darkness came again. Emily ate nothing, perhaps sipped some weak, milky tea, and then when the meal was over, crossed the hallway to the dining room and took up her sewing, only to drop it into her lap almost immediately out of sheer weakness.

Charlotte sat at the dining room table and did the only thing she *could* do: she wrote to Ellen of the great calamity that seemed to be battering at the parsonage door and windows no less insistently than the December winds outdoors: "I should have written to you before, if I had had one word of hope to say; but I had not. She grows daily weaker. The physician's opinion was expressed too obscurely to be of use. He sent some medicine which she would not take. Moments so dark as these I have never known" (II, p. 293).

*Reprinted from K. Frank, *Emily Brontë: A Chainless Soul* (Boston: Houghton Mifflin, 1990), 259–61.

Later in the morning Charlotte left the house for the first time in weeks to scour the snow-covered, frozen moors for a spray of heather to bring to Emily. It took her several hours to find a withered but still scarlet-purple branch, but by the time she returned home Emily's "dim and indifferent eyes" could no longer recognize the gift or the giver. Charlotte, in fact, was only just in time, for above all things she feared Emily dying alone. Much of the anguish of Emily's illness had been that Charlotte could not share it, that Emily had locked her out. It would be beyond endurance if Emily found her way out of the world alone.

Emily was too far away now to offer resistance, so Charlotte and Anne moved her to the sofa where she could lie down. Then there seemed nothing else to do. To watch the person you love most in the world die is both an agony and a mystery. The passage is an uncharted, unfathomable one and the watcher stands desolate on the shore. Emily was both there and not there; Charlotte and Anne could see her, touch her, but not *reach* her. Emily was somewhere else, in that dark space that is the horizon of death. Like Catherine Earnshaw, she "was all bewildered; she sighed, and moaned and knew nobody." Or rather, knew not Charlotte and Anne and her father. But some other, inaccessible life was going on within her even though Charlotte couldn't break the code of her utterances. Emily was speaking at last in her delirium, but in the foreign tongue of the "world within."

At noon, however, she came part of the way back to them. The delirium subsided for a moment the way a wave recedes from the shore only to prepare for a larger one behind it. And now, when Emily was able to recognize and respond to Charlotte again, she gave the permission she had withheld for so long. She said they might send for the doctor. Perhaps the darkness from which she had emerged and which lay ahead made her falter; more likely, the stricken faces of her sisters made Emily yield, at last and too late, to their fears and their love. At two in the afternoon, before the doctor arrived, she "turned her dying eyes from the pleasant sun."

POETRY

Introduction

THOMAS JOHN WINNIFRITH

The greatness of Emily Brontë's poetry has generally been recognized. Anthologies of nineteenth-century poetry and of women's poetry would be incomplete without some of her masterpieces. Critical commentary has been sadly lacking, and in making a representative selection one has not a very wide choice. This is a strange contrast to the embarrassing wealth of articles about *Wuthering Heights*. It is naturally difficult to detach *Wuthering Heights* from the poems or vice versa, and many studies, notably one by Mary Visick, really conflate the two, although of course ideally each poem should be considered as a separate entity. Others, especially Chitham in his biography, have used the poems as a means for providing insights into Emily's life. This is dangerous, although it is useful, as Hewish's biographical chapter shows, to know the circumstances of her life when considering her poetry.

It is also useful to know the publishing history of this poetry. Charlotte discovered some poems by Emily in the autumn of 1845. The discovery was not popular, but eventually the three sisters decided to publish a selection of their poems. This appeared in 1846 and attracted little attention, although there were reviews favorable to Emily, whose work undoubtedly suffered, and perhaps still suffers today, by being linked to the inferior poems of her sisters. Charlotte included a few more poems by Emily and Anne in her second editions of *Wuthering Heights* and *Agnes Grey,* published in 1851. Her editing of her sister's poetry was not above reproach. The manuscripts of the poems passed into the hands of Mr. Nicholls but were then acquired by C. K. Shorter, who published two very unsatisfactory editions in 1910 and 1923. In the meantime, thanks to the nefarious activities of T. J. Wise, the manuscripts were widely scattered. A reasonable edition by C. W Hatfield appeared in 1941, and a scholarly edition by D. Roper and Chitham is imminent. Details of more accessible collections by J. Gezari and B. Lloyd Evans and selections by J. Barker, Chitham and S. Davies, all with some critical commentary, can be found in the bibliography.

Even with this recently improved availability, there are still obstacles to the proper appreciation of Brontë's poems. The first and most formidable obstacle is Gondal. Just as Charlotte and Branwell wrote numerous poems and prose stories about an imaginary realm in Africa called Angria, so Emily and Anne created a similar country in the Pacific called Gondal and wrote poetry and prose about it. But only the poems survive, and much of their meaning is lost without a knowledge of the Gondal context. F. Ratchford tried to work out from the poems the story of Gondal, and we open our selection with her findings. It should be noted, however, that these cannot be taken for granted, since the characters in these poems are referred to frequently only by their initials, and Ratchford's account makes several bold assumptions in linking initials together. Quite a few characters in *Wuthering Heights* and *The Tenant of Wildfell Hall* have names beginning with the letter *H*. A different version of the Gondal story appears in Denis Donoghue's article. Charlotte's Angrian prose stories have characters dying and being restored to life; this fluid structure suggests that it is probably a mistake to look for a single coherent narrative in Gondal. In addition Ratchford, whose pioneer work on the juvenilia cannot be ignored, became obsessed by Gondal, and saw all of the poetry as belonging to the saga, although there is both internal and external evidence against this thesis. Emily would seem to have divided her poems into two notebooks, only one of which dealt with Gondal, and many of the best poems appear to be personal statements that have nothing to do with Gondal.

Another barrier to the appreciation of the poetry is, oddly enough, the existence of *Wuthering Heights*. It is easy to interpret the poems in the light of the novel, since both poetry and prose deal with thwarted love, savage revenge, rugged scenery, dark passions, and prolonged mourning, all linked by baffled and baffling metaphysical questioning. But Visick, whose book is appropriately called *The Genesis of "Wuthering Heights,"* aims to prove that the poems, especially the Gondal poems, were trial runs for *Wuthering Heights*. This thesis, though well argued, is perhaps demeaning to some of the superior poetry while it elevates inferior poems because they seem thematically connected to the novel. Her long extract contains an impressive selection of poems, but these are of varying quality.

It is the great merit of Donoghue's article that he is able to get away from Gondal and *Wuthering Heights* and start considering Brontë's poems in their own right. He also gives some idea of the core of the poems, suggesting that there are about thirty poems of intrinsic merit. A collection of articles edited by Anne Smith and entitled *The Art of Emily Brontë* contains three essays on the poetry, of which we print one. Hardy concentrates on the best poems and is able to show Brontë's peculiar strain of romanticism. The two other articles in this collection, by Rosalind Miles and Robin Grove, do not alter Donoghue's thesis: Grove is indeed fairly rude about some inferior poems whose crude emphasis on doom and gloom tends to blind the average reader to the subtlety of Brontë's finer work. We conclude this section with an extract from one of Davies's books on Brontë as a feminist revolutionary, showing that the poems as well as *Wuthering Heights* are capable of being interpreted in an innovative fashion.

A Reconstruction of Gondal

FANNY RATCHFORD*

Augusta Geraldine Almeda or A.G.A., known also as Rosina, Princess of Alcona, a province in Gondal, was born under the predominating auspices of the planet Venus. From a "glorious child," loving and generous, courageous and truthful, a messenger of joy and gladness, she developed into a true daughter of her brilliant star, ardent in temperament, poetic in thought, fickle and changeable in love. Worshipped of all men who came under her charms, she brought tragedy to those upon whom her amorous light shone—death in battle to Lord Elbë; exile and death to Amedeus; exile and suicide to Lord Alfred; imprisonment, madness and suicide to Fernando; assassination to Julius.

In Julius Brenzaida, Prince of Angora, A.G.A. found the one true and lasting passion of her life. Urged on by her ambition, and with her political and military help, he defeated his rivals, the princes of the House of Exina, treacherously making himself emperor of all Gondal and Gaaldine. At the height of his power he was assassinated by political and personal enemies led by Angelica, A.G.A.'s onetime stepdaughter, and by Angelica's foster brother, Amedeus, who together struck in revenge at A.G.A. through Julius.

With the overthrow of the Julian empire, A.G.A., or Rosina, became a fugitive with her child, whom she left to die in a mountain snowstorm. In time she rallied her forces and regained her throne, reigning brilliantly for fifteen years or longer, though grieving bitterly for Julius all the while.

One day her old enemy, Angelica, finding her upon the moors alone except for two unarmed attendants, lovers blindly absorbed in each other, incited Douglas, a fellow outlaw, to murder first the lovers and then the Queen herself. A.G.A.'s lifeless body was discovered by Lord Eldred, Captain of the Queen's Guard. Sending his men in pursuit of the assassin, he himself kept watch over the corpse, reviewing in thought the tempestuous career of this woman once "so adored, so deified," now lying "a wreck of desolate despair" in the moonlight before him.

*Reprinted from F. Ratchford, *Gondal's Queen* (Austin:University of Texas Press, 1953), 41–42.

61

The Gondal Saga

MARY VISICK*

To investigate the origins of this amazing novel is a critical task worth undertaking. These origins may be found quite specifically in the Gondal poems. Emily Brontë's earliest dated poem was written towards the end of her eighteenth year; by February 1844, when she was nearly twenty-six, she had accumulated enough poetry to begin transcribing it into two manuscript books, which presumably contain all she wished to preserve. Fortunately other manuscripts have survived which, although the verse they contain is often inferior, occasionally supply some significant variations, or provide Gondal poems which help us to piece the story together. Of the two transcript books one bears simply her initials and the date; the other is headed *Gondal Poems*. Of the 151 fully finished poems in Mr Hatfield's edition, these two books account for seventy-six. There is a third manuscript book, now in the British Museum, and there are also three collections of loose sheets, in the hands of various collectors; but neither the third book nor the sheets contains any poem dated later than February 1844. The two transcript books, then, superseded them. The books escaped the holocaust which consumed all the Gondal prose, and were obviously prepared with great care—whether for publication or not it is impossible to say. The story they can be shown to tell is the story of *Wuthering Heights*.

Charlotte's well-known account of her accidental discovery of "a MS volume of verse in my sister Emily's handwriting" implies that Emily Brontë did not intend to publish her poems, that in fact she shrank from the idea and had to be persuaded by Charlotte that her poems "merited publication." On this a good deal of fine writing on Emily's morbidly fastidious shyness has been produced; it seems rather beside the point, for the poems which finally appeared in *Poems by Currer, Ellis and Acton Bell* published in 1846 are not the least personal—they include the most personal of all her poems, *The Prisoner, Stars, The Old Stoic, Plead for me, The Philosopher;* they are, quite simply, the best poems. If she had shrunk from revealing her "quivering sensibility" to the world these would, one imagines, have been the ones she would have torn

*Reprinted from M. Visick, *The Genesis of "Wuthering Heights"* (Hong Kong: Hong Kong University Press, 1948), 10–32.

from Charlotte's rapacious grasp. We may make the not-very-rash assumption that Charlotte was right when she represented the diffidence mingled with Emily's anger (and it seems she was angry: "it took hours to reconcile her to the discovery") as doubt whether the poems would be acceptable. Furthermore, although Charlotte only mentions one book, the poems in the sisters' volume are actually drawn from two manuscripts. Either Charlotte found two, or Emily voluntarily produced the second, and selected from both those poems which she felt to be the most satisfactory. Possibly she was ready to let the poems go because her mind was turning towards her novel, of which the poems represent a kind of foreshadowing.

To return to the manuscripts themselves. It is clear by the inscription *Gondal Poems* that Emily Brontë made a distinction in her mind between Gondal and non-Gondal verse. This manuscript (referred to by Mr Hatfield as MS B) was begun in 1844, but contains poems of a much earlier date. These poems are not copied in the order of their composition; it seems fair to assume that there is some other order rather than that their sequence is purely haphazard, especially since Emily Brontë seems to have been a methodical worker. The verse dates back some years. A note written by Anne Brontë in July 1845 says that she and her sister began writing the (presumably prose) Gondal Chronicles "three and a half years ago"; but some of the poems are dated much earlier. The birthday notes written by Emily and Anne in 1845, exchanged, and intended to be opened on Emily's birthday in 1848, suggest that the prose chronicles related to a later generation of Gondalians than that of the chief characters of the verse, the heroes and heroines of *Gondal's Queen* and also, I believe, recognizably the chief characters of *Wuthering Heights:* probably the people belonging to this older generation were evolved in the early stages of the Gondal game, and matured in their creator's mind. If, in 1845, the current Gondal prose might be regarded as an account of contemporary Gondal, the people of the poems were historical figures out of a stormier past. The main action of *Wuthering Heights* takes place in the past—about the year 1775 and onwards. It is in fact a historical novel.

A clue to the Gondal story, then, might be found in the order in which Emily Brontë arranged the poems in her *Gondal Poems* manuscript. Poems written before 1844 are copied in their sequence in the Gondal story. For poems written after April 1844, however, the order is roughly chronological, as if she copied them in as they were written without regard for their place in the Gondal story. Many of them amplify sections of the story already told in the earlier part of the manuscript. On this theory there are two poems in the later part which are out of sequence; but since there are other Gondal poems preserved in the "odd" manuscripts but not transcribed she may originally have intended to reject these, and changed her mind later.

The first seventeen poems in the manuscript fall into five sections each referring to an episode in the life of the heroine, Augusta Geraldine Almeda or Rosina. Miss Ratchford thinks these are two names for the same heroine,

Miss Laura Hinkley thinks they are in fact two people. This sounds like a fundamental and violent difference; but it is unimportant when we are considering the relationship between Gondal and *Wuthering Heights,* since if they were
indeed two their personalities coalesced in the figure of Catherine Earnshaw.

Emily Brontë usually refers to the heroine as "A.G.A.," which is a useful
abbreviation for a somewhat cumbersome name. A.G.A.—Rosina, then, has
four lovers. The first is Alexander, Lord of Elbë, to whom the first two poems
refer. He is killed in battle. An early figure in the saga, he contributes nothing
to the *Wuthering Heights* theme, and has no particular interest. One might, of
course, catch a whiff of the Napoleonic legend in his title "Elbë": and the
foundling Heathcliff might well be a quasi-Napoleonic figure. Charlotte was
a great partisan of the Duke of Wellington who appears, somewhat translated, in her imaginary kingdom of Angria; Emily who does not seem to have
shared Charlotte's high Toryism may have felt some admiration for Napoleon.
However, conjecture cannot build on this. The next six poems relate to Lord
Alfred of Aspin Castle, another lover of A.G.A. He looks like a prototype of
Edgar Linton; and the poems show that the original story of his relationship
with the heroine was altered, becoming more like that of Catherine and
Edgar in *Wuthering Heights.* This point will be developed later. The third
group, of four poems, refers to a political assassination; it is not clear whether
the "sovereign" who has been murdered is a man or a woman, but Miss
Ratchford's earlier reconstruction identified him with one Julius Brenzaida,
another of A.G.A.'s lovers, who, though apparently of obscure birth, rose to
be emperor of Gondal. The poem "Rosina," which seems to belong to this
group, certainly refers to the murder of Julius. The fourth group obviously
preceded the third, since it concerns a relationship between Julius and a girl
called Geraldine; and the fifth concerns yet another lover, Fernando de
Samara, who was driven to suicide by A.G.A. and in whose reproaches we can
catch a note of Heathcliff. Thus each group is defined but the groups are not
in sequence in the story. It is as if already in 1844 Emily Brontë was dissect-
ing the Gondal story, seeing it as isolated episodes. Possibly she was already
considering the regrouping of the episodes into another story, which in the
end led her beyond Gondal to the novel.

After these sets of poems come three which have a rather obscure relation to the main story. Then the twenty-first and twenty-third refer to the
death of the heroine A.G.A. This brings us to the point at which Emily
Brontë caught up with herself in transcribing; from now on most of the
poems bear dates which suggest that they were copied into the transcript
book as soon as, or soon after, they were written. Two concern Julius, of which
one is Rosina's lament "Cold in the earth, and the deep snow piled above thee
. . ." which has struck many readers as prefiguring the eighteen years of
Heathcliff's mourning for Catherine. However another poem which also
occurs late in the manuscript is even closer in verbal expression to Heathcliff;
and here, as in "No coward soul . . ." the reference is not to ordinary human

love but to some other order of experience. It is a long Gondal narrative of which some self-contained stanzas were published in the 1846 volume as "The Prisoner, a fragment":

> Then dawns the Invisible, the Unseen its truth reveals;
> My outward sense is gone, my inward essence feels—
> Its wings are almost free, its home, its harbour found;
> Measuring the gulf it stoops and dares the final bound!
>
> Oh, dreadful is the check—intense the agony
> When the ear begins to hear, and the eye begins to see;
> When the pulse begins to throb, the brain to think again,
> The soul to feel the flesh, and the flesh to feel the chain. (p. 239)

In *Wuthering Heights* Heathcliff's dead love, or rather the sense of her presence, is at the core of the invisible world he cannot reach:

> I have neither a fear, nor a presentiment, nor a hope of death. Why should I? With my hard constitution and temperate mode of living, and unperilous occupation, I ought to, and probably *shall* remain above ground, till there is scarcely a black hair on my head—And yet I cannot continue in this condition! I have to remind myself to breathe—almost to remind my heart to beat! And it is like bending back a stiff spring: it is by compulsion that I do the slightest act not prompted by one thought, and by compulsion that I notice anything alive or dead, which is not associated with one universal idea. I have a single wish, and my whole being and faculties are yearning to attain it. They have yearned towards it so long, and so unwaveringly, that I'm convinced it *will* be reached—and soon—because it has devoured my existence: I am swallowed up in the anticipation of its fulfillment . . . O, God! It is a long fight, I wish it were over! (xxxiii)

Here is another indication that the love between Catherine and Heathcliff is Emily Brontë's way of giving expression to some all-devouring spiritual experience.

Among several other themes in *Gondal Poems,* many of which are undeveloped and may or may not have any relation to the novel, we find one emerging as a well-marked interest towards the end of the manuscript. The figures in the foreground are two children, a dark boy and a fair and happy girl, who seem to belong to a different generation. The former is to be found in several very early Gondal poems, but by 1845 he is becoming rather like Hareton Earnshaw, and the girl is beginning to look like Cathy Linton.

In two poems grouped together by Charlotte Brontë in her edition of 1850, and which she called "The Two Children" it is possible that the second-generation theme of *Wuthering Heights* is beginning to appear. This statement assumes that Emily Brontë intended the two poems to be read as one, for which there is some evidence. The first has a Gondal heading, "A. E. and R.

C." and the date, May 28, 1845. The second poem has no heading and no date. It is rare for Emily Brontë not to date a poem, and from the two sets of initials we might expect to find two characters in the poems; but there is only one in the first. It seems safe to assume, then, that A. E. is the boy and R. C. the girl. This double poem is certainly one of the loveliest of Emily Brontë's lyrics—a too-little-known Song of Innocence:

> Heavy hangs the raindrop
> From the burdened spray;
> Heavy broods the damp mist
> On uplands far away;
>
> Heavy looms the dull sky,
> Heavy rolls the sea—
> And heavy beats the young heart
> Beneath that lonely tree.
>
> Never has a blue streak
> Cleft the clouds since morn—
> Never has his grim Fate
> Smiled since he was born.
>
> Frowning on the infant,
> Shadowing childhood's joy,
> Guardian angel knows not
> That melancholy boy.
>
> Day is passing swiftly
> Its sad and sombre prime;
> Youth is fast invading
> Sterner manhood's time.
>
> All the flowers are praying
> For sun before they close,
> And he prays too, unknowing,
> That sunless human rose!
>
> Blossoms, that the west wind
> Has never wooed to blow,
> Scentless are your petals,
> Your dew as cold as snow.
>
> Soul, where kindred kindness
> No early promise woke,
> Barren is your beauty
> As weeds upon the rock.

Wither, brothers, wither,
You were vainly given—
Earth reserves no blessing
For the unblessed of Heaven!

Child of Delight! with sunbright hair,
And seablue, seadeep eyes;
Spirit of Bliss, what brings thee here,
Beneath these sullen skies?

Thou should'st live in eternal spring,
Where endless day is never dim;
Why, seraph, has thy erring wing
Borne thee down to weep with him?

"Ah, not from heaven am I descended,
And I do not come to mingle tears;
But sweet is day, though with shadows blended;
And, though clouded, sweet are youthful years.

"I, the image of light and gladness
Saw and pitied that mournful boy,
And I swore to take his gloomy sadness,
And give to him my beamy joy.

"Heavy and dark the night is closing;
Heavy and dark may its biding be:
Better for all from grief reposing,
And better for all who watch like me.

"Guardian angel he lacks no longer;
Evil fortune he needs not fear:
Fate is strong, but Love is stronger;
And more unsleeping than angel's care." (pp. 228–30)

Another poem, written much earlier—in May 1842—is placed nearly next to "The Two Children" in the manuscript and, like it, is concerned with a dark boy and a fair girl:

In the same place, when Nature wore
The same celestial glow,
I'm sure I've seen those forms before
But many springs ago;

And only *he* had locks of light,
And *she* had raven hair;

> While now, his curls are dark as night,
> And hers as morning fair . . . (p. 173)

The place of this poem is obscure; but the older generation sound like Edgar and Catherine, and the children might well foreshadow Hareton and Cathy. It is interesting to see Emily Brontë working out that relation between inner self and personal appearance which is so important in *Wuthering Heights*.

Thus we may summarise the parts of the Gondal story which concern A.G.A.: After the death of Alexander Elbë the heroine is associated with three men, one of whom, Julius Brenzaida, Emperor of Gondal, is murdered, leaving her to lament him through "fifteen wild Decembers." At some period in her career she has deserted him for the gentle, fair-haired Lord Alfred (whose fate will be discussed later). She is also loved by the guitar-player Fernando de Samara, who commits suicide. After her death a dark boy is rescued from some kind of misery by a fair girl.

In the unfolding story of Lord Alfred of Aspin Castle as it is told in *Gondal Poems* I believe we can see a significant modification of both the Gondal people and the story—a change which entails a much deeper scrutiny of the motives of the characters than is usual in Gondal and which also brings the Gondal plot much closer to that of the novel. Other Gondal poems not in the transcript book help to make the stages of this revision clear.

The contention that the third to the eighth entries in *Gondal Poems* refer to Lord Alfred can only be upheld at risk of some disagreement with Miss Ratchford's reconstruction. But she has not taken into account the arrangement Emily Brontë imposed on her poems in transcribing them, and that Emily Brontë did make a deliberate arrangement of at least the earlier poems in the manuscript seems clear. We find, then, the following poems, in the order in which they are placed in *Gondal Poems;* the numbers are those given the poems by Mr Hatfield in his edition:

I. No. 137. A.G.A. To A.S. May 6, 1840
                            July 28, 1843

Here the heroine expresses her happiness in the love of Alfred, for whom she feels something like veneration:

> At such a time, in such a spot,
> The world seems made of light;
> Our blissful hearts remember not
> How surely follows night.
>
> I cannot, Alfred, dream of aught
> That casts a shade of woe;
> That heaven is reigning in my thought,

Which wood and wave and earth have caught
From skies that overflow.

That heaven which my sweet lover's brow
Has won me to adore,
Which from his blue eyes beaming now
Reflects a still intenser glow
Than nature's heaven can pour.

I know our souls are all divine;
I know that when we die,
What seems the vilest, even like thine
A part of God himself shall shine
In perfect purity.

But coldly breaks November's day;
Its changes, charmless all;
Unmarked, unloved, they pass away;
We do not wish one hour to stay,
Nor sigh at evening's fall.

And glorious is the gladsome rise
Of June's rejoicing morn;
And who with unregretful eyes
Can watch the lustre leave its skies
To twilight's shade forlorn?

And art thou not my golden June
All mist and tempest free?
As shines earth's sun in summer noon,
So heaven's sun shines in thee.

Let others seek its beams divine
In cell and cloister drear;
But I have found a fairer shrine
And happier worship here.

By dismal rites they win their bliss—
By penance, fasts and fears;
I have one rite: a gentle kiss;
One penance: tender tears.

O could it thus forever be
That I might so adore;
I'd ask for all eternity
To make a paradise for me,
My love—and nothing more! (p. 143)

This recalls Catherine in the first days of her marriage in the summer world of Thrushcross Grange—"almost over-fond" of Edgar. Again, the mainspring of Edgar's character is a gentle, firm Christianity, at the opposite pole from the hell-fire cant of old Joseph: ineffectual against Heathcliff and Catherine, but none the less real. He might well have developed from the Alfred of this poem. It would seem that the mood of this poem, highly uncharacteristic of A.G.A., is shattered by the appearance of another lover, who is to Lord Alfred as the sun is to the moon.

II. No. 110. To A.G.A.

This poem is undated. In it someone taxes A.G.A. with unfaithfulness and she replies that "morning . . . and ardent noon" have destroyed her "moon of life":

> "Thou standest in the greenwood now
> The place, the hour the same—
> And here the fresh leaves gleam and glow
> And there, down in the lake below,
> The tiny ripples flame.
>
> "The breeze sings like a summer breeze
> Should sing in summer skies
> And tower-like rocks and tent-like trees
> In mingled glory rise.
>
> "But where is he to-day, to-day?"
> "O question not with me."
> "I will not, Lady; only say
> Where may thy lover be?
>
> "Is he upon some distant shore
> Or is he on the sea
> Or is the heart thou dost adore
> A faithless heart to thee?"
>
> "The heart I love, whate'er betide,
> Is faithful as the grave
> And neither foreign lands divide
> Nor yet the rolling wave."
>
> "Then why should sorrow cloud that brow
> And tears those eyes bedim?
> Reply this once—is it that thou
> Hast faithless been to him?"
>
> "I gazed upon the cloudless moon
> And loved her all the night

Till morning came, and ardent noon,
Then I forgot her light—

"No—not forgot—eternally
Remains its memory dear;
But could the day seem dark to me
Because the night was fair?

"I well may mourn that only one
Can light my future sky
Even though by such a radiant sun
My moon of life must die." (p. 117)

III. No. 169. A.G.A. To A.S., is a farewell, penitent but irrevocable, to the
gentle lover she is deserting. Its date is March 2, 1844:

This summer wind, with thee and me
Roams in the dawn of day;
But thou must be where it shall be,
Ere Evening—far away.

The farewell's echo from thy soul
Shall not depart before
Hills rise and distant rivers roll
Between us evermore.

I know that I have done thee wrong—
Have wronged both thee and Heaven—
And I may mourn my lifetime long
Yet may not be forgiven.

Repentant tears will vainly fall
To cancel deeds untrue;
But for no grief can I recall
The dreary word—Adieu.

Yet thou a future peace shalt win
Because thy soul is clear;
And I who had the heart to sin
Will find a heart to bear.

Till far beyond earth's frenzied strife
That makes destruction joy,
Thy perished faith shall spring to life
And my remorse shall die. (p. 197)

IV. No. 61. A.G.A. To A.S. March 20, 1838

In this much earlier poem, A.G.A. laments not her desertion but the death of her lover. Miss Ratchford's rigid reconstruction of the plot forces her to see in this A.S. an unidentified lover: but A.S. often, though not always, stands for Lord Alfred, and the poem suggests the same gentle personality in the same summery setting as the first of the Lord Alfred poems.

> . . . The woods—even now their small leaves hide
> The blackbird and the stockdove well;
> And high in heaven, so blue and wide,
> A thousand strains of music swell . . .
>
> . . . Well, pass away with the other flowers:
> Too dark for them, too dark for thee
> Are the hours to come, the joyless hours
> That Time is treasuring up for me.
>
> If thou hast sinned in this world of care,
> 'Twas but the dust of thy drear abode—
> Thy soul was pure when it entered here,
> And pure it will go again to God. (p. 70)

V. No. 100. A.G.A. To the Bluebell May 9, 1839

Miss Ratchford takes this to be a lament for a child; but there seems no reason why, coming where it does in the manuscript, it should not refer to Lord Alfred:

> Sacred watcher, wave thy bells!
> Fair hill flower and woodland child!
> Dear to me in deep green dells—
> Dearest on the mountains wild.
>
> Bluebell, even as all divine
> I have seen my darling shine—
> Bluebell, even as wan and frail
> I have seen my darling fail—
> Thou hast found a voice for me,
> And soothing words are breathed by thee.
>
> Thus they murmur, "Summer's sun
> Warms me till my life is done.
> Would I rather choose to die
> Under winter's ruthless sky?
>
> "Glad I bloom and calm I fade;
> Weeping twilight dews my bed;
> Mourner, mourner, dry thy tears—
> Sorrow comes with lengthened years!" (p. 106)

VI. No. 154. Written in Aspin Castle. There are two dates at the head of this long semi-narrative poem: 20 August 1842 and 6 February 1843 (p. 175).

It would seem that the ghost of Lord Alfred "walks" unquietly: that he died far away and in despair; and that the heroine of the saga in some way destroyed him. This poem may thus be taken to refer to the desertion of A.G.A's "moon of life." In passing, we may notice that a portrait of Lord Alfred is described, and it sounds not unlike the portrait of Edgar which Nelly shows Lockwood in *Wuthering Heights*.

While it is not certain that all these poems refer to Lord Alfred it is clear that they all refer to some gentle, fair character, the prototype of Edgar Linton. It seems that as late as May 1839 the Gondal story included the death of this character simply; the more intricate situation in which A.G.A. forsakes him for another man is worked out by 1842; Emily Brontë was in Brussels this year, away from Anne with whom she planned new stories. Perhaps it was a time for meditating on past Gondal games and even modifying the story. The undated poem "Thou standest in the greenwood now . . ." contains a hint of the kind of contrast which is drawn in *Wuthering Heights* between Heathcliff and Linton. In her confession to Nelly Catherine says:

> I've no more business to marry Edgar Linton than I have to be in heaven . . .
> It would degrade me to marry Heathcliff now; so he shall never know how I love him: and that, not because he's handsome, Nelly, but because he's more myself than I am. Whatever our souls are made of, his and mine are the same; and Linton's is as different as a moonbeam from lightning, or frost from fire. (ix)

The mention of heaven here, and its association with Linton, seems a link with the cruder personality of the Gondal man as we see it in the poem "At such a time, in such a spot . . ."; but the main point is the use of natural imagery to point the contrast. The stanzas about the "cloudless moon" and the bright day, which suggest two kinds of love, appear only in the later draft of the poem, the one which was copied into *Gondal Poems*. It seems as if some new experience is being worked into the story of A.G.A. and Alfred.

The earliest draft of "Thou standest in the greenwood now . . ." is to be found on a loose sheet. The poem is undated; but the poem on the reverse side (No. 109 in Hatfield) is dated July 19, 1839. Thus there is some indication that the idea of a forsaken lover, probably already Lord Alfred, comes later than those poems in which the fair-haired lover is represented as dying rather than as committing suicide. The first draft ends with the line "Hast faithless been to him," and with two following lines which do not appear in any other draft: "I dreamt, one dark and stormy night When winter winds were wild." Here the draft stops abruptly.

On another sheet appear two stanzas later worked into "Thou standest in the greenwood now . . ." which make the contrast between the sun and the moon. The final stanza of the *Gondal Poems* version ("I needs must mourn . . .") is found only in that, the final, form.

Like the earliest draft, the two stanzas may be tentatively dated by another poem occupying the same sheet. This poem also concerns forsaking, and must also be mentioned. Mr Hatfield gives the date as July 26, 1843, though he points out that the last figure of the date is obscure, and might be a "2"; in any case the two stanzas are later than the early draft, and show no connection with it.

Thus in its final form "Thou standest in the greenwood . . ." is made up of three strata: the first, unfinished draft probably written in 1839; the two stanzas ending "But could the day seem dark to me Because the night was fair?"; and the final summing-up stanza. No other poem shows such evidence that the writer was preoccupied with it over an extended period. It seems as if this part of the Gondal story underwent severe revision.

Furthermore, the poem dated July 26, 1843—or 1842—may be assumed to be on the same theme; Emily Brontë did not copy it into *Gondal Poems* but the final stanza is nearly identical with the first stanza of the repentant poem "This summer wind . . ." which she did use in *Gondal Poems,* and which she headed "A.G.A. to A.S." It is an expression of the mood which the writer is later to associate with Thrushcross Grange:

> Yes, holy be thy resting-place
> Wherever thou mayst lie;
> The sweetest winds breathe on thy face,
> The softest of the sky.
>
> And will not guardian Angels send
> Kind dreams and thoughts of love,
> Though I no more may watchful bend
> Thy loved repose above?
>
> And will not heaven itself bestow
> A beam of glory there
> That summer's grass more green may grow,
> And summer's flowers more fair?
>
> Farewell, farewell, 'tis hard to part
> Yet, loved one, it must be:
> I would not rend another heart
> Not even by blessing thee.
>
> Go! we must break affection's chain,
> Forget the hope of years:
> Nay, grieve not—willest thou remain
> To waken wilder tears?

> This wild breeze with thee and me
> Roved in the dawning day;
> And thou shouldst be where it shall be
> Ere evening, far away. (p. 189)

Here is a Linton-like figure—entitled to a "holy" resting-place, religious, slightly devitalized (even Nelly, Edgar's most consistent partisan, says "he wanted spirits in general") and also, like Edgar, not small or ridiculous. Successive revisions have brought him closer and closer to the later figure of Edgar. From his personality and fate spring the sense of irretrievable wrong, which checks even the passionate A.G.A. and which destroys Catherine. "If I have done wrong, I'm dying for it" she moans; but in the more complex world of *Wuthering Heights* it is hard to see who has been most deeply wronged. Emily Brontë makes Nelly acknowledge this when, although she dislikes Catherine, distrusts Heathcliff and admires Edgar, she twists a lock of Heathcliff's hair round one of Edgar's, and lays them together in the locket round the dead Catherine's neck.

As for the sunlike lover, Miss Ratchford argues convincingly that he is Julius Brenzaida, the low-born emperor of Gondal. Julius wins power by violence and treachery; so Heathcliff deliberately corrupts Hindley, gets possession of the Heights, possibly murders him, or at least does not encourage him to live, traps Isabella and later Cathy, ruthlessly exploits his own son, and so becomes master of the fate of all the people round him. Julius, like him, is vivid, unscrupulous and violent.

Gondal Poems also contains two songs by "Julius Brenzaida" addressed to "Geraldine": the first is a kind of serenade, in which he recalls to her the moors where they have once been happy:

> . . . Wild the road, and rough and dreary;
> Barren all the moorland round;
> Rude the couch that rests us weary;
> Mossy stone and heathy ground.
>
> But, when winter storms were meeting
> In the moonless, midnight dome,
> Did we heed the tempest's beating,
> Howling round our spirits' home?
>
> No; that tree with branches riven,
> Whitening in the whirl of snow,
> As it tossed against the heaven,
> Sheltered happy hearts below . . . (p. 82)

There is no need to labour the parallel; in October 1838 the two figures who were to become Heathcliff and Catherine in their childhood at the Heights were already sketched out in Emily Brontë's mind. And the second *Song,* of the same date, shows how the story was shaping:

> I knew not 'twas so dire a crime
> To say the word, Adieu;
> But this shall be the only time
> My slighted heart shall sue.
>
> The wild moorside, the winter morn,
> The gnarled and ancient tree—
> If in your breast they waken scorn,
> Shall wake the same in me . . . (p. 83)

Miss Ratchford's reconstruction, in which the heroine first loves Julius, then abandons him for various lovers the last of whom is Lord Alfred, and finally leaves Alfred and returns to him, seems justified, among other reasons, because it is a sketch of the relations between Catherine, Heathcliff and Edgar in the first part of *Wuthering Heights.*

Emily Brontë: The Latitude of Interpretation

Denis Donoghue*

I

Her poems were first published in *Poems by Currer, Ellis and Acton Bell* (1846). When the second edition of *Wuthering Heights* was issued in 1850, in a volume which also contained *Agnes Grey* and a selection of poems by Emily and Anne, Charlotte Brontë added a biographical notice of the two sisters. Of Emily's poems she wrote:

> One day, in the autumn of 1845, I accidentally lighted on a MS. volume of verse in my sister Emily's handwriting. Of course, I was not surprised, knowing that she could and did write verse: I looked it over, and something more than surprise seized me,—a deep conviction that these were not common effusions, nor at all like the poetry women generally write. I thought them condensed and terse, vigorous and genuine. To my ear, they had also a peculiar music—wild, melancholy, and elevating.

Some of the poems were written as early as 1834, when Emily Brontë was sixteen. Between that date and 1846, she wrote about two hundred poems, most of them short pieces, and some fragments. In February 1844 she transcribed a selection of verses into two notebooks: one contained thirty-one poems, autobiographical lyrics; the other, forty-four poems from the Gondal saga, a childhood legend propounded by Emily and Anne. Charlotte speaks of one volume, but the first printed poems come variously from both sources, the personal poems as well as the Gondal pieces; no distinction is announced. This has caused some confusion. The reader who comes upon "The Night is Darkening Round Me" in, say, W. H. Auden's anthology *Nineteenth Century Minor Poets* is likely to assume that it is a personal lyric, unless he happens to know that it is a dramatic lyric spoken by the guilty Augusta in the Gondal saga. The paralysis of will which is represented in the poem is Augusta's, not Emily Brontë's. Again, "Heavy Hangs the Raindrop" does not express the relation between

*Reprinted from *The Interpretation of Narrative Theory and Practice*, Harvard English Studies 1, ed. M. Bloomfield, (Cambridge, Mass.: Harvard University Press, 1970), 106–24.

Emily Brontë and Nature; it marks a moment in the relation between the imprisoned Arthur of Exina and the little fair-haired girl who loves him.

In fact, most of Emily Brontë's poems, including several of her most celebrated pieces, are Gondal poems. We are to think of a mythical island in the North Pacific, divided into several hostile kingdoms. Julius Brenzaida, Prince of Angora in Northern Gondal, is loved by Rosina, Princess of Alcona in the south. He conquers the kingdom of Almedore and sacks the city of Zalona. Then he secretly marries Geraldine Sidonia, daughter of a conquered family. Soon, however, he leaves her, possibly to return to Rosina. Geraldine has a child, Augusta Geraldine Almeda, and she decides to bring the infant to Julius. But on the voyage the ship is wrecked, and Geraldine is drowned. The child is saved and brought to Julius, who arranges to have her reared in the mountains of Angora. Julius then marries Rosina. A child is born to them, a beautiful boy. Julius captures the city of Tyndarum. Shortly after, he betrays Gerald of Exina, and casts him into prison along with Gerald's son Arthur. But a rebellion is raised against Julius, and he is murdered. (Rosina mourns him in the famous threnody "Cold in the Earth, and the Deep Snow piled above Thee.")

The personal poems issue directly from Emily Brontë's experience; many of them testify to her isolation, her sense of decay and mutability, the melancholy to which Charlotte referred, Emily's "dark world," her dreams, visions, fancies, Branwell's tragedy. A few poems are direct invocations of her muse, sometimes called Imagination as opposed to "stern Reason," the admonishing voice of daylight and law. These are moorland poems, in the sense that they praise the visionary power by which the bleakness of the moors is transformed and enriched. "My sister Emily loved the moors," Charlotte wrote; yet, as Charlotte remarked in the introduction to *Wuthering Heights* the moors do not provide the desired beauty from their own resources; rather, they provoke it in the perceiver, compelling the visionary power to invent it. "If she demand beauty to inspire her," Charlotte wrote, "she must bring it inborn; these moors are too stern to yield any product so delicate." That product must come from within. "The eye of the gazer," Charlotte said "must *itself* brim with a 'purple light,' intense enough to perpetuate the brief flower-flush of August on the heather, or the rare sunset-smile of June; out of his heart must well the freshness, that in latter spring and early summer brightens the bracken, nurtures the moss, and cherishes the starry flowers that spangle for a few weeks the pasture of the moor-sheep." Finally, "unless that light and freshness are innate and self-sustained, the drear prospect of a Yorkshire moor will be found as barren of poetic as of agricultural interest." But to Emily Brontë's imagination, absence and bareness were just as provocative as presence. Her characteristic powers were innate and self-sustained; they did not delight in a given plenitude, if the gift seemed independent of her imagination.

We distinguish between these autobiographical poems and the Gondal poems, but we should not push them too far apart. Beneath the overt difference, there is continuity. Demonstrably, and in more than the obvious sense, every poem issues from a single imagination, bearing Emily Brontë's signature. Moving from *Wuthering Heights* to the Gondal saga and then to the autobiographical poems, we mark the obvious differences of genre, but we are also aware of a landscape of feeling shared by all these works. The landscape is given in certain pervasive images, recurring figures, patterns, rhythms. Some of these are so distinctive that they assert themselves. When Emily Dickinson read Emily Brontë's poems, she found one stanza lodging in her mind; it struck her as somehow definitive, and she quoted it in several letters:

> Though Earth and Man were gone
> And Suns and Universes ceased to be
> And thou wert left alone,
> Every existence would exist in thee—(p. 243)

The first line should read "Though Earth and Moon were gone"; but it hardly matters. What matters is a certain gesture. Emily Dickinson recognized it as Emily Brontë's particular sign, ostensibly a syntax of excess, of hyperbole, but in the declared case not excess at all, since the feeling lives up to the declaration. It is a characteristic cadence, especially in the verve with which All is identified with One. The cadence is memorable in the poems, and it is one of the definitive tropes of *Wuthering Heights,* as in Chapter IX, where Catherine says of Heathcliff: "If all else perished, and *he* remained, *I* should still continue to be; and if all else remained, and he were annihilated, the universe would turn to a mighty stranger: I should not seem a part of it." It is typical of Emily Brontë's imagination that it runs to the extreme case, or to the extreme form of a common case, and that it is impatient with mediate things, relative or provisional moods. It is also typical of her imagination to define character by its extremity, and to make extremes meet. So Augusta, the fatal heroine of the Gondal saga, is a trial account of Cathy in *Wuthering Heights;* when we add Julius to that account, we see that Heathcliff is already in a measure defined. Emily Brontë did not possess, in any Shakespearean sense, a dramatic imagination. Her characters, in the novel as in the poems, are functions or projections, if not of herself, then of certain forces which belong to her as intimately as her desires. These forces are few, but each is definitive. Each is absolute. The novel and the poems are continuous in this respect, that they release these forces, at whatever cost to other forces which are ignored. Emily Brontë's limit is the outer limit of those forces which she releases, separately or in powerful conjunction. Her fictive world is not, indeed, complete. It is not, in the common sense, rich, diverse, plenary. Rather, it compels by the power of its limitation. Many images of life are absent, but we are forced to feel that they are absent because they have been rejected as irrelevant. Whatever beauty she needs, she invents, but her necessities are not of that order. Her deepest need is to make a clear space for her imagination; what she demands of space is that, for her sake, it be empty.

Indeed, her imagination is so exclusive that it discloses itself in a certain pattern, a plot. The plot is a fiction; it is not to be found in any single poem or in the novel, but in the configuration of her whole work. It suggests itself as an abstract or virtual fiction, compounded of a few typical figures and motifs. It is often said of Shakespeare's plays that they constitute a single work, a single poem. The remark is not fanciful. Emily Brontë's entire work constitutes a single poem, a single fiction. Its plot runs somewhat as follows. The story begins in childhood; the young spirit is in harmony with nature, delighting in "the splashing of the surge, / The changing heaven, the breezy weather." "Laughing mirth's most joyous swell" is delightful for the same reason, the swell, the great sense of life as motion and action. Spirit conceives itself as action, and recognizes action in every natural appearance. Indeed, life itself is unified by this terminology, so that no gap is disclosed between consciousness and experience. But in the next period a change occurs. Natural events are felt to have changed their character. The terminology of action persists, but its characters and signs are altered. Breezes become storms, malignant because independent; change becomes decay. The splashing of the surge now denotes the violence and hostility of nature; there is no kinship:

> O cold, cold is my heart!
> It will not, cannot rise;
> It feels no sympathy
> With those refulgent skies. (p. 108)

Everything is felt as external. Sometimes this feeling is embodied in imagery of imprisonment, severance, and burial. The spirit feels itself defeated by a "tyrant spell." "I hear my dungeon bars recoil." The hidden God has turned tyrant. In other moods, the feeling comes as a sense of guilt, either a categorical feeling of guilt as innate and original, or else guilt arising from a specific sin, perhaps a sinful passion. Both feelings now merge in an archetypal figure, to be discussed later in the present essay, the child lost in a forest. The child is lost, abandoned, either because of a malicious God or because of an original sin. In the next period there is a corresponding desire for rest, release, silence, calm. The terminology of action is given up altogether, since it has proved itself fallacious. The pervasive images in this new period are quietist:

> How still, how happy! Those are words
> That once would scarce agree together; (p. 96)

But now they agree together. In this condition the ideal imagery features the loss of definition and character; states once welcomed as separate and therefore rich are now dissolved. Sometimes the old images of rigor, ice, and snow are melted; there is consolation in nullity, when all things are returned to an original, undifferentiated source. The earth itself is tolerable when bare and silent, but the only joy is in absence. Finally, there is a movement of feeling beyond earth and time; the things of earth and time are transcended, or retained only as shadows of themselves. The relative appearances offered to the senses are translated into their absolute equivalents, so that the appearances themselves may be discarded:

> But first a hush of peace, a soundless calm descends;
> The struggle of distress and fierce impatience ends;
> Mute music soothes my breast—unuttered harmony
> That I could never dream till earth was lost to me.
>
> Then dawns the Invisible, the Unseen its truth reveals;
> My outward sense is gone, my inward essence feels—
> (p. 239)

Death is the only good thing, after all; the spirit frees itself from the heard melodies of time, since the divine malice resides in melody itself. "O for the time when I shall sleep / Without identity." The motto for this period is given in one of the poems: "I'm happiest when most away" (p. 63). In another, the spirit speaks of the terror felt when, after such happiness, the senses reassert themselves:

> Oh, dreadful is the check—intense the agony
> When the ear begins to hear and the eye begins to see;
> When the pulse begins to throb, the brain to think again,
> The soul to feel the flesh and the flesh to feel the chain!
>
> Yet I would lose no sting, would wish no torture less;
> The more that anguish racks the earlier it will bless;
> And robed in fires of Hell, or bright with heavenly shine,
> If it but herald Death, the vision is divine. (p. 239)

The vision is divine; specifically, these transcendental desires are addressed toward an angelic figure, variously called messenger, idol, "visitant of air," or "Strange Power." Sometimes the power is invoked as God, sometimes it is identified with the creative power of the imagination. Under any name, its place is "the steadfast, changeless shore," otherwise "Eternity" or "Immortality." One poem begins with "Death" and ends with "Eternity" (pp. 224–25), a characteristic sequence, but Eternity here has nothing to do with the Christian hope of resurrection. The tone is different. The dominant feeling is deemed to be fulfilled in rest, calm, obliteration, as in those Renaissance manuals of iconography in which Night is featured as a woman with black wings, "in one, a sleeping white child to signify Sleep, in the other a black one that seems asleep, and signifies Death."

One way of describing the *figura* in Emily Brontë's work is to say that it marks the gradual discovery, on her part, that the periphery was lost, the world of objects a deceit. In her "first" moments she was herself part of the sustaining periphery; progressively, as the world of objects lost its consoling force, she discovered that her own imagination must occupy the creative center of whatever circle might be drawn. The result is that her characteristic poems do not explore the objective world; they do not even define or test a sense of the world as already formed. These poems act on the assumption that the world of objects is, indeed, given, but given as foreign and indifferent. To know the world in greater depth or in richer detail would not alter that new sense of its character; it would merely confirm it. Emily Brontë has already passed sentence upon the world. In "The Night Wind" and "Shall earth no more inspire thee?" the genius of Earth woos her, persuading her to return to his favor and protection. But the spirit answers that the music of Earth has no power over her; her feelings run in another course. Emily Brontë writes, in fact, as if a knowledge of the world were not in question; before speech begins, that knowledge is present. She writes as if, on that theme, there is nothing further to be said. A knowledge of the world is already her possession, and therefore her fate. What each poem proposes, therefore, is not so much to confirm her sense of the world but rather to define the self in which that sense has been formed. Inevitably, her sense of the world comes to seem crucial because it is her nature, not because it bears upon such an object. Emily Brontë's romanticism is indeed her subjectivity, her sense of herself as center.

The more this sense was developed, the more inward it appeared. The inward essence is increasingly distinguished from the outward sense; the distinction is, in several poems, between God and man. Whether the ostensible object of invocation is the imagination, fancy, or the angelic messenger, it is in fact a function of Emily Brontë's nature. Finally, the imagination must identify itself with God, if the logic of the imagery is to prevail. The distinction between God and man may persist as an interim rhetoric, but it cannot remain when the one center becomes All. At that moment the only relevant circle is the new circle formed by the center which expands itself, occupying ground laid waste for that purpose. The center begins to expand when "the world without" is sharply and critically distinguished from "the world within." In "To Imagination" the creative power within is invoked to "call a lovelier life from death, / And whisper with a voice divine / Of real worlds as bright as thine" (p. 206). The principle is Coleridgean—the imagination as the secular version of the divine power, the infinite I AM. In "No Coward Soul is Mine" Emily Brontë writes:

> O God within my breast,
> Almighty ever-present Deity
> Life, that in me has rest
> As I Undying Life, have power in thee. (p. 243)

The theology itself is circular, as it must be when the only vivid terms move about an ever-expanding center. In another poem to Imagination, Emily Brontë writes:

> And am I wrong to worship where
> Faith cannot doubt nor Hope despair
> Since my own soul can grant my prayer? (p. 209)

It could hardly be a more explicit assertion. In this idiom poetry and religion become one, faith and aesthetics become one. A new world arises when the old world, discredited, is transcended. The old world was based upon the primacy of object; the new world is based upon the primacy of subject.

But this pleasure, this vertigo, as Hélène Tuzet describes it, is available only when the child-spirit feels that it may invent a new world, emanating from the self as center. The child does not then negotiate with the forest, since to deal with the world in those terms is to be compromised. The answer to loss is willful disengagement:

> Fall, leaves, fall; die, flowers, away;
> Lengthen night and shorten day;
> Every leaf speaks bliss to me
> Fluttering from the autumn tree.
> I shall smile when wreaths of snow
> Blossom where the rose should grow;
> I shall sing when night's decay
> Ushers in a drearier day. (p. 82)

The ultimate ideal is to answer one rejection by another, the spirit transmuting everything into itself:

> When I am not and none beside—
> Nor earth nor sea nor cloudless sky—
> But only spirit wandering wide
> Through infinite immensity. (p. 63)

When we speak of the expansion of the center to fill the entire circle, we posit a continuous act of will. Nothing less will answer. If the objective world is maintained by God or by some other force, the subjective world is maintained only by the subject—the imagination, endlessly creative, sustained by that form of itself which is called the will. It is a commonplace that *Wuthering Heights* is a fiction remarkable for its representation of life in terms of will; indeed, the novel owes little to any other manifestation of human life. We make the point when we say, and it is again a commonplace, that Heathcliff and Cathy are more readily understandable as forms of energy than as characters, absolute because self-sustaining. Their identity, upon which Cathy insists, is the center, the vortex, from which the relevant forms of energy issue. It is in this sense that passion in *Wuthering Heights* is given as a natural force, natural and therefore immune to the moral considerations of men and women in the historical world. Heathcliff is a purer form of energy than Cathy, a point made in the novel by the multiplicity of considerations which are deemed irrelevant to him. Indeed, what gives the book its uncanny power is the verve with which so much of human life is set aside as irrelevant. Here again the continuity between Emily Brontë's imagination and Heathcliff as one of its characteristic projections is clear. Both are defined by the nature of their wills; in both, sublimity is egotistical.

There is a famous passage in Hazlitt's lecture on Shakespeare and Milton, one of the *Lectures on the English Poets,* in which Hazlitt speaks of the "generic quality" of Shakespeare's mind, "its power of communication with all other minds—so that it contained a universe of thought and feeling within itself, and had no one peculiar bias, or exclusive excellence more than another." He goes on: "He was the least of an egotist that it was possible to be. He was nothing in himself; but he was all that others were, or that they could become." Keats extended Hazlitt's description of the Shakespearean imagination, distinguishing it from the Wordsworthian or egotistical sublime. "When I am in a room with People," he wrote to Richard Woodhouse on October 27, 1818, "if I ever am free from speculating on creations of my own brain, then not myself goes home to myself: but the identity of every one in the room begins to press upon me (so) that I am in a very little time annihilated." It is the special mark of Emily Brontë's imagination that it resists annihilation by maintaining itself at the center of its circle. So her Gondal poems are not, or not entirely, dramatic monologues: they are in another sense soliloquies, diverse only in their settings. What is different, in each case, is the circumstance. The difference does not require a variation in the demonstrated character of the world, only in the feeling of the perceiver. To Emily Brontë, even in the Gondal poems, soliloquy is a mode of introspection; the circumstance provides the occasion, but it does not offer itself as the object of consciousness. If we distinguish between the Gondal poems and the personal poems, the distinction should admit the consideration that, at a certain level of description, the local differences tend to disappear. It is not necessary to force the argument. Hazlitt rebuked certain contemporary poets for trying to "reduce poetry to a mere effusion of natural sensibility," surrounding the meanest objects "with the morbid feelings and devouring egotism of the writers' own minds." In Emily Brontë's imagination there is, indeed, a trace of the morbid, but she does not parade her sensibility: she is concerned with sensibility only as a form of the will. She takes no pride in the expression of will; the will is supreme because innate and categorical.

Her imagination, that is to say, does not allow the identity of an object to assert itself in her presence. The ideal moment, for that imagination, is when the plenary objects of the world are either hidden or transcended. Emily

Brontë is a lunar poet, if we distinguish between poets lunar and solar. The solar poet delights in the manifold richness of objects. The lunar poet waits until night, when objects lose their force, the earth withdraws, and the imagination proceeds to fill the empty space between itself and the stars. The muse invoked in "The Prisoner" is akin to Emily Brontë's muse in the poem "Stars":

> O Stars and Dreams and Gentle Night;
> O Night and Stars return!
> And hide me from the hostile light
> That does not warm, but burn—
>
> That drains the blood of suffering men;
> Drinks tears, instead of dew:
> Let me sleep through his blinding reign,
> And only wake with you! (pp. 226–27)

But my account is too general if it does not specify the choice poems and observe them. Henry James complained, in "The Lesson of Balzac," that the romantic tradition associated with the Brontës had virtually prevented any critical attention to their works. The image of "their dreary, their tragic history, their loneliness and poverty of life" stood as a force "independent of any one of their applied faculties." That image, he maintained, had supplanted the works themselves, had offered itself more insistently than *Jane Eyre* or *Wuthering Heights,* so that the question of the Brontës "has scarce indeed been accepted as belonging to literature at all." Literature, he argued, is "an objective, a projected result; it is life that is the unconscious, the agitated, the struggling, floundering cause." The case is somewhat different now, but there is always, and preeminently in the consideration of Emily Brontë, a disposition to allow the causes to speak for the results. Indeed, the best claim I can reasonably make for the paradigm, the *figura* as I have called it, in Emily Brontë's poems is that it mediates between cause and result, between the original agitation and the resultant forms. The paradigm is not merely agitation; but it is not yet form. It is a mediating fiction, no more. Its chief merit may be that it recalls the agitation and foresees its probable forms.

A reasonable showing among the two hundred poems would include these, listed in no particular order but with an implication of weight and representative merit: "Sacred watcher, wave thy bells"; "Fall, leaves, fall"; "A little while, a little while"; "How still, how happy"; "The night is darkening round me"; "If grief for grief can touch thee"; "'Tis Moonlight"; "Aye, there it is"; "In Summer's Mellow Midnight"; "I See Around Me Tombstones Grey"; "The Day is Done"; "How Clear She Shines"; "Well Hast Thou Spoken"; "The Linnet in the Rocky Dells"; "When Weary with the Long Day's Care"; "O Thy Bright Eyes"; "Enough of Thought, Philosopher"; "Cold in the Earth"; "Death, that Struck when I was Most Confiding"; "Heavy Hangs the Raindrop"; "How Beautiful the Earth is Still"; "Often Rebuked"; "In the

Dungeon Crypts"; "Silent is the House"; "No Coward Soul." One of these will help to show some of Emily Brontë's "applied faculties":

> Aye, there it is! It wakes to-night
> Sweet thoughts that will not die
> And feeling's fires flash all as bright
> As in the years gone by!
>
> And I can tell by thine altered cheek
> And by thy kindled gaze
> And by the word thou scarce dost speak,
> How wildly fancy plays.
>
> Yes, I could swear that glorious wind
> Has swept the world aside,
> Has dashed its memory from thy mind
> Like foam-bells from the tide—
>
> And thou art now a spirit pouring
> Thy presence into all—
> The essence of the Tempest's roaring
> And of the Tempest's fall—
>
> A universal influence
> From Thine own influence free—
> A principle of life, intense,
> Lost to mortality.
>
> Thus truly when that breast is cold
> Thy prisoned soul shall rise,
> The dungeon mingle with the mould—
> The captive with the skies. (p. 165)

The motif is characteristically Romantic. The wind is invoked as the natural force of action, the Aeolian lyre, the "correspondent breeze," life itself as motion and spirit. Spirit is universal, wind is the form it takes, and the form of the poem is the process by which, from first word to last, every objective image is transformed into spirit. This interchange of state is the motive of the poem. The wind, waking sweet thoughts and feelings in the recipient, begins the process of changing him into its own terms. The first signs of change are the "altered cheek," the "kindled gaze," of the second stanza. In the second stage of transformation the terms of earth and time are dissolved, "the world" and its memory. The change is complete when the recipient is entirely spirit. At that stage wind and recipient are one, alike in function and power: "And thou art now a spirit pouring / Thy presence into all"; like the original wind itself. Appropriately, existence is purified to essence, while essence retains, like the wind, its proper terminology of action: "The essence of the Tempest's roaring / And of the Tempest's fall." In the next stanza the terms are moral rather than philosophical. Just as the recipient's existence was purified, transformed into its proper essence, so now his finite "influence" is transformed into that "universal influence" which is spirit in its moral idiom. "From Thine own influence free"; free, as prefiguring the freedom from mortality invoked in the next lines. "A principle of life intense"; intense, since principles and absolutes do not obliterate the manifestations they transform, in this case manifestations of force and power. The last stanza is a vision of the future, the transformation complete, soul released to the skies. This is more than freedom, commonly understood, since it enforces the victory of a subjective terminology over every alien power.

The poem is, then, a ritual, designed to break the chains of time, place, and body. Most of the work, so far as the language goes, is done by the verbs; assertively in the third stanza, where the "glorious wind / Has swept the world aside, / Has dashed its memory from thy mind." "Glorious" is not a mere tag, given that the wind's achievement is martial and heroic. In fact all the verbs are verbs of transformation, changing every state into its spiritual equivalent: wakes, flash, plays, swept aside, dashed, rise, mingle. The verbs testify to a formative principle of change and are themselves, preeminently, the vehicles of that change. The nouns are, for the most part, the great subjective terms—feeling, fancy, memory, mind, spirit, presence, influence, soul, principle, essence—with their descriptive cousins—fire, wind, cheek, gaze, breast, thought. The adjectives are those of human and natural relations, with a supporting air of extremity and change: sweet, bright, wild, kindled, glorious, intense. But in saying that the main work is done by the verbs we should also remark that the essential movement of feeling is a stanzaic movement, where each stanza is a lyric moment, sustained and effected by the action of the verbs, for the most part, up to that point. Within each stanza there is little change; rather, a change is registered, defined in the stanza. The plot of the poem, if the term is permissible, is a sequence of lyric moments, each stanza marking a certain stage in the large cadence of feeling. The process is subjective, but only because the relevant transformation is personal, an act of will. Nature does not, in this case, enforce itself: it is invoked in that character. The movement of feeling arises from within the soul of the speaker; the transformation is effected by calling upon a natural force already hospitable to such changes. This explains the typical grammar of the poem. Emily Brontë begins with the indicative, "Aye, there it is"; simple because true. But gradually she uses indicatives as if they were imperatives: or rather, a poet with less confidence in the transforming power of will and the subjective idiom generally would be obliged to use imperatives where Emily Brontë uses indicatives. "And thou art now a spirit" means "Be thou now a spirit," but it is unnecessary to change to the imperative mood, since the indicative already has the air of an assumption. "Already with thee!" is Keats's equivalent in the "Ode to a Nightingale." The point is that Emily Brontë's poem is doing the traditional work of metaphor, but in slow motion, and by degrees. The process of metaphor is the process of transformation, metamorphosis. Metaphor acts suddenly, in a flash; the poem achieves a metaphorical object, but slowly, earning the right to do so as it moves along, stanza by stanza.

But a critical difficulty persists. I have reached the stage of describing Emily Brontë's poems as soliloquies; but if they are soliloquies, they cannot be dramatic lyrics, Gondal monologues. So, according to the logic, the Gondal saga is irrelevant, at best a romantic smoke screen. I hope to show that the contradiction is more apparent than real, but it must be faced, perhaps along the following lines.

It is clear that Emily Brontë's imagination found in Gondal sustenance not available in the daily life of Haworth. Gondal was an invented kingdom, neither England in general nor Haworth in particular; that it was the joint invention of Emily and Anne increased its distinction, giving the invention a note of conspiracy. It made, for the two sisters, a "world elsewhere": that world is the source of the "peculiar music" which Charlotte heard in Emily's poems. Gondal was a fiction, not necessarily better than historical fact in every respect but certainly better in respect of freedom. To Emily it offered a world in which she could play roles far more diverse than those available to her at Haworth. The roles she chose to play are now male, now female, now adult, now child: but, more important, the roles are played in an aboriginal world. We are to think of Gondal as a place not yet marked out by conventions, laws, morals, society. These forces have not yet arrived: to Emily Brontë, so much the better. The only laws are those of passion and will: punishment is primitive, but natural. Gondal is anthropological, Haworth is historical. Like *Wuthering Heights,* it proposes a mode of life which exists, powerful and intransigent, beneath the accretions of manners, morals, and society. That Emily Brontë's imagination needed such a world can hardly be disputed.

But the creation of Gondal did not really extend her imagination: it fulfilled the needs of that imagination without changing its nature or composition. Emily Brontë could not suppress herself in favor of her invented characters: could not, or would not. The characters, once invented, are allowed to move and live in Gondal, but they are still extreme functions of Emily Brontë's own personality. She does not release them: she endows them not with free will, but with her own will in diverse forms. When they speak, therefore, what we hear is a kind of ventriloquism. There is no precise term for this, as far as I know. "Dramatic monologue" will not do, because this proposes a strict separation of speaker and poet. "Soliloquy" will not do, because this implies a speaker communing with her own feelings. The term we need is somewhere between these two phrases; but where, precisely, and what word?

Perhaps we can approach it by noting a certain sequence. We call that imagination "Shakespearean" which delights in registering modes of feeling not its own. We may call another kind of imagination "Yeatsian" if it has a particular flair for registering modes of feeling related to its own by contrast and opposition: we have in mind, for this description, Yeats's account of the imagination as operating in terms of mask, role-playing, anti-self, and so forth. *A Vision* and "Ego Dominus Tuus" are the theoretical occasions. There is also, for a third stage, the imagination which we may call "Proustian," thinking of a remark by Roland Barthes in *Le Degré zéro de l'Écriture* that "a character of Proust materializes into the opacity of a particular language, and it is really at this level that his whole historical situation . . . is integrated and ordered." Finally, there is an imagination which we call "Eliotic," which delights in secreting "characters" from materials entirely verbal, the characters therefore being merely virtual or ostensible. Thus Hugh Kenner has observed in *The Invisible Poet* that "J. Alfred Prufrock is a name plus a Voice: he isn't a 'character' cut out of the rest of the universe and equipped with a history and a little necessary context, like the speaker of a Browning monologue." So there are several identifiable positions between the two extremes, soliloquy and drama; more, indeed, than the standard critical terminologies encourage us to recognize. Josiah Royce has shown in his *Lectures on Modern Idealism* that it was characteristic of nineteenth-century idealists to develop by way of dialectics, truth being a process, the grappling of opposites. Arnold spoke, in his Preface to the 1853 edition of his *Poems,* of "the dialogue of the mind with itself" as constituting the modern element in literature. But Emily Brontë does not commit herself to these procedures. The relation between her and, say, Augusta in the Gondal poems is not Shakespearean; Emily is not willing to suppress herself for Augusta's sake. Augusta is established only in the sense that Emily's subjective imagination secretes her: her fictive existence is not independent; it depends upon Emily's will and is, indeed, an extreme manifestation of that will. In the Gondal poems generally Emily Brontë's will sets an outer limit beyond which her imagination, in the creation of characters, may not go. In detail, the same limit is marked by the opacity of the language; the comparison with Proust may be retained but need not be forced. In *Wuthering Heights* the minor characters are equably released from the control of her will; with Joseph, Zillah, Lockwood, and Mrs. Dean, Emily Brontë's will takes a holiday—they present no danger to her imaginative world. But upon the central characters she exerts a particularly imperious claim, requiring them to contain themselves within her circle. She cannot release them.

The Lyricism of Emily Brontë

BARBARA HARDY*

Some of the poems belonging to the Gondal saga contain fine lyrical passages in a context of weak, banal or melodramatic narrative. Most readers will have their own anthology of lyrical fragments filched from bad verse:

> Sleep brings no strength to me,
> No power renewed to brave,
> I only sail a wilder sea,
> A darker wave. (p. 54)

> I'm happiest when most away
> I can bear my soul from its home of clay
> On a windy night when the moon is bright
> And the eye can wander through worlds of light—(p. 63)

> Yet, still steeped in memory's dyes,
> They come sailing on,
> Darkening all my summer skies,
> Shutting out my sun. (p. 69)

> The world seems made of light; (p. 143)

> But Death has stolen our company. (p. 203)

> Blow, west wind, by the lonely mound,
> And murmur, summer streams,
> There is no need of other sound
> To soothe my Lady's dreams. (p. 205)

> Come, the wind may never again
> Blow as now it blows for us;
> And the stars may never again shine as now they shine; (p. 207)

There are fragments we take from poems, and also some fragments that are all we have: "I'm happiest when most away" (p. 63) or "Fall, leaves, fall" (p. 82).

*Reprinted from *The Art of Emily Brontë*, ed. A. Smith (London: Vision Press, 1976), 96–118.

Some fragments are much larger pieces whose language, imagery and rhythmical line are powerfully individual in expression, but companioned by trite action, language and music. Poem 163 has an impressive beginning:

> In the earth, the earth, thou shalt be laid,
> A grey stone standing over thee;
> Black mould beneath thee spread
> And black mould to cover thee.
>
> "Well, there is rest there,
> So fast come thy prophecy;
> The time when my sunny hair
> Shall with grass roots twinèd be."

And there is one other stanza where a movement of feeling seems to be generated:

> Farewell, then, all that love,
> All that deep sympathy:
> Sleep on; heaven laughs above,
> Earth never misses thee.

But the rest of the poem consists of three extremely crude and exaggerated exclamations, unfortunately typical of much of Emily Brontë's verse-writing. The last verse can stand as an example.

> Turf—sod and tombstone drear
> Part human company;
> One heart broke only there—
> *That* heart was worthy thee! (p. 190)

The best known of her poetic fragments, powerful in a weak context, and gaining immeasurably when extracted from that context, is the description of Hope from "Julian M. and A. G. Rochelle" (p. 238):

> He comes with western winds, with evening's wandering airs,
> With that clear dusk of heaven that brings the thickest stars;
> Winds take a pensive tone, and stars a tender fire,
> And visions rise and change which kill me with desire—
>
> "Desire for nothing known in my maturer years
> When joy grew mad with awe at counting future tears;
> When, if my spirit's sky was full of flashes warm,
> I knew not whence they came, from sun or thunderstorm;
>
> "But first a hush of peace, a soundless calm descends;
> The struggle of distress and fierce impatience ends;

Mute music soothes my breast—unuttered harmony
That I could never dream till earth was lost to me.

"Then dawns the Invisible, the Unseen its truth reveals;
My outward sense is gone, my inward essence feels—
Its wings are almost free, its home, its harbour found;
Measuring the gulf it stoops and dares the final bound!

"Oh, dreadful is the check—intense the agony
When the ear begins to hear and the eye begins to see;
When the pulse begins to throb, the brain to think again,
The soul to feel the flesh and the flesh to feel the chain!

"Yet I would lose no sting, would wish no torture less;
The more that anguish racks the earlier it will bless;
And robed in fires of Hell, or bright with heavenly shine,
If it but herald Death, the vision is divine."

She ceased to speak, and I, unanswering, watched her there,
Not daring now to touch one lock of silken hair—
As I had knelt in scorn, on the dank floor I knelt still,
My fingers in the links of that iron hard and chill.

This intense evocation was printed separately in *Poems by Currer, Ellis and Acton Bell,* in 1846, and is the classical example of Emily Brontë's visionary verse. The visionary feeling, though present in the complete narrative poem, which belongs to the Gondal saga, is greatly intensified and transformed when background, story and character are eliminated. It is sometimes described as mystical, and the startling physical account of the withdrawal of vision does resemble accounts of mystical experience. The surrounding verses are undistinguished in language and uninteresting in character and action, and were evidently eliminated because of these inferiorities. As in her novel, vagueness becomes powerful. But the missing stanzas indicate that she had no aim of deliberate vagueness at the start. They provide explanations which make it hard to take the seven stanzas as being about spiritual trance or ecstasy. When we put the lines back in the context of its story of imprisonment and rescue, the first thing that changes is metaphor. In context, "chain," "torture" and "rack" are not images of spirit tormented by flesh but mean precisely what they say, literally describing a physical imprisonment. The "flesh" which feels "the chain" does not refer to the indifference of flesh to spirit, but to the metal chains, bolts and fetters which bind the lady in the dungeon. The stings, tortures and racks refer to physical punishment, and not to the torture of life-in-the-flesh. The check and agony describe the pain and discomfort of being fettered. The "Desire for nothing known in my maturer years," and "The more that anguish racks the earlier it will bless" refer not to a desire for identity with spirit but to a hoped-for release by Death. Any death and any life-after-death will do. She is indifferent to the theological implications of her vision, "robed in fires of Hell, or bright with heavenly shine, / If it but herald Death, the vision is divine." The vision of hope, and the return of reality, are more resonantly suggestive of rapture, ecstasy and liberation when removed from their setting but such reverberations are accidents of selection. Even the divine or diabolical vision, which sounds so interestingly reckless out of context, is conditioned by the imprisonment. Once there is a glimpse of possible rescue by the hero, the vision is indeed rejected: "Earth's hope was not so dead, heaven's home was not so dear; / I read it in that flash of longing quelled by fear."

Were Emily Brontë's powers of shaping feeling less, such transformation would of course not be possible. The religious and sexual penumbra of imagery does exist, but in the narrative context there is a restriction not only of feelings but of action and development. The heroine prefers release by rescue to the vision of death. The context of history and character is banal and histrionic, like most of Emily Brontë's narrative verse, but its sifting down to elemental feeling lends it an unearned strength.

What critical taste and accident have done to this poem reflect Emily Brontë's tendency to exaggerated intensity. What is excess in a particular context becomes interestingly expansive when melodrama is cut out. And the act of selection reflects the work of the poetic process itself. When James Joyce reproduces the act of making a poem in *A Portrait of the Artist as a Young Man*, he shows how event decomposes into feeling, how action reduces to image, how narratives of laborious memory are compressed under stress of sensation and feeling. Stephen Dedalus's villanelle concentrates events to distil feeling, standing as a lyrical "transubstantiation," as he calls it, between two passages of narrative sequence. What Joyce illustrates is the transformation of history into lyric by that process of elimination which reshapes and telescopes event, bringing out new implications by removing context, exposing suggestion, developing nuance and turning actuality into metaphor, sequence into image. Emily Brontë seems to have conceived and written much of her lyric poetry in an expansive narrative context. There is no doubt about the patchiness of her writing in the Gondal poems where character and action are usually so wooden or strained as to be self-eliminating. Many of the lyric poems have gained from being broken off from the full history or story in which they once took a part. The Gondal saga is full of bondage and imprisonment, subjects that roused her sharpest sensations, and it may be that the powerful short poem, often known as "Spellbound" (p. 56), originally existed in a fuller context which explained what was happening, to whom, and why:

> The night is darkening round me,
> The wild winds coldly blow;

But a tyrant spell has bound me
And I cannot, cannot go.

The giant trees are bending
Their bare boughs weighed with snow,
And the storm is fast descending
And yet I cannot go.

Clouds beyond clouds above me,
Wastes beyond wastes below;
But nothing drear can move me;
I will not, cannot go.

The poem as it stands is an extreme example of lyric isolation. The withdrawal of narrative is not to be wished away. Lyric poetry removes more than it keeps in order to reproduce or produce pure forms of feeling. This poem is self-generative, growing and coming to an end when growth is complete. To move beyond feeling into explanation would not be an advantage. The first stanza may suggest some direct connection between the night, the weather, and the tyrant spell, since the night's darkening and the winds' wildness and coldness are aggressive and threatening. "And I cannot, cannot go" aids this preliminary sense of connection which continues into the second stanza, where the epithet "giant," more anthropomorphic than anything in the previous lines, adds its weight. But just as the identification seems to become clearer, it is checked by "And yet I cannot go," which discourages the identification of the tyrant spell with hostile nature. In the third stanza the dissociation from nature is complete, "But nothing drear can move me." The tyrant spell is left disturbingly unidentified as the poem's movement ends in the climax and conclusion of the last line. It is more than a negation, "I will not, cannot go." The will now seems to submit to the tyranny. We have gone further than the "cannot, cannot" of the first refrain. Moreover, nature's limited hostility is made clear; it defines constraint by its force of dreariness, but does not explain it. Nature does not explain the bondage. The dreariness accumulates, but only to create a theatre for feeling. And the reader is oppressed by the enclosure and refusal to tell, checked by the frustrated movement towards knowledge. The poem slowly acts out the state of bondage it describes, so going beyond description.

Such apparent opening and final enclosure depend on absence of information. The suggestiveness of what is not defined by nature, but is intensified by the natural harshness, reverberates like Catherine's dream and Heathcliff's vision, answering to Coleridge's praise of poetry that moves best by being imperfectly understood. For the lyric poetry of vision, this seems true. But the short poem's suggestiveness manages to combine feeling with idea, presenting the action of bondage in a way which is reflective and self-conscious, "nothing drear can move me." The self-consciousness, like Catherine's discriminations of love, stops short of analytic control. It is self-reflective but scarcely self-possessed, and its brief moment only occupies a small part of the poem and is perfectly compatible with the enactment of bondage.

The natural world often exists for Emily Brontë in order to suggest what is unnatural, and in this poem unnatural feelings are all we are given. Emily Brontë's lyric poetry is usually less extreme in reserve, but it is often inclined to be enigmatic. Sometimes a fully detailed and narrated action can stress feeling by withholding conventional development, arranging feeling in an erratic or unexpected way. Narrative is often allegorical in Emily Brontë's poetry, but the allegory is evasive, meanings and correlations often being suggested provisionally and then modified or withdrawn. In the incantatory poem, "Far away is the land of rest" (p. 53), the land of rest is not identified until the concluding stanza, and in the third stanza there is a deceptive possibility that it is not death:

> Often he looks to the ruthless sky,
> Often he looks o'er his dreary road,
> Often he wishes down to lie
> And render up life's tiresome load.

This permits a strange argument or apostrophe, in which the mournful man is encouraged—if that is the word—to continue, on the grounds of what has already been achieved: "Leagues on leagues are left behind / Since your sunless course began." The second stage of the poem's own progress, in the fourth and fifth stanza, seems to continue this argument from sheer mileage, and the poem's conclusion can only assert that the goal is rest. This is a limited goal, but rest cannot be timed to choice or convenience. It is an exhausted poem, exhausted perhaps in diction as in mood, and the attempt to prolong its own energy charges the abstract journey of life with feeling. Death was always the goal, but it has to be worked and waited for.

In the powerfully bizarre allegory, "Death, that struck when I was most confiding" (p. 224), Emily Brontë astonishingly creates symbols of faith and hope only to let them be destroyed. The poem describes a lost "certain Faith" most vividly, lusciously and vigorously, through a combination of images which are at once abstract and sensuously particular:

> Leaves, upon Time's branch, were growing brightly,
> Full of sap and full of silver dew;
> Birds, beneath its shelter, gathered nightly;
> Daily, round its flowers, the wild bees flew.

The human actor in this poem has a faith in the seasonal rhythm of the symbolism, and suggests it in the vigour of sapful leaves, sheltered birds, and fertilizing wild bees:

> And behold, with tenfold increase blessing
> Spring adorned the beauty-burdened spray;

> Wind and rain and fervent heat caressing
> Lavished glory on its second May.
>
> High it rose; no wingèd grief could sweep it;
> Sin was scared to distance with its shine:
> Love and its own life had power to keep it
> From all wrong, from every blight but thine!

The vitality can only be destroyed by Death, and the seasonal symbol is checked in its implications in order to make absolutely clear the frustration of human feeling. "Time for me must never blossom more!" is not allowed to be the last word. That is given to an image which is logical enough, "Strike it down, that other boughs may flourish / Where that perished sapling used to be," and—somewhat oddly—appropriates the imagery of natural decay and regeneration: "Thus, at least, its mouldering corpse will nourish / That from which it sprung—Eternity." Much of the passion in the poem goes into the imagery and action of frustration, but this is framed between the last verse and the first. The poem initially insists, before the story was told, that what is wanted is for Death to strike again—apparently for a third time, as we know by the time we get to the end:

> Death, that struck when I was most confiding
> In my certain Faith of Joy to be,
> Strike again, Time's withered branch dividing
> From the fresh root of Eternity!

The poem manages to contain, without conflict or rancour, the narrative of pain and loss, and the declaration of faith.

"The Night-Wind" (p. 146) is a full narrative argument, with a tense and developing dialogue establishing the relationship between the speaker and the wind. At each stage in the action there is an illusory sense of progress. What the wind first does and says is gentle, like the scene established in the poem's first lines:

> In summer's mellow midnight,
> A cloudless moon shone through
> Our open parlour window
> And rosetrees wet with dew.
>
> I sat in silent musing,
> The soft wind waved my hair;
> It told me Heaven was glorious,
> And sleeping Earth was fair.

The speaker's first rejection of the wind is simply made on the grounds that its thoughts are not necessary: "I needed not its breathing / To bring such thoughts to me," but this argument is immediately followed by a different suggestion:

> But still it whispered lowly,
> "How dark the woods will be!
>
> "The thick leaves in my murmur
> Are rustling like a dream,
> And all their myriad voices
> Instinct with spirit seem."

This seductive whisper seems distinct from the first, with the stress placed on darkness—echoed in Robert Frost's "Stopping by Woods on a Snowy Evening." The darkness is qualified by a larger dream-like lure, and the plea seems to me to be made for spirit rather than humanity. The human actor now rejects the voice on the new grounds that its music has not "power to reach" the mind and recommending that it

> "Play with the scented flower
> The young tree's supple bough,
> And leave my human feelings
> In their own course to flow."

We then reach the last stage in the seductive appeal to old acquaintance, "Have we not been from childhood friends?" strengthened and made sinister by the suggestion, however sweetly sighed, that it can overpower the will. There is a seductive deepening of friendship to love. It is love on both sides, but what the wind has loved is the human being, while her love is not just for the wind, but also for "the night / Whose silence wakes my song." The invocation of beloved darkness introduces something new into the argument:

> "And when thy heart is laid at rest
> Beneath the church-yard stone
> I shall have time enough to mourn
> And thou to be alone."

All the lures and arguments are joined in these last words: death includes the darkness of the woods, the voices instinct with spirit, and the silent night. The conclusion implicitly explains the several rejections, the human being's sense of Heaven and earth, her desire for her human feelings to flow in their own course, the implication that this course is distinct from the world of vegetable nature, and her old affection for darkness, night, silence and the wind itself.

Only when we reach the conclusion do the various rebuttals and appeals become clear. This final darkness, silence, solitude and lamentation is what the wind has always been uttering, as it speaks both for surviving nature and for natural mortality. It can outlast the individual, like Keats's nightingale, but what this sweetness sings is less a solace than a threat. The attempts to distinguish what is human from what is natural meet the inevitable frustration.

Such an attempt to paraphrase calls attention to the poem's reliance on an erratic course of feeling. It does not move towards a climax but gradually and obliquely notes a shift in feelings. The speaker never fully comprehends what the wind's last words can tell the reader, for the telling turns back, giving the process a new and ironic sadness in the recapitulation. Feeling is met with feeling. Meaning is created by a wayward assembly of experiences, not by an intellectual argument. The feelings stop and start, rather than accumulate in an orderly curve.

Although Emily Brontë's poems show a variety of theme and passion, their symbolism and their attitudes come to cohere. There is, for instance, a body of poetry which enacts a clash of will, and an experience of half-desired, half-feared bondage. There is also a community and variety of conclusions about nature, spirit and death. The night-wind itself belongs to a set of images of wind, darkness, moonlight and starlight, which often represent an imaginative force which both bind and are bound by the human speaker. At times it utters an affinity with her mind, "Have we not been from childhood friends? Have I not loved thee long?" and "I needed not its breathing / To bring such thoughts to me," and at times speaks for a nature or a spirit which transcends the individual. The force may be expressed naturally and supernaturally, as in "The Night-Wind" or "Spellbound." There are theological rather than naturalistic implications in "No coward soul is mine" (p. 243), where the sense of a "God within" seems to create the imaginative realization of a God which exists outside, and beyond:

> With wide-embracing love
> Thy spirit animates eternal years
> Pervades and broods above,
> Changes, sustains, dissolves, creates and rears.
>
> Though Earth and moon were gone
> And suns and universes ceased to be
> And thou wert left alone
> Every Existence would exist in thee.
>
> There is not room for Death
> Nor atom that his might could render void
> Since thou art Being and Breath
> And what thou art may never be destroyed.

Emily Brontë often questions Imagination by analyzing and evaluating its capacities. She does not regard Imagination as a monolithic power. In

"Often rebuked, yet always back returning"[1] there is a separation between the natural imagination and a more fantastic creative effort. The poem's typically expansive inclusions create a tension between two efforts of mind. The poem begins with a large negative invocation of an energy and area of imagination which is to be rejected:

> Often rebuked, yet always back returning
>   To those first feelings that were born with me,
> And leaving busy chase of wealth and learning
>   For idle dreams of things which cannot be:
>
> To-day, I will seek not the shadowy region;
>   Its unsustaining vastness waxes drear;
> And visions rising, legion after legion,
>   Bring the unreal world too strangely near.
>
> I'll walk, but not in old heroic traces,
>   And not in paths of high morality,
> And not among the half-distinguished faces,
>   The clouded forms of long-past history.

The "I will seek not" and "I'll walk, but not" are embedded in the long and detailed account of imaginative rejection, and the rejection, while clearly dismissive—"unsustaining," "drear," "unreal," "too strangely near," "clouded forms"—is sufficiently evocative to make the lure felt.

The positive movement of natural Imagination occupies only seven lines, of these only six remain uninterrupted and unqualified by negatives and rejections. The poem first registers effort, then the last undisturbed six lines create relief after struggle, in the two lines of simple natural celebration: "Where the grey flocks in ferny glens are feeding; / Where the wild wind blows on the mountain side," and the concluding stanza of energetic defence:

> What have those lonely mountains worth revealing?
>   More glory and more grief than I can tell:
> The earth that wakes *one* human heart to feeling
>   Can centre both the worlds of Heaven and Hell.

Everything that the shadowy region might hold can be found here—glory, grief, Heaven and Hell. Once more, there is the insistence that the individual Imagination can focus, concentrate, and contain extremity and multiplicities. The amorality of the last line, reminiscent of *Wuthering Heights* in its claim for Imagination, also makes a claim for something small and personal, "*one* human heart," and something large and impersonal, "both the worlds of Heaven and Hell." Both are claims for creativity. The retreat to "my own nature" and to earth's nature is not made in the interests of a simplified pastoral repose or pleasure. There is a defiant refusal of restriction, a claim for liberty made in the interests of bravely claiming and facing extremes of experience. But the defiance works both ways, to affirm and to state the pull away from nature. The poems dealing more explicitly and precisely with Imagination show a similar division, and a similar inclusiveness. They offer not a system but a variety of passionate moods which image ideas, and particularize abstraction, though neither steadily nor consistently. At times Imagination compels, at times it frees. At times it is fantastic, at times claims authenticity for vision. At times it seems lost, then found. At times there seems no incompatibility between the extent and force of the individual Imagination and a sense of totally reliable meaning, in a God, an Immortality, and an Eternity. At times, there is a gap between the sense of imaginative power and its guarantees in religious experience.

Her poetry of Imagination always dramatizes effort and sometimes frustration. In the poem "Ah! why, because the dazzling sun" (p. 225) there is a severance between a rejoicing nature, lit and warmed by daylight, and the poet's Imagination, needing the nourishment of night and stars:

> All through the night, your glorious eyes
> Were gazing down in mine,
> And with a full heart's thankful sighs
> I blessed that watch divine!
>
> I was at peace, and drank your beams
> As they were life to me
> And revelled in my changeful dreams
> Like petrel on the sea.
>
> Thought followed thought—star followed star
> Through boundless regions on,
> While one sweet influence, near and far,
> Thrilled through and proved us one.
>
> Why did the morning rise to break
> So great, so pure a spell,
> And scorch with fire the tranquil cheek
> Where your cool radiance fell?

The night ended, the necessary day rises, and the imagery of the sun is aggressive, threatening and hostile, though it is what Nature needs:

> Blood-red he rose, and arrow-straight
> His fierce beams struck my brow:
> The soul of Nature sprang elate,
> But mine sank sad and low!

> My lids closed down—yet through their veil
> I saw him blazing still;
> And bathe in gold the misty dale,
> And flash upon the hill.

The poet tries to turn back to Night, and the imagery of unextinguishable day cannot be wholly harsh or unpleasant, though there is a clever blurring of beneficence and discomfort:

> It would not do—the pillow glowed
> And glowed both roof and floor,
> And birds sang loudly in the wood,
> And fresh winds shook the door.
>
> The curtains waved, the wakened flies
> Were murmuring round my room,
> Imprisoned there, till I should rise
> And give them leave to roam.

This violently physical invocation of day establishes the identification of creativity with night, partly through the logical associations of dream, magic, vastness, concentration, and solitude, the concept of the Imagination's dependence on the sleep of consciousness and the banishment of routine, but partly through invocations of purity, coolness and sweetness. The starlight can be gazed at, "I . . . drank your beams," as the sunlight cannot. The relationship between this brilliant piece of antithetical sensation and "Often rebuked, yet always back returning," brings out the impossibility of imposing a consistent pattern on this poetry.

In another poem about Imagination, "My Comforter" (p. 196), the imagery tells a very different story. There is a clear distinction between a hidden light in the soul, and a hysterically rendered gloom in daylit existence:

> Deep down—concealed within my soul,
> That light lies hid from men,
> Yet glows unquenched—though shadows roll,
> Its gentle ray can not control—
> About the sullen den.
>
> Was I not vexed, in these gloomy ways
> To walk unlit so long?
> Around me, wretches uttering praise,
> Or howling o'er their hopeless days,
> And each with Frenzy's tongue—

But the imagery blurs the simplicity: the outer experience is rendered in terms of an admittedly glorious sunlight, but this is accompanied and qualified by another glare, "the glare of Hell." The central statement of suffering transforms and restates a much weaker verse which describes rather than expresses feeling:

> So stood I, in Heaven's glorious sun
> And in the glare of Hell
> My spirit drank a mingled tone
> Of seraph's song and demon's moan—
> What my soul bore my soul alone
> Within its self may tell.

The refusal to tell is more powerful than the telling. Similarly, although the soothing power of Imagination's comfort is evoked, it is provisional and tentative, ushering in and dismissing images that will not quite render the solace:

> Like a soft air above a sea
> Tossed by the tempest's stir—
> A thaw-wind melting quietly
> The snowdrift on some wintery lea;
> No—what sweet thing can match with thee,
> My thoughtful Comforter?

And the poem ends where it began, with the beginning only of comfort:

> And yet a little longer speak,
> Calm this resentful mood,
> And while the savage heart grows meek,
> For other token do not seek,
> But let the tear upon my cheek
> Evince my gratitude.

Emily Brontë likes to record imaginative effort and essay, the process of feeling a mingled pain and consolation. Her concept of Imagination is not stated but experienced, not understood or perceived statically, but through particulars. In "How Clear She Shines!" (p. 184) there is an impassioned invocation of Fancy made in the full knowledge that dream will not last:

> How clear she shines! How quietly
> I lie beneath her silver light
> While Heaven and Earth are whispering me,
> "To-morrow wake, but dream to-night."
>
> Yes, Fancy, come, my Fairy love!
> These throbbing temples, softly kiss;
> And bend my lonely couch above
> And bring me rest and bring me bliss.

> The world is going—Dark world, adieu!
> Grim world, go hide thee till the day;
> The heart thou canst not all subdue
> Must still resist if thou delay!

The poem reverses the process of "Often rebuked, yet always back returning," beginning with the willing of Fancy and dream, and then stating Imagination's *fiat* through a string of bitter personifications. They make their presence felt so powerfully that the poem turns from the hope of consolation to an irony unusual though not unparalleled in Emily Brontë. Irony admits what Imagination will have to deny:

> And this shall be my dream to-night—
> I'll think the heaven of glorious spheres
> Is rolling on its course of light
> In endless bliss through endless years;
>
> I'll think there's not one world above,
> Far as these straining eyes can see,
> Where Wisdom ever laughed at Love,
> Or Virtue crouched to Infamy.

The concluding four stanzas admit the presences of everything that will have to be dismissed. The poem dramatizes will and imaginative intent, but then travels fast and harshly from moonlight to the unlit world. The dismissal of Joy, Peace and especially Hope, "a phantom of the soul," makes the invocation a startling gathering-up of hostility and cynicism. The world which needs to be changed by dreaming is established in all its undiminished horrors. The poem moves through extremes of feeling, as does "O Dream, where art thou now" (p. 87) where the feeling is a complex one in which the memory of vision seems intolerable. Emily Brontë uses Imagination while she probes its certainties and uncertainties:

> Alas, alas for me
> Thou wert so bright and fair,
> I could not think thy memory
> Would yield me nought but care!

There are more poems energetically praising Imagination than poems which lament its passage. The transience is almost always acknowledged, even in poems of praise like "To Imagination" (p. 205) which prizes the world within, admitting the "hopeless" world without. This poem vacillates from doubt to assertion, claiming that the important principle is

> . . . a bright unsullied sky,
> Warm with ten thousand mingled rays
> Of suns that know no winter days

but adding Reason's intrusive complaints and Truth's destruction. So it seems right that the concluding stanza gathers together welcome and trust:

> I trust not to thy phantom bliss,
> Yet still in evening's quiet hour
> With never-failing thankfulness
> I welcome thee, benignant power,
> Sure solacer of human cares
> And brighter hope when hope despairs.

One of the best-known poems about Imagination is "O thy bright eyes must answer now" (p. 208), which offers the most complex analysis of Imagination's struggle with Reason, defending Imagination as a "radiant angel" but one which has to speak eloquently at the Judgement seat of Stern Reason. The analysis runs through the sense of bondage and the sense of power:

> So with a ready heart I swore
> To seek their altar-stone no more,
> And gave my spirit to adore
> Thee, ever present, phantom thing—
> My slave, my comrade, and my King!
>
> A slave because I rule thee still;
> Incline thee to my changeful will
> And make thy influence good or ill—
> A comrade, for by day and night
> Thou art my intimate delight—
>
> My Darling Pain that wounds and sears
> And wrings a blessing out from tears
> By deadening me to real cares;
> And yet, a king—though prudence well
> Have taught thy subject to rebel.

The poem becomes more lucidly a poem about itself, the constant process of qualification offers a rational yet tense account of imaginative complexity and tension. It is sufficiently assertive to tolerate uncertainty, sufficiently uncertain to confront objections. The final summons admits question, expects an affirmative answer, and asserts the personal and individual guarantee. It tries to claim at the same time the authority of a universal, in the apostrophe to a God, and a God of "Visions":

> And am I wrong to worship where
> Faith cannot doubt nor Hope despair
> Since my own soul can grant my prayer?
> Speak, God of Visions, plead for me
> And tell why I have chosen thee!

The constant entertainment of acceptance and rejection is subtly at work in the strange poem "Enough of Thought, Philosopher" (p. 220). At the heart of this poem is an elaborately detailed vision of a Spirit standing by the golden, blood-red and sapphire rivers, and finding his unity in an ocean first darkened and troubled by the joined waters, and then radiantly whitened. The transformation seems inseparable from an intensity of vision formed to see its splendour:

> "The Spirit bent his dazzling gaze
> Down on that Ocean's gloomy night,
> Then—kindling all with sudden blaze,
> The glad deep sparkled wide and bright—
> White as the sun; far, far more fair
> Than the divided sources were!"

The vision is asserted as an explanation, apparently made by the speaker to the "Space-sweeping soul" who uncaringly looks for annihilation since he believes in no possible Heaven or Hell. The speaker's position is different, since he has imagined what the Philosopher has never conceived, and shares the wish for a sleep without identity only because it has been seen but not found. The poem sets a defence of one state of unbelief against another, but its religious feelings self-consciously rest on the dazzling but unreliable findings of Imagination. It weighs poetry against philosophy, to assert the poet's vision, lovingly but doubtingly. "It is too late to call thee now" (p. 141) declares the pointlessness of dream, since "every joy that lit my brow / Would bring its after-storm of pain." The most powerful image combines barrenness and radiance:

> Besides, the mist is half withdrawn;
> The barren mountain-side lies bare;
> And sunshine and awaking morn
> Paint no more golden visions there.

The poem moves from the strongly asserted refusal to dream to the weaker expression of gratitude for past dreaming:

> Yet, ever in my grateful breast,
> Thy darling shade shall cherished be;
> For God alone doth know how blest
> My early years have been in thee!

In "No coward soul is mine" (p. 243) Imagination goes beyond nature, and the natural images are mostly sterile, "withered weeds / Or idlest froth." There is a striking attempt to use natural images to define transience, though it is not carried out with complete consistency, for the imagery of light, "I see Heaven's glories shine" and strength, "The steadfast rock of Immortality," are natural images, invoked, magnified, and generalized in traditional religious language. As we have seen, the poem invokes the familiar sense of a vast existence beyond the individual by invoking and then dismissing nature:

> There is not room for Death
> Nor atom that his might could render void
> Since thou art Being and Breath
> And what thou art may never be destroyed.

Emily Brontë can only imagine spirit through nature. "Atom" and "Breath" are physiological terms being made into absolutes. The mind is felt to be capable of apprehending what is outside the mind; its light is part of the light outside: "I see Heaven's glories shine / And Faith shines equal arming me from Fear." The effort involved in this invocation is rare in her poetry.[2] Whether dealing with the passions of love, nature, death or religious faith, her poetry commonly involves a sense of the gap between the human Imagination and the consequences of its powers. The poetry only once states that perfect equivalence between a light in Heaven and the light of the mind, an image made conventional in many hymns, but given a personal voice here. In the earlier poems, "Spellbound" (p. 56), written in 1837, and "The Night-Wind" (p. 146), written in 1840, there are affinity and acquiescence, but also struggle, reluctance and pain. In this respect, Emily Brontë's self-consciousness about vision is close to that of Wordsworth's and Keats's, also inclined to see the vision as impaired, doubtful, unstable or lost.

Even Emily Brontë's rare love poetry makes the same accommodation, and creates the same tension. In "R. Alcona to J. Brenzaida" (p. 222), the first three stanzas make a strong claim to fidelity in the form of question, not assertion:

> Cold in the earth, and the deep snow piled above thee!
> Far, far removed, cold in the dreary grave!
> Have I forgot, my Only Love, to love thee,
> Severed at last by Time's all-wearing wave?
>
> Now when alone, do my thoughts no longer hover
> Over the mountains on Angora's shore;
> Resting their wings where heath and fern-leaves cover
> That noble heart for ever, ever more?

The question, however, does not receive a negative answer. As with "The Philosopher" the mode is that of painful candour, not irony. The questioning prepares for a complex definition of remembrance, not through a claim of unchanged emotion, but through the admission of necessary change. The third stanza, with its memorable image, "fifteen wild Decembers / From those brown hills have melted into spring," creates movement and plurality to reduce time and yet to measure it. The last two lines of this stanza first appear commonplace in what they say about "years of change," but are then seen to assert a kind of forgetting:

> Cold in the earth, and fifteen wild Decembers
> From those brown hills have melted into spring—
> Faithful indeed is the spirit that remembers
> After such years of change and suffering!

The poem is no trite assertion of remembrance, but explains the nature of a survival of love, scrupulously allowing for the passage of time. Love has to forgive the necessary process of forgetting. The explanation makes a melancholy and rational account of a feeling which, though subject to change, remains a feeling of personal love. The speaker, Rosina Alcona, is no Heathcliff; she joins passionate lament with an unobsessed remembrance, eroded and distracted. Bliss has gone, but life has continued:

> No other Sun has lightened up my heaven;
> No other Star has ever shone for me:
> All my life's bliss from thy dear life was given—
> All my life's bliss is in the grave with thee.

Dreams have gone too, and passion has had to live on, qualified by dreamlessness. We are told this somewhat baldly:

> But when the days of golden dreams had perished
> And even Despair was powerless to destroy,
> Then did I learn how existence could be cherished,
> Strengthened and fed without the aid of joy

It is not simply a life and love-in-memory which is expressed. The memory has dangerously regenerated feeling, as imaginative memory can, and the poem moves out of its rational explanation to the point where reason is in danger of losing control. The individual words are flat, but what is being said is spiritedly conveyed. The poem must end at this point, because energy of remembrance is the force which it resists:

> And even yet, I dare not let it languish,
> Dare not indulge in Memory's rapturous pain;
> Once drinking deep of that divinest anguish,
> How could I seek the empty world again?

Emily Brontë's best love poem is imaginative in the fullest and most exact sense of the word. It recognizes the limits and the indulgences of Imagination, and controls its own passion by that act of recognition. Its dynamism and order show her lyricism once more melting abstraction into particulars. The growth of feeling seems to rely on the powerful syntax which checks, permits, drives and shapes sharp feeling. Like much of her poetry, it has lapses. Its phrases are weak, often conventional. Her ecstatic description often partakes of the vague and uncontrolled hyperbole of hymns: "rapturous pain" and "divinest anguish" are uncomfortably overintense. But the direct utterance, while flouting restraint, does act as a medium for passion. The poem is characteristic of her strengths and her weaknesses. Emily Brontë can muster more intensity than greater masters of language.

Notes

    1.   This poem is not included in the numbered collection of Emily Brontë's poems because Hatfield conjectures it is by Charlotte Brontë (p. 255). There seems to be little basis for this speculation.
    2.   "No coward soul is mine" is one of Emily Brontë's last poems, written in 1846.

Brontë as Heretic

STEVIE DAVIES*

To find an English version we have only to turn to the corpus of Emily Brontë's lyric poetry. Here the search for liberty and peace is consistently associated with the sanctuary of a moorland vista, the nocturnal dreamworld traditionally allied with the feminine, and with the more threatening but ultimately benign realm of the underworld in its ancient treaty and concord with the upper world (figured in the Persephone / Demeter myth, which has been shown to shape so many nineteenth century novels by women, including, to some degree, *Wuthering Heights*).[1] The pull of earth invariably disenchants her poetic personae with the allure of heaven, to such a degree as to arrest allegiance at source. Here I shall look closely at one of the most telling of the lyrics, "I see around me tombstones grey" (p. 166), where the persona names as *mother* the archetypal affinity which binds her to earth and the mother-religion. Acknowledging the unhealing pain of terrestrial life, she analyses it out of intrinsic connection with heaven:

> Sweet land of light! thy children fair
> Know nought akin to our despair
>
> . . . .
> Well, may they live in extasy
> Their long eternity of joy;
> At least we would not bring them down
> With us to weep, with us to groan.
> No—Earth would wish no other sphere
> To taste her cup of sufferings drear;
> She turns from Heaven a careless eye
> And only mourns that *we* must die!
> (ll. 15–16, 21–8)

The immune "children of heaven" live in a self-absorbed trance of bliss, narcissistically disconnected from knowledge of their proximity to the incurable and chaotic pain endured on earth. To know would be to compassionate, and to feel compassion would be to fall into a share of pain. The Father's children must be allowed to retain their hard hearts. The children of Earth (personalised as

*Reprinted from S. Davies, *Emily Brontë* (Hemel Hempstead: Harvester, 1998), 36–41.

"she," hence the children of the Mother) are a race of implicit moral superiority, who "would not bring them down" to fall into human comprehension of pain. Angels and mortals, as in Byron's mystery play, *Heaven and Earth*, whose influence I shall assess later inhabit the poles of a contradictory universe. This poem is a declaration of primary allegiance to the mother-principle, affirming with characteristic hauteur a creation separable from its God and denying the necessity of a contract between them. To deny the fact or desirability of mediation between heaven and earth is by implication to deny Christ. The persona speaks for human nature in refusing to invoke intercession from the Father: "we would not bring them down / With us to weep." Such strategic withdrawal from the Divine scheme ironically indicates that human autonomy is essential to preserve the scheme itself intact and pure, contaminating no "child of heaven" (such as Christ the Son) with the crude matter of human clay. Incarnation and atonement would challenge the perfect polarities upon which the universe is founded. They would indict the Father's logic. The children of the Mother announce their superiority over the refinements of the irrelevantly perfect heaven. From the vantage-point of such elevation, the mother-world can afford to deny the possibility of any redemptive passage or communication between heaven and earth. "Earth would wish no other sphere / To taste her cup of sufferings drear," remembering—but rebuking—Christ at Gethsemane. Emily Brontë's earth, self-defending in her proud isolation from any bending-down of the intercessive skies, turns a "careless" eye to heaven and broods inwardly upon her own children. The very existence of memory in human beings makes it impossible that heaven could palliate one's knowledge of bygone pain. The poem emphasises the passionate love-bond between earth and earth's children: it stands as a statement of affiliation, not to the authority of a commanding and omniscient Divine Parent, but to the maternal principle perceived as being *like ourselves* in vulnerability and in staunch commitment to the defence of its young in a world it does not control.[2] Taut abstraction expresses the remote beatitude of the Blessed ("Well, may they live in extasy / Their long eternity of joy"), which is almost metaphysical in its dashingly casual manner. The circle of the octosyllabic couplet closes in half-rhyme, playing a subtle verbal music (*live / long, extasy / eternity*) to imply the repetitious circularity of the timeless realm, in which the tautology of "*long* eternity" reflects a possible routine of ennui unknown to the lower world. Earth as *mater dolorosa,* mutely alienated from an unatoning heaven, claims from the speaker a passionately personal affiliation:

> Ah mother, what shall comfort thee
> In all this boundless misery?
>
> (ll. 29–30)

The poetic voice lends its power to articulate the "deep *unutterable* woe" of the parent planet. For Milton's allegiance to the power and glory of the Father

("Hail, holy Light . . .") Emily Brontë substitutes an invocation to the earth named as mortal mother. Orphaned of her natural mother since the age of three, she consecrates the earth which contains her dead mother's remains in a poem which declares conscious recognition of the archetypal vision upon which her heretical religion and sinistral perception are founded:

> Indeed, no dazzling land above
> Can cheat thee of thy children's love.
> We all, in life's departing shine,
> Our last dear longings blend with thine;
> And struggle still and strive to trace
> With clouded gaze, thy darling face.
> We would not leave our native home
> For *any* world beyond the Tomb.
> No—rather on thy kindly breast
> Let us be laid in lasting rest;
> Or waken but to share with thee
> A mutual immortality.
>
> (II. 35–46)

Earth's "darling face" and "kindly breast" are loved as human and succouring in a way that the delusive glory of heaven cannot match. Indeed, the radiant children of heaven inhabit a country whose luminous perfection is understood as potential corruption of clear vision. *Dazzle* is an ironic Miltonism, alluding to *Paradise Lost*'s heaven of too intense Light that bears into the surcharged vision of the angel host as a kind of darkness:

> Dark with excessive bright thy skirts appear
> Yet dazzle heaven, that brightest seraphim
> Approach not, but with both wings veil their eyes.
>
> (II. 380–2)

To reject transcendence in quintessential Light in favour of immanence within the dying planet is, for the poetic persona, a choice against moral blindness. Fidelity is Emily Brontë's cardinal virtue: both her poetry and fiction are pre-occupied with the keeping of faith to one's source and earliest allegiances, if necessary across the boundary of the grave. The pledge to the mother-world ("no dazzling world above / Can cheat thee of thy children's love") affirms that mortality's love of its home is faithful as the child to the mother, in wanting to rest its eyes on that face and no other. The eternal reciprocity of shared sleep—featured in *Wuthering Heights* in the shared bed and shared grave of Catherine and Heathcliff, or the (gloriously phrased) "mutual immortality" of earth with earth's child—is the final focus of desire.

As a self-acknowledged "child of the Mother," Emily Brontë, as we shall see recognises and does not disclaim kinship with the predatory chain of

being which characterises nature. But she denies man's and nature's responsibility for their impaired condition, grafting responsibility for the fall on to the
God who has unpardonably stigmatised his creation. Her heroine chooses to
fall with Lucifer from the reprehensible perfection of the angels back into the
world of early affinity: the heath and Heathcliff. My study opens its account
of these central themes of *Wuthering Heights* by reflecting on the likeness of
the linguistic norms of the novel—apparently so prohibitively opaque—to an
original language of childhood desire.

Notes

1.   See D. Athas, "Goddesses, Heroines and Women Writers," *St Andrew's Review* 3
(Fall-Winter 1975): 5–13.
2.   This equivalence and at-oneness between the mother-goddess and human nature is
a familiar mythic archetype in the ancient mother-religions, e.g. the stricken Ceres in the
Eleusinian mystery cult (see my *The Idea of Woman in Renaissance Literature* [Lexington: University Press of Kentucky, 1986], 17–22 for an account and sources). Here I am not claiming cul-
tic influence on Emily Brontë, but rather the natural coincidence of corresponding clusters of
ideas and images around an identical archetype.

WUTHERING HEIGHTS:
THE FIRST HUNDRED YEARS
◆

Introduction

THOMAS JOHN WINNIFRITH

Both in her admirable collection of reviews and articles on the Brontë sisters in *The Brontës: The Critical Heritage* series and in the shorter but equally comprehensive selection of Victorian criticism of *Wuthering Heights* in the Macmillian Casebook Series, Miriam Allott is at pains to stress that it is a myth that Emily Brontë's novel was either ignored or reviled for the first 50 years after its publication. She quotes a series of contemporary reviews and later comments that the novel had power in spite of its unattractive features. Charlotte's preface to the second edition, praising her sister's work with faint damns, sets the tone for Victorian comment; indeed, modern critics, notably Philip Drew, and more recently Juliet Barker, have put some of the blame on Charlotte for Emily's comparatively poor standing. It is possible that Allott, although quite rightly drawing our attention to the fact that *Wuthering Heights* was not totally neglected in the nineteenth century, slightly underestimates the initial hostility to this novel and the tendency to regard Charlotte as the only Brontë worth studying.

Contemporary reviews of *Wuthering Heights* were fewer and less laudatory than those of *Jane Eyre*. In *The Brontës and their Background* I was able to show that all the Brontës were attacked for "coarseness," a somewhat blanket term hinting vaguely at sexual immorality of thought or expression but encompassing brutality and irreligion. These charges were most frequently leveled at *The Tenant of Wildfell Hall,* but the publication of this novel led to a reexamination of *Wuthering Heights*, which began to be seen as the worst of a bad lot. American reviews were particularly harsh. As Charlotte recalls, a month before her death, Emily, drawing breath with difficulty, sat by the fire, smiling sardonically, as she read the description of herself in *The North American Review* by E. Whipple as "a man of uncommon talents, but dogged, brutal and morose."

Sidney Dobell thought highly of *Wuthering Heights,* but he was eccentric, especially in his insistence that Charlotte must have been the author. Most Victorian reviewers felt obliged to give a long summary of the plot and to include long passages from the work reviewed. They found this difficult to do in the case of *Wuthering Heights.* After Charlotte's biographical preface it became less easy to condemn Ellis Bell as a dogged and morose man, but G. H. Lewes still called Emily's novel "sombre, rude, brutal, yet true." The publication of Mrs. Gaskell's *Life of Charlotte Brontë* brought about more sympathy, and Allott rightly draws attention to praise of *Wuthering Heights* from Skelton, Dallas, Roscoe, and Montégut, but Roscoe calls the book revolting, and Montégut says the characters are criminal. The *Christian Remembrancer* described *Wuthering Heights* as a monstrous performance, and the *North American Review*, though kinder than in 1848, still talked of a distorted fancy and said that the power of the creations is as great as it is grotesque.

Critical opinion did not change much until the last decades of Victoria's reign, and even then praise of Emily was intermittent. Allott quotes a long article on Emily's poetry and prose in the American periodical *Galaxy* of February 1873, but in fact, as well as apologizing for the neglect and vilification of Brontë, the author of this article aims to praise her poetry rather than her novel, whose "faults are too prominent to admit of either glozing or concealment." Writing a new biography of Charlotte Brontë, T. Wermyss Reid in 1877 said that *Wuthering Heights* was practically unread. Swinburne leapt to Emily's defence, but Swinburne is not the voice of the Victorian establishment. For a more representative view we should look at the verdicts of Leslie Stephen and George Saintsbury.

Saintsbury, now seen as typical of wrongheaded Victorian literary criticism but nevertheless a man of considerable energy and a fair representative of the spirit of his age, actually ascribed *Wuthering Heights* to Acton Bell. Leslie Stephen, another eminent Victorian, in replying to Swinburne in the *Cornhill Magazine* for December 1877, said very little about Emily Brontë, but he did say that her feeble grasp of external facts made her book a kind of baseless nightmare. Swinburne mounted a more impassioned defence of the poetic quality of *Wuthering Heights* in 1883, when Mary Robinson's rather thin and unsatisfactory biography appeared, but Stephen had the last word when, in the *Dictionary of National Biography,* he devoted more space in his article on Charlotte Brontë to Branwell's disgraceful behavior than he did to Emily's literary achievements.

The *Dictionary of National Biography* was edited by Stephen and published by George Smith, both, in their remorseless energy, typifying the Victorian age, as indeed does the massive dictionary. Stephen's connection with the Brontës was an odd one; his father had assisted the Robinson family when protesting against their portrayal in Mrs. Gaskell's life, and his daughter, Virginia Woolf, wrote one of the most famous statements preferring Emily to Charlotte. But it was not to Stephen that Smith turned when he wanted to publish a new edition of the Brontë novels. Instead he asked a figure as firmly set in the English establishment but one who looked forward to the new century.

We open our selection of modern criticism of *Wuthering Heights* where Allott closes her *Critical Heritage* volume, with the preface to the Haworth edition of *Wuthering Heights* written just before the turn of the century by Mrs. Humphry Ward. This preface is important because it clearly puts Emily ahead of Charlotte as the greater writer; Ward is in the equivalent preface to *Jane Eyre* fairly disparaging about the faults of Charlotte's novel. The preface to *Wuthering Heights* represents something of a watershed, and conveniently it was written at or near the turn of the century, the end of Queen Victoria's reign and the 50th anniversary of the publication of *Wuthering Heights*. Ward herself is less easy to fit into a nineteenth-century or Victorian straitjacket. She was the niece of Matthew Arnold and the granddaughter of Thomas Arnold, seen by some as the epitome of Victorian religious earnestness and derided by Lytton Strachey in *Eminent Victorians*. When Ward died in 1920, two years after Strachey's book was published, she was hailed as England's greatest woman of letters, but her star had already begun to wane, and her books, bestsellers in their day, are now virtually unread, although *Robert Elsmere* (1893), the story of a clergyman who lost his faith, has a certain historical interest and shows that Ward was not stuck in a totally Victorian time warp.

In her criticism of the Brontës, Ward certainly looks forward as well as back, and in setting Emily above Charlotte she prepared the way for the next half century of Brontë criticism. It is true that in stressing Emily's links with English and Continental Romanticism, Ward still follows the Victorian idea that Brontë was a savage writer, and there are criticisms of Heathcliff's character and the inconsistencies in the portrayal of Nelly Dean. These are mild when compared to the attacks on the glaring faults to be found in *Jane Eyre*.

It was left to the twentieth century to complete the transformation of Brontë from a rough, rude, romantic writer with power as her only virtue to a consummate artist whose novel is constructed with great skill. There were still uninformed writers, very often using inaccurate biographical information, who persisted in the Victorian view; there is an interesting account of these in Melvin Watson's article "Wuthering Heights and the Critics." But a more penetrating analysis came from Bloomsbury, the same intellectual coterie that inspired *Eminent Victorians*.

Virginia Woolf's preference for Emily over Charlotte stresses her universality as the reason for her greatness. When Victorian values fell out of fashion, Charlotte, writing with and for these values, fell out of fashion, but Emily writes for all places and all times, so Woolf argues in an essay originally written in 1916. This essay, published in *The Common Reader* (London, 1925), is usually shortened in anthologies so that it ends with the rather baffling words "the sentence remains unfinished." This may reinforce the impression that Brontë, though stating universal truths, is somehow incoherent, but in fact, as the concluding part of the essay shows, Woolf is at pains to stress the realism and creditability of the characters in *Wuthering Heights*.

It was, however, left to another writer with Bloomsbury connections to stress the care and accuracy of the construction of Brontë's novel. Sanger was a lawyer by training, as could perhaps be guessed from his careful analysis of legal points in the story, but he is equally strong on chronology. Various attempts have been made to improve and refine his chronological scheme, the most recent being that by A. Stuart Daley in *Brontë Society Transactions* for 1995. Nobody has really been able to solve the problem of what exactly the ghost of Catherine means when she says in Lockwood's dream that she has been an outcast for twenty years.

Cecil's thesis was very influential, although many later critics mention it only to attack it. He never quite explains how the mixed marriages of the second generation succeed in resolving the apparently irreconcilable division between calm and storm, although he tried to do so in a later address to the Brontë Society, printed in *Brontë Society Transactions* for 1973, pages 169-76.

Cecil was a university teacher, although his book was written for the general public. The immense proliferation of critical books and articles on the Brontës occurred after the Second World War, when expanding universities required their teachers to publish their research. The centenary of the publication of the Brontës' novels provided a pretext for some observations. We have already noted Watson's harsh review of amateur critics of *Wuthering Heights*. There is a good summary of mid-century opinion on the Brontës by Richard Chase, entitled "The Brontës: A Centennial Observation," in the *Kenyon Review*. We conclude this account of early criticism, straying slightly over the first hundred years, with two academic appreciations of *Wuthering Heights,* one from England and one from the United States.

Both Watson and Kettle take issue with Cecil; Kettle takes on Woolf, too. Watson thinks Cecil pays not enough attention to Heathcliff and sees the principal struggle in the book not between calm and storm, but between love and hate in Heathcliff's soul. Kettle thinks that we do take sides in the book, and that we are on Heathcliff's side. Watson, Kettle, and Cecil agree in their high opinion of the novel and that it has one distinct meaning. Over the next forty-five years, few could be found to challenge *Wuthering Heights*'s greatness, but even fewer were so confident or so naive as to try to tie Brontë's novel to a single level of meaning.

Wuthering Heights

MARY WARD*

Emily Brontë, like her sister, inherited Celtic blood, together with a stern and stoical tradition of daily life. She was a wayward, imaginative girl, physically delicate, brought up in loneliness and poverty, amid a harsh yet noble landscape of hill, moor and stream. Owing to the fact that her father had some literary cultivation, and an Irish quickness of intelligence beyond that of his brother-clergy, this child of genius had from the beginning a certain access to good books, and through books and newspapers to the central world of thought and of affairs. In 1827, when Emily was nine, she and her sisters used to amuse themselves in the wintry firelight by choosing imaginary islands to govern, and peopling them with famous men. Emily chose the Isle of Arran, and for inhabitants Sir Walter Scott and the Lockharts; while Charlotte chose the Duke of Wellington and Christopher North. In 1829, Charlotte, in a fragment of journal, describes the newspapers taken by the family in those troubled days of Catholic emancipation and reform, and lets us know that a neighbour lent them *Blackwood's Magazine*, "the most able periodical there is." It was, indeed, by the reading of *Blackwood* in its days of most influence and vigour, and, later, of *Fraser* (from 1832 apparently), that the Brontë household was mainly kept in touch with the current literature, the criticism, poetry, and fiction of their day. During their eager enthusiastic youth the Brontë sisters, then, were readers of Christopher North, Hogg, De Quincey, and Maginn in *Blackwood,* of Carlyle's early essays and translations in *Fraser,* of Scott and Lockhart, no less than of Wordsworth, Southey, and Coleridge. Charlotte asked Southey and Coleridge for an opinion on her poems; Branwell did the same with Hartley Coleridge; and no careful reader of Emily Brontë's verse can fail to see in it the fiery and decisive influence of S. T. C.

So much for the influences of youth. There can be no question that they were "romantic" influences, and it can be easily shown that among them were many kindling sparks from that "unextinguished hearth" of German poetry and fiction which played so large a part in English imagination during the first half of the century. In 1800, Hannah More, protesting against the Germanising invasion, and scandalised by the news that Schiller's "Räuber" "is

*Reprinted from the Haworth edition of the Brontë novel (London: Smith Elder, 1900), XIX–XXXIX.

now acting in England by persons of quality," sees, "with indignation and astonishment, the Huns and Vandals once more overpowering the Greeks and Romans," and English minds "hurried back to the reign of Chaos and old Night by distorted and unprincipled compositions, which, in spite of strong flashes of genius, unite the taste of the Goths" with the morals of the "road." In 1830, Carlyle, quoting the passage, and measuring the progress of English knowledge and opinion, reports triumphantly "a rapidly growing favour for German literature." "There is no one of our younger, more vigorous periodicals," he says, "but has its German craftsman gleaning what he can"; and for twenty years or more he himself did more than any other single writer to bring the German and English worlds together. During the time that he was writing and translating for the *Edinburgh,* the *Foreign Review* and *Fraser,*—in *Blackwood* also, through the years when Charlotte and Emily Brontë, then at the most plastic stage of thought and imagination, were delighting in it, one may find a constant series of translations from the German, of articles on German memoirs and German poets, and of literary reflections and estimates, which testify abundantly to the vogue of all things Teutonic, both with men of letters and the public. In 1840, *Maga,* in the inflated phrase of the time, says, indeed, that the Germans are aspiring "to wield the literary sceptre, with as lordly a sway as ever graced the dynasty of Voltaire. No one who is even superficially acquainted with the floating literature of the day can fail to have observed how flauntingly long-despised Germanism spreads its phylacteries on every side." In the year before (1839), *Blackwood* published a translation of Tieck's *Pietro d'Abano,* a wild robber-and-magician story, of the type which spread the love of monster and vampire, witch and werewolf, through a Europe tired for the moment of eighteenth-century commonsense; and, more important still, a long section, excellently rendered, from Goethe's *Dichtung und Wahrheit.* In that year Emily Brontë was alone with her father and aunt at Haworth, while her two sisters were teaching as governesses. *Blackwood* came as usual, and one may surely imagine the long, thin girl bending in the firelight over these pages from Goethe, receiving the impress of their lucidity, their charm, their sentiment and "natural magic," nourishing from them the vivid and masterly intelligence which eight years later produced *Wuthering Heights.*

But she was to make a nearer acquaintance with German thought and fancy than could be got from the pages of *Blackwood* and *Fraser.* In 1842 she and Charlotte journeyed to Brussels, and there a certain divergence seems to have declared itself between the literary tastes and affinities of the two sisters. While Charlotte, who had already become an eager reader of French books, and was at all times more ready to take the colour of an environment than Emily, was carried, by the teaching of M. Héger acting upon her special qualities and capacities, into that profounder appreciation of the French Romantic spirit and method which shows itself thenceforward in all her books, Emily set herself against Brussels, against M. Héger, and against the French models that he was constantly proposing to the sisters. She was homesick and miserable; her attitude of mind was partly obstinacy, partly, perhaps, a matter of instinctive and passionate preference. She learnt German diligently, and it has always been assumed, though I hardly know on what first authority, that she read a good deal of German fiction, and especially Hoffmann's tales, at Brussels. Certainly, we hear of her in the following year, when she was once more at Haworth, and Charlotte was still at Brussels, as doing her household work "with a German book open beside her," though we are not told what the books were; and, as I learn from Mr. Shorter, there are indications that the small library Emily left behind her contained much German literature.

Two years later, Charlotte, in 1845, discovered the poems which, at least since 1834, Emily had been writing. "It took hours," says the elder sister, "to reconcile her to the discovery I had made, and days to persuade her that such poems merited publication." But Charlotte prevailed, and in 1846 Messrs. Aylott & Jones published the little volume of *Poems by Currer, Ellis, and Acton Bell.* It obtained no success; but "the mere effort to succeed," says Charlotte, "had given a wonderful zest to existence; it must be pursued. We each set to work on a prose tale: Ellis Bell produced *Wuthering Heights,* Acton Bell *Agnes Grey,* and Currer Bell also wrote a narrative in one volume—*The Professor."* For a year and a half *Wuthering Heights,* in common with *Agnes Grey* and *The Professor,* travelled wearily from publisher to publisher. At last Messrs. Newby accepted the first two. But they lingered in the press for months, and *Wuthering Heights* appeared at last, after the publication of *Jane Eyre,* and amid the full noise of its fame, only to be received as an earlier and cruder work of Currer Bell's, for which even those who admired *Jane Eyre* could find little praise and small excuse. Emily seems to have shown not a touch of jealousy or discouragement. She is not known, however, to have written anything more than a few verses—amongst them, indeed, the immortal "Last Lines"—later than *Wuthering Heights,* and during the last year of her life she seems to have given herself—true heart, and tameless soul!—now to supporting her wretched brother through the final stages of his physical and moral decay, and now to consultation with and sympathy for Charlotte in the writing of *Shirley.* Branwell died in September, and Emily was already ill on the day of his funeral. By the middle of December, at the age of thirty, she was dead; the struggle of her iron will and passionate vitality with hampering circumstance was over. The story of that marvelous dying has been often told, by Charlotte first of all, then by Mrs. Gaskell, and again by Madame Darmesteter, in the vivid study of Emily Brontë, which represents the homage of a new poetic generation. Let us recall Charlotte's poignant sentences:—

Never in all her life had she lingered over any task that lay before her, and she did not linger now. She sank rapidly. She made haste to leave us. Yet while physically she perished, mentally she grew stronger than we had yet known her. Day by day, when I saw with what a front she met suffering, I looked on her with an anguish of wonder and love. I have seen nothing like it; but indeed I have never seen her parallel in anything. Stronger than a man, simpler than a child, her nature stood alone. The awful point was, that while full of ruth for others, on herself she had no pity; the spirit was inexorable to the flesh; from the trembling hand, the unnerved limbs, the faded eyes, the same service was exacted as in health . . . She died December 19, 1848.

"Stronger than a man, simpler than a child:"—these words are Emily Brontë's true epitaph, both as an artist and as a human being. Her strength of will and imagination struck those who knew her and those who read her as often inhuman or terrible; and with this was combined a simplicity partly of genius partly of a strange innocence and spirituality, which gives her a place apart in English letters. It is important to realise that of the three books written simultaneously by the three sisters, Emily's alone shows genius already matured and master of its tools. Charlotte had a steady development before her, especially in matters of method and style; the comparative dulness of *The Professor* and the crudities of *Jane Eyre* made way for the accomplished variety and brilliance of *Villette*. But though Emily, had she lived, might have chosen many happier subjects, treated with a more flowing unity than she achieved in *Wuthering Heights,* the full competence of genius is already present in her book. The common, hasty, didactic note that Charlotte often strikes is never heard in *Wuthering Heights.* The artist remains hidden and self-contained; the work, however morbid and violent may be the scenes and creatures it presents, has always that distinction which belongs to high talent working solely for its own joy and satisfaction, with no thought of a spectator, or any aim but that of an ideal and imaginative whole. Charlotte stops to think of objectors, to teach and argue, to avenge her own personal grievances, or cheat her own personal longings. For pages together she often is little more than the clever clergyman's daughter, with a sharp tongue, a dislike to Ritualism and Romanism, a shrewd memory for persecutions and affronts, and a weakness for that masterful lover of whom most young women dream. But Emily is pure mind and passion; no one, from the pages of *Wuthering Heights,* can guess at the small likes and dislikes, the religious or critical antipathies, the personal weaknesses of the artist who wrote it. She has that highest power— which was typically Shakespeare's power, and which in our day is typically the power of such an artist as Turgueniev—the power which gives life, intensest life, to the creatures of imagination, and, in doing so, endows them with an independence behind which the maker is forgotten. The puppet show is everything; and, till it is over, the manager—nothing. And it is his delight and triumph to have it so.

Yet, at the same time, *Wuthering Heights* is a book of the later Romantic movement, betraying the influences of German Romantic imagination, as Charlotte's work betrays the influences of Victor Hugo and George Sand. The Romantic tendency to invent and delight in monsters, the *exaltation du moi,* which has been said to be the secret of the whole Romantic revolt against classical models and restraints; the love of violence in speech and action, the preference for the hideous in character and the abnormal in situation—of all these there are abundant examples in *Wuthering Heights*. The dream of Mr. Lockwood in Catherine's box bed, when in the terror of nightmare he pulled the wrist of the little wailing ghost outside on to the broken glass of the window, "and rubbed it to and fro till the blood ran down and soaked the bedclothes"—one of the most gruesome fancies of literature!—Heathcliff's long and fiendish revenge on Hindley Earnshaw; the ghastly quarrel between Linton and Heathcliff in Catherine's presence after Heathcliff's return; Catherine's three days' fast, and her delirium when she "tore the pillow with her teeth"; Heathcliff dashing his head against the trees of her garden, leaving his blood upon their bark, and "howling, not like a man, but like a savage beast being goaded to death with knives and spears"; the fight between Heathcliff and Earnshaw after Heathcliff's marriage to Isabella; the kidnapping of the younger Catherine, and the horror rather suggested than described of Heathcliff's brutality towards his sickly son:—all these things would not have been written precisely as they were written but for the "Germanism" of the thirties and forties, but for the translations of *Blackwood* and *Fraser,* and but for those German tales, whether of Hoffmann or others, which there is evidence that Emily Brontë read both at Brussels and after her return.

As to the "exaltation of the Self," its claims, sensibilities and passions, in defiance of all social law and duty, there is no more vivid expression of it throughout Romantic literature than is contained in the conversation between the elder Catherine and Nelly Dean before Catherine marries Edgar Linton. And the violent, clashing egotisms of Heathcliff and Catherine in the last scene of passion before Catherine's death, are as it were an epitome of a whole *genre* in literature, and a whole phase of European feeling.

Nevertheless, horror and extravagance are not really the characteristic mark and quality of *Wuthering Heights*. If they were, it would have no more claim upon us than a hundred other forgotten books—Lady Caroline Lamb's *Glenarvon* amongst them—which represent the dregs and refuse of a great literary movement. As in the case of Charlotte Brontë, the peculiar force of Emily's work lies in the fact that it represents the grafting of a European tradition upon a mind already richly stored with English and local reality, possessing at command a style at once strong and simple, capable both of homeliness and magnificence. The form of Romantic imagination which influenced Emily was not the same as that which influenced Charlotte; whether from a secret stubbornness and desire of difference, or no, there is not a mention of the French language, or of French books, in Emily's work, while Charlotte's abounds in a kind of display of French affinities, and French scholarship. The dithyrambs of *Shirley* and *Villette,* the "Vision of Eve" of *Shirley,* and the description of Rachel in *Villette,* would have been impossible to Emily; they come to a great extent from the reading of Victor Hugo and George Sand.

But in both sisters there is a similar *fonds* of stern and simple realism; a similar faculty of observation at once shrewd, and passionate; and it is by these that they produce their ultimate literary effect. The difference between them is almost wholly in Emily's favour. The uneven, amateurish manner of so many pages in *Jane Eyre* and *Shirley;* the lack of literary reticence which is responsible for Charlotte's frequent intrusion of her own personality, and for her occasional temptations to scream and preach, which are not wholly resisted even in her masterpiece, *Villette;* the ugly, tawdry sentences which disfigure some of her noblest passages, and make quotation from her so difficult:—you will find none of these things in *Wuthering Heights.* Emily is never flurried, never self-conscious; she is master of herself at the most rushing moments of feeling or narrative; her style is simple, sensuous, adequate and varied from first to last; she has fewer purple patches than Charlotte, but at its best, her insight no less than her power of phrase, is of a diviner and more exquisite quality.

Wuthering Heights, then, is the product of romantic imagination, working probably under influences from German literature, and marvelously fused with local knowledge and a realistic power which, within its own range, has seldom been surpassed. Its few great faults are soon enumerated. The tendency to extravagance and monstrosity may, as we have seen, be taken to some extent as belonging more to a literary fashion than to the artist. Tieck and Hoffmann are full of raving and lunatic beings who sob, shout, tear out their hair by the roots, and live in a perpetual state of personal violence both towards themselves and their neighbours. Emily Brontë probably received from them an additional impulse towards a certain wildness of manner and conception which was already natural to her Irish blood, to a woman brought up amid the solitudes of the moors and the ruggedness of Yorkshire life fifty years ago, and natural also, alas! to the sister of the opium-eater and drunkard, Branwell Brontë.

To this let us add a certain awkwardness and confusion of structure; a strain of ruthless exaggeration in the character of Heathcliff; and some absurdities and contradictions in the character of Nelly Dean. The latter criticism indeed is bound up with the first. Nelly Dean is presented as the faithful and affectionate nurse, the only good angel both of the elder and the younger Catherine. But Nelly Dean does the most treacherous, cruel, and indefensible things, simply that the story may move. She becomes the go-between for Catherine and Heathcliff; she knowingly allows her charge Catherine, on the eve of her confinement, to fast in solitude and delirium for three days and nights, without saying a word to Edgar Linton, Catherine's affectionate husband, and her master, who was in the house all the time. It is her breach of trust which brings about Catherine's dying scene with Heathcliff, just as it is her disobedience and unfaith which really betray Catherine's child into the hands of her enemies. Without these lapses and indiscretions indeed the story could not maintain itself; but the clumsiness or carelessness of them is hardly to be denied. In the case of Heathcliff, the blemish lies rather in a certain deliberate and passionate defiance of the reader's sense of humanity and possibility; partly also in the innocence of the writer, who, in a world of sex and passion, has invented a situation charged with the full forces of both, without any true realisation of what she has done. Heathcliff's murderous language to Catherine about the husband whom she loves with an affection only second to that which she cherishes for his hateful self; his sordid and incredible courtship of Isabella under Catherine's eyes; the long horror of his pursuit and capture of the younger Catherine, his dead love's child; the total incompatibility between his passion for the mother and his mean ruffianism towards the daughter; the utter absence of any touch of kindness even in his love for Catherine, whom he scolds and rates on the very threshold of death; the mingling in him of high passion with the vilest arts of the sharper and the thief:—these things o'erleap themselves, so that again and again the sense of tragedy is lost in mere violence and excess, and what might have been a man becomes a monster. There are speeches and actions of Catherine's, moreover, contained in these central pages which have no relation to any life of men and women that the true world knows. It may be said, indeed, that the writer's very ignorance of certain facts and relations of life, combined with the force of imaginative passion which she throws into her conceptions, produces a special poetic effect—a strange and bodiless tragedy—unique in literature. And there is much truth in this; but not enough to vindicate these scenes of the book from radical weakness and falsity, nor to preserve in the reader that illusion, that inner consent, which is the final test of all imaginative effort.

Nevertheless, there are whole sections of the story during which the character of Heathcliff is presented to us with a marvelous and essential truth. The scenes of childhood and youth; the up-growing of the two desolate children, drawn to each other by some strange primal sympathy—Heathcliff "the little black thing, harboured by a good man to his bane," Catherine who "was never so happy as when we were all scolding her at once, and she defying us with her bold saucy look, and her ready words"; the gradual development of the natural distance between them, he the ill-mannered, ruffianly no-man's-child, she the young lady of the house; his pride and jealous pain; her young fondness for Edgar Linton, as inevitable as a girl's yearning for pretty finery, and a new frock with the spring; Heathcliff's boyish vow of vengeance on the brutal Hindley and his race; Cathy's passionate discrimination, in the scene with Nelly Dean which ends as it were the first act of the play, between her affection for Linton and her identity with Heathcliff's life and being:—for the mingling of daring poetry with the easiest and most masterly command of local truth, for sharpness and felicity of phrase, for exuberance of creative force, for invention and freshness of detail, there are few things in English fiction to match it. One might almost say that the first volume of *Adam Bede* is false and mannered beside it,—the first volumes of *Waverley* or *Guy Mannering* flat and diffuse. Certainly, the first volume of *Jane Eyre,* admirable as it is, can hardly be set on the same level with the careless ease and effortless power of these first nine chapters. There is almost nothing in them but shares in the force and the effect of all true "vision"—Joseph, "the wearisomest self-right-eous Pharisee that ever ransacked a Bible to rake the promises to himself, and fling the curses to his neighbours"; old Earnshaw himself, stupid, obstinate and kindly; the bullying Hindley with his lackadaisical consumptive wife; the delicate nurture and superior wealth of the Lintons; the very animals of the farm, the very rain- and snow-storms of the moors,—all live, all grow together, like the tangled heather itself, harsh and gnarled and ugly in one aspect, in another beautiful by its mere unfettered life and freedom, capable too of wild moments of colour and blossoming.

And as far as the lesser elements of style, the mere technique of writing, are concerned, one may notice the short elastic vigour of the sentences, the rightness of epithet and detail, the absence of any care for effect, and the flashes of beauty which suddenly emerge like the cistus upon the rock.

"Nelly, do you never dream queer dreams?" said Catherine suddenly, after some minutes' reflection.

"Yes, now and then," I answered.

"And so do I. I've dreamt in my life dreams that have stayed with me ever after and changed my ideas: they've gone through and through me like wine through water, and altered the colour of my mind. And this one; I'm going to tell it—but take care not to smile at any part of it." (ix)

Nelly Dean tries to avoid the dream but Catherine persists:—

"I dreamt once that I was in heaven."

"I tell you I won't hearken to your dreams, Miss Catherine! I'll go to bed," I interrupted again.

She laughed, and held me down; for I made a motion to leave my chair.

"This is nothing," cried she: "I was only going to say that heaven did not seem to be my home; and I broke my heart with weeping to come back to earth; and the angels were so angry that they flung me out into the middle of the heath on the top of Wuthering Heights; where I woke sobbing for joy! That will do to explain my secret, as well as the other. I've no more business to marry Edgar Linton than I have to be in heaven; and if the wicked man in there had not brought Heathcliff so low, I shouldn't have thought of it. It would degrade me to marry Heathcliff now; so he shall never know how I love him: and that, not because he's handsome, Nelly, but because he's more myself than I am. Whatever our souls are made of, his and mine are the same; and Linton's is as different as a moonbeam from lightning, or frost from fire." (ix)

"The angels flung me out into the middle of the heath—where I woke sobbing for joy"—the wild words have in them the very essence and life-blood not only of Catherine but of her creator!

The inferior central scenes of the book, after Catherine's marriage, for all their teasing faults, have passages of extraordinary poetry. Take the detail of

Catherine's fevered dream after she shuts herself into her room, at the close of the frightful scene between her husband and Heathcliff, or the weird realism of her half-delirious talk with Nelly Dean. In her "feverish bewilderment" she tears her pillow, and then finds

> childish diversion in pulling the feathers from the rents she had just made, and ranging them on the sheet according to their different species: her mind had strayed to other associations.

> "That's a turkey's," she murmured to herself; "and this is a wild duck's; and this is a pigeon's. Ah, they put pigeons' feathers in the pillows—no wonder I couldn't die! Let me take care to throw it on the floor when I lie down. And here is a moor-cock's; and this—I should know it among a thousand—it's a lapwing's. Bonny bird; wheeling over our heads in the middle of the moor. It wanted to get to its nest, for the clouds had touched the swells, and it felt rain coming. This feather was picked up from the heath, the bird was not shot: we saw its nest in the winter, full of little skeletons. Heathcliff set a trap over it, and the old ones dared not come. I made him promise he'd never shoot a lapwing after that, and he didn't. Yes, here are more! Did he shoot my lapwings, Nelly? Are they red, any of them? Let me look."
> "Give over with that baby-work!" I interrupted, dragging the pillow away, and turning the holes towards the mattress, for she was removing its contents by handfuls. "Lie down, and shut your eyes: you're wandering. There's a mess! The down is flying about like snow."
> I went here and there collecting it.
> "I see in you, Nelly," she continued, dreamily, "an aged woman: you have grey hair and bent shoulders. This bed is the fairy cave under Penistone Crags, and you are gathering elf-bolts to hurt our heifers; pretending, while I am near, that they are only locks of wool. That's what you'll come to fifty years hence: I know you are not so now. I'm not wandering: you're mistaken, or else I should believe you really *were* that withered hag, and I should think I *was* under Penistone Crags; and I'm conscious it's night, and there are two candles on the table making the black press shine like jet." (xii)

To these may be added the charming and tender passage describing Catherine's early convalescence, and her yearnings—so true to such a child of nature and feeling—for the first flowers and first mild breathings of the spring; and the later picture of her, the wrecked and doomed Catherine, sitting in "dreamy and melancholy softness" by the open window, listening for the sounds of the moorland, before the approach of Heathcliff and death:—

> Gimmerton chapel bells were still ringing; and the full mellow flow of the beck in the valley came soothingly on the ear. It was a sweet substitute for the yet absent murmur of the summer foliage, which drowned that music about the Grange when the trees were in leaf. At Wuthering Heights it always sounded on quiet days following a great thaw or a season of steady rain. (xv)

8

Lines which, for their "sharp and eager observation," may surely be matched with these of Coleridge, her master in poetic magic, her inferior in all that concerns the passionate and dramatic sense of life:—

> All is still,
> A balmy night! and though the stars be dim,
> Yet let us think upon the vernal showers
> That gladden the green earth, and we shall find
> A pleasure in the dimness of the stars.

Of what we may call the third and last act of *Wuthering Heights,* which extends from the childhood of the younger Catherine to the death of Heathcliff, much might be said. It is no less masterly than the first section of the book and much more complex in plan. The key to it lies in two earlier passages—in Heathcliff's boyish vow of vengeance on Hindley Earnshaw, and in his fierce appeal to his lost love to haunt him, rather than leave him "in this abyss where I cannot find her." The conduct of the whole "act" is intricate and difficult; the initial awkwardness implied in Nelly Dean's function as narrator is felt now and then; but as a whole, the strength of the intention is no less clear than the deliberate and triumphant power with which the artist achieves it. These chapters are not always easy to read, but they repay the closest attention. Not an incident, not a fragment of conversation is thrown away, and in the end the effect is complete. It is gained by that fusion of terror and beauty, of ugliness and a flying magic—"settling unawares"—which is the characteristic note of the Brontës, and of all that is best in Romantic literature. Never for a moment do you lose hold upon the Yorkshire landscape and the Yorkshire folk—look at the picture of Isabella's wasteful porridge-making and of Joseph's grumbling rage, amid her gruesome experience as a bride; never are you allowed to forget a single sordid element in Heathcliff's ruffianism; and yet through it all the inevitable end develops, the double end which only a master could have conceived. Life and love rebel and reassert themselves in the wild slight love-story of Hareton and Cathy, which breaks the final darkness like a gleam of dawn upon the moors; and death tames and silences for ever all that remains of Heathcliff's futile cruelties and wasted fury.

But what a death! Heathcliff has tormented and oppressed Catherine's daughter; and it is Catherine's shadow that lures him to his doom, through every stage and degree of haunting feverish ecstasy, of reunion promised and delayed, of joy for ever offered and for ever withdrawn. And yet how simple the method, how true the "vision" to the end! Around Heathcliff's last hours the farm-life flows on as usual. There is no hurry in the sentences; no blurring of the scene. Catherine's haunting presence closes upon the man who murdered her happiness and youth, interposes between him and all bodily needs, deprives him of food and drink and sleep, till the madman is dead of his "strange happiness," straining after the phantom that slays him, dying of the love whereby alone he remains human, through which fate strikes at last—and strikes home.

"Is he a ghoul or vampire?" I mused. "I had read of such hideous incarnate demons" (xxxiv). So says Nelly Dean just before Heathcliff's death. The remark is not hers in truth, but Emily Brontë's, and where it stands it is of great significance. It points to the world of German horror and romance, to which we know that she had access. That world was congenial to her, as it was congenial to Southey, Scott, and Coleridge; and it has left some ugly and disfiguring traces upon the detail of *Wuthering Heights*. But *essentially* her imagination escaped from it and mastered it. As the haunting of Heathcliff is to the coarser horrors of Tieck and Hoffmann, so is her place to theirs. For all her crudity and inexperience, she is in the end with Goethe, rather than with Hoffmann,[1] and thereby with all that is sane, strong, and living in literature. "A great work requires many-sidedness, and on this rock the young author splits," said Goethe to Eckermann, praising at the same time the art which starts from the simplest realities and the subject nearest at hand, to reach at last by a natural expansion the loftiest heights of poetry. But this was the art of Emily Brontë. It started from her own heart and life; it was nourished by the sights and sounds of a lonely yet sheltering nature; it was responsive to the art of others, yet always independent; and in the rich and tangled truth of *Wuthering Heights* it showed promise at least of a many-sidedness to which only the greatest attain.

Note

1.   For any one who has waded through Hoffmann's *Serapion-brüder*—which has become for our generation all but unreadable,—in spite of the partial explanation which the *physical violence* of these tales may perhaps offer of some of the minor detail of *Wuthering Heights,* there is only one passage which memory will in the end connect with Emily Brontë. The leading idea of the stories which make up the Serapion-collection—if they can be said to have a leading idea—is that all which the imagination really *sees*—man or goblin, monster or reality—it may lawfully report. "Let each of us try and examine himself well, as whether he has really *seen* what he is going to describe, before he sets to work to put it in words." The vividness of the Romantics,—as compared with the measure of the Classicalists; there is here a typical expression of it, and it is one which may well have lingered in Emily Brontë's mind.

Jane Eyre and Wuthering Heights

Virginia Woolf*

The meaning of a book, which lies so often apart from what happens and what is said and consists rather in some connection which things in themselves different have had for the writer, is necessarily hard to grasp. Especially this is so when, like the Brontës, the writer is poetic, and his meaning inseparable from his language, and itself rather a mood than a particular observation. *Wuthering Heights* is a more difficult book to understand than *Jane Eyre,* because Emily was a greater poet than Charlotte. When Charlotte wrote she said with eloquence and splendour and passion "I love," "I hate," "I suffer." Her experience, though more intense, is on a level with our own. But there is no "I" in *Wuthering Heights*. There are no governesses. There are no employers. There is love, but it is not the love of men and women. Emily was inspired by some more general conception. The impulse which urged her to create was not her own suffering or her own injuries. She looked out upon a world cleft into gigantic disorder and felt within her the power to unite it in a book. That gigantic ambition is to be felt throughout the novel—a struggle, half thwarted but of superb conviction, to say something through the mouths of her characters which is not merely "I love" or "I hate," but "we, the whole human race" and "you, the eternal powers . . ." the sentence remains unfinished. It is not strange that it should be so; rather it is astonishing that she can make us feel what she had it in her to say at all. It surges up in the half-articulate words of Catherine Earnshaw, "If all else perished and *he* remained, I should still continue to be; and if all else remained and he were annihilated, the universe would turn to a mighty stranger; I should not seem part of it." It breaks out again in the presence of the dead. "I see a repose that neither earth nor hell can break, and I feel an assurance of the endless and shadowless hereafter—the eternity they have entered—where life is boundless in its duration, and love in its sympathy and joy in its fulness." It is this suggestion of power underlying the apparitions of human nature and lifting them up into the presence of greatness that gives the book its huge stature among other novels. But it was not enough for Emily Brontë to write a few lyrics, to utter a cry, to express a creed. In her poems she did this once and for all, and her

*Reprinted from V. Woolf, *The Common Reader,* first series (London: The Hogarth Press, 1925), 201–4.

poems will perhaps outlast her novel. But she was novelist as well as poet. She must take upon herself a more laborious and a more ungrateful task. She must face the fact of other existences, grapple with the mechanism of external things, build up, in recognisable shape, farms and houses and report the speeches of men and women who existed independently of herself. And so we reach these summits of emotion not by rant or rhapsody but by hearing a girl sing old songs to herself as she rocks in the branches of a tree; by watching the moor sheep crop the turf; by listening to the soft wind breathing through the grass. The life at the farm with all its absurdities and its improbability is laid open to us. We are given every opportunity of comparing *Wuthering Heights* with a real farm and Heathcliff with a real man. How, we are allowed to ask, can there be truth or insight or the finer shades of emotion in men and women who so little resemble what we have seen ourselves? But even as we ask it we see in Heathcliff the brother that a sister of genius might have seen; he is impossible we say, but nevertheless no boy in literature has a more vivid existence than his. So it is with the two Catherines; never could women feel as they do or act in their manner, we say. All the same, they are the most lovable women in English fiction. It is as if she could tear up all that we know human beings by, and fill these unrecognisable transparences with such a gust of life that they transcend reality. Hers, then, is the rarest of all powers. She could free life from its dependence on facts; with a few touches indicate the spirit of a face so that it needs no body; by speaking of the moor make the wind blow and the thunder roar.

The Structure of *Wuthering Heights*

C. P. SANGER*

By common consent *Wuthering Heights* is a remarkable book. I do not propose to discuss its literary merits, but to confine myself to the humbler task of investigating its structure, which presents certain peculiarities. Whether this is worth doing I do not know, but I found that it added to my interest in the book and made the tale much more vivid for me.

The main theme is how a sort of human cuckoo, called Heathcliff, sets out with success to acquire all the property of two families, the Earnshaws and the Lintons. The tale is a fairly complicated one, and the incidents extend over a period of more than thirty years. Stated as baldly and shortly as I can, the plot is as follows: Mr. and Mrs. Earnshaw live at Wuthering Heights, a farmhouse on a Yorkshire moor. They have two children, a son called Hindley and a daughter Catherine. One day Mr. Earnshaw, who has been to Liverpool on business, brings home a waif he has picked up there. This waif, Heathcliff, is brought up at Wuthering Heights. Not long after, Mrs. Earnshaw dies. Heathcliff is Mr. Earnshaw's favourite; he is also great friends with Catherine, but Hindley, who is older, bullies him. At last, Hindley is sent off to college. When Mr. Earnshaw dies, Hindley returns for the funeral, bringing with him a young wife. He takes possession, ill-treats Heathcliff, thrusts him into the position of a mere servant, and allows him no more education. But Catherine and Heathcliff have remained great friends, and one Sunday they go for a walk, and out of curiosity look at Thrushcross Grange, a gentleman's house in a park four miles off where Mr. and Mrs. Linton live. Catherine and Heathcliff peep in through the drawing-room window and see the two Linton children—Edgar and Isabella. The Lintons, hearing Heathcliff and Catherine and taking them for robbers, let the bulldog loose on them; the dog seizes Catherine and hurts her ankle badly. She is taken in and looked after at Thrushcross Grange for five weeks, and returns to Wuthering Heights elegantly dressed. Heathcliff, who is very dirty and untidy, is ashamed. The next day the two Lintons come to dinner; Heathcliff behaves ill and is punished by Hindley. The next year Hindley's wife gives birth to a son—Hareton. She, however, is consumptive and does not survive long. In despair at her death Hindley takes

*Reprinted from C. P. Sanger, *Hogarth Essay* 19 (London: The Hogarth Press, 1926).

to drink. When Catherine is fifteen Edgar Linton proposes to her. She accepts him, feeling all the time that she is doing wrong because she loves Heathcliff. She tells Hareton's nurse, Ellen Dean, about it; Heathcliff overhears part of the conversation, runs off and vanishes. Catherine is distracted by this, gets fever, and when convalescent goes to stay at Thrushcross Grange. Her host and hostess, Mr. and Mrs. Linton, both catch the fever and die. This may be considered the end of the first stage of the story. The elder generation are all dead. The next generation are all alive—Hindley and Catherine at Wuthering Heights, Edgar and Isabella at Thrushcross Grange. Hindley's wife is dead, but his son Hareton—the only representative of the third generation— is alive. Heathcliff has disappeared. His passion for Catherine and his revenge is the main theme of the root of the story.

Catherine in due course marries Edgar and goes to live at Thrushcross Grange. After six months of happiness, Heathcliff, who has meanwhile mysteriously got some education and money, reappears. He sets himself to ruin Hindley, who gambles and drinks. He also finds that Isabella is in love with him, and decides to marry her to get her money. One day, after a violent scene between Heathcliff and Edgar, Catherine goes on hunger strike and gets brain fever. Isabella elopes with Heathcliff, who treats her abominably, and finally brings her back to Wuthering Heights. One Sunday while Edgar is at church, Heathcliff comes to see Catherine. There is a passionate scene. That night Catherine gives birth to a daughter and dies. On the night after the funeral, Hindley tries to kill Heathcliff but is nearly killed by him. Isabella escapes from Wuthering Heights and goes to the South of England, where she gives birth to a sickly child named Linton Heathcliff. Soon after this Hindley dies of drink, and Heathcliff is left in possession of Wuthering Heights with Hareton, whom, out of revenge for the way he was treated as a boy, he brings up as a mere brute. At this stage there is a long gap in the story. Edgar's daughter, who is also called Catherine, lives with him at Thrushcross Grange; Isabella's son, Linton, lives in the South of England with her. Catherine is kept in ignorance of both her cousins Linton and Hareton.

Edgar hears that Isabella is dying and goes to see her. Catherine in his absence goes to Penistone Crags, and in doing so has to pass Wuthering Heights, where she sees Hareton. On Isabella's death, Edgar comes home with Linton, but Heathcliff claims him, and he is taken to Wuthering Heights. Catherine is not allowed by Edgar, her father, to go there. One day, after some time, Catherine on a walk meets Heathcliff and Hareton and goes to Wuthering Heights, where she sees her cousin, Linton. Catherine and Linton correspond secretly. The correspondence is detected and stopped. Catherine's father, Edgar, becomes ill. Heathcliff meets Catherine and tells her that Linton is seriously ill. She goes to see him, and many times visits him secretly. One day, just before her father dies, she is kidnapped by Heathcliff and forced to marry Linton. Soon after Linton dies, having made a will leaving all his personal property to his father, Heathcliff. Heathcliff takes possession of

Thrushcross Grange, and lets it to Mr. Lockwood, who tells the story. But Heathcliff dies soon after, and Hareton and Catherine marry.

How is a long story like this to be told? How is the reader's interest to be excited? How is the tale to be kept together? How are we to be made to feel the lapse of time without being pestered by dates? How far did the authoress accurately visualize the ages of the characters in the different incidents, the topography, and so on? And how did Heathcliff succeed in getting the property? These are the questions I attempt to answer.

The most obvious thing about the structure of the story which deals with three generations is the symmetry of the pedigree. Mr. and Mrs. Earnshaw at Wuthering Heights and Mr. and Mrs. Linton at Thrushcross Grange each have one son and one daughter. Mr. Linton's son marries Mr. Earnshaw's daughter, and their only child Catherine marries successively her two cousins—Mr. Linton's grandson and Mr. Earnshaw's grandson. See the pedigree on the next page.

In actual life I have never come across a pedigree of such absolute symmetry. I shall have to refer to this pedigree again later. It is a remarkable piece of symmetry in a tempestuous book.

The method adopted to arouse the reader's interest and to give vividness and reality to the tale is one which has been used with great success by Joseph Conrad. But it requires great skill.

After Edgar Linton's death, Mr. Lockwood, the narrator, takes Thrushcross Grange for a year. He goes to call on his landlord, Heathcliff, at Wuthering Heights, and is puzzled to find there a *farouche* young woman and an awkward boor. At first he supposes Catherine to be Heathcliff's wife; when told she is his daughter-in-law, he then supposes that Hareton is Heathcliff's son, and has again to be corrected. He, and the reader, are naturally puzzled at this strange trio. Lockwood calls again, and is forced to spend the night because of a heavy fall of snow. In his room he finds some books with the name Catherine Earnshaw and Catherine Linton, and a sort of diary of Catherine's in a childish hand which gives a vivid picture of the situation just after her father's death. Mr. Lockwood has a nightmare in which Catherine's spirit comes to the window, and he also witnesses a strange scene of Heathcliff imploring Catherine's spirit. Our interest cannot fail now to be excited. What is this strange man and this strange ménage? Who was this Catherine who died years before? What were her relations with Heathcliff? Naturally, Lockwood is much intrigued. On his way back next day he catches a chill and becomes ill. To pass the time he asks Ellen Dean, the housekeeper at Thrushcross Grange, what she knows about the family at Wuthering Heights. She, who was first Hareton's nurse and then the younger Catherine's, tells him the story of the past thirty years in considerable detail. So that during the major part of the book Mr. Lockwood is telling us what Ellen Dean told him, but sometimes, also, what Ellen Dean told him that someone

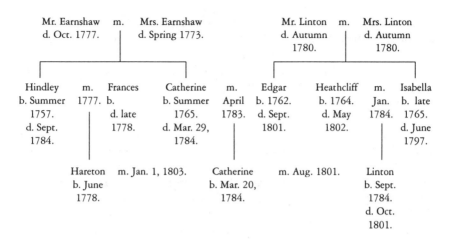

else—for instance, Isabella—had told her. Only a small part, perhaps one tenth of the book, consists of direct narrative by Lockwood from his own knowledge. But such a scheme may be confusing, and it is easy to muddle the time. Did Emily Brontë realize and let us know the dates when each event happened? She did, but not by giving them directly. Look again at the pedigree. The dates there have all been derived from the book, yet only one is directly stated. What first brought me to study the book more closely was when I noticed that the first word in the book was a date—1801. I thought this must have some significance. Similarly, the first word of Chapter XXXII is 1802. Apart from this, only one other date is given directly. In the last sentence of Chapter VII, Ellen Dean says, "I will be content to pass on to the next summer—the summer of 1778, that is, nearly twenty-three years ago." This gives no further information, as 1801 is twenty-three years after 1778, but in the first sentence of the next chapter she tells us that Hareton was born in June. This is how I get June 1778 for Hareton's birth in the pedigree. But what about the rest of the dates, not only those in the pedigree but of all the incidents in the story? There are a considerable number (perhaps nearly a hundred) indications of various kinds to help us—intervals of time, ages of characters, the months, the harvest moon, the last grouse, and so forth, and we learn, incidentally, that the younger Catherine's birthday was on 20th March. Sometimes, too, we know the day of the week—thus Ellen Dean will remember something which happened on a Sunday, or on a Christmas Eve. Taking all these indications, it is, I think, possible to ascertain the year, and, in most cases, the month of the year in which every event takes place—also the ages of the various characters, except, naturally, there is a slight doubt as to Heathcliff, because no one knows his exact age when he was found by Mr. Earnshaw. But one has to go warily and consider all the indications together, for there is a curious subtlety that sometimes the characters are described as *looking* some ages which are not exact. Thus Lockwood when he first describes them says that Heathcliff was about forty and Catherine did not look seventeen. In fact, Catherine was seventeen and three-quarters and Heathcliff cannot have been more than thirty-eight. It would be too tedious to state the process by which I have discovered each date (see Appendix). But I will give one or two illustrations. We already know that Hareton was born in June 1778; we are told that he was nearly five when Catherine Earnshaw married Edgar Linton, so that the marriage was before June 1783. But Heathcliff returned in September after they had been happily married for six months. Thus the marriage was in April 1783. We are told that the scene that led to Catherine's death was a Sunday in the March after Heathcliff's return, and that her daughter, Catherine, was born about midnight, and the mother died two hours later. Later on we learn that Catherine's birthday was the 20th (and that this was also treated as the day of her mother's death). Hence Catherine died at 2 a.m. on Monday, 20th March 1784.

I will give only one other instance. Lockwood begins his account in 1801; it is snowy weather, which might be in January or February or in November or December. But he returns in 1802 before his year's tenancy is out. Hence the story begins at the end of 1801. A Michaelmas tenancy begins on the 10th October—not on 29th September—because when the calendar was reformed eleven days were left out. Therefore the story begins after 10th October 1801. Now after Lockwood has been ill three weeks Heathcliff sends him some grouse, the last of the season. Since the Game Act, 1831, grouse may not be shot after 10th December, so we may take this as about the date for the last grouse. Thus the story begins about the middle of November, and this fits pretty well with the later indications. That is sufficient to illustrate the process. Sometimes it is only by fitting together several indications, each rather vague, that one can find the month. There is, however, one curious fact. We can ascertain Hindley's age. Now Ellen Dean was of the same age. She was his foster sister, and the doctor also refers to her as being of the same age as Hindley. Yet she makes two mistakes about her own age. Middle-aged people do, of course, make mistakes about their age, and these slips may have been intentional on the part of Emily Brontë but, if so, it seems to me a little over-subtle.

The topography is equally precise. On going from Thrushcross Grange to the village of Gimmerton a highway branches off to the moor on the left. There is a stone pillar there. Thrushcross Grange lies to the south-west, Gimmerton to the east, and Wuthering Heights to the north. The distance from Thrushcross Grange to Wuthering Heights is four miles, and Penistone Crags lie a mile and a half farther on. It was half an hour from Gimmerton to Thrushcross Grange.

The botany is sure to be correct. Emily Brontë loved the country. I was a little surprised to find an ash tree in bud as early as 20th March, but then I realized that it was not on the moor but in the park at Thrushcross Grange, which lay low and was no doubt sheltered.

I now come to the final problem. Heathcliff schemed to get all the property of both the Earnshaws and the Lintons. How did he do it? Emily Brontë clearly had a considerable knowledge of the law. We know the source of George Eliot's use of a base fee for the plot of Felix Holt. We do not know the source of Jane Austen's unerring grasp of the law of real property; but she lived among people who had settled estates and could easily have obtained it. But how Emily Brontë acquired her knowledge I cannot guess. There is also this difficulty. *Wuthering Heights* was written in the eighteen-forties. It was published in 1847. But the period of the tale is from 1771 to 1803. The Inheritance Act of 1834, the Wills Act of 1837, and, I think, the Game Act of 1831, had changed the law. Did Emily Brontë apply the law at the time she wrote or that at the period of the tale? In one case, as we shall see, she used the earlier law.

Novelists sometimes make their plots depend on the law and use legal terms. But they frequently make mistakes and sometimes are absurd as Trollope is in *Orley Farm*. What is remarkable about *Wuthering Heights* is that the ten or twelve legal references are, I think, sufficient to enable us to ascertain the various legal processes by which Heathcliff obtained the property. It is not a simple matter. There was a fundamental difference between the law of land (real property) and that of money and goods (personal property).

Let us begin with Wuthering Heights. The Earnshaws were farmers and not likely to have their estate settled. The property had been in their family since 1500. We may take it then that Mr. Earnshaw was owner in fee-simple, that is in effect absolute owner, of Wuthering Heights, and was not likely to have possessed any investments. It is more likely that there was a mortgage on the house and farm. On Mr. Earnshaw's death the land descended to Hindley as his heir-at-law. There is no mention of a will. The personal property, which, probably, was only the farming stock and the furniture, would go equally to his children, Hindley and Catherine, subject to the payment of his debts out of it. On Catherine's marriage Edgar would have become entitled to her personal property. Now Hindley drinks and gambles away all he has, and at his death the property is mortgaged up to the hilt. Heathcliff we find is the mortgagee. The personal property would also be liable to the debts, so that Heathcliff is mortgagee in possession and, for practical purposes, owner of all the Earnshaw property except any personalty that had gone to Catherine. This is all fairly simple; but it is more difficult when we come to the Linton property. They were landed gentry; they had a park, they had tenants. Mr. Linton, and Edgar after him, was a magistrate. Such people, generally, had a settlement of their land, and we find, in fact, that Mr. Linton had settled it by his will. To understand what happens it is necessary to go into the intricacies of real property law and to look at the pedigree.

I must explain very shortly the law of entails. What is called an estate tail is an estate which descends according to the following rules: (1) Males are preferred to females; (2) males take in order according to seniority of birth, but females take equally; (3) descendants represent their ancestor. In case of a conflict between them, rule (3) prevails. A tenant in tail of full age in possession could by means of a fictitious action (for which a deed was substituted by the Fines and Recoveries Act, 1833) bar the entail and obtain the fee-simple, which practically amounts to absolute ownership. By his will a testator could settle his land on living persons for life, but could not give life estates to the children of such persons who were not alive at the testator's death. Consequently, if he wanted to tie up his estate as long as possible, he gave life estates to such of his descendants as were living at his death, followed by estates tail to their children.

Now the settlement made by Mr. Linton's will must have been as follows: The estate was devised to Edgar, his only son, for life, then to Edgar's sons in tail; Edgar's daughters were passed over in favour of Mr. Linton's daughter, Isabella, who, presumably, had a life interest with remainder to her sons in tail. This is the usual form. Thus on Edgar Linton's death, Linton Heathcliff became tenant in tail in possession during the few weeks he survived his uncle. As a minor he could not bar the entail. It is most improbable that he had an estate in fee-simple; that would have been too unusual. Isabella might have had an estate tail instead of a life interest. This is most improbable, but if she did, her son, Linton Heathcliff, would have become tenant in tail by descent, so the result is the same. Heathcliff claims the property—by what right? Ellen Dean says that he claimed and kept the Thrushcross Grange estate in his wife's right and in his son's also. She adds: "I suppose, legally at any rate, Catherine, destitute of cash and friends, cannot disturb his possession." She is quite right in her suspicions. Even if Isabella had had an estate tail, or even an estate in fee-simple, Heathcliff would not have had any right as husband to an estate for life—the estate known as an estate by courtesy—because Isabella was never in possession. And even if, which to my mind is not possible, Linton Heathcliff had had an estate in fee-simple, his father would not have been his heir before the Inheritance Act, 1833, because it was considered unnatural that an inheritance should ascend directly; and, as Ellen Dean knows and states, Linton Heathcliff as a minor could not dispose of his land by will. There is no difficulty as to the personal property. Whatever Isabella had Heathcliff got by marrying her. There was no Married Women's Property Act in these days. They eloped, so there was no question of a marriage-settlement. Edgar Linton had saved out of his rents to make a provision for his daughter, Catherine. When dying he decides, in order to prevent Heathcliff getting at them, to alter his will so as to settle them on Catherine for life and then for her children. The attorney for whom he sends is, however, kept from going by Heathcliff, and Edgar dies before his will is altered, so the money passes to Catherine and then to her husband, Linton. He, though a minor, could (before the year 1838) make a will of personalty. He is induced or forced to do so, and leaves it all to Heathcliff.

Thus, at Heathcliff's death, the position seems to be that he has acquired all the personal property of both families: he is mortgagee in possession of Wuthering Heights, and is, though wrongfully, in possession of Thrushcross Grange, which he has let to Lockwood. He thinks of making a will but does not do so. What then happens on his death? He has no relations, so that his real property will escheat, and his personal property will go to the Crown as *bona vacantia*. What then becomes of Hareton and Catherine who, when the tale ends, are to be happily married on New Year's Day, 1803? At one time I thought this was the climax of the tragedy. These young people, ill-educated and incompetent, were to be left destitute. But that would be going too far. Catherine, as you will see from the pedigree, is the sole living descendant of Mr. Linton. In some way or other, I need not go through the various alternatives, she must have become entitled to Thrushcross Grange, which is plainly by far the most valuable property. Heathcliff had been mortgagee in possession of Wuthering Heights for eighteen years, but this was not long enough to obtain an absolute title by adverse possession. Hareton, as Hindley's heir, would be entitled to the equity of redemption. Now if Heathcliff, who managed well, properly accounted for his profits during the eighteen years as he could be made to do, it may well be that they were sufficient, if he was charged a proper occupation rent, to pay off the mortgage. So that Hareton would get the house and land unencumbered or, at any rate, only slightly burdened. The personal property was comparatively unimportant, and we can only hope that the Crown did not insist on its rights, if it knew of them, or that if it did insist, the happy couple could buy out the Crown's claim out of the rent which Lockwood, as we know, paid.

There is, so far as I know, no other novel in the world which it is possible to subject to an analysis of the kind I have tried to make. This in itself makes the book very unusual. Did the authoress carry all the dates in her head, or did she work with a calendar? Was 20th March 1784, for example, on a Monday? According to my calculations it was not, it was a Saturday, but I should like to have this confirmed by some competent chronologist; for if I am right, it shows that Emily Brontë did not use a calendar, and that nothing will be gained by finding out, for instance, the date of Easter in 1803.

However dull and technical the above details may be, they do, I believe, throw a light on the character of Emily Brontë and her book. German romances can hardly have been the source of her knowledge of English law. A great critic has spoken of the passionate chastity of the book; but the extreme care in realizing the ages of the characters at the time of each incident which is described seems to me a more unusual characteristic of a novel. It demonstrates the vividness of the author's imagination.

CHRONOLOGY OF WUTHERING HEIGHTS

CHAP.

	1757, before September.	Hindley Earnshaw born.
	1762, "	Edgar Linton born.
	1764, "	Heathcliff born.
	1765, summer.	Catherine Earnshaw born.
	" late.	Isabella Linton born.
IV.	1771, summer, beginning of harvest.	Heathcliff brought to Wuthering Heights.
	1773, spring or early summer.	Mrs. Earnshaw dies.
V.	1774, October.	Hindley sent to college.
	1777,	Hindley marries.
	" "	Mr. Earnshaw dies.
VI.	" "	Hindley returns with his wife.
III.	" October or November.	The scene described by Catherine.
VI.	" November, third week, Sunday.	Catherine and Heathcliff go to Thrushcross Grange.
VII.	" Christmas Eve.	Catherine returns to W. H.
	" Christmas Day.	The Lintons visit W. H.
VIII.	1778, June.	Hareton Earnshaw born.
	" late.	Frances Earnshaw dies.
	1780, summer.	Edgar Linton calls at W. H. and proposes to Catherine.
IX.	" "	Hindley returns drunk.
	" "	Catherine tells Ellen about Edgar.
	" "	Heathcliff goes off.
IX.	1780, summer.	Catherine gets wet through and catches fever.
	" autumn.	Catherine, convalescent, goes to Thrushcross Grange. Mr and Mrs Linton catch the fever and die.
	1783, April.	Edgar marries Catherine.

X.	"	September.	Heathcliff returns and sees Catherine.
	"	autumn.	Isabella falls in love with Heathcliff, who visits Thrushcross Grange from time to time.
XI.	"	December.	Ellen Dean sees Hareton. Heathcliff kisses Isabella.
	1784,	January 6, Monday.	Violent scene at Thrushcross Grange. Heathcliff is turned out and Catherine goes on hunger strike.
XII.	"	January 10, Friday.	Catherine delirious.
	"	" " 2 a.m.	Isabella elopes with Heathcliff.
XIII.	"	March 13, Monday.	The Heathcliffs return to W. H.
XIV.	"	March 15, Wednesday.	Ellen Dean goes to W. H.
XV.	"	March 19, Sunday.	Heathcliff sees Catherine: violent scene.
XVI.	"	" midnight.	Catherine Linton born.
	"	March 20, Monday, 2 a.m.	Catherine (the elder) dies.
	"	March 21, Tuesday.	Heathcliff puts a lock of hair in Catherine's locket.
	"	March 24, Friday.	Catherine's funeral.
XVII.	"	same day, midnight.	Heathcliff nearly kills Hindley, who tried to kill him.
	"	March 25, Saturday.	Isabella runs off.
XVII.	1784,	September.	Linton Heathcliff born.
	"	September or October.	Hindley Earnshaw dies. All his property is mortgaged to Heathcliff.
XVIII.	1797,	early June.	Catherine goes to Penistone Crags and meets Hareton.
XIX.	"	June.	Isabella dies. Edgar brings back Linton Heathcliff.

XX.	"	"	Linton Heathcliff is taken to live at Wuthering Heights.
XXI.	1800,	March 20.	Catherine and Ellen meet Hareton, and go to Wuthering Heights where they see Linton.
	"	March or April.	Catherine and Linton correspond.
XXII.	"	late October or November.	Catherine sees Heathcliff, who says that Linton is seriously ill.
XXIII.	"	late October or November.	Catherine and Ellen go to see Linton. Ellen catches cold and is ill for three weeks.
XXIV.	"	November.	During Ellen's illness Catherine visits Linton secretly.
XXV.	1801,	March 20.	Edgar too ill to visit his wife's grave.
	"	June.	Edgar declining.
XXVI.	"	August.	Ellen and Catherine go to meet Linton.
	"	August, Thursday, a week	They are kidnapped.
	"	later. Monday?	Catherine and Linton marry.
XXVII.	"	August or September.	Ellen is let out.
	"	next Tuesday.	Edgar is dying; he sends for Mr Green, the lawyer, who does not come.
XXVIII.	1801,	Wednesday, 3 a.m., harvest moon.	Catherine escapes and comes to Thrushcross Grange. Edgar Linton dies.
XXIX.	1801,	September, evening after the funeral	Heathcliff comes to the Grange and takes off Catherine.
XXX.	"	October	Linton Heathcliff dies. Hareton tries to please Catherine.

I.	"	late November.	Lockwood calls at W.H.
II.	"	next day.	He calls again and has to stay the night. He finds Catherine's diary and sees Heathcliff's outburst.
	"	next day.	Leaves at eight. Catches cold.
IV.	"	"	Ellen Dean begins her story.
X.	"	three weeks later.	Heathcliff sends grouse.
	"	one week later.	Heathcliff calls.
XV.	1802,	January, one week later.	Lockwood continues his account.
XXXI.	"	January, 2nd week.	Lockwood calls at W. H.
XXXII.	"	beginning of February.	Ellen goes to live at W. H.
	"	March.	Hareton has an accident.
	"	Easter Monday.	Catherine is nice to Hareton.
XXXIII.	"	Easter Tuesday.	Scene about altering garden.
	"	(after March 18).	Heathcliff getting odd.
XXXIV.	"	April.	Heathcliff goes on hunger strike.
	"	May.	Heathcliff dies.
	"	September.	Lockwood visits Thrushcross Grange and Wuthering Heights.
XXXIV.	1803,	January 1.	Catherine and Hareton marry.

Emily Brontë and *Wuthering Heights*

DAVID CECIL*

W*uthering Heights*—the very name is enough to set the imagination vibrating. We hear it perhaps spoken in a London street, for a moment the intricate roar of traffic and chattering people fades into stillness: and instead our mental ear is filled by the rush of streams, the shock and reverberation of thunder, the whistling of the wind over the moors. Nor is the sound fainter to us than it was to its contemporaries. Alone of Victorian novels *Wuthering Heights* is undimmed, even partially, by the dust of time. Alone it stirs us as freshly today as the day it was written.

Yet Emily Brontë has never been generally appreciated as she deserved. In her own time she was hardly appreciated at all: and though since she has slowly pushed her way to the front rank of Victorian novelists, she is still regarded, even by admirers, as an unequal genius, revealing some flashes of extraordinary imagination, but remote from the central interests of human life, often clumsy and exaggerated, and incapable of expressing her inspiration in a coherent form.

As a matter of fact she is a great deal more than that. Yet it is not odd that people should have failed to realise it. We tend to judge a work of art by a preconceived standard drawn from the masterpieces of the form and school of which it is representative. We take for granted that an author writing a novel in the Victorian age is trying to write an orthodox Victorian novel; and we estimate it accordingly. Now by any such criterion there is no doubt that Emily Brontë is a very imperfect novelist indeed. If *Wuthering Heights* was meant to be the same sort of novel as *Vanity Fair* or *David Copperfield,* it is a lamentable failure.

But it was never meant to be anything of the kind. The first fact to be realised about Emily Brontë, if we are ever to appreciate her properly, is that her achievement is of an intrinsically different kind from that of any of her contemporaries. Like that of Dickens, indeed, it is specially distinguished by the power of its imagination. And like his, hers is an English imagination. There is nothing exotic about Emily Brontë. *Wuthering Heights* is not like *Esther Waters,* a French novel written in English, in accordance with French

*Reprinted from D. Cecil, *Early Victorian Novelists* (London: Constable, 1934), 161–69.

ideals and with French limitations. The imagination that informs it is characteristically English, violent, unself-conscious, spiritual. And the mode in which it expresses itself is wholly the product of native influences. Its every fibre smells of the Northern soil where it had its root. But though Emily Brontë is characteristic of England, she is not characteristic of Victorian England. No generalisation that is true of Thackeray and Dickens, Trollope and Mrs. Gaskell, is true of her. She writes about different subjects in a different manner and from a different point of view. She stands outside the main current of nineteenth-century fiction as markedly as Blake stands outside the main current of eighteenth-century poetry.

For one thing she writes about a different world from the other novelists of her age. She spent her short tense aloof life almost entirely in her father's parsonage in Yorkshire. And Yorkshire, in those days of slow, infrequent communications and before the industrial revolution, was pretty well cut off from the influence of those forces that shaped the main trend of the time. Its life remained essentially the same as it had been in the days of Queen Elizabeth; a life as rugged and unchanging as the fells and storm-scarred moors and lonely valleys which were its setting: a primitive life of confined interests and unbridled passions, of simple earthy activities and complex demon-haunted imaginings; where feuds endured for generations, and a whole existence could concentrate itself with fanatical frenzy upon a single object.

Nor did she, like her sister Charlotte, ever turn from this life to contemplate the world outside. She drew mankind only from the grim race who inhabited the land of her childhood and from her own grimmer relations. So that if we are accustomed to the picture presented by Dickens or Thackeray, hers seems, to say the least of it, odd. That bustling, prosaic, progressive world of nineteenth-century middle-class England, which is the background of their whole picture, simply does not come into her view at all. Finally, since she was unconscious of this world, she did not, as all the other Victorians did, write to please it. So that its conventions and preoccupations and moral preferences left as little mark on the world of her creation as if she had lived and died in China.

But even if she had lived and died at Brighton, her books would still have been essentially unlike those of Dickens or Thackeray. For she looked at the human life which was their common subject from a different point of view. I have said that she stood outside her age as Blake stood outside his. It is for the same reason. Like Blake, Emily Brontë is concerned solely with those primary aspects of life which are unaffected by time and place. Looking at the world, she asks herself not, how does it work? what are its variations?—but what does it mean? None of the other Victorian novelists are concerned with such a question. And the fact that she is so occupied makes Emily Brontë's view of life essentially different from theirs. For it means that she sees human beings, not as they do in relation to other human beings, or to human civilisations and societies and codes of conduct, but only in relation to the cosmic scheme of which they form a part. Mrs. Brown appears not as to Jane Austen in relation to Mr. Brown, or as to Scott in relation to her ancestors, or as to Trollope in relation to her place in the social structure, or as to Proust in relation to herself; but in relation to time and eternity, to death and fate and the nature of things. Nature plays a much larger part in Emily Brontë's books than it does in most novelists'. On the other hand those individual and social aspects of life which fill their canvasses do not appear on hers. Her great characters exist in virtue of the reality of their attitude to the universe; they loom before us in the simple epic outline which is all that we see of man when revealed against the huge landscape of the cosmic scheme.

This does not make her unique even in English literature; Hardy is primarily interested in man's relation to the universe. And, as a matter of fact, she is more like Hardy than anyone else. But she is not very like him. Essentially, her view of human nature is more unlike his than his is unlike that of Thackeray or Dickens. For though she was concerned with the same aspects of it as he was, she looked at them from a different angle. Hardy sees man and nature in a different proportion to one another from Thackeray and Dickens, but they have the same significance for him. Hardy's heroes were concerned with fate and freewill, Dickens' with their marriages and their careers; but fate and freewill meant much the same thing to them as they would have to Dickens' heroes if they had happened to consider them.

Not so the heroes and heroines of Emily Brontë. It is here we come to the determining factor in her personality. She was—once more like Blake—a mystic. She had on certain occasions in her life known moments of vision— far and away the most profound of her experiences—in which her eyes seemed opened to behold a transcendental reality usually hidden from mortal sight. And it is in the light of these moments of vision that she envisages the world of mortal things; they endow it with a new significance; they are the foundation of the philosophy on which her picture of life rests. What precisely this philosophy was she never tells us in explicit terms. She was an artist, not a professor. Moreover, founded as it was on sporadic flashes of vision, she seems never to have made it wholly clear even to herself. And any attempt to state it explicitly reveals it as full of dark places and baffling inconsistencies of detail. However, its main features are clear enough.

The first is that the whole created cosmos, animate and inanimate, mental and physical alike, is the expression of certain living spiritual principles— on the one hand what may be called the principle of storm—of the harsh, the ruthless, the wild, the dynamic; and on the other the principle of calm—of the gentle, the merciful, the passive and the tame.

Secondly, in spite of their apparent opposition these principles are not conflicting. Either—Emily Brontë does not make clear which she thinks— each is the expression of a different aspect of a single pervading spirit; or they are the component parts of a harmony. They may not seem so to us. The world of our experience is, on the face of it, full of discord. But that is only because in the cramped condition of their earthly incarnation these principles are diverted from following the course that their nature dictates, and get in each other's way. They are changed from positive into negative forces; the calm becomes a source of weakness, not of harmony, in the natural scheme, the storm a source not of fruitful vigour, but of disturbance. But when they are free from fleshly bonds they flow unimpeded and unconflicting; and even in this world their discords are transitory. The single principle that ultimately directs them sooner or later imposes an equilibrium.

Such convictions inevitably set Emily Brontë's view of human life in a perspective fundamentally different from that presented to us by other English novelists. For they do away with those antitheses which are the basis of these novelists' conceptions. The antithesis between man and nature to begin with: Emily Brontë does not see animate man revealed against inanimate nature, as Mrs. Gaskell does. She does not even see suffering, pitiful, individual man in conflict with unfeeling, impersonal, ruthless natural forces, like Hardy. Men and nature to her are equally living and in the same way. To her an angry man and an angry sky are not just metaphorically alike, they are actually alike in kind; different manifestations of a single spiritual reality.

"'One time, however,'"—it is Catherine Linton speaking of Linton Heathcliff—"'we were near quarrelling. He said the pleasantest manner of spending a hot July day was lying from morning till evening on a bank of heath in the middle of the moors, with the bees humming dreamily about among the bloom, and the larks singing high up overhead, and the blue sky and bright sun shining steadily and cloudlessly. That was his most perfect idea of heaven's happiness: mine was rocking in a rustling green tree, with a west wind blowing, and bright white clouds flitting rapidly above; and not only larks, but throstles, and blackbirds, and linnets, and cuckoos pouring music on every side and the moors seen at a distance, broken into cool dusky dells; but close by great swells of long grass undulating in waves to the breeze; and woods and sounding water, and the whole world awake and wild with joy. He wanted all to lie in an ecstasy of peace; I wanted all to sparkle and dance in a glorious jubilee. I said his heaven would be only half alive; and he said mine would be drunk; I said I should fall asleep in his; and he said he could not breathe in mine'" (xxiv).

In this passage Linton's and Catherine's choices represent no chance preference, but the fundamental bias of their different natures. Each is expressing his or her instinctively-felt kinship with that aspect of nature of which he or she is the human counterpart. When Linton says that he could not "breathe" in Catherine's heaven he is stating a profound truth. He draws the breath of his life from a different spiritual principle.

Again, and more important, Emily Brontë's vision of life does away with the ordinary antithesis between good and evil. To call some aspects of life good and some evil is to accept some experiences and to reject others. But it is an essential trait of Emily Brontë's attitude that it accepts all experience. Not that she is an optimist who believes that the pleasant parts of life are its only real aspects. The storm is as much part of her universe as the calm. Indeed, she is peculiarly aware of the storm: she makes out the harsh elements of life to be as harsh as they can be. Her characters set no bridle on their destructive passions; nor do they repent of their destructive deeds. But since these deeds and passions do not spring from essentially destructive impulses, but impulses only destructive because they are diverted from pursuing their natural course, they are not "bad." Further, their fierceness and ruthlessness have, when confined to their true sphere, a necessary part to play in the cosmic scheme, and as such are to be accepted. Emily Brontë's outlook is not immoral, but it is pre-moral. It concerns itself not with moral standards, but with those conditioning forces of life on which the naïve erections of the human mind that we call moral standards are built up.

In consequence that conflict between right and wrong which is the distinguishing feature in the Victorian view of life does not come into her view. Human nature, to her, is not a mixture of good and bad elements, as it is to Thackeray. It cannot be grouped into the virtuous and the wicked, as it is by Charlotte Brontë or Dickens. The conflict in her books is not between right and wrong, but between like and unlike. No doubt she herself did find some characters more sympathetic than others. But this did not lead her to think them "better," in the strict sense of the word. Sympathetic and unsympathetic alike, they act only according to the dictates of the principle of which they are the manifestation; and are not, therefore, to be blamed or praised. Even when one of her characters undergoes a change of heart, she never represents this as a moral process. Catherine Linton is first cruel to Hareton, and then kind: but she shows no remorse for her cruelty; nor does her creator give any sign that she thinks she ought to have.

Emily Brontë's attitude to human emotion is equally different from that of her contemporaries. Her characters have extremely intense emotions, the most intense in English fiction. They are implacable and irresistible as the elemental forces they resemble; unchanging as the hills, fierce as the lightning; beside them, even Mr. Rochester's passions seem tame and tea-party affairs. But they are not awoken by the same causes as the emotions in other Victorian novels. Emily Brontë's heroes and heroines do not love each other because they find each other's personalities pleasant, or because they admire each other's characters. They may be superficially attracted for such reasons, as Catherine Earnshaw is attracted to Edgar Linton. But their deeper feelings are only roused for someone for whom they feel a sense of affinity, that comes from the fact that they are both expressions of the same spiritual principle. Catherine does not "like" Heathcliff, but she loves him with all the strength of her being. For he, like her, is a child of the storm; and this makes a bond between them, which interweaves itself with the very nature of their existence. In a sublime passage she tells Nelly Dean that she loves him "'not because he's handsome, Nelly, but because he's more myself than I am.

Whatever our souls are made of, his and mine are the same, and Linton's is as different as a moonbeam from lightning, or frost from fire. . . . My great miseries in this world have been Heathcliff's miseries, and I watched and felt each from the beginning: my great thought in living is himself. If all else perished, and *he* remained, *I* should still continue to be; and if all else remained, and he were annihilated, the universe would turn to a mighty stranger: I should not seem a part of it. My love for Linton is like the foliage in the woods: time will change it, I'm well aware, as winter changes the trees. My love for Heathcliff resembles the eternal rocks beneath: a source of little visible delight, but necessary. Nelly, I *am* Heathcliff! He's always, always in my mind; not as a pleasure, any more than I am always a pleasure to myself, but as my own being' " (ix). The quality of these emotions is as remote from that of the ordinary lover's passion as its origin. For all its intensity, Catherine's love is sexless; as devoid of sensuality as the attraction that draws the tide to the moon, the steel to the magnet; and it is as little tender as if it were hate itself. Catherine does not care whether her death will make Heathcliff unhappy or not. She fears only lest it may break the bond between them. If inconsolable anguish will keep him faithful to her, she is glad of it.

    " 'You and Edgar have broken my heart, Heathcliff! And you both come to bewail the deed to me, as if *you* were the people to be pitied! I shall not pity you, not I. You have killed me—and thriven on it, I think. How strong you are! How many years do you mean to live after I am gone? . . . I wish I could hold you till we were both dead! I shouldn't care what you suffered. I care nothing for your sufferings. Why shouldn't *you* suffer? I do! Will you forget me? Will you be happy when I am in the earth? Will you say twenty years hence, "That's the grave of Catherine Earnshaw? I loved her long ago, and was wretched to lose her; but it is past. I've loved many others since: my children are dearer to me than she was; and, at death, I shall not rejoice that I am going to her: I shall be sorry that I must leave them!" ' " (xv).

    Finally, Emily Brontë does away with the most universally accepted of all antitheses—the antithesis between life and death. She believes in the immortality of the soul. If the individual life be the expression of a spiritual principle, it is clear that the mere dissolution of its fleshly integument will not destroy it. But she does more than believe in the immortality of the soul in the orthodox Christian sense. She believes in the immortality of the soul *in this world*. The spiritual principle of which the soul is a manifestation is active in this life: therefore, the disembodied soul continues to be active in this life. Its ruling preoccupations remain the same after death as before. Here she is different from other Victorian novelists: and, as far as I know, from any novelists of any time. Emily Brontë does not see human conflict as ending with death. Catherine Earnshaw dreams that she goes to heaven, but is miserable there because she is homesick for Wuthering Heights, the native country of her spirit. Nor is this a parable: it is a sort of prophecy. For when in fact she comes to die, her spirit does take up its abode at Wuthering Heights. And not just as an ineffective ghost: as much as in life she exerts an active influence over Heathcliff, besieges him with her passion.

Thus the supernatural plays a different part in *Wuthering Heights* from that which it does in other novels. Most novelists, intent on trying to give a picture of life as they know it, do not bring in the supernatural at all. Those who do, either use it as a symbol, not to be believed literally, like Nathaniel Hawthorne—or like Scott, as an extraneous anomaly at variance with the laws of nature. With Emily Brontë it is an expression of those laws. It is, in truth, misleading to call it supernatural: it is a natural feature of the world as she sees it.

Her characters hold this view of death as much as she does. They may regret dying, but it is only because death means a temporary separation from those with whom they feel an affinity. For themselves they welcome it as a gateway to a condition in which at last their natures will be able to flow out unhampered and at peace; a peace not of annihilation, but of fulfilment. "'And,' " cries the dying Catherine, "'the thing that irks me most is this shattered prison, after all. I'm tired of being enclosed here. I'm wearying to escape into that glorious world, and to be always there: not seeing it dimly through tears, and yearning for it through the walls of an aching heart: but really with it, and in it. Nelly, you think you are better and more fortunate than I; in full health and strength: you are sorry for me—very soon that will be altered. I shall be sorry for *you*. I shall be incomparably beyond and above you all' " (xv). And Nelly, gazing on her dead body, has the same thought. "'I see a repose that neither earth nor hell can break, and I feel an assurance of the endless and shadowless hereafter—the Eternity they have entered— where life is boundless in its duration, and love in its sympathy, and joy in its fulness' " (xvi).

Tempest in the Soul:
The Theme and Structure of *Wuthering Heights*

MELVIN WATSON*

I

In the century since its publication, *Wuthering Heights,* like the plays of Shakespeare with which it has often been compared, has been the subject of many diverse criticisms and interpretations. Almost no one has been audacious enough to deny its power and its unique place in the development of English fiction, but few have made an unprejudiced attempt to understand what Emily Brontë strove for in her one full-length study of human nature—its impulses and its desires, its loves and its hates, its disasters and its triumphs, its defeats and its victories. Because of its strange, elemental fierceness and barbarity, its stormy setting, divorced from the world as we know it, its seemingly crude, inartistic structure, and its superhuman emotions, *Wuthering Heights* is not an easy book to discuss. Yet if it is the masterpiece that it is admitted to be, it must present a valid interpretation of life in people who are believable, however seldom their prototypes may appear in the world as we know it; it must concern itself with a theme which we can all understand; and it must show a power of architectonics, however unconventional or imperfect from the inexperience of the architect that power might be.

Certainly *Wuthering Heights* is different, primarily, perhaps, because its author was an individualist who spurned the easy road of convention. Not for her was the typical Victorian novel with its study of normal men and women in the ordinary pursuits of life. Considered as a novel of that kind, it is a miserable failure, badly organized and badly told, with two heroes—Edgar Linton and Hareton Earnshaw—neither of whom is strong or prominent enough to carry the story, and with a villain who overrides the action and is at last triumphantly united with the heroine who has died midway through the book. The plan then becomes incontrovertibly confusing, the point of view too blatantly awkward, the presence of two generations unnecessary, and the conclusion a travesty of poetic justice.

*Reprinted from *Nineteenth Century Fiction* 4 (1949): 87–100.

Nor are other possibilities any more feasible as a complete explanation of what Emily Brontë was doing. Although revenge plays a large part in the story, it cannot be considered merely a revenge tragedy analogous to the dramas of Kyd, Chapman, or Marston. The dissolution of the revenge motif in the last chapters and the supreme happiness of Heathcliff as he prepares for his reunion with Catherine rule out such an explanation. To consider this merely the account of Heathcliff's and Catherine's love is equally fantastic. Love there is of a superhuman strength, and thwarted love it is which motivates much—but not all—of Heathcliff's hatred; but if this is a love story and nothing more, the importance of Hindley, Hareton, Cathy, and Linton is misplaced, the entire last half is ill-proportioned, and the ending is off key. If, on the other hand, we assume that *Wuthering Heights* is nothing more than a Gothic romance, we automatically exclude it as a serious study of any human problem.

One last possibility must be considered. In his detailed and provocative essay on Emily Brontë, Lord David Cecil contends that what we have is an allegory setting forth her conception of the universe, a universe built up from two opposing forces—storm and calm—and that the theme is the reëstablishment of the cosmic order which has been disturbed by faulty external actions, by an improper mixture of the two forces in the marriages of Catherine and Edgar, and of Isabella and Heathcliff, which produce children of love and hate respectively, and by the introduction of an extraneous element in the person of Heathcliff. Two principal weaknesses of this interpretation suggest themselves. *Wuthering Heights* is not, I believe, a metaphysical dissertation in which the Heights and Thrushcross Grange are a microcosm and their inhabitants only allegorical puppets whose wooden actions serve to envision a Brontëan universe. Doubtless, Emily Brontë had her own unconventional views of the world, which inevitably became a part of the fabric of *Wuthering Heights,* but surely she was attempting something more concrete, more closely related to human experience than this. But, more important, such an analysis relegates Heathcliff to a position of less prominence than he occupies. Heathcliff *is* the story. He not only acts and suffers, but causes others to act and suffer; his strength permeates the story; his power for good and for evil shocks and surprises the reader; his deeds and his reactions from the ghastly beginning to the pastoral close make a coherent whole out of what might have been a chaotic heap.

Wuthering Heights, then, is a psychological study of an elemental man whose soul is torn between love and hate. He is a creature about whose past nothing is known. A dark, dirty beggar, he was picked up on the Liverpool streets by Mr. Earnshaw and brought to the secluded part of the world known as the moors, where he has ample space to work out his destiny. Only the elemental passions of love and hate receive any development in the elemental environment by which he was molded. His strength of will and steadfastness of purpose he brought with him to the moors, but there they were prevented by external events from following their natural course. There he was hardened by his physical surroundings, toughened and embittered by the harsh treatment of Hindley, disillusioned by what he considered the treachery of Catherine, on whom he had poured love out of his boundless store. Then he resolves to even scores by crushing everyone who has stood in his way, everyone who has helped to thwart his happiness, the specter of which haunts him for seventeen long years during which he works out the venom which has accumulated in his soul. As soon as part of the venom is removed and the day of happiness begins to dawn, he no longer has the will to keep up his torturing.

This is a daring theme, subject to much misinterpretation, for during most of the action Heathcliff performs like a villain or like a hero who has consciously chosen evil for his companion. When completely understood, however, he is neither an Iago for whom evil is a divinity nor a Macbeth who consciously chooses evil because of his overpowering ambition, but rather a Hamlet without Hamlet's fatal irresolution. Like Hamlet, he was precipitated into a world in which he saw cruelty and unfaithfulness operating. His dilemma was not Hamlet's, for he has no father to avenge or mother to protect, but in a way he has evil thrust upon him if he is to survive among harsh surroundings. And Heathcliff was not one to hesitate when faced with an alternative, however tragic the consequences might be.

Though Heathcliff is not perhaps more sinned against than sinning, his actions are produced by the distortion of his natural personality. This distortion had already begun when Mr. Earnshaw brought him into Wuthering Heights, a "dirty, ragged, black-haired child." Already he was inured to hardship and blows; already he uncomplainingly accepted suffering, as when he had the measles, and ill treatment from Hindley if he got what he wanted. From the very first he showed great courage, steadfastness, and love. But with Mr. Earnshaw's death Hindley has the power to degrade Heathcliff to the status of a servant. A weak, vindictive character, as cruel as Heathcliff without Heathcliff's strength, Hindley prepares for his own destruction by his inhumanity to Heathcliff and the other inhabitants of the Heights. Though Heathcliff was forced down to an animal level, he took a silent delight in watching his persecutor sinking also into a life of debauchery. Nor was he alone, for he had Cathy, on whom he poured his devotion and love. They were inseparable. On the moors by day or in the chimney corner by night, they chatted and dreamed whenever Heathcliff was not busy with the chores. But the visit to Thrushcross Grange introduced Cathy to another world to which she opened her arms, and that world contained Edgar Linton. Edgar held a superficial attraction for Cathy which Heathcliff could never understand and which he feared, for, having possessed Cathy for some years, he feared losing even part of her attention. The final blow, a blow which turns Heathcliff from sullen acquiescence to tragic determination, comes when Cathy confesses to Ellen her infatuation with Edgar and her resolve to marry him so that she and

Heathcliff can escape from the repressive world of Wuthering Heights. Not once did she think of giving up Heathcliff, but Heathcliff inadvertently over-hears only the first part of the conversation. Cathy has deserted him for a mess of pottage, for fine clothes and refined manners; she is ashamed of his rough exterior, of his lack of polish; she would be degraded to marry him as he is. Heathcliff doesn't stay to hear Cathy confess her oneness with him:

> If all else perished, and *he* remained, *I* should still continue to be; and if all else remained, and he were annihilated, the universe would turn to a mighty stranger: I should not seem a part of it. My love for Linton is like the foliage in the woods: time will change it, I'm well aware, as winter changes the trees. My love for Heathcliff resembles the eternal rocks beneath: a source of little visible delight, but necessary. Nelly, I *am* Heathcliff. He's always, always in my mind: not as a pleasure, any more than I am always a pleasure to myself, but as my own being. (ix)

His mind is made up. If love alone is insufficient to hold Cathy, he will secure the necessary money and polish; if his only happiness is to be snatched from him, he will turn to hate; and now not only Hindley will be the object of his wrath, but Edgar also. As long as he had Cathy, his worldly condition, his suf-fering, was as nothing; without her, all is chaff to be trampled underfoot.

For three years, during which he vanishes from sight, he prepares him-self, the poison in his system increasing all the time until love is submerged in a sea of hate which he must drain off before love can reassert itself. Union with Cathy is his one desire. Since physical union is made impossible by her death—not that it was ever important—the union must be spiritual, but the world and the people of the world must be subjugated before such happiness can be achieved. The course is set, the wind is strong, the bark is sturdy, the journey long. For seventeen years Heathcliff wreaks his vengeance on Hind-ley, Edgar, and Isabella and on their children Hareton, young Cathy, and Lin-ton. The account of the trip is not pretty. Even in the love scenes before the elder Cathy's death there is a savage passion which strikes terror to the heart of the beholder, unlike any other scenes in the course of English fiction; and before the masochistic treatment of Isabella, Hareton, young Cathy, and Lin-ton we cringe. Here is a man haunted by a ghost of happiness for which he must exorcise his soul, a soul filled with accumulated hatred. That he ceases his reign of terror before Hareton and young Cathy have been completely broken is due not to any loss of spiritual strength but to the realization that the end of the voyage is near, that the tempest is subsiding, and that reunion with Cathy is about to be consummated. In Heathcliff one looks in vain for Christian morals or virtues; his is a primitive, pagan soul; yet love conquers even a Heathcliff in the end—after his soul has been purged of the hate in and with which he has lived for decades. The evil that he does springs not from a love of evil itself, but from the thwarting of the natural processes of love.

In the development of this theme everyone, even Catherine, is subordinated to Heathcliff, as important as many of them are in molding Heathcliff's character, in serving as contrasts to him, or in receiving the force of his hatred. Mr. Earnshaw introduces him to the Heights but exits too early to be more than a puppet, except as he favors Heathcliff over Hindley and thus encourages the waif's willful ways and prepares for the tragedy that is to follow. Hindley reverses his father's actions. He has inherited all the cruelty of the moors without any of their saving strength; he vents his accumulated wrath on Heathcliff but treads himself the primrose path of dalliance. His habits of drinking and gambling make him a clay pigeon when Heathcliff has prepared himself for revenge. He is a despicable character whose downfall calls forth no sympathizing tear. Edgar Linton, on the other hand, contrasts with Heathcliff in another way. In another novel he might have been a conventional Victorian hero; he is presentable and well-mannered, sincere but somewhat smug, honest but thoroughly conventional, good-looking but pallid, devoted to Catherine but incapable of understanding or possessing her. His moral sense the Victorian reader could comprehend and sympathize with. In *Wuthering Heights,* however, he is an anomaly, owning Catherine without possessing her, resenting Heathcliff but lacking the power to thwart him. Though he lives under the shadow of the volcano, he suffers only as he sees those whom he loves—Isabella, Cathy, and Linton—submerged by the lava of hate. And Edgar is as helpless as the peasants who lived near Vesuvius. Isabella, as weak as Catherine is strong, as conventional as Catherine is unconventional, as superficially attracted to Heathcliff as Catherine was to Edgar, allows Heathcliff to make his first inroads on Thruschcross Grange. An emotional, giddy girl who had no knowledge of men or their motives, she felt only the physical attraction of a dark, handsome, well-dressed newcomer to her small circle of acquaintances. Too late she discovered that she was to be only a tool, used briefly and then cast aside to be worn away by rust. Though completely convincing in her role, she is significant only as the device which enables Heathcliff to gain control of Thrushcross Grange.

Catherine alone stands as a near equal to Heathcliff. Beautiful, selfish, willful, she strides through the first part of *Wuthering Heights* like the queen that she is. She understands Heathcliff because she is like him. She could control him, but she forfeits that power by her marriage to Edgar. One of the greater ironies of the book is this: that by her action intended primarily to help Heathcliff she partly alienates herself from him and blows to flame the fire of hatred which produces an eruption lasting seventeen years. She failed to think her decisions through. When she makes her fatal confession to Ellen, not once does she consider the effect of her choice on Heathcliff. She assumes that she can continue to rule both Edgar and Heathcliff as she has done in the past, but she reckons without his pride. Catherine, however, was no hypocrite; she loved both Edgar and Heathcliff—in entirely different ways; she was faithful to her marriage vows, but they could not prevent her feeling a spiritual kinship with Heathcliff. The love scene in chapter xv, overpowering as it is, contains nothing gross, nothing merely physical. It is symbolic of a union which the two cannot resist, for it expresses a likeness of the two souls. But Catherine had deserted him and brings upon herself the curses of heaven and hell that she shall wander as a ghost until he has subjugated the world and attained spiritual union with her. During the last half of the book, Catherine is present only as a spirit, an influence which continually goads Heathcliff like the Furies of old. In the final analysis it is her *spirit,* not Catherine herself, that is important for the novel as a whole.

The presence of the second generation caused many early commentators to stumble, for they failed to recognize that Hareton, young Cathy, and Linton are essential to the theme. Time is necessary for Heathcliff to eradicate the hate from his soul in order that love can reassert itself; furthermore, in order to gain the wealth and power which, he feels, separated him from Catherine, he must possess not only Wuthering Heights but Thrushcross Grange as well. This he can accomplish only through the marriage of Cathy and Linton. His relation to Hareton is peculiar. Though he once ironically saved him from death when Hindley in a drunken fit let him fall over the banisters, he takes a savage delight in degrading him as he was once degraded by Hindley. Hareton is saved by the absence of hatred in his heart, and the fondness between him and young Cathy blossoms in time to prevent his becoming just an animal. The love which develops out of and in spite of the hate which surrounds them—but develops as that hate is subsiding—provides the calm and symbolic ending of the book.

II

The structure of *Wuthering Heights* is as different and unconventional as the theme. How could it be otherwise? New wine should not be poured into old bottles. Though there are superficial awkwardnesses and old-fashioned conventions in the point of view, this seems to be the inevitable way of telling such a story. The structure provides yet another analogy with Elizabethan drama, for it is consciously organized like a five-act tragedy, with breaks always indicated at the appropriate points. The method of telling the story, "in terms of autobiography thrice involved," as William Dean Howells said, is necessary for this structure. Mr. Lockwood, the relative nonentity who records the story as told to him by Ellen Dean, lives in the community only a few months before Heathcliff dies; yet representing, as he does, normal humanity, and experiencing enough of the confusion of Wuthering Heights to make him believe anything about these creatures, and being the audience before whom their past is unfolded, a past which is broken into segments by

Ellen's or Mr. Lockwood's interruptions, he lends credibility to the events and serves as a curtain marking off the divisions of the story.

The Prologue (chapters i-iii), like that of a Greek tragedy, sets the tone and character of the book. Here, through a perfectly detached spectator, an ordinary person from the outside world, we are catapulted into the story at a point just before the denouement. Lockwood observes the primitive quality of the life at Wuthering Heights, the brutality and the coldness evident on every hand, both inside and out; he witnesses the inhumanity and the hatred of Heathcliff; he experiences the ghastly night in Catherine's old bedchamber, with Cathy's spirit crying for entrance—or was it a dream? He is as confused, as shocked, and as mystified as any reader could be; naturally he is curious to discover more about these strange inhabitants of this peculiar establishment. This beginning is not accidental; it is the triumph of an artistic spirit that realized the difficulties inherent in her material. If the strange behavior of her characters was to be made believable, she must storm the citadel with the first assault; she must make Lockwood's reactions coincide with the reader's and cause both to suspend their disbelief until they have discovered the background for the present situation. Ellen Dean, fortunately, is able to satisfy all his curiosity.

Though this minor-character point of view seems the only possible one for this story, certain disadvantages loom before us. Ellen is at moments plot-ridden. The climactic last scene between Cathy and Heathcliff is arranged by Ellen, and she is the direct cause of young Cathy's and Linton's getting so friendly; yet we feel that here Ellen is merely the agent of fate; these things would have happened whether or not Ellen had intervened. Certain time-honored but slightly unnatural conventions, also, are used. Ellen gets part of the story in a letter from Isabella—hardly a person to correspond with a servant; she secures needed information about the situation at Wuthering Heights by gossiping with Zillah, the new servant there; but, more significant, she acquires mental reactions and attitudes from the confessions to her, such as Catherine's in chapter ix, Heathcliff's in chapter xxi, and Edgar's in chapter xxv. Except for the first, these are really soliloquies in the Elizabethan sense and should be accepted as such. Finally, to have Ellen Dean as narrator, we must accept the fact that a servant can be in many places where she would not ordinarily be and hear many things that she would not ordinarily hear: for example, the last scene between Cathy and Heathcliff in chapter xv, or Heathcliff's description of what he did on Catherine's burial day and of his looking at her corpse after many years, in chapter xxix. But the advantages gained by having the story told by an eyewitness are weighty enough to balance all these disadvantages. Dramatic intensity is secured by seeing the story unfold with all the freshness and vigor with which Ellen saw it. Ellen relates the story with breaks to set off the divisions as it actually happened. She has no favorites; though she may at moments betray partialities, she makes no consistent attempt to whitewash any of the characters or events. And she lends further credibility to the story by recounting only what she has seen or heard.

Act I, including chapters iv-vii, introduces the first generation, provides the initial complications in Hindley's treatment of Heathcliff, and the effect on Cathy of her visit to the Grange, and ends with Heathcliff's defiance of Hindley: "I'm trying to settle how I shall pay Hindley back. I don't care how long I wait, if I can only do it at last. I hope he will not die before I do!" Mrs. Dean interrupts herself to remind Lockwood that she should stop, but is persuaded to continue her tale.

The next section, containing only two chapters, includes the birth of the first member of the second generation, Hareton, develops Cathy's relation with Edgar Linton, and climbs to a minor climax when Heathcliff inadvertently hears Cathy declare that she has accepted Edgar's proposal of marriage. The last few pages of the act hurry over three years, at the end of which Cathy and Edgar are married. Here Ellen Dean stops because of the lateness of the hour.

After Lockwood has recovered from a four weeks' illness brought on by his first visit to Wuthering Heights, he demands more of "the history of Mr. Heathcliff." Ellen responds with Act III, leading up in its five chapters to the main climax of the novel. From the first meeting of Cathy and Heathcliff after her marriage to the arrangement for their last scene a few hours before her death, this act runs the gamut of emotional intensity. Heathcliff finishes the ruin of Hindley by catering to his taste for drink and gambling and secures mortgages on Wuthering Heights; he elopes with Isabella after she has thrown herself at his feet; he physically chastises Edgar for daring to interfere in his talks with Catherine; he alternates between passionate love and fierce hatred in his attitude toward Catherine and helps produce in her a fever from which she dies. Instead of ending this act with the climactic scene between Cathy and Heathcliff from which she never recovers, Emily Brontë only prepares for it, but presents the climax itself at the beginning of the next act. Again her technique seems right, for not only does this break give the reader a chance to catch his breath, but it makes of Act IV a more symmetrical structure.

The interruption at the end of chapter xiv is the last one until Mrs. Dean has brought the story up to date at the close of chapter xxx. In the week intervening between the close of chapter xiv and the beginning of chapter xv, Mrs. Dean has told Mr. Lockwood the rest of the story, which he has determined to continue in her own words. Since the structural breaks in Act IV and the beginning of Act V are not so important as the others, there is no necessity for inventing interruptions. Casual comments are enough to mark the breaks now, of which there are three, one at the beginning of chapter xviii ("continued Mrs. Dean") to indicate the last part of Act IV, and another in the opening line of chapter xxv ("said Mrs. Dean") to indicate the start of Act V. The other break, slightly more prominent than these, sets off the climactic scene, the birth of young Cathy, and the death of Catherine from the rest of this section and occurs in the middle of chapter xvi. These events, though a bridge between the rising and the falling actions, were to be clearly marked off from the less dramatic events of this act: the birth of Linton after Isabella's escape from Wuthering Heights, the mention of her death some years later, the death of Hindley—these occupy the middle of the act—and the development of the second generation, which fills up the last "scene" of the act.

By the close of the first "scene" of Act V, Nelly Dean has brought Lockwood up to date. The machinations of Heathcliff have accomplished the marriage of young Cathy and Linton, and with the death of Edgar, and then of Linton, Heathcliff has come into possession of Thrushcross Grange. Lockwood's visit to Wuthering Heights after his recovery, described in chapter xxxi and forming the second part of this last act, prepares the reader for the final resolution of the drama. Several crucial months have elapsed since the memorable night spent in Catherine's former bedchamber, months during which the inhabitants of the Heights have changed. Heathcliff now wonders about the wisdom of his treatment of Hareton, for when he looks for Hindley in his face, he sees only Catherine. Hareton is making gigantic efforts to pull himself up by his bootstraps by learning to read in order to impress Cathy. Cathy, though still bitter and morose from her harsh treatment, and changed less than the other two, totters on the verge of a readjustment. Wisely, this scene has been inserted to make the reformation in the last chapters easier to accept.

When Lockwood saw Wuthering Heights for the first time, he was impressed in this manner:

> Pure, bracing ventilation they must have up there at all times, indeed; one may guess the power of the north wind blowing over the edge, by the excessive slant of a few stunted firs at the end of the house; and by a range of gaunt thorns all stretching their limbs one way, as if craving alms of the sun. Happily, the architect had foresight to build it strong; the narrow windows are deeply set in the wall, and the corners defended with large jutting stones.

The locked gate, the padlocked door, and the fierce dogs added to his sense of awe. On his last visit, after a nine months' absence from the moors, he was struck by a different atmosphere:

> Before I arrived in sight of it, all that remained of day was a beamless amber light along the west: but I could see every pebble on the path, and every blade of grass, by that splendid moon. I had neither to climb the gate nor to knock—it yielded to my hand. That is an improvement, I thought. And I noticed another, by the aid of my nostrils; a fragrance of stocks and wallflowers wafted on the air from amongst the homely fruit-trees.

The explanation for the difference both in external and internal atmosphere is supplied by Nelly Dean as she once again brings Lockwood up to date, detailing the increasing friendship and then love between Cathy and Hareton and the dissolution and final death of Heathcliff as the possibility of permanent reunion with his Cathy makes his face glow with a ghastly happiness. To escape the lovers, Lockwood vanishes through the kitchen door; and as he later meditates on the quietness of the kirk where Edgar, Cathy, and Heathcliff lie buried side by side, the story whispers itself out.

As careful as she was in constructing the story, so meticulous was Emily Brontë in maintaining unity of place and tone. The reader never leaves the moors, once he has arrived there with Mr. Lockwood. He travels between Wuthering Heights and Thrushcross Grange; he sees the graves on the hillside and catches an occasional glimpse of Peniston Crag; he knows where the road to Gimmerton branches off from the road with which he is well acquainted, but never does he follow that road to the outer world. When Mr. Earnshaw travels to Liverpool, when Heathcliff disappears, when Isabella escapes, when Edgar goes to get Isabella's son, the reader remains on the moors, awaiting their return or news of their death. Wuthering Heights, Thrushcross Grange, and the rippling moors between—these are the physical bounds of the story. And so with the tone. No comic scenes or characters lighten the dramatic intensity of the action. Even Joseph is more ironic than comic, and Mr. Lockwood's occasional facetious comments are outside the action and have no influence upon it. Though incapable of understanding the book, Charlotte Brontë sensed the power attained through this unity: "Its power fills me with renewed admiration; but yet I am oppressed; the reader is scarcely ever permitted a taste of unalloyed pleasure; every beam of sunshine is poured down through black bars of threatening cloud; every page is surcharged with a sort of moral electricity."

Wuthering Heights is not the "work of immature genius," "awkwardly and illogically constructed," a study of "unnatural passion"; nor is it, I believe, the "one perfect work of art amid all the vast varied canvases of Victorian fiction." In theme and structure, however, it is the product of a mature artist who knew what effects she wished to achieve and possessed the ability to carry her scheme through to a logical and satisfying conclusion. Her theme of the relationship between love and hate is universal in its significance; her structure, if not unique in English fiction, is the ideal one for this story which could not be confined within the relatively narrow bounds of the drama.

Emily Brontë: *Wuthering Heights* (1847)

ARNOLD KETTLE*

W*uthering Heights,* like all the greatest works of art, is at once concrete and yet general, local and yet universal. Because so much nonsense has been written and spoken about the Brontës and because Emily in particular has been so often presented to us as a ghost-like figure surrounded entirely by endless moorland, cut off from anything so banal as human society, not of her time but of eternity, it is necessary to emphasize at the outset the local quality of the book.

Wuthering Heights is about England in 1847. The people it reveals live not in a never-never land but in Yorkshire. Heathcliff was born not in the pages of Byron, but in a Liverpool slum. The language of Nelly, Joseph and Hareton is the language of Yorkshire people. The story of *Wuthering Heights* is concerned not with love in the abstract but with the passions of living people, with property-ownership, the attraction of social comforts, the arrangement of marriages, the importance of education, the validity of religion, the relations of rich and poor.

There is nothing vague about this novel; the mists in it are the mists of the Yorkshire moors; if we speak of it as having an elemental quality it is because the very elements, the great forces of nature are evoked, which change so slowly that in the span of a human life they seem unchanging. But in this evocation there is nothing sloppy or uncontrolled. On the contrary the realization is intensely concrete: we seem to smell the kitchen of Wuthering Heights, to feel the force of the wind across the moors, to sense the very changes of the seasons. Such concreteness is achieved not by mistiness but by precision.

It is necessary to stress this point but not, of course, to force it to a false conclusion. The power and wonder of Emily Brontë's novel does not lie in naturalistic description, nor in a detailed analysis of the hour-by-hour issues of social living. Her approach is, quite obviously, not the approach of Jane Austen; it is much nearer to the approach of Dickens. Indeed, *Wuthering Heights* is essentially the same kind of novel as *Oliver Twist*. It is not a romance, not (despite the film bearing the same title) an escape from life to the wild

*Reprinted from A. Kettle, *An Introduction to the English Novel* (London: Hutchinson, 1951), 139–54.

moors and romantic lovers. It is certainly not a picaresque novel and it cannot adequately be described as a moral fable, though it has a strong, insistent pattern. But the pattern, like that of Dickens's novel, cannot be abstracted as a neat sentence: its germ is not an intellectualized idea or concept.

Emily Brontë works not in ideas but in symbols, that is to say concepts which have a significance and validity on a level different from that of logical thought. Just as the significance of the workhouse in *Oliver Twist* cannot adequately be conceived in merely logical terms but depends on a host of associations—including its physical shape and colour—which logical analysis may penetrate but is unlikely adequately to convey, so the significance of the moors in *Wuthering Heights* cannot be suggested in the cold words of logic (which does not mean that it is illogical). The symbolic novel is an advance on the moral fable just in the sense that a symbol can be richer—can touch on more of life—than an abstract moral concept.

The opening sentence of the *Social Contract* gives a simple example: "Man was born free, but everywhere he is in chains." Of the two statements in this sentence the first is abstract, the second symbolic. And the impact of the second on our imagination is greater than that of the first for this very reason. (If one were concerned to go deeper into the matter one might suggest that Rousseau *knew* that man was in chains but merely speculated that he had been born free.) Now, whereas the symbolism of the moral fable (and the fable is itself a kind of extended symbol) is inherently limited by the abstract concept behind it, the symbolism of *Wuthering Heights* or the good part of *Oliver Twist* is the expression of the very terms in which the novel has been conceived. In fact, it *is* the novel and the novel stands or falls by its validity, its total adequacy to life.

Wuthering Heights is a vision of what life in 1847 was like. Whether it can be described as a vision of what life as such—all life—is like is a question we will consider later. It is, for all its appearance of casualness and the complexity of its family relationships, a very well-constructed book, in which the technical problems of presentation have been most carefully thought out. The roles of the two narrators, Lockwood and Nelly Dean, are not casual. Their function (they the two most "normal" people in the book) is partly to keep the story close to the earth, to make it believable, partly to comment on it from a common-sense point of view and thereby to reveal in part the inadequacy of such common sense. They act as a kind of sieve to the story, sometimes a double sieve, which has the purpose not simply of separating off the chaff, but of making us aware of the difficulty of passing easy judgments. One is left always with the sense that the last word has not been said.

The narrators do not as a rule talk realistically, though sometimes Nelly's part is to slip into a Yorkshire dialect that "places" what she is describing and counteracts any tendency (inherent in symbolic art) to the pretentious. At critical points in the narrative we are not conscious of their existence at all; there is no attempt at a limiting verisimilitude of speech. They do not impose themselves between us and the scene. But at other times their attitudes are important.

One of the subtleties of the book is the way these attitudes change and develop; Lockwood and Nelly, like us, learn from what they experience, though at first their limitations are made use of, as in the very first scene when the expectations of the conventional Lockwood are so completely shocked by what he finds at Wuthering Heights. He goes there, he the normal Victorian gentleman, expecting to find the normal Victorian middle-class family. And what he finds—a house seething with hatred, conflict, horror—is a shock to us, too. The attack on our complacency, moral, social and spiritual, has already begun.

The centre and core of the book is the story of Catherine and Heathcliff. It is a story which has four stages. The first part, ending in the visit to Thrushcross Grange, tells of the establishing of a special relationship between Catherine and Heathcliff and of their common rebellion against Hindley and his régime in Wuthering Heights. In the second part is revealed Catherine's betrayal of Heathcliff, culminating in her death. The third part deals with Heathcliff's revenge, and the final section, shorter than the others, tells of the change that comes over Heathcliff and of his death. Even in the last two sections, after her death, the relationship with Catherine remains the dominant theme, underlying all else that occurs.

It is not easy to suggest with any precision the quality of feeling that binds Catherine and Heathcliff. It is not primarily a sexual relationship. Emily Brontë is not, as is sometimes suggested, afraid of sexual love; the scene at Catherine's death is proof enough that this is no platonic passion, yet to describe the attraction as sexual is surely quite inadequate. Catherine tries to express her feelings to Nelly (she is about to marry Linton).

> "My great miseries in this world have been Heathcliff's miseries, and I watched and felt each from the beginning: my great thought in living is himself. If all else perished, and *he* remained, *I* should still continue to be; and if all else remained, and he were annihilated, the universe would turn to a mighty stranger: I should not seem a part of it. My love for Linton is like the foliage in the woods: time will change it, I'm well aware, as winter changes the trees. My love for Heathcliff resembles the eternal rocks beneath: a source of little visible delight, but necessary. Nelly, I *am* Heathcliff! He's always, always in my mind: not as a pleasure, any more than I am always a pleasure to myself, but as my own being." (ix)

And Heathcliff cries, when Catherine is dying: "I *cannot* live without my life, I *cannot* live without my soul" (xv). What is conveyed to us here is the sense of an affinity deeper than sexual attraction, something which it is not enough to describe as romantic love.

This affinity is forged in rebellion and, in order to grasp the concrete and unromantic nature of this book, it is necessary to recall the nature of that rebellion. Heathcliff, the waif from the Liverpool slums, is treated kindly by old Mr. Earnshaw but insulted and degraded by Hindley. After his father's death Hindley reduces the boy to the status of a serf. "He drove him from their company to the servants, deprived him of the instructions of the curate, and insisted that he should labour out of doors instead; compelling him to do so as hard as any other hand on the farm" (vi). The situation at Wuthering Heights is wonderfully evoked in the passage from Catherine's journal, which Lockwood finds in his bedroom:

"An awful Sunday!" commenced the paragraph beneath. "I wish my father were back again. Hindley is a detestable substitute—his conduct to Heathcliff is atrocious—H. and I are going to rebel—we took our initiatory step this evening.

"All day had been flooding with rain; we could not go to church, so Joseph must needs get up a congregation in the garret, and, while Hindley and his wife basked downstairs before a comfortable fire—doing anything but reading the Bibles, I'll answer for it—Heathcliff, myself, and the unhappy plough-boy, were commanded to take our Prayer-books, and mount: were ranged in a row, on a sack of corn, groaning and shivering, and hoping that Joseph would shiver too, so that he might give us a short homily for his own sake. A vain idea! The service lasted precisely three hours: and yet my brother had the face to exclaim, when he saw us descending, 'What, done already?' On Sunday evenings we used to be permitted to play, if we did not make much noise; now a mere titter is sufficient to send us into corners!

" 'You forget you have a master here,' says the tyrant. 'I'll demolish the first who puts me out of temper! I insist on perfect sobriety and silence. Oh, boy! was that you? Frances darling, pull his hair as you go by: I heard him snap his fingers.' Frances pulled his hair heartily, and then went and seated herself on her husband's knee: and there they were, like two babies, kissing and talking nonsense by the hour—foolish palaver that we should be ashamed of. We made ourselves as snug as our means allowed in the arch of the dresser. I had just fastened our pinafores together, and hung them up for a curtain, when in comes Joseph on an errand from the stables. He tears down my handiwork boxes my ears and croaks—

" 'T' maister nobbut just buried, and Sabbath no o'ered, and t' sound o' t' gospel still i' yer lugs, and ye darr be laiking! Shame on ye! Sit ye down, ill childer! There's good books enough if ye'll read em! sit ye down, and think of yer sowls!'

"Saying this, he compelled us so to square our positions that we might receive from the far-off fire a dull ray to show us the text of the lumber he thrust upon us. I could not bear the employment. I took my dingy volume by the scroop, and hurled it into the dogkennel, vowing I hated a good book. Heathcliff kicked his to the same place. Then there was a hubbub!

" 'Maister Hindley!' shouted our chaplain. 'Maister, coom hither! Miss Cathy's riven th' back of "Th' Helmet O' Salvation," un Heathcliff's pawsed his fit into t' first part o' "T' Broad Way to Destruction." It's fair flaysome, that ye let 'em go on this gait. Ech! th' owd man wad ha' laced 'em properly—but he's goan!'

"Hindley hurried up from his paradise on the hearth, and seizing one of us by the collar, and the other by the arm, hurled both into the back kitchen, where, Joseph asseverated, 'owd Nick' would fetch us as sure as we were living, and, so comforted, we each sought a separate nook to await his advent." (iii)

This passage reveals, in itself, a great deal of the extraordinary quality of *Wuthering Heights*. It is a passage which, in the typical manner of the novel, evokes, in language which involves the kind of attention we give to poetry, a world far larger than the scene it describes, and evokes it through the very force and concreteness of the particular scene. The rebellion of Catherine and Heathcliff is made completely concrete. They are not vague romantic dreamers. Their rebellion is against the régime in which Hindley and his wife sit in fatuous comfort by the fire whilst they are relegated to the arch of the dresser and compelled for the good of their souls to read the *Broad Way to Destruction* under the tutelage of the canting hypocrite Joseph. It is a situation not confined, in the year 1847, to the more distant homesteads of the Yorkshire moors.

Against this degradation Catherine and Heathcliff rebel, hurling their pious books into the dog-kennel. And in their revolt they discover their deep and passionate need of each other. He, the outcast slummy, turns to the lively, spirited, fearless girl who alone offers him human understanding and comradeship. And she, born into the world of Wuthering Heights, senses that to achieve a full humanity, to be true to herself as a human being, she must associate herself totally with him in his rebellion against the tyranny of the Earnshaws and all that tyranny involves.

It is this rebellion that immediately, in this early section of the book, wins over our sympathy to Heathcliff. We know he is on the side of humanity and we are with him just as we are with Oliver Twist, and for much the same reasons. But whereas Oliver is presented with a sentimental passivity, which limits our concern, Heathcliff is active and intelligent and able to carry the positive values of human aspiration on his shoulders. He is a conscious rebel. And it is from his association in rebellion with Catherine that the particular quality of their relationship arises. It is the reason why each feels that a betrayal of what binds them together is in some obscure and mysterious way a betrayal of everything, of all that is most valuable in life and death.

Yet Catherine betrays Heathcliff and marries Edgar Linton, kidding herself that she can keep them both, and then discovering that in denying Heathcliff she has chosen death. The conflict here is, quite explicitly, a social one. Thrushcross Grange, embodying as it does the prettier, more comfortable side of bourgeois life, seduces Catherine. She begins to despise Heathcliff's lack of "culture." He has no conversation, he does not brush his hair, he is dirty, whereas Edgar, besides being handsome, "will be rich and I shall like to be the greatest woman of the neighbourhood, and I shall be proud of having such a husband" (ix). And so Heathcliff runs away and Catherine becomes mistress of Thrushcross Grange.

Heathcliff returns, adult and prosperous, and at once the social conflict is re-emphasized. Edgar, understandably, does not want to receive Heathcliff, but Catherine is insistent:

> "I know you didn't like him," she answered, repressing a little the intensity of her delight. "Yet, for my sake, you must be friends now. Shall I tell him to come up?"
> "Here," he said, "into the parlour?"
> "Where else?" she asked.
> He looked vexed, and suggested the kitchen as a more suitable place for him. Mrs. Linton eyed him with a droll expression—half angry, half laughing at his fastidiousness.
> "No," she added after a while; "I cannot sit in the kitchen. Set two tables here, Ellen: one for your master and Miss Isabella, being gentry, the other for Heathcliff and myself, being the lower orders. Will that please you, dear? . . ." (x)

And from the moment of Heathcliff's reappearance Catherine's attempts to reconcile herself to Thrushcross Grange are doomed. In their relationship now there is no tenderness, they trample on each other's nerves, madly try to destroy each other; but, once Heathcliff is near, Catherine can maintain no illusions about the Lintons. The two are united only in their contempt for the values of Thrushcross Grange. "There it is," Catherine taunts Edgar, speaking of her grave, "not among the Lintons, mind, under the chapel roof, but in the open air, with a headstone" (xii). The open air, nature, the moors are contrasted with the world of Thrushcross Grange. And the contempt for the Lintons is *moral* contempt, not a jealous one. When Nelly tells Heathcliff that Catherine is going mad, his comment is:

> "You talk of her mind being unsettled. How the devil could it be otherwise in her frightful isolation? And that insipid paltry creature attending her from *duty* and *humanity*! From *pity* and *charity*! He might as well plant an oak in a flower pot, and expect it to thrive, as imagine he can restore her to vigour in the soil of his shallow cares!" (xiv)

The moral passion here is so intense, so deeply imbedded in the rhythm and imagery of the prose, that it is easy to be swept along without grasping its full and extraordinary significance. Heathcliff at this point has just perpetrated the first of his callous and ghastly acts of revenge, his marriage to Isabella. It is an act so morally repulsive that it is almost inconceivable that we should be able now to take seriously his attack on Edgar Linton, who has, after all, by conventional, respectable standards, done nobody any harm. And yet we *do* take the attack seriously because Emily Brontë makes us. The passion of the passage just quoted has the quality of great poetry. Why?

We continue to sympathize with Heathcliff, even after his marriage with Isabella, because Emily Brontë convinces us that what Heathcliff stands for is morally superior to what the Lintons stand for. This is, it must be insisted, not a case of some mysterious "emotional" power with which Heathcliff is charged. The emotion behind his denunciation of Edgar is *moral* emotion. The words "duty" and "humanity," "pity" and "charity" have precisely the kind of force Blake gives such words in his poetry.[2]

They are used not so much paradoxically as in a sense inverted but more profound than the conventional usage. Heathcliff speaks, apparently paradoxically, of Catherine's "frightful isolation," when to all appearances she is in Thrushcross Grange less isolated, more subject to care and society, than she could possibly be with him. But in truth Heathcliff's assertion is a paradox only to those who do not understand his meaning. What he is asserting with such intense emotional conviction that we, too, are convinced, is that what he stands for, the alternative life *he* has offered Catherine is more natural (the image of the oak enforces this), more social and more moral than the world of Thrushcross Grange. Most of those who criticize Heathcliff adversely (on the grounds that he is unbelievable, or that he is a neurotic creation, or that he is merely the Byronic satan-hero revived) fail to appreciate his significance because they fail to recognize this moral force. And as a rule they fail to recognize the moral force because they are themselves, consciously or not, of the Linton party.

The climax of this inversion by Heathcliff and Catherine of the common standards of bourgeois morality comes at the death of Catherine. To recognize the revolutionary force of this scene one has only to imagine what a different novelist might have made of it.

The stage is all set for a moment of conventional drama. Catherine is dying, Heathcliff appears out of the night. Two possibilities present themselves: either Catherine will at the last reject Heathcliff, the marriage vow will be vindicated and wickedness meet its reward; or true love will triumph and reconciliation proclaim the world well lost. It is hard to imagine that either possibility ever crossed Emily Brontë's mind, for either would destroy the pattern of her book, but her rejection of them is a measure of her moral and artistic power. For instead of its conventional potentialities the scene acquires an astonishing moral power. Heathcliff confronted with the dying Catherine, is ruthless, morally ruthless: instead of easy comfort he offers her a brutal analysis of what she has done.

> "You teach me now how cruel you've been—cruel and false. *Why* did you despise me? *Why* did you betray your own heart Cathy? I have not one word of comfort. You deserve this. You have killed yourself. Yes, you may kiss me, and cry: and wring out my kisses and tears: they'll blight you—they'll damn you. You loved me—then what *right* had you to leave me? What right—answer me—for the poor fancy you felt for Linton? Because misery and degradation, and death, and nothing that God or Satan could inflict would have parted us, *you,* of your own will, did it. I have not broken your heart—*you* have broken it;

and in breaking it you have broken mine. So much the worse that I am strong. Do I want to live? What kind of living will it be when you—oh, God! would *you* like to live with your soul in the grave?" (xv)

It is one of the harshest passages in all literature, but it is also one of the most moving. For the brutality is not neurotic, nor sadistic, nor romantic. The Catherine-Heathcliff relationship, standing as it does for a humanity finer and more morally profound than the standards of the Lintons and Earnshaws has to undergo the kind of examination Heathcliff here brings to it. Anything less, anything which smudged or sweetened the issues involved, would be inadequate, unworthy. Heathcliff knows that nothing can save Catherine from death but that one thing alone can give her peace, a full and utterly honest understanding and acceptance of their relationship and what it implies. There is no hope in comfort or compromise. Any such weakness would debase them both and make a futile waste of their lives and death. For Heathcliff and Catherine, who reject the Lintons' chapel roof and the consolations of Christianity, know, too, that their relationship is more important than death.

In the section of the book that follows Catherine's death Heathcliff continues the revenge he has begun with his marriage to Isabella. It is the most peculiar section of the novel and the most difficult because the quality of Heathcliff's feeling is of a kind most of us find hard to comprehend. All normal and healthy human feeling is rejected. He cries:

"I have no pity! I have no pity! The more the worms writhe, the more I yearn to crush out their entrails! It is a moral teething; and I grind with greater energy, in proportion to the increase of pain." (xiv)

"It is a moral teething"—the phrase is both odd and significant, giving as it does the answer to our temptation to treat this whole section as a delineation of pathological neurosis. Heathcliff becomes a monster: what he does to Isabella, to Hareton, to Cathy, to his son, even to the wretched Hindley, is cruel and inhuman beyond normal thought. He seems concerned to achieve new refinements of horror, new depths of degradation. And we tend to feel, perhaps, unless we read with full care and responsiveness, that Emily Brontë has gone too far, that the revenge (especially the marriage of Cathy and Linton Heathcliff) has o'erflown the measure.

And yet it is only one side of our minds, the conscious, limited side that refers what we are reading to our everyday measures of experience that makes this objection. Another side, which is more completely responding to Emily Brontë's art, is carried on. And the astonishing achievement of this part of the book is that, despite our protests about probability (protests which, incidentally, a good deal of twentieth-century history makes a little complacent), despite everything he does and is, we continue to sympathize with Heathcliff—not, obviously, to admire him or defend him, but to give him our inmost sympathy, to continue in an obscure way to identify ourselves with him *against* the other characters.

The secret of this achievement lies in such a phrase as "it is a moral teething" and in the gradually clarifying pattern of the book. Heathcliff's revenge may involve a pathological condition of hatred, but it is not at bottom merely neurotic. It has a moral force. For what Heathcliff does is to use against his enemies with complete ruthlessness their own weapons, to turn on them (stripped of their romantic veils) their own standards, to beat them at their own game. The weapons he uses against the Earnshaws and Lintons are their own weapons of money and arranged marriages. He gets power over them by the classic methods of the ruling class, expropriation and property deals. He buys out Hindley and reduces him to drunken impotency, he marries Isabella and then organizes the marriage of his son to Catherine Linton, so that the entire property of the two families shall be controlled by himself. He systematically degrades Hareton Earnshaw to servility and illiteracy. "I want the triumph of seeing *my* descendant fairly lord of *their* estates! My child hiring their children to till their father's lands for wages" (xx). (This is a novel which, some critics will tell you, has nothing to do with anything as humdrum as society or life as it is actually lived.) And what particularly tickles Heathcliff's fancy is his achievement of the supreme ruling-class triumph of making Hareton, the boy he degrades, feel a deep and even passionate attachment towards himself.

Heathcliff retains our sympathy throughout this dreadful section of the book because instinctively we recognize a rough moral justice in what he has done to his oppressors and because, though he is inhuman, we understand *why* he is inhuman. Obviously we do not approve of what he does, but we understand it; the deep and complex issues behind his actions are revealed to us. We recognize that the very forces which drove him to rebellion for a higher freedom have themselves entrapped him in their own values and determined the nature of his revenge.

If *Wuthering Heights* were to stop at this point it would still be a great book, but a wholly sombre and depressing one. Man would be revealed as inevitably caught up in the meshes of his own creating; against the tragic horror of Heathcliff's appalling rebellion the limited but complacent world of Thrushcross Grange would seem a tempting haven and the novel would resolve itself into the false antithesis of Thrushcross Grange / Wuthering Heights, just as in *Oliver Twist* the real antithesis becomes sidetracked into the false one of Brownlow / Fagin. But *Wuthering Heights*, a work of supreme and astonishing genius, does not stop here. We have not done with Heathcliff yet.

For at the moment of his horrible triumph a change begins to come over Heathcliff.

"It is a poor conclusion, is it not?" he observed, having brooded a while on the scene he had just witnessed: "an absurd termination to my violent exertions? I get levers and mattocks to demolish the two houses, and train myself to be capable of working like Hercules, and when everything is ready and in my power, I find the will to lift a slate off either roof has vanished! My old enemies have not beaten me; now would be the precise time to revenge myself on their representatives: I could do it, and none could hinder me. But where is the use? I don't care for striking; I can't take the trouble to raise my hand! That sounds as if I had been labouring the whole time only to exhibit a fine trait of magnanimity. It is far from being the case: I have lost the faculty of enjoying their destruction, and I am too idle to destroy for nothing.

"Nelly, there is a strange change approaching: I'm in its shadow at present." (xxxiii)

and he goes on to speak of Cathy and Hareton, who "seemed a personification of my youth, not a human being." "Hareton's aspect was the ghost of my immortal love; of my wild endeavour to hold my right; my degradation, my pride, my happiness and my anguish." When Nelly asks "But what do you mean by a *change,* Mr. Heathcliff?" he can only answer "I shall not know that till it comes," he said, "I'm only half conscious of it now." Once more the stage is set for a familiar scene, the conversion of the wicked who will in the final chapter turn from his wickedness. And once more the conventional must look again.

The change that comes over Heathcliff and the novel and leads us on to the wonderful, quiet, gentle, tentative evocation of nature in the final sentence, is a very subtle one. It has something of the quality of the last two acts of *The Winter's Tale* but is much less complete, less confident. Mr. Klingopulos in his interesting essay on *Wuthering Heights*[3] has commented on the ambiguous nature of this final tranquility. I do not agree with his analysis but he has caught the tone most convincingly. Heathcliff, watching the love of Cathy and Hareton grow, comes to understand something of the failure of his own revenge. As Cathy teaches Hareton to write and stops laughing at his ignorance we too are taken back to the first Catherine.

Cathy and Hareton are not in the novel an easy re-creation of Catherine and Heathcliff; they are, as Mr. Klingopulos remarks, different people, even lesser people, certainly people conceived on a less intense and passionate scale than the older lovers. But they do symbolize the continuity of life and human aspirations, and it is through them that Heathcliff comes to understand the hollowness of his triumph. It is when Hareton, who loves him, comes to Cathy's aid when he strikes her that the full meaning of his own relationship with Catherine comes back to him and he becomes aware that in the feeling between Cathy and Hareton there is something of the same quality. From the moment that Cathy and Hareton are drawn together as rebels the change begins. For now for the first time Heathcliff is confronted not with those who accept the values of Wuthering Heights and Thrushcross Grange but with those who share, however remotely, his own wild endeavours to hold his right.

Heathcliff does not repent. Nelly tries to make him turn to the consolations of religion.

> "You are aware, Mr. Heathcliff," I said, "that from the time you were thirteen
> years old, you have lived a selfish, unchristian life; and probably hardly had a
> Bible in your hands during all that period. You must have forgotten the contents of the Book, and you may not have space to search it now. Could it be
> hurtful to send for some one—some minister of any denomination, it does not
> matter which—to explain it, and show you how very far you have erred from
> its precepts; and how unfit you will be for its heaven, unless a change takes
> place before you die?"
> "I'm rather obliged than angry, Nelly," he said, "for you remind me of the
> manner in which I desire to be buried. It is to be carried to the churchyard in
> the evening. You and Hareton may, if you please, accompany me: and mind,
> particularly, to notice that the sexton obeys my directions concerning the two
> coffins! No minister need come; nor need anything be said over me.—I tell you
> I have nearly attained my heaven, and that of others is altogether unvalued and
> uncoveted by me." (xxxiv)

One sentence here, in its limpid simplicity, especially evokes the state of mind Heathcliff has come to. He speaks of the manner in which he wishes to be buried. "It is to be carried to the churchyard in the evening." The great rage has died in him. He has come to see the pointlessness of his fight to revenge himself on the world of power and property through its own values. Just as Catherine had to face the full moral horror of her betrayal of their love, he must face the full horror of his betrayal too. And once he has faced it he can die, not nobly or triumphantly, but at least as a man, leaving with Cathy and Hareton the possibility of carrying on the struggle he has begun, and in his death he will achieve again human dignity, "to be carried to the churchyard in the evening."

It is this re-achievement of manhood by Heathcliff, an understanding reached with no help from the world he despises, which, together with the developing relationship of Cathy and Hareton and the sense of the continuity of life in nature, gives to the last pages of *Wuthering Heights* a sense of positive and unsentimental hope. The Catherine-Heathcliff relationship has been vindicated. Life will go on and others will rebel against the oppressors. Nothing has been solved but much has been experienced. Lies, complacencies and errors, appalling errors, have been revealed. A veil has been drawn from the conventional face of bourgeois man; he has been revealed, through Heathcliff, without his mask.

Above all, the quality of the feeling that binds Catherine and Heathcliff has been conveyed to us. Their love, which Heathcliff can without idealism call immortal, is something beyond the individualist dream of two soul-mates finding full realization in one another; it is an expression of the necessity of man, if he is to choose life rather than death, to revolt against all that would destroy his inmost needs and aspirations, of the necessity of all human beings to become, through acting together, more fully human. Catherine, responding to this deep human necessity, rebels with Heathcliff but in marrying Edgar (a "good" marriage if ever there was one) betrays her own humanity; Heathcliff, by revenging himself on the tyrants through the adoption of their own standards makes more clear those standards but betrays too his humanity and destroys his relationship with the dead Catherine whose spirit must haunt the moors in terror and dismay.

Only when the new change has come over Heathcliff and he again recognizes through Hareton (and remotely, therefore, through Catherine herself) the full claims of humanity can Catherine be released from torment and their relationship re-established. Death is a matter of little importance in *Wuthering Heights* because the issues the novel is concerned with are greater than the individual life and death. The deaths of Catherine and Heathcliff are indeed a kind of triumph because ultimately each faces death honestly, keeping faith. But there is no suggestion that death itself is a triumph: on the contrary it is life that asserts itself, continues, blossoms again.

Mr. David Wilson in his excellent essay on Emily Brontë[4] to which I am deeply indebted (though I do not agree with all of his interpretation) suggests an identification, not necessarily conscious in Emily Brontë's mind, of Heathcliff with the rebellious working men of the hungry "forties" and of Catherine with that part of the educated class which felt compelled to identify itself with their cause. Such a formulation, suggestive as it is, seems to me to be too far removed from the actual impact of *Wuthering Heights* as a novel, to be satisfactory. But Mr. Wilson has done a valuable service in rescuing *Wuthering Heights* from the transcendentalists and in insisting on the place of Haworth (generally assumed to be a remote country village) in the industrial revolution and its attendant social unrest.[5] The value of his suggestion with regard to Heathcliff and Catherine seems to me in the emphasis it gives to the concrete, local particularity of the book.

It is very necessary to be reminded that just as the values of Wuthering Heights and Thrushcross Grange are not simply the values of *any* tyranny but specifically those of Victorian society, so is the rebellion of Heathcliff a particular rebellion, that of the worker physically and spiritually degraded by the conditions and relationships of this same society. That Heathcliff ceases to be one of the exploited is true, but it is also true that just in so far as he adopts (with a ruthlessness that frightens even the ruling class itself) the standards of the ruling class, so do the human values implicit in his early rebellion and in his love for Catherine vanish. All that is involved in the Catherine-Heathcliff relationship, all that it stands for in human needs and hopes, can be realized only through the active rebellion of the oppressed.

Wuthering Heights then is an expression in the imaginative terms of art of the stresses and tensions and conflicts, personal and spiritual, of nineteenth-century capitalist society. It is a novel without idealism, without false comforts, without any implication that power over their destinies rests outside the struggles and actions of human beings themselves. Its powerful evocation of nature, of moorland and storm, of the stars and the seasons is an essential part of its revelation of the very movement of life itself. The men and women of *Wuthering Heights* are not the prisoners of nature; they live in the world and strive to change it, sometimes successfully, always painfully, with almost infinite difficulty and error.

This unending struggle, of which the struggle to advance from class society to the higher humanity of a classless world is but an episode, is conveyed to us in *Wuthering Heights* precisely because the novel is conceived in actual, concrete, particular terms, because the quality of oppression revealed in the novel is not abstract but concrete, not vague but particular. And that is why Emily Brontë's novel is at the same time a statement about the life she knew, the life of Victorian England, and a statement about life as such. Virginia Woolf, writing about it, said:

> That gigantic ambition is to be felt throughout the novel, a struggle half thwarted but of superb conviction, to say something through the mouths of characters which is not merely "I love" or "I hate" but "we, the whole human race" and "You; the eternal powers . . ." the sentence remains unfinished.[6]

I do not think it remains unfinished.

Notes

1.   A simple, though not infallible, indication of the kind of novel one is dealing with is given by the naming of characters. In allegory and the novel of "humours" names always denote character—e.g., Faithful and Squire Allworthy. In totally non-symbolic novelists like Jane Austen the names are quite without significance: Emma Woodhouse might equally well be called Anne Elliot. In novels which have a certain symbolic quality the names of characters generally have a peculiar rightness of their own: Heathcliff, Noah Claypole, Henry James's characters.

2.   E.g. Pity would be no more

> If we did not make somebody Poor;
> And Mercy no more could be
> If all were as happy as we
> or
> Was Jesus humble? or did he
> Give any proofs of Humility.

3.   G. Klingopulos, "The Novel as a Dramatic Poem" (II), *Wuthering Heights, Scrutiny* 14 (1946-7): 69-86.

4.   D. Wilson, "Emily Brontë, First of the Moderns," *Modern Quarterly Miscellany* 1 (1947): 94-115.

5.   One of the most interesting exhibits in the Haworth museum today is a proclamation of the Queen ordering the Riot Act against the rebellious workers of the West Riding.

6.   V. Woolf, *The Common Reader,* first series (London: The Hogarth Press, 1925), 202.

WUTHERING HEIGHTS: CRITICISM 1950–1975

◆

Introduction

THOMAS JOHN WINNIFRITH

We have shown how in the first half of the twentieth century, *Wuthering Heights* lost its reputation as a brutal, incoherent book, with the power of its wild, passionate romanticism to commend it, and instead was shown to be a work of great craft, a parcel neatly tied up with no loose ends showing. All the essays in the last section adopt this position, although they show a certain amount of disagreement as to what was in the parcel. Melvin Watson's two articles, one cited, one quoted, may be taken as typical of mid-century opinion. In his summary of previous criticism, he is rightly contemptuous of romantic biographical amateurs: in his article on the centrality of Heathcliff, he tries to find the central meaning of *Wuthering Heights,* and he finds it in a different place from David Cecil.

Watson published his articles in *Nineteenth Century Fiction,* previously known as *The Trollopian.* This periodical published many articles on *Wuthering Heights,* most of them emerging from what is still called the New Criticism, an approach that was contemptuous of biography. Watson's hostility to silly biographical approaches and even John Mathison's hostility to Nelly Dean, a figure much revered by local admirers of Brontë in Yorkshire, may seem to have emanated from the New Criticism, although in fact both their articles included in this selection are hardly typical of the New Critics, many of whom are cited in Mathison's omitted first footnote. What the new critics were often trying to do was to seize upon a few remaining loose ends in *Wuthering Heights* and tie them together more fiercely. What was the meaning of Lockwood's dream? Why did Mr. Earnshaw adopt Heathcliff? Very often the explanation offered was a sexual one. Heathcliff was the illegitimate son of Earnshaw, and Lockwood's harshness to the waif through the window seemed after Freud to have sexual undertones. These theories, though clearly interesting and obviously at variance with any theories interested in the life of Brontë (which are unlikely to discuss illegitimacy and Freudian symbols at Haworth Parsonage), tend to hinder rather than help the average Brontë student. They focus attention on small if important parts of a complicated whole and thus distort our appreciation of this whole.

In looking at other representative criticism of the third quarter of this century, I have chosen five writers who try to reveal what is in the parcel through the process of undoing a few knots. Three of the five writers wrote books, not articles, on *Wuthering Heights;* the two exceptions are Mathison and Miriam Allott, but Mathison's articles were collected into a book after his death, and Allott is a prodigious Brontë anthologist. Matthew Arnold saw the dangers of *Wuthering Heights* as a work like *King Lear,* difficult to see steadily and whole, impossible to appreciate in its entirety, a huge rugged mountain of a work to which various narrow paths give partial access. The New Critics began to climb these paths.

Heroically, if not wholly successfully, the five essays face the perilous ascent to the summit. All five interestingly enough tend to concentrate on one or more of the interesting bifurcations in *Wuthering Heights,* a work like *Oedipus Rex,* full of literal and metaphorical crossroads. *Wuthering Heights* has, as critics of previous generations have established, a careful interplay between two houses, two narrators, two generations, and two attitudes to our appreciation of Heathcliff. Critics between 1950 and 1975 understood the difficulty of trying to establish one central meaning to the novel, in the process disagreeing with previous writers like Cecil and articles in *Nineteenth Century Fiction.* Mathison asks why it is that we like Nelly Dean but do not trust her, a question answered in rather a different way by an article, both famous and infamous, entitled "The Villain of *Wuthering Heights,*" by James Hafley, published in *Nineteenth Century Fiction* 13 (1958): 199–215. Hafley's article is regularly pilloried by Yorkshire admirers of Brontë, dedicated to the biographical approach, who see Nelly Dean as she sees herself, as a model of common sense; he is of course far too definitive in his approach. Allott disagrees with Cecil, and is perhaps surprisingly sympathetic to the younger generation. The intriguing question mark in her title leaves us, like Lockwood, a little baffled about the end of the novel. Queenie Leavis is on the side of Terry Eagleton about preferring Wuthering Heights to Thrushcross Grange, yet she moves the debate against Heathcliff by seeing the novel from the elder Catherine's point of view, and for this reason, she has been hailed as a proto-feminist. Frank Kermode, by his brilliant analysis of Lockwood's first night at Wuthering Heights, exposes the essential ambiguities and various meanings of *Wuthering Heights* but restores Heathcliff to his central position. Terry Eagleton, writing well before he had become a leading luminary of literary theory, is surprisingly keen on the physical and historical detail of *Wuthering Heights* and is again on Heathcliff's side, although he seems to ignore a little victory for Heathcliff when he says that Cathy in her bourgeois way orders Hareton to dig up the black currants and replace them with flowers but overlooks the fact that Heathcliff orders the black currants to be restored.

Interestingly, both Allott in the second edition of her critical anthology and Eagleton in the second edition of *Myths of Power* are on record as admitting that their initial approach to *Wuthering Heights* did not take enough factors into consideration. Eagleton apologizes for not considering psychological and feminist approaches, which will be discussed in the next section. All the critics of this section are aware that there are many sides to *Wuthering Heights,* and all interestingly try to relate two or more of the bifurcations we have previously noted. Beginners approaching *Wuthering Heights* could do worse than concentrate on this generation of Brontë criticism, standing midway between the simplistic approach of the first hundred years and the complex articles that have emerged in the last twenty years.

Nelly Dean and the Power of *Wuthering Heights*

JOHN MATHISON*

I

The memorable quality of *Wuthering Heights,* its power, has often been mentioned; numerous elements of the work have been considered the source of this power. No one element can be expected to account completely for it, and no combination of causes is likely to produce an answer that is fully satisfying. But examinations of the various elements in the structure of the novel have suggested clear connections between method and results, between technique and meaning.

In this essay I am attempting a partial explanation of the power of the book through a detailed examination not of the general question of the use of a narrator but specifically of the fully developed character of Nelly Dean. Nelly Dean is not a mere technical device: we cannot forget as the story progresses that we are hearing it from her rather than from the author. She is a minute interpreter. She tells us what events mean, what is right or wrong, what is praiseworthy or despicable or unforgivable behaviour. Her morality is a result of her training, experiences, and reading, combined with her native temperament. The reader's degree of acceptance of her explanations and moral judgments determines his understanding of the meaning of the story and its power over him.

Nelly is an admirable woman whose point of view, I believe, the reader must reject. She is good-natured, warmhearted, wholesome, practical, and physically healthy. Her interpretation of her reading and her experiences, her feelings on various occasions, are, to a large extent, the consequence of her physical health. When the reader refuses to accept her view of things, which he continually does and must do, he is forced to feel the inadequacy of the normal, healthy, hearty, good-natured person's understanding of life and human nature. He is consequently forced into an active participation in the book. He cannot sit back and accept what is given him as the explanation of the actions of the characters. He must continually provide his own version.

*Reprinted from *Nineteenth Century Fiction* 11 (1956): 106–29.

For the reader to disagree with Nelly would be easy, if Nelly were not admirable. But to prevent the reader's turning Nelly into a cliché of simple and narrow piety, Emily Brontë has provided Joseph. He makes clear through his actions and his explicit statements to Nelly that she is not conventionally or rigidly pious. Her condemnations and approvals do not result from an unintelligent or fanatical acceptance of rigid rules of conduct. Joseph is sure she is destined for hell because of her warmth and human kindness, and because of her enjoyment of such pleasures as folk song and dancing. Joseph's strictures intensify the reader's favourable impressions of Nelly, the favourable impressions that make his rejection of her views more intense and significant.

And enough other servants are introduced to increase still further our realization of Nelly's superiority, intellectual and moral. Her pipe-smoking successor at the Grange is apparently what might be expected of a servant. One need not more than mention Zillah, who has some mental alertness, to be made strongly aware of Nelly's superiority.

But more strongly than her superiority is shown by contrast with Joseph, with Zillah, or with the servant Lockwood finds at the Grange on his return, it is shown by the affection of the major characters, including Heathcliff, for her, as seen not in their words but in their behaviour to her. And of course there is her narrative, full as it is of her ideas. In spite of all her fine qualities, nevertheless, she fails to understand the other characters and, more important, fails in her behaviour in important crises of the action. From the emphasis on her admirable qualities, and from her final inadequacy, the reader is led to see that the insight of the normal, wholesome person cannot penetrate into all feelings justly: the reader becomes the active advocate of the extremes of passion of Cathy and Heathcliff, troublesome as they are to a peaceful, domestic routine.

Emily Brontë could not have succeeded in a direct attempt to demand our sympathy for or understanding of two such characters as Heathcliff and Cathy. Approached directly, the reader would not have to exercise his own perceptions; he would remain passive. Some readers might say that such violent behaviour is exciting enough to read about in romantic novels, but that in real life it would not do to encourage such people as Cathy and Heathcliff. To other readers, the novel might have appeared merely as a tremendous protest against conventional standards, but the interest in it would be merely biographical, sociological, or psychological.

By indirection, Emily Brontë has produced not a personal protest but a work of art. The reader's reaction is not, of course, the precise opposite of any of those mentioned above, not a simple stamp of approval bestowed on Heathcliff and Cathy, but a realization that the "normal" person is often incapable of feeling for the tortured, emotionally distraught person, and that the latter's tortured failure to understand himself and the sources of his misery partly results from the failure of imagination of the majority. The question is not whether Heathcliff and Cathy are good or bad. They are the result of psychological isolation and misunderstanding working on a particular native temperament, and the "good" are as much the doers of the damage as the "bad," either Hindley or Joseph.

The better we come to know Nelly, the more we recognize her lack of understanding of the principals. To know her we need to watch her character as it is revealed through her opinions, and even more, through her reports of her own actions. It is this person, whom we come to know well, whose judgments we finally interpret. Not abstract judgments of a merely nominal narrator, they are the particular limited judgments of a person of a distinct emotional and intellectual viewpoint. Knowing the judge, or interpreter, knowing the giver of advice as well as the advice given, we realize the inadequacy of the interpretation, the advice, and the judgments; we become as we read active interpreters, protesters, explicators, and possibly judges.

II

Nelly's physical vigour is emphatically part of her character. Impressing us generally from her account of her actions throughout the novel, her abundant good health is specifically alluded to as well. Her one illness, a bad cold after she had been obliged to sit for a long while in "soaked shoes and stockings," was a great surprise to her; up to the time of the narrative it is the only indisposition in her life that she can recall. By this accident, which most would accept as in the course of things, her spirits were depressed: "It is wearisome, to a stirring active body—but few have slighter reasons for complaint than I had" (xxiii). Elsewhere, responding to the terrors of Cathy, who fears that everyone she knows may die and leave her alone, Nelly confidently boasts: ". . . I am strong, and hardly forty-five. My mother lived till eighty, a canty dame to the last" (xxii). Numerous examples of illness, decline, wasting away, and death in her experience make little impression on her, who feels herself so strong. Although she once remarks "I am stout, and soon put out of breath" (xxvii), this reference confirms rather than contradicts her feeling of "ruddy" health; the picture is that of the Shepherd's wife in *The Winter's Tale*:

> when my old wife liv'd, upon
> This day she was both pantler, butler, cook;
> Both dame and servant; welcom'd all, serv'd all,
> Would sing her song and dance her turn; now here,
> At upper end o' the table, now i' the middle;
> On his shoulder, and his; her face o' fire
> With labour and the thing she took to quench it . . .
>
> (IV, iii, 55–61)

Her own health makes her a poor sympathizer with the illnesses of others; she tends to view even those illnesses in the novel which end in death as partly wilful, partly acting. The physique and the temperament which goes with it of the weak or sick she cannot really believe in. An early example is her view of Hindley's consumptive wife; throughout the book further examples abound, to the last case of the frail son of Isabella whom she finds revolting largely because he will not exert himself and be vigorous. But to resume, of Hindley's wife, who had expressed fear of dying, she says:

> I imagined her as little likely to die as myself. She was rather thin, but young, and fresh complexioned, and her eyes sparkled as bright as diamonds. I did remark, to be sure, that mounting the stairs made her breathe very quick, that the least sudden noise set her all in a quiver, and that she coughed troublesomely sometimes: but, I knew nothing of what these symptoms portended, and had no impulse to sympathize with her. We don't in general take to foreigners here, Mr Lockwood, unless they take to us first. (vi)

Since Nelly regards the idea of her own death as absurd, she sees no reason that Hindley's wife should be entitled to a fear of death. Such nonsense is just what one expects of foreigners (from a different county of England). This passage, very early in the novel, makes the reader aware of Nelly's fallibility of judgment combined with her satisfaction with her own attitudes. It conditions our expectations regarding her probable actions in later episodes, and helps us know her and hence discount her judgments and substitute our own. These early suspicions are confirmed when Cathy becomes ill:

> . . . Mr. Kenneth, as soon as he saw her, pronounced her dangerously ill; she had a fever.
> He bled her, and he told her to let her live on whey, and water gruel; and take care she did not throw herself down stairs, or out of the window; and then he left. . . .
> Though I cannot say I made a gentle nurse, and Joseph and the master were no better; and though our patient was as wearisome and headstrong as a patient could be, she weathered it through. (ix)

Why should Cathy have chosen to come down with a fever, become dangerously delirious, and consequently be "wearisome" to healthy, reasonable people?

If we knew less of Nelly we might be able to sympathize with her jogging of Lockwood during his illness: " 'You shouldn't lie till ten. There's the very prime of the morning gone long before that time. A person who has not done one half his day's work by ten o'clock, runs a chance of leaving the other half undone' " (vii). As it is, however, we know her advice is little more than justification of her own natural urges to be "busy and stirring" always; it is her failure to grasp the possibility of people's being less vigorous than herself.

Most serious is her deficiency in Cathy's later illness and delirium, fore-shadowed by the illness already mentioned. Inevitably, she views it as an act:

> "Catherine ill?" he [Edgar Linton] said, hastening to us. "Shut the window, Ellen! Catherine! why . . ."
>
> He was silent; the haggardness of Mrs. Linton's appearance smote him speechless, and he could only glance from her to me in horrified astonishment.
>
> "She's been fretting here," I continued, "and eating scarcely anything, and never complaining, she would admit none of us till this evening, and so we couldn't inform you of her state, as we were not aware of it ourselves, *but it is nothing*" [italics mine]. (xii)

One might suppose Ellen's "it is nothing" were a well-meant if unsuc-cessful effort to cheer Edgar, if the scene ended at this point, and if we had not begun to know Nelly rather well, but as it continues, it becomes clear that she really considers the illness both wilful and minor:

> "Her mind wanders, sir," I interposed. "She has been talking nonsense the whole evening; but let her have quiet and proper attendance, and she'll rally. Hereafter, we must be cautious how we vex her."
>
> "I desire no further advice from you," answered Mr. Linton. "You knew your mistress's nature, and you encouraged me to harass her. And not to give me one hint of how she has been these three days! It was heartless! Months of sick-ness could not cause such a change!"
>
> I began to defend myself, thinking it too bad to be blamed for another's wicked waywardness! (xii)

As Edgar Linton says, Nelly had had a lifetime of experience with Cathy, but the last quoted sentence alone makes clear the triumph of constitution and temperament over experience. Nelly never will grasp the less wholesome, physically or emotionally.

It may need to be said that objectively it would be possible for the reader to find Cathy a difficult person. But the healthy Nelly's complacent self-justi-fication and lack of surmise of stronger passions and more highly strung tem-peraments, make the reader Cathy's advocate in the context, and while he reads they lower his enthusiasm for the vigorously normal and, it appears, consequently obtuse.

Nelly's health is only one, though a significant, feature of the total char-acter. Her "philosophy" on all sorts of matters is presented in detail. It is pri-marily a matter of avoiding any really strong passions, but continually encouraging a good deal of "natural affection." Children must "take to her." On a visit to the Heights she encounters the five-year-old Hareton near the building, and he begins to throw stones at her, and curses, distorting "his baby features into a shocking expression of malignity." Her reaction is unper-ceptively conventional.

You may be certain this grieved, more than angered me. Fit to cry, I took an orange from my pocket, and offered it to propitiate him.

He hesitated, and then snatched it from my hold, as if he fancied I only intended to tempt and disappoint him. (xi)

Here, too, she is clearly more concerned with her picture of herself as affectionately motherly, than with understanding.

She believes in forgiving one's enemies, but she herself, not having to struggle hard in this respect, does not realize that for others placid domestic normality may not be the strongest drive. After a serious crisis in which Hindley had confined Heathcliff (during childhood) fasting in the garret for more than twenty-four hours, she broke Hindley's commands by letting him into the kitchen to feed him: "he was sick and could eat little . . ."; he remained "wrapt in dumb meditation."

On my inquiring the subject of his thoughts, he answered gravely—

"I'm trying to settle how I shall pay Hindley back. I don't care how long I wait, if I can only do it, at last. I hope he will not die before I do!"

"For shame, Heathcliff!" said I. "It is for God to punish wicked people; we should learn to forgive."

"No, God won't have the satisfaction that I shall," he returned. "I only wish I knew the best way! Let me alone, and I'll plan it out: while I'm thinking of that, I don't feel pain."

But, Mr. Lockwood, I forget these tales cannot divert you. I'm annoyed how I should dream of chattering on at such a rate . . . I could have told Heathcliff's history, all that you need hear, in half a dozen words. (vi)

Nelly is sorry for Heathcliff and sneaks him some supper. As usual she compromises, helping Heathcliff a little and disobeying Hindley a little. Perhaps that is what was possible. But in her role as narrator she looks back upon the event, having seen the whole history of the subsequent years, and takes it in stride, still blaming Heathcliff conventionally for his lapses, still blaming others moderately, and still keeping her picture of herself as normally affectionate and good. Heathcliff should have listened to her and forgiven his enemies.

She allows, of course, for normal selfishness. Since the marriage of Cathy to Edgar Linton does take place, she hopefully finds signs that there is a "deep and growing happiness" in their union. At least she is able to be a bustling housekeeper; there are no domestic storms. But this happy period ended. "Well, we *must* be for ourselves in the long run; the mild and generous are only more justly selfish than the domineering—and it ended when circumstances caused each to feel that the one's interest was not the chief consideration in the other's thoughts" (x). To her this situation is normal. No allowance is made for the enduring passion of Cathy and Heathcliff. No doubt Cathy's marriage would have appeared more successful had she forgotten Heathcliff, but it is too easy for Nelly to take this stand for the reader to go along with her. He begins to sympathize with the course that Cathy and Heathcliff did take.

Later when the reader might have been exasperated with a tantrum of Cathy's, Nelly's stolidity makes him take Cathy's part against the printed interpretation:

> The stolidity with which I received these instructions was, no doubt, rather exasperating; for they were delivered in perfect sincerity; but I believed a person who could plan the turning of her fits of passion to account, beforehand, might, by exerting her will, manage to control herself tolerably even while under their influence; and I did not wish to "frighten" her husband, as she said, and multiply his annoyances for the purpose of serving her selfishness. (xi)

For Nelly to control "fits of passion" and "manage to control herself while under their influence" have never required a struggle. She is too ruddy, healthy, physically busy and emotionally placid to know what such a struggle would be. When a few pages later she confidently announces that "the Grange had but one sensible soul in its walls, and that lodged in my body" (xii) we agree, but the value we place on being "sensible" is far lower than hers.

Nelly is as much opposed to cold lack of visible affection as to violent passion. Normally approving of Edgar Linton, she fails to understand the feeling behind his apparent coldness and is quite ready to condemn him in his treatment of Isabella:

> "And you won't write her a little note, sir?" I asked imploringly.
> "No," he answered. "It is needless. My communication with Heathcliff's family shall be as sparing as his with mine. It shall not exist!"
> Mr. Edgar's coldness depressed me exceedingly; and all the way from the Grange, I puzzled my brains how to put more heart into what he said, when I repeated it; and how to soften his refusal of even a few lines to console Isabella. (xiv)

She is "depressed" by "coldness," although all she wants from Edgar is a few futilely affectionate, meaningless, brotherly words not calculated to achieve any helpful result. That there is more "heart" in his coldness than in her superficiality does not occur to her. To make things well, and it really seems so to those like her, she will soften his refusal, in some compromising way, and thus receive the congratulations of her own conscience. On arriving at the Heights a few minutes later, she is actually able to say, "There never was such a dreary, dismal scene as the *formerly cheerful* house presented" [italics mine] (xiv).

The reader's first view of the house had been Lockwood's on his first visit, the history Nelly has told started with the discord resulting from the

introduction into the house of the orphan Heathcliff (and the reactions to this
say little enough in favour of the Earnshaws), and he has subsequently been
concerned with Heathcliff, Cathy, and their agonized growing up in the
house, not to mention Hindley, Joseph, and Hindley's consumptive wife. The
reader, consequently, cannot help placing a low value on the judgment of the
wholesome Nelly, and he reassesses her narrative with quite a different
emphasis.

Edgar, except for his coldness to Isabella, is admired by Nelly. No
unleashed and distressing passions are usually his, but a sensible and quiet
affection, comforting to the housekeeper. Referring to Edgar's mourning for
his deceased wife, Nelly approvingly says: "But he was too good to be thoroughly unhappy long. *He* didn't pray for Catherine's soul to haunt him: Time
brought resignation, and a melancholy sweeter than common joy. He recalled
her memory with ardent, tender love, and hopeful aspiring to the better
world, where, he doubted not, she was gone" (xvii). How much of this is
Nelly's attribution and how much was Edgar's real state remain doubtful;
surely the part about "melancholy sweeter than common joy" is something
she picked up from her boasted reading in the Linton library, but much is her
natural wholesomely sentimental feeling about the decorous way for a
bereaved husband to act. Possibly, too, Emily Brontë is indicating a tendency
in Nelly to show off her elegance to impress Lockwood, a gentleman.

Of those aspects of experience which threaten to upset her outlook she
forbids discussion, admitting her uneasiness, but willing to push aside the difficulty. Cathy, wishing to reveal a seriously troubling dream to Nelly, is
abruptly halted: "'Oh! don't, Miss Catherine!' I cried. 'We're dismal enough
without conjuring up ghosts and visions to perplex us. Come, come, be merry,
and like yourself! Look at little Hareton—*he's* dreaming nothing dreary. How
sweetly he smiles in his sleep!'" (ix). Apart from the unwillingness to hear the
dream, for Nelly to characterize Cathy as "merry, and like yourself" is a
stretch in making the desired the actual at any time during Cathy's adolescence, and her preference for babies is again apparent. Cathy replies: "'Yes;
and how sweetly his father curses in his solitude! You remember him, I dare
say, when he was just such another as that chubby thing—nearly as young
and innocent.'" Nelly interrupted her story to explain the situation to Lockwood:

> I was superstitious about dreams then, and am still; and Catherine had an
> unusual gloom in her aspect, that made me dread something from which I
> might shape a prophecy, and foresee a dreadful catastrophe.
> She was vexed, but she did not proceed. Apparently taking up another sub-
> ject, she recommenced in a short time.
> "If I were in heaven, Nelly, I should be extremely miserable."
> "Because you are not fit to go there," I answered. "All sinners would be mis-
> erable in heaven."

"But it is not for that. I dreamt, once, that I was there."
"I tell you I won't hearken to your dreams, Miss Catherine! I'll go to bed," I interrupted again. (ix)

Little help can the distracted girl get from the only one from whom she can even try to get it. Nothing must interfere with Nelly's determination to impose her own meaning on events, and that meaning must be ordinary and cheerful. But Cathy and Heathcliff persist in a fatal tendency to try to confide in Nelly. Even at the end of his life Heathcliff confesses to her, although, dreading to hear anything unsettlingly appalling, she half refuses to listen.

The customary always triumphs with Nelly. Admirable feelings in Heathcliff, if strange or uncustomary, are shut out of her mind. Far from admirable attitudes in Edgar are approved without question, if they would be shared by most normal people in his station. When Isabella is attracted to Heathcliff, Nelly observes it merely as a new trouble to Edgar: "Leaving aside the degradation of an alliance with a nameless man, and the possible fact that his property, in default of heirs male, might pass into such a one's power, he had sense to comprehend Heathcliff's disposition . . ." (x). No reader can approve such merely conventional objections, introduced without a qualm. Such attitudes had been responsible for much of the maiming of Heathcliff already. And Heathcliff is here blamed, as often, merely for not knowing his place.

Nelly is similarly imperceptive when Isabella, who has really suffered from Heathcliff, reviles him. Nelly's attempt is simply to "hush" her railings. To Isabella's "would that he could be blotted out of creation, and out of my memory!" Nelly replies, "Hush, hush! He's a human being . . . Be more charitable; there are worse men than he is yet!" (xvii). What appears is her hatred of extremes; she does not want even Heathcliff to be unique, but merely a normally bad man, one of the well-known class of sinners. What she advocates is some conventional verbal charity and to forget, to proceed as if nothing had happened.

Nelly is a woman whom everyone in her circle, employers, the children of employers, the other servants in the neighbourhood, the people of Gimmerton, and Lockwood have recognized as superior, and admirable. How superior to Joseph, Zillah, and to various other characters the reader readily perceives. To insist that she should have shown a full understanding of Cathy and Heathcliff would be to show a lack of understanding of what is possible or probable. From day to day she did her best, with regard to her own welfare and peace of comfort; few would have done better.

None the less, her character, a representation of the normal at its best, is inadequate to the situation. As will be shown, failing to understand them, she advises them poorly, and her actions in relation to them are also harmful. Emily Brontë does not plead for them. She lets us see them as they were seen and dealt with by a good woman. The reader must progressively lower his estimate of the value of the normal and healthy, develop a comprehension of and sympathy for genuine emotions however extreme and destructive, and in so doing become an active interpreter of the meaning of the novel. The reader's active involvement and sympathy with the conventionally despicable makes the power of the book.

III

Resulting from qualities in themselves admirable, Nelly's judgments based on her understanding of events and other people result in advice and action which are parts of the total harm done to Cathy and Heathcliff. Describing the first days of Heathcliff in the Earnshaw household, she makes it apparent to the reader that her presence there will do nothing to better the little Heathcliff's situation. Speaking of the child's silent endurance of Hindley's torments, she says:

> This endurance made old Earnshaw furious when he discovered his son perse-cuting the poor, fatherless child, as he called him. He took to Heathcliff strangely believing all he said (for that matter, he said precious little, and gen-erally the truth), and petting him up far above Cathy, who was too mischievous and wayward for a favourite.
>
> So, from the very beginning, he bred bad feeling in the house . . . (iv)

Heathcliff is, at this early point in the story, obviously blameless, yet Nelly sides with the persecutors, concerned with the trouble caused by an unusual, and hence somehow wrong situation. Looking back through the years, she can only suppose that all would have been well had Mr. Earnshaw never had so freakish a notion as to introduce a waif into the neighbourhood, not that the waif become warped through continued mistreatment and helpless suffer-ing. The parenthetical words, whose significance she disregards, reveal the almost inevitable obtuseness of interpretation by a person of her type.

One page further on, another anecdote makes a point opposite from what Nelly intends it to. Heathcliff's colt (a gift from old Earnshaw) becoming lame, the boy tries to exchange it for Hindley's sound one. " 'You must exchange horses with me; I don't like mine, and if you won't I shall tell your father of the three thrashings you've given me this week, and show him my arm, which is black to the shoulder' ". The result is that Hindley "cuffs his ears," then threatens him with an iron weight, which he finally hurls at him, hitting him in the chest. Nelly prevents Heathcliff from revealing this blow to old Earnshaw, and Hindley suddenly says: " 'Take my colt, gipsy, then! . . . And I pray that he may break your neck; take him, and be damned, you beg-garly interloper! and wheedle my father out of all he has, only afterwards show him what you are, imp of Satan—and take that, I hope he'll kick out your brains!' " Of the words or blows, which were more damaging to young Heathcliff may be debated, but Nelly's actively taking the part of Hindley certainly contributes to the harm. And beyond that, she teaches Heathcliff to lie about the episode; "I persuaded him easily to let me lay the blame of his bruises on the horse; he minded little what tale was told since he had what he wanted. He complained so seldom, indeed of such stirs as these, that I really thought him not vindictive—I was deceived, completely, as you will hear." From the beginning, Nelly deals with Heathcliff through a policy of expediency, preserving outward tranquility, preventing "stirs" in the family. Later when events demand even more of her, we recollect her habitual patterns of behaviour, and know she will continue to fail, with increasingly serious results.

After old Earnshaw's death when Hindley becames "Master," Nelly is not much troubled by the resulting deliberate degradation of Heathcliff. "He bore his degradation pretty well at first, because Cathy taught him what she learnt, and worked or played with him in the fields. They both promised fair to grow up as rude as savages . . ." (v). More surprising is her assumption that the fanatical Joseph's discipline would have been successful unless there was something basically wrong with Heathcliff and Cathy: "The curate might set as many chapters as he pleased for Catherine to get by heart, and Joseph might thrash Heathcliff till his arm ached; they forgot everything the minute they were together again, at least the minute they had contrived some naughty plan of revenge . . ." (vi). Another of her methods of helping Heathcliff is seen slightly later in a reproof: " 'You are incurable, Heathcliff, and Mr. Hindley will have to proceed to extremities, see if he won't' " (vi).

Dramatically, with no recourse to the essay technique of Fielding as he restores the wayward Tom Jones to the favour of the reader, the reader's sympathies are being directed powerfully towards Heathcliff, and Cathy. More powerfully, perhaps, because unless he is making a deliberate analysis of the book he does not feel his sympathies being directed by a device of the author. Fielding's reader, directly exhorted, may argue back; Emily Brontë's reader reacts spontaneously in favour of Heathcliff.

The most Nelly can admit is that Hindley was a bad "example" for Heathcliff. This way of going to ruin—evil companions showing the way to vice—is familiar, and she makes allowance for Heathcliff in this way. It is a qualified allowance, for Heathcliff, she says, seemed "possessed of something diabolical at that period" (viii). Her evidence is that Heathcliff rejoiced to see Hindley degrade himself. But the portrait of Heathcliff is far from the depravity suggested in miscellaneous remarks:

In the first place, he had, by that time, lost the benefit of his early education: continual hard work, begun soon and concluded late, had extinguished any curiosity he once possessed in pursuit of knowledge, and any love for books or learning. His childhood's sense of superiority, instilled into him by the favours of old Mr. Earnshaw, was faded away. He struggled long to keep up an equality with Catherine in her studies, and yielded with poignant though silent regret: but he yielded completely; and there was no prevailing on him to take a step in the way of moving upward, when he found he must, necessarily, sink beneath his former level. (viii)

It is hard to see how Nelly could account for Heathcliff's behaviour at the same time both by diabolical possession and as she does here, but her ability to describe accurately, and yet disregard the facts in favour of explanation by a conventional formula, is a major feature of her character and her inadequacy as a counsellor.

Usually, of course, Cathy and Heathcliff are being simultaneously influenced. When Cathy returns from her stay at Thrushcross Grange, Nelly is deceived by the surface improvement in her manners (vii). But Heathcliff's consequent desire for reform and self-improvement gets discouragingly brisk treatment:

> "Nelly, make me decent, I'm going to be good."
> "High time, Heathcliff," I said; "you have grieved Catherine; she's sorry she ever came home, I dare say! It looks as if you envied her, because she is more thought of than you". (vii)

Nelly, complacently quoting herself in such passages, still realizes no shortcomings in herself (her questions to Lockwood on moral problems from time to time never touch such failings). Had Heathcliff told his story, excusing all his actions through harsh portraits of these adults, the effect would be reversed: the reader would excuse the adults and blame Heathcliff, saying that they were no worse than most normal conventional people, and that others have survived better in worse circumstances.

Nelly's major failure (though few could have done better) is in the decisive episode during which Cathy reveals her intention of marrying Linton, despite her lack of love for him, and her intense love for, her identity with, Heathcliff. Nelly dissembles her knowledge of Heathcliff's presence, but worse, her knowledge of his departure at the worst possible moment: "Having noticed a slight movement, I turned my head, and saw him rise from the bench, and steal out, noiselessly. He had listened till he heard Catherine say it would degrade her to marry him, and then he stayed to hear no farther" (ix). And when Catherine wants to be assured that Heathcliff, unlike herself, does not know what deep love is, Nelly answers equivocally, " 'I see no reason that he should not know, as well as you . . . and if *you* are his choice, he'll be the most unfortunate creature that ever was born!' " (*ibid.*), automatically putting Cathy in the wrong, getting herself over a difficult moment. What this moment has done is let Heathcliff overhear and leave, and the plans for marriage to Edgar go forward; Nelly has not let Cathy know that Heathcliff has heard her say that it would degrade her to marry him, but has not heard her say the words describing her real feelings, leading up to "I am Heathcliff." Nelly's view of the scene, in which her own inconvenience is more important than either Heathcliff's or Cathy's sufferings, is summarized by herself at the conclusion of Cathy's tremendous confession: "She paused, and hid her face in the folds of my gown; but I jerked it forcibly away. I was out of patience with her folly!" (ix).

The reader, prepared by earlier passages in which Nelly has shown, on lesser occasions, her inevitable adherence to expediency or her own comfort, is not surprised by the major failure here: moral habits are not likely to be overcome in a crisis where there is little time for struggle and deliberation. Heathcliff enters and leaves while Cathy is talking and Nelly cannot but act from habit, on the spur of the moment, but the defects revealed in this scene are her customary ones. Here, perhaps more than anywhere, the reader is sharply aware not only of her failure as an interpreter of the past, but more important, of her failure as a counsellor at the time of the action. Both failures cooperate to affect the reader and produce the power of the scene.

The following page, on which Nelly admits that Heathcliff had heard much, confirms the disaster: Cathy searches for Heathcliff during the storm, and stays up all night in wet clothes while Nelly, at one here with Joseph, is chiefly concerned about the interruption in the household routine, even after Heathcliff is clearly gone and Cathy has come down with a serious illness. This whole passage, too well remembered to need detailed citation, is the turning-point. We see it as Nelly tells it. Our necessity of disagreeing completely with the narrator's version, made very easy owing to the great detail, gives our total sympathy to Cathy and Heathcliff. We give, perhaps, more than they deserve; we become unduly severe towards Nelly, but to make us feel powerfully the inadequacy of the "steady reasonable kind of body," Emily Brontë's technique could not be improved. Neither a direct plea nor a narrator who was a moralizing, narrow-minded, hypocritically pious guardian could have placed us so completely with Heathcliff and Cathy. It needs above all Nelly's admirable qualities including particularly the affection she arouses in both Cathy and Heathcliff, and the awareness that her failure is the result of them. Heathcliff and Cathy would have fared better with worse parental guidance. The failure of the ordinarily good being made apparent, the reader, attempting to supply the fuller comprehension, becomes fully involved in the novel.

To emphasize the significance of the whole scene, Emily Brontë has Nelly sum up her attitude:

One day, I had the misfortune, when she provoked me exceedingly, to lay the blame of his disappearance on her (where indeed it belonged, as she well knew). From that period for several months, she ceased to hold any communication with me, save in the relation of a mere servant. Joseph fell under a ban also; he *would* speak his mind, and lecture her all the same as if she were a little girl. . . . (ix)

Later on, a dialogue between Heathcliff and Nelly emphasizes this superficiality of hers by contrasting her explanation with his. To his inquiry, after Cathy's marriage and illness, concerning her condition, Nelly first replies, "I blamed her, as she deserved, for bringing it all on herself," and continues, "the person [Edgar] who is compelled, of necessity, to be her companion, will only sustain his affection hereafter, by the remembrance of what she once was, by common humanity, and a sense of duty!" She is speaking not out of any true knowledge of Edgar, but out of her determination to edify Heathcliff. His refusal to be edified produces his reply and reveals once more Nelly's inadequacy: " 'That is quite possible,' remarked Heathcliff, forcing himself to seem calm, 'quite possible that your master should have nothing but common humanity and a sense of duty to fall back upon. But do you imagine that I shall leave Catherine to his *duty* and *humanity?* and can you compare my feelings respecting Catherine, to his?' " (xiv).

Heathcliff finally forces her to agree to arrange an interview between him and Cathy; her motives are not a genuine feeling for the two, but the desire to avoid an "explosion":

> Was it right or wrong? I fear it was wrong, though expedient. I thought I prevented another explosion by my compliance; and I thought, too, it might create a favourable crisis in Catherine's mental illness: and then I remembered Mr. Edgar's stern rebuke of my carrying tales; and I tried to smooth away all disquietude on the subject, by affirming, with frequent iteration, that betrayal of trust, if it merited so harsh an appellation, should be the last. (xiv)

Worse is the smugness in reporting the actual meeting when she sarcastically remarks "it seemed Heathcliff *could* weep on a great occasion like this" (xv). And conventionally, she weeps herself for Heathcliff after Cathy's death:

> "She's dead!" he said; "I've not waited for you to learn that. Put your handkerchief away—don't snivel before me. Damn you all! she wants none of *your* tears!"
>
> I was weeping as much for him as her: we do sometimes pity creatures that have none of the feeling either for themselves or others; and when I first looked into his face, I perceived that he had got intelligence of the catastrophe; and a foolish notion struck me that his heart was quelled, and he prayed, because his lips moved, and his gaze was bent on the ground.
>
> "Yes, she's dead!" I answered, checking my sobs, and drying my cheeks. "Gone to heaven, I hope, where we may, every one, join her, if we take due warning, and leave our evil ways to follow good!"
>
> "Did *she* take due warning, then?" asked Heathcliff, attempting a sneer. "Did she die like a saint? Come, give me a true history of the event. How did . . ." (xvi)

The death of Cathy and its repercussions, however, do not end Nelly's failures that result from the great good fortune, for her own survival, of her native endowments. There remain young Cathy and the sickly son of Isabella for her to fail to comprehend. Dealing with them, she reveals her unimpaired self-confidence. Suspecting that young Cathy is corresponding with Linton, rather than question Cathy as might seem her duty as a guardian, she automatically uses the method of trying all her household keys on Cathy's locked drawer:

> . . . I emptied the whole contents into my apron, and took them with me to examine at leisure in my own chamber. . . .
> Some of them struck me as singularly odd compounds of ardour and flatness; commencing in strong feeling, and concluding in the affected, wordy way that a schoolboy might use to a fancied, incorporeal sweetheart.
> Whether they satisfied Cathy, I don't know, but they appeared very worthless trash to me.
> After turning over as many as I thought proper, I tied them in a handkerchief and set them aside, re-locking the vacant drawer. (xxi)

Catherine's agony on realizing that the letters have been discovered is great, but Nelly sympathizes with her not at all, since to her both the letters and their author are contemptible.

Still harsher is her treatment of Cathy after the revelation of the visits to Wuthering Heights:

> "Now, Ellen, you have heard all; and I can't be prevented from going to Wuthering Heights, except by inflicting misery on two people—whereas, if you'll only not tell papa, my going need disturb the tranquillity of none. You'll not tell, will you? It will be very heartless if you do."
> "I'll make up my mind on that point by to-morrow, Miss Catherine," I replied. "It requires some study; and so I'll leave you to your rest, and go think it over."
> I thought it over aloud, in my master's presence; walking straight from her room to his, and relating the whole story, with the exception of her conversations with her cousin, and any mention of Hareton. (xxv)

Though Edgar, no doubt, should know of the activities of his daughter, Nelly's methods are shown first in her promise to Cathy to consider the problem (the easy and immediate way of "smoothing over" that difficulty), second, in her immediate and unreflective revelation to Edgar, and third, in her holding back from Edgar those items that might cause her some trouble with him. Most revelatory of all, of course, is the more than satisfied manner in which she narrates the whole episode to Lockwood.

One can also contrast the superficiality of Nelly's understanding even with that of young Cathy in two passages very close together (xx). Cathy, now his daughter-in-law, says in the former,

> "Mr. Heathcliff, *you* have *nobody* to love you; and, however miserable you make us, we shall still have the revenge of thinking that your cruelty arises from your

greater misery! You *are* miserable, are you not? Lonely, like the devil, and envious like him? *Nobody* loves you—*nobody* will cry for you, when you die! I wouldn't be you!"

The realization of cruelty as the consequence of misery is beyond Nelly who had once explained his character as due to the evil example of Hindley. To emphasize Nelly's inability to understand, immediately after the passage just quoted, Emily Brontë has Heathcliff tell Nelly of his opening of Cathy's grave, and the reader is more than ever aware of the torments he has suffered, especially when he ends, "It was a strange way of killing, not by inches, but by fractions of hairbreadths, to beguile me with the spectre of a hope, through eighteen years." To this she comments to Lockwood:

> Mr. Heathcliff paused and wiped his forehead—his hair clung to it, wet with perspiration; his eyes were fixed on the red embers of the fire; the brows not contracted, but raised next the temples, diminishing the grim aspect of his countenance, but imparting a peculiar look of trouble, and a painful appearance of mental tension towards one absorbing subject. He only half addressed me, and I maintained silence—*I didn't like to hear him talk* [italics mine].

And while he had been talking, she had interrupted him with, " 'You were very wicked, Mr. Heathcliff!' I exclaimed; 'were you not ashamed to disturb the dead?' " (p. 305), quick to register conventional horror at a breach of custom, but apparently oblivious of the overwhelming torment that had caused the breach. Here, with particular intensity, the reader revolts from accepting the wholesome, normal person as a criterion of thought and behaviour, and tends to accept any passion so long as it is real, and in so doing becomes his own active interpreter of the true state of affairs and is powerfully affected by the genuine insight into human emotion.

Yet he may not be allowed to forget that Nelly is a fine woman nevertheless; she is once more contrasted with Joseph when Lockwood finds both of them together on his unexpected visit in September 1802, just after, furthermore, he had encountered her cloddish successor at the Grange:

> . . . at the door, sat my old friend, Nelly Dean, sewing and singing a song, which was often interrupted from within, by harsh words of scorn and intolerance, uttered in far from musical accents.
>
> "Aw'd rayther, by the haulf, hev 'em swearing i' my lugs frough morn tuh neeght, nur hearken yah, hahsiver!" said the tenant of the kitchen, in answer to an unheard speech of Nelly's. "It's a blazing shaime, ut Aw cannut oppen t' Blessed Book, bud yah set up them glories tuh sattan, un' all t' flaysome wickednesses ut iver wer born intuh t' warld. . . . O Lord, judge 'em fur they's norther law nur justice amang wer rullers!"
>
> "No! Or we should be sitting in flaming fagots, I suppose," retorted the singer. "But wisht, old man, and read your Bible like a christian, and never mind me. This is 'Fairy Annie's Wedding'—a bonny tune—it goes to a dance." (xxxii)

With this picture of Nelly's natural attractiveness and gaiety in mind we reach her narration of Heathcliff's end, his "queer" end, as she calls it.

As any reader of the novel will have guessed, Nelly was taken by surprise at Heathcliff's death: as with all the other now dead characters, she had supposed him sound in all ways:

> "But what do you mean by a *change,* Mr. Heathcliff?" I said, alarmed at his manner, though he was neither in danger of losing his senses, nor dying; according to my judgment he was quite strong and healthy; and, as to his reason, from childhood, he had a delight in dwelling on dark things, and entertaining odd fancies. He might have had a monomania on the subject of his departed idol; but on every point his wits were as sound as mine. (xxxiii)

Such phrases as "delight in dwelling on dark things," "monomania on the subject of his idol!" are perhaps a climax in Nelly's brushing aside of all powerful emotion, and above all, it should be noted that the only thing that here alarms her is Heathcliff's unwholesome manner.

As his death approaches, Nelly finally begins to worry about him; she fears for a short time, as the only way of explaining him, that he must be some "ghoul, or a vampire," but rejects that explanation and tries to conjure up some type of parentage that would account for his nature, but concludes by turning her attention aside to a serious abnormality, that he will not be able to have a proper tombstone, since his age and true name are unknown: "We were obliged to content ourselves with the single word, 'Heathcliff.' . . . If you enter the kirkyard, you'll read on his headstone, only that, and the date of his death." Her final words show how well for her own tranquility she has settled the whole violent tale, when in response to Lockwood's half jest that the ghosts of Cathy and Heathcliff will be the future inhabitants of Wuthering Heights, " 'No, Mr. Lockwood,' said Nelly, shaking her head. 'I believe the dead are at peace, but it is not right to speak of them with levity'" (xxxiv).

We have received the story almost entirely from Nelly, a representative of an admirable type of person, a character developed in great detail and with great skill, no obvious technical device, but a genuinely memorable character. In the circumstances in which she had been forced to live, she has revealed the futility of a tolerant, common-sense attitude which is the result of a desire merely to avoid trouble, to deny serious problems, and of a failure to grasp genuinely the emotions of others; the futility of compromise which is a mere improvisation from day to day in the interest of averting "explosions," of the futility of a constant attempt to preserve surface decorum and tranquillity on the grounds that what does not appear will not do any harm, and she has made the reader feel that her action has been throughout the best that can be expected of the type she represents. The reader continually decreases in sympathy with a type that he would usually admire, as she goes healthily and happily singing about her household duties and amusing the babies, since her so consistently emphasized good qualities turn out to be of so little use.

Thus, constantly rejecting her explanations, the reader substitutes his own, based always on the available evidence which she supplies but does not take into account or understand, and he becomes through his own perceptions increasingly sympathetic with the thoughts, feelings, and deeds of Heathcliff and Cathy.

The engaging of the reader actively as one who does a large part of the work of comprehending is an important cause of the power of the novel. As Nelly contentedly provides her superficial interpretations of motive, and contentedly recounts her inadequate parental behaviour, we are constantly directed towards feeling the inadequacy of the wholesome, and towards sympathy with genuine passions, no matter how destructive or violent.

The Rejection of Heathcliff?

MIRIAM ALLOTT*

The altered emphasis in the second part of the book is apparent at once in the changed character of one of Emily Brontë's most important pieces of dramatic apparatus: her nature imagery. The predominantly sombre nature imagery expressive of the elder Catherine's love for Heathcliff now gives place to the brighter images of summer landscape and summer weather which surround the younger Catherine. The conflict eventually destroying the first Catherine, which is given its most forceful expression in some of the book's best-known passages, is presented figuratively in a whole series of contrasted alternatives: "a bleak hilly coal country" or "a beautiful fertile valley" (Chapter VIII); moonbeam or lightning; frost or fire (Chapter IX). Catherine's love for Linton, "like foliage in the woods: time will change it . . . as winter changes the trees," is set against her love for Heathcliff, which "resembles the eternal rocks beneath: a source of little visible delight but necessary" (Chapter IX). Again, Heathcliff is "an unreclaimed creature, without refinement, without cultivation"; and if Isabella Linton marries him it will be "like putting a little canary into the park on a winter's day" (Chapter X). The opposition that these contrasts present to us is a direct one between the extremes of "storm" and "calm," between "Earth" in her dark guise and "Earth" in her fairer aspect, and the complication arises because Catherine. identifies herself with the darker element while allying herself with the fairer one.

The way in which this opposition is modified in the second-generation story is perhaps best illustrated by the account of the younger Catherine's quarrel with Linton in Chapter XXIV. Catherine has fallen in love with her young and sickly cousin, Heathcliff's child by Isabella Linton, and she steals away from the "valley" and Thrushcross Grange in order to be with him as often as she can. But Linton is peevish, irritable and mortally ill, and their relationship is not harmonious:

"One time . . . we were near quarrelling. He said the pleasantest manner of spending a hot July day was lying from morning till evening on the bank of heath in the middle of the moors, with the bees humming dreamily about

*Reprinted from *Essays in Criticism* 10 (1958): 38–47.

among the bloom, and the larks singing high up overhead, and the blue sky and bright sun shining steadily and cloudlessly. That was his most perfect idea of heaven's happiness: mine was rocking in a rustling green tree, with a west wind blowing, and bright white clouds flitting rapidly above; and not only larks, but throstles, and blackbirds, and linnets, and cuckoos pouring out music on every side, and the moors seen at a distance, broken into cool dusky dells; but close by great swells of long grass undulating in waves to the breeze; and woods and sounding water, and the whole world awake and wild with joy. He wanted all to lie in an ecstacy of peace; I wanted all to sparkle and dance in a glorious jubilee. I said his heaven would be only half-alive; and he said mine would be drunk: I said I should fall asleep in his; and he said he could not breathe in mine, and began to grow very snappish . . ."

The splendid literary qualities of this passage help to strengthen the point it is trying to make. It is a vivid re-statement in fresh terms and with a different emphasis of the conflict expressed in the elder Catherine's dream in Chapter IX. Emily Brontë's intention, almost certainly, is that we should recall this dream now when the child of the first Catherine and the child of Heathcliff in their turn discuss ideas of "heaven's happiness." It is only one of the many oblique comments that this passage makes on the first-generation story that the whole incident should be quite devoid of the more troubled feelings that accompany the account of the elder Catherine's dream; the "quarrel" is a brief one—"and then we kissed each other, and were friends." More importantly, the passage shows that whereas for the elder Catherine the bare hard moor is "heaven's happiness," for her daughter that happiness is identified with a bright animated landscape in which the moors are "seen at a distance." More-over, the brilliant sunlit moors in which Linton lies in his "ecstasy of peace" have nothing to do with the bleak moors in which his father ran wild when he was young. In fact we now find qualities earlier associated with the "valley" imposed on the Heights, and *vice versa*. Each quality is modified in transit: "storm" retains its energy but sheds its destructiveness; while calm, losing its positive qualities, is lulled in a delicious but languorous inactivity (the atti-tude of the first Lintons to the elder Catherine had involved much more than passiveness—"the honeysuckles embracing the thorn" as Nelly Dean tells us in Chapter X).

In using this passage as part of her commentary on the first-generation story, Emily Brontë also makes her nature imagery contrast the characters of her two Catherines. The younger Catherine's ideal landscape includes larks, thrushes, blackbirds, linnets and cuckoos, all "pouring out music on every side." Her description recalls the delirious fantasies of Chapter XII, where her mother, the elder Catherine, tears her pillow in a frenzy, and then pulls out the feathers, arranging them in groups and remembering the creatures to whom they once belonged. It is in keeping with the differences in texture in the two parts of the story that the elder Catherine's birds (she mentions lap-wings, moorcocks and wild duck) should not only be more identifiable with a northern, moorland countryside but should also bring with them ideas of violence, vanished childhood, winter and death—ideas which are associated with "Heathcliff" feelings, and have no comparable urgency in the story of the younger Catherine. The younger Catherine's birds, on the contrary, suggest notions of summer and sunshine and happy vitality.

Emily Brontë's determination to prognosticate a brighter future for the new Linton-Earnshaws is revealed to us in the good-weather imagery which she lavishes on her account of the younger Catherine's childhood and adolescence. One of her earliest Gondal poems, "Will the day be bright or cloudy," is concerned with weather omens presiding over a child's birth: the poem sketches three alternative kinds of destiny, tranquil, troubled or vitally active, according to the omens, and these alternatives do more or less anticipate the differences between Linton and the two Catherines. Now, in her novel, Emily Brontë stresses the fact that for the younger Catherine—and also for Hareton, whom she will marry—the weather omens are favourable. Both children are born in fine weather, the one in spring, the other in the hay-making season. They are both children of love, and it is established that Catherine was conceived in the "calm" period of Edgar's and the first Catherine's "deep and growing happiness" before Heathcliff's return, the predominant mood of the six months since their marriage being suggested by the scene that Nelly Dean describes in Chapter X when she tells Lockwood about Heathcliff's sudden return. Though the second Catherine is "puny" and unwelcome to begin with (her mother dies in giving birth to her), her first morning is "bright and cheerful out of doors": and this fine weather lasts throughout the week. There is a resurgence of first-generation violence in Chapter XVII, when the first Catherine is buried on the Friday, and so enters her "glorious world" of the moors: "That Friday made the last of our fine days for a month . . . the wind shifted and brought rain first, and then sleet and snow." This intervening chapter of storm marks Heathcliff's violent emotional reaction to her death and underlines the supernatural element (explained later, in the "flashback" of Chapter XXIX, when Heathcliff tells Nelly Dean that he was prevented from opening Catherine's coffin only by the sense that her spirit was already standing beside him in the darkness). From the beginning of the next chapter (Chapter XVIII), however, when we are led steadily on into the second-generation story, all this violence dies away. Spring and summer images indicate the untroubled years of Catherine's childhood in the valley—her first twelve years are described by Nelly Dean as "the happiest of my life." In these years she is almost as secure from the troubling associations of Wuthering Heights as a princess in an enchanted castle, and Penistone Crags in the distance are "golden rocks," even though Nelly Dean had to explain "that they were bare masses of stone, with hardly enough earth in their clefts to nourish a stunted tree" (Chapter XVIII). Catherine's sixteenth birthday is "a beautiful spring day," and Nelly Dean describes her vivacity and joy:

She bounded before me, and returned to my side and was off again like a young greyhound; and, at first, I found plenty of entertainment in listening to the larks singing far and near, and enjoying the sweet warm sunshine; and watching her, my pet, and my delight, with her golden ringlets flying loose behind, and her bright cheek, as soft and pure in its bloom as a wild rose, and her eyes radiant with cloudless pleasure. She was a happy creature, and an angel in those days. It's a pity she could not be content. (Chapter XXI)

On other occasions she climbs trees, "swinging twenty feet above the ground" and "lying from dinner to tea in her breeze-rocked cradle," singing. (Much of this reminds us of Ellen Nussey's account of the Brontë girls out on the moors.)

Attention is naturally centred on Catherine, since Nelly Dean loses Hareton when Heathcliff takes possession of him after Hindley's death (the loss is commemorated in the sensitively recorded episode of Chapter XI); but the importance of Hareton's birth is stressed by the break in Nelly Dean's narrative at the end of Chapter VII, when she takes up the story again at his birthday in "the summer of 1778, that is nearly twenty-three years ago," and her next words, placed prominently at the opening of Chapter VIII, suggest the auspiciousness of the day and the excitement attending the arrival of this latest member of the ancient Earnshaw family:

On the morning of a fine Sunday, my first bonny nursling, and the last of the Earnshaw stock was born. We were busy with the hay in a far-away field, and the girl that usually brought our breakfasts came running out an hour too soon, across the meadow and up the lane, calling as she ran: "Oh, such a grand bairn," she panted out. "The finest lad that ever breathed . . ."

And in almost all the scenes in which Hareton appears in the second-generation story his connection with the fertile earth and his gentleness with living things are kept before our eyes. Nelly Dean, seeing him for the first time after his many years with Heathcliff (in Chapter XVIII), realises that he is not altogether spoilt:

I thought I could detect in his physiognomy a mind owning better qualities than his father ever possessed. Good things lost amid a wilderness of weeds, to be sure . . . yet, notwithstanding, evidence of a wealthy soil, that might yield luxuriant crops under other and favourable circumstances.

These "other and favourable circumstances" begin on Easter Monday in 1802, when Catherine opens her friendly campaign to reclaim the neglected "soil" by offering to teach Hareton to read. The whole process is symbolised by the clearing of the ground in the garden of Wuthering Heights, where, to Joseph's horror, Catherine plans with Hareton to plant flowers imported from the Grange. By April she and Hareton are working in the garden, and Nelly is "comfortably revelling in the spring fragrance around and the beautiful blue overhead . . ." (Chapter XXXIV).

To reach this point the characters in the second-generation story have to contend with Heathcliff's animosity, but their "dark" scenes of conflict are totally unlike those of the first-generation story. In the earlier part of the book storm images establish the prevailing emotional atmosphere from the beginning. Lockwood's visit in frost and snow to Wuthering Heights, his dream in the first Catherine's oak bed with its accompaniment of "gusty wind, and the driving of snow," the ice-cold fingers of the child-ghost, all prepare us for the bleakness and wildness of the first Catherine's childhood—of which she herself leaves a record:

> "An awful Sunday! . . . All day had been flooding with rain . . . we were ranged in a row, on a sack of corn, groaning and shivering . . . we cannot be damper, or colder, in the rain than we are here."

When Heathcliff vanishes, in Chapter IX, the event is dramatised by storm and lightning (the first Catherine catches a fever hunting for him in the downpour), and storm and tempest emphasise his grief at the time of Catherine's death. There is no comparable "stormy" weather in the later story: the "dark" scenes are not so much different in degree as in kind, for their final effect is no more sombre than clouds passing over a sunny landscape, an idea suggested to us more than once by Nelly Dean's descriptions of the second Catherine.

What, then, becomes of the storm-centre, Heathcliff himself, in this second half of the book? Our attention is turned to him once more when he traps Catherine into staying at Wuthering Heights, and we see that his behaviour is as outrageous as ever. He inveigles Catherine into the marriage with Linton, he prevents her from joining her dying father, he makes her nurse the mortally sick Linton unaided, he secures her property once Linton is dead, he treats her with systematic harshness. Yet, for most of the time, his behaviour is hardly more sinister than a stage villain's. The strongest emotion Heathcliff arouses in us throughout the greater part of the later narrative is a kind of angry exasperation at his injustice. He is still capable of making ferocious remarks:

> ". . . what a savage feeling I have to anything that seems afraid of me! Had I been born where laws are less strict and tastes less dainty, I should treat myself to a slow vivisection of those two, as an evening's amusement . . ."

but this lacks the resonance of such passionate outbursts as his speech to "Cathy" before her death:

> ". . . You deserve this. You have killed yourself. Yes, you may kiss me, and cry; and ring out my kisses and tears: they'll blight you—they'll damn you. You loved me—then what *right* had you to leave me? What right—answer me—

for the poor fancy you felt for Linton? Because misery and degradation, and death, and nothing that God or Satan could inflict would have parted us, *you,* of your own will, did it. I have not broken your heart—*you* have broken it; and in breaking it, you have broken mine. So much the worse for me, that I am strong. Do I want to live? What kind of living will it be when you—oh, God! would *you* like to live with your soul in the grave?" (Chapter XV)

Angry exasperation is an emotion on too small a scale to suit the earlier Heathcliff. On the other hand, Emily Brontë's portrayal of Heathcliff still communicates the kind of sympathy which makes the earlier story so remarkable—it is a story, after all, which not only depicts the "heroine" and the "villain" falling in love with each other, but describes their passion with a sympathetic power so intense that it makes nonsense of the more usual responses to such a situation and completely upsets conventional value judgments. This sympathy is now partly suggested through Nelly Dean—whose function for Heathcliff is rather more than that of *confidante*—and partly through such mitigating circumstances as Hareton's persistent love for him, a feeling that is not unreturned (we also remember that Heathcliff saved Hareton's life in Chapter IX). Again, the bad effect on us of Heathcliff's callousness to his son is complicated by the fact that Linton is a sorry mixture of peevishness and irritability (Linton, at his worst, sometimes recalls genuine Heathcliff violence: he can scream and rage, so that old Joseph croaks out, "Theear, that's t'father . . . We've allas summat o' either side in us . . ."). We also realise that Heathcliff fails to break Catherine's spirit—indeed, before the end, he no longer wants to break it.

But at the very point where his need for vengeance dies, Heathcliff does in fact fully revive *as* Heathcliff, that is to say, as the powerfully compelling and complex figure of the first part of the story. Hitherto, in the second half of the book, Emily Brontë has concentrated on her "calm" figures, who represent alternatives to Heathcliff and to everything that he stands for, and as long as she makes him serve as a foil to these figures he is merely their vindictive enemy. But when she turns to look directly and exclusively at him again, she sees and feels what she saw and felt earlier. This is apparent in her handling of the monologue she gives to Heathcliff late in the story (in Chapter XXIX), when he tells Nelly Dean about his two attempts to open the first Catherine's coffin—once on the night of her funeral, and a second time, successfully, when—years later—Edgar's grave is being prepared beside hers, and, with the help of the sexton, he at last sees her dead face ("It is hers still"). As he watches the growing alliance between the second Catherine and Hareton (the latter resembling the first Catherine in appearance more and more, "because his senses were alert, and his mental faculties wakened to unwanted activity"), Heathcliff senses the "strange change approaching," and in another outburst to Nelly Dean, in Chapter XXXIII, he resumes much of the intensity and passion of his earlier appearances:

". . . In every cloud, in every tree—filling the air at night, and caught by glimpses in every object by day—I am surrounded with her image! The most ordinary faces of men and women—my own features—mock me with a resemblance. The entire world is a dreadful collection of memoranda that she did exist, and that I have lost her! Well, Hareton's aspect was the ghost of my immortal love; of my wild endeavours to hold my right, my degradation, my pride, my happiness, and my anguish—."

Later still, when the tale is nearly at its end and Catherine's ghost seems to walk once more, the old feelings are fully revived, the obsessional pattern of *motifs* reappears, and Nelly Dean, finding Heathcliff lying motionless and soaking wet in the oak bed, his eyes staring, his wrist grazed by the open lattice, cries, "I could not think him dead," and tries "to extinguish, if possible, that frightful life-like gaze of exultation."

It is now that the first of the story's two "arcs" approaches its final point of rest. It reaches this point, moreover, at the same moment that the second-generation story is coming to its own conclusion, and this "coincidence" draws attention to the nature and degree of Emily Brontë's resolution of her conflict. At the last, within the space of a single page, we turn from the phantoms of Heathcliff and the elder Catherine restlessly walking the Heights in rain and thunder—they are now as ominous in their own way as Henry James's Peter Quint and Miss Jessel are in theirs—to contemplate those other "ramblers" on the moors, Hareton and the younger Catherine, who halt on the threshold of the old house to take "a last look at the moon—or, more correctly, at each other by her light." The closing passage of the book might suggest to an unwary reader that the final victory is to them. It is possible to mistake this last comment of Lockwood's, indicating "calm" after "storm," for a statement of calm's ultimate triumph. But such a reading overlooks the departure of Hareton and the younger Catherine to the valley, and their abandonment of the old house to the spirits of the still restless Heathcliff and the elder Catherine. There is, after all, no escape for Emily Brontë from her emotional commitment to Heathcliff; there can only be an intellectual judgment that for the purposes of ordinary life he will not do. It is the artist's business, Tchekov tells us, to set questions, not solve them, and Emily Brontë sets her very personal question in terms that establish the greatness of her art. It is less a sign of any flaw in her achievement than an indication of the urgency of her internal conflict that the tones of her own voice can be heard even through her admirably controlled "oblique and indirect view" of Catherine's and Heathcliff's fated alliance. The tones are those of someone aware that the claims of head and heart remain unreconciled.

A Fresh Approach to *Wuthering Heights*

QUEENIE LEAVIS*

Of course, in general one attempts to achieve a reading of a text which includes all its elements, but here I believe we must be satisfied with being able to account for some of them and concentrate on what remains. It is better to admit that some of the difficulties of grasping what is truly creative in *Wuthering Heights* are due to the other parts—to the author in her inexperience having made false starts, changing her mind (as tone and style suggest) probably because of rewriting from earlier stories with themes she had lost interest in and which have become submerged, though not assimilated, in the final work. Another source of confusion to the reader is that she tried to do too much, too many different things (a common trouble in first novels and in most Victorian novels) and that some of these interfere with her deeper intentions—though of course this is also one source of the richness of this novel and we wouldn't care to sacrifice many of these, I think. The novel has all the signs of having been written at different times (because in different styles) and with varying intentions; we must sort these out in order to decide what *is* the novel. In spite of the brilliantly successful time-shifts and what has been called, not very happily, the "Chinese box" ingenuity of construction, it certainly isn't a seamless "work of art," and candour obliges us to admit ultimately that some things in the novel are incompatible with the rest, so much so that one seems at times to find oneself in really different novels.

Even criticism that is felt to be very helpful because unusually honest and sensitive may end by leaving the stress in the wrong place. I will instance a pioneer critique, Mr Klingopulos's revaluation of *Wuthering Heights* in *Scrutiny* under our collaborative heading "The Novel as Dramatic Poem." In 1947, when we published it, it was very salutary that *Wuthering Heights* should thus be rescued from the woolly treatment that was then current (e.g., in Lord David Cecil's *Early Victorian Novelists*). But in order to make the case and points he felt needed making, Mr Klingopulos ignores or slights elements and scenes which impinge on me, at least, as of fundamental importance. For instance, though he starts by saying, very properly, that "the main problems in any account of the book are these: to decide on the status of Catherine and her relationship with Edgar and Heathcliff: to decide on the

*Reprinted from F. and Q. Leavis, *Lectures in America* (London: Chatto and Windus, 1969), 86–104.

status of the Cathy-Hareton relationship and the appropriateness of reading it as a comment on what happened earlier,"—nothing could be better than this clearing of the ground—yet he makes Catherine as a matter of course the splendid and valuable creature of conventional esteem (without noting Nelly's, Edgar's and at times Heathcliff's "placing" of her, as well as more subtle insights of the novelist's own), and he goes so far as to assert as a general truth of *Wuthering Heights* that "the author's preferences are not shown" and therefore, he deduces, it is not "a moral tale." Actually, I shall argue, the author's preferences *are* shown, Catherine is judged by the author in the parallel but notably different history of the daughter who, inheriting her mother's name, and likenesses both physical and psychological, is shown by deliberate choice, and trial and error, developing the maturity and therefore achieving the happiness, that the mother failed in, whereas we have seen the mother hardening into a fatal immaturity which destroys herself and those (Heathcliff and Edgar principally) involved with her. Nor is the author's impersonality (deliberately maintained by the device of a narrator who records other narrators and all of whom are much less like their creator than Conrad's Marlow his)—nor is that impersonality inconsistent with a moral intention. That is, the reader is obliged to draw moral conclusions, from the very nature of the scenes and actors in whose lives he is involved by sympathy and compassion or horror and repulsion.

I would first like to clear out of the way the *confusions* of the plot and note the different levels on which the novel operates at different times. It seems clear to me that Emily Brontë had some trouble in getting free of a false start—a start which suggests that we are going to have a regional version of the sub-plot of *Lear* (Shakespeare being generally the inspiration for those early nineteenth-century novelists who rejected the eighteenth-century idea of the novel). In fact, the Lear-world of violence, cruelty, unnatural crimes, family disruption and physical horrors remains the world of the household at Wuthering Heights, a characteristic due not to sadism or perversion in the novelist (some of the physical violence is quite unrealized)[1] but to the Shakespearian intention. The troubles of the Earnshaws started when the father brought home the boy Heathcliff (of which he gives an unconvincing explanation and for whom he shows an unaccountable weakness) and forced him on the protesting family; Heathcliff "the cuckoo" by intrigue soon ousts the legitimate son Hindley and, like Edmund, Gloucester's natural son in *Lear,* his malice brings about the ruin of two families (the Earnshaws and the Lintons, his rival getting the name Edgar by attraction from *Lear*). Clearly, Heathcliff was originally the illegitimate son and Catherine's half-brother, which would explain why, though so attached to him by early associations and natural sympathies, Catherine never really thinks of him as a possible lover either before or after marriage;[2] it also explains why all the children slept in one bed at the Heights till adolescence, we gather (we learn later from Catherine (Chapter XII) that being removed at puberty from this bed became a turning-point in her inner life, and this is only one of the remark-able insights which *Wuthering Heights* adds to the Romantic poets' exploration of childhood experience). The favourite Romantic theme of incest therefore must have been the impulsion behind the earliest conception of *Wuthering Heights*. Rejecting this story for a more mature intention, Emily Brontë was left with hopeless inconsistencies on her hands, for while Catherine's feelings about Heathcliff are never sexual (though she feels the bond of sympathy with a brother to be more important to her than her feelings for her young husband), Heathcliff's feelings for her are always those of a lover. As Heath-cliff has been written out as a half-brother, Catherine's innocent refusal to see that there is anything in her relation to him incompatible with her position as a wife, becomes preposterous and the impropriety which she refuses to recog-nize is translated into social terms—Edgar thinks the kitchen the suitable place for Heathcliff's reception by Mrs Linton while she insists on the parlour. Another trace of the immature draft of the novel is the fairy-tale opening of the Earnshaw story, where the father, like the merchant in *Beauty and the Beast,* goes off to the city promising to bring his children back the presents each has commanded: but the fiddle was smashed and the whip lost so the only present he brings for them is the Beast himself, really a "prince in dis-guise" (as Nelly tells the boy he should consider himself rightly); Catherine's tragedy then was that she forgot her prince and he was forced to remain the monster, destroying her; invoking this pattern brought in much more from the fairy-tale world of magic, folk-lore and ballads, the oral tradition of the folk, that the Brontë children learnt principally from their nurses and their servant Tabby.[3] This element surges up in Chapter XII, the important scene of Catherine's illness, where the dark superstitions about premonitions of death, about ghosts and primitive beliefs about the soul, come into play so significantly; and again in the excessive attention given to Heathcliff's gob-lin-characteristics and especially to the prolonged account of his uncanny obsession and death. That this last should have an air of being infected by Hoffman too is not surprising in a contemporary of Poe's; Emily is likely to have read Hoffmann when studying German at the Brussels boarding-school and certainly read the ghastly supernatural stories by James Hogg and others in the magazines at home. It is a proof of her immaturity at the time of the original conception of *Wuthering Heights* that she should express real psycho-logical insights in such inappropriate forms.

In the novel as we read it Heathcliff's part either as Edmund in *Lear* or as the Prince doomed to Beast's form, is now suspended in boyhood while another influence, very much of the period, is developed, the Romantic image of childhood,[4] with a corresponding change of tone. Heathcliff and Cather-ine are idyllically and innocently happy together (and see also the end of Chapter V) roaming the countryside as hardy, primitive Wordsworthian chil-dren, "half savage and hardy and free." Catherine recalls it longingly when she feels she is dying trapped in Thrushcross Grange. (This boy Heathcliff is

of course not assimilable with the vicious, scheming and morally heartless—
"simply insensible"—boy of Chapter IV who plays Edmund to old Earnshaw's Gloucester.) Catherine's dramatic introduction to the genteel world of
Thrushcross Grange—narrated with contempt by Heathcliff who is rejected
by it as a ploughboy unfit to associate with Catherine—is the turning-point
in her life in *this* form of the novel; her return, got up as a young lady in
absurdly unsuitable clothes for a farmhouse life, and "displaying fingers wonderfully whitened with doing nothing and staying indoors"[5] etc. visibly sepa-
rates her from the "natural" life, as her inward succumbing to the temptations of social superiority and riches parts her from Heathcliff. Heathcliff's
animus against his social degradation by his new master Hindley is barbed by
his being made to suffer (like Pip at the hands of Estella in *Great Expectations*)[6]
taunts and insults—mainly from Edgar Linton—based on class and externals
alone. They are suffered again (thus making Emily Brontë's points
inescapable) in the second half of the novel by Hindley's son Hareton at the
hands of Catherine's and Edgar's daughter Cathy as well as from his other
cousin Linton Heathcliff, Isabella's son. And this makes us sympathetic to
Heathcliff as later to Hareton; we identify here with Nelly who with her
wholesome classlessness and her spontaneous maternal impulses supports
Heathcliff morally while he is ill-used (and even tries to persuade Catherine
not to let Edgar supplant him in her life)—she retains this generous sympathy for him until she transfers it to her foster-child Hareton when in turn he
becomes a victim (of Heathcliff's schemes). Her sympathy for Heathcliff's
hard luck, even when she sees that his return is a threat to the Lintons' happiness, is at odds with her loyalty to her new master Edgar, and leads her to
consent to some ill-advised interviews between Catherine and the desperate
Heathcliff—though she also feels that to consent to help him there is the
lesser of two evils (as it probably was), and she has no doubts about her duty
to protect Isabella from becoming Heathcliff's victim.

Nelly Dean is most carefully, consistently and convincingly created for
us as the normal woman, whose truly feminine nature satisfies itself in nur-
turing all the children in the book in turn.[7] To give this salience we have the
beginning of Chapter VIII when the farm-girl runs out to the hayfield where
Nelly is busy to announce the birth of "a grand bairn" and to give her artless
(normal feminine) congratulations to Nelly for being chosen to nurse it since
it will soon be motherless: "I wish I were you, because it will be all yours
when there is no missus." Nelly's greater sensibility in realizing that from the
bairn's point of view this is not altogether a matter for rejoicing is shown in
the next chapter when she says "I went into the kitchen, and sat down to lull
my little lamb to sleep . . . I was rocking Hareton on my knee, and humming
a song that began

> " *'It was far in the night, and the bairnies grat,*
> *The mither beneath the mools heard that'* . . ."

The ballad is evidently one expressing the widespread belief, in folk-song and folk tale, that a prematurely dead mother cannot rest in the grave but returns to suckle the babe or help her child in the hour of need,[8] an indication of what is going on in Nelly's compassionate mind. But the whole episode of Hareton's birth and childhood exposes Catherine's insensibility, that her self-centred nature is essentially loveless. (Her only reference to her own pregnancy later is the hope that a son's birth will "erase Isabella's title" to be Edgar's heir.) Yet Nelly's limitations are made clear and the novelist's distinct position of true insight, where necessary. Like Dolly in *Anna Karénina* who is also the normal maternal woman, Nelly is inevitably too *terre-à-terre* (Vronsky's complaint about Dolly), therefore unable to sympathize with difficulties that seem to her the result only of will, and a perverse will at that ("'I should not have spoken so, if I had known her true condition, but I could not get rid of the notion that she acted a part of her disorder'"). These limitations and not ill-will are of course the reason why Nelly makes some mistakes in trying to act for the best in situations where no easy or right solution offered itself. But in doing Catherine full justice ("'she was not artful, never played the coquette'") and giving her sound advice in her "perplexities and untold troubles," Nelly convinces us of her right to take a thoroughly disenchanted view of Catherine's disposition. In fact, both Heathcliff and Edgar know the truth about Catherine and Hindley is under no illusions— "'You lie, Cathy, no doubt'" he remarks (correctly) of her explanation of Edgar Linton's visit in his absence. One of the most successful indications of the passage of time is Nelly Dean's change, from the quick-moving and quick-witted girl who for little Hareton's sake copes with the drunken murderous Hindley, to the stout, breathless, middle-aged woman who, though still spirited, cannot save Cathy from a forced marriage.

To hark back to Heathcliff: it follows from this "social" development of the theme that Heathcliff should go out into the world to make his fortune and come back to avenge himself, "a cruel hard landlord," "near, close-handed" and given over to "avarice, meanness and greed," plotting to secure the property of both Earnshaws and Lintons and also to claim equality with them socially—we are now in the Victorian world of *Great Expectations* where money, as Magwitch the convict learnt, makes a gentleman. Emily Brontë took no trouble to explain the hiatus in Heathcliff's life—irrelevant to her purposes—and in fact it is enough for us to gather that he comes back a professional gambler at cards; a real flaw however is wholly inadequate illustration of the shared life and interests of himself and Catherine that makes it plausible that on his return she should be so absorbed in conversing with him as to cut out immediately and altogether her young husband. After all, we reflect, they couldn't always have been talking about their childhood escapades—that is to say, we recognize a failure in creative interest here in the novelist; nor do we ever hear what they talk about till Catherine attacks him over Isabella and they quarrel, when it becomes clear even to Catherine that he can be only the monster he has been made by his history. This aspect of him is kept before us from now till the end and accounts for his brutalities and violent outbreaks. For various reasons, therefore, after envisaging several alternative conceptions of Heathcliff, Emily Brontë ended by keeping and making use of them all, so that like Dostoievsky's Stavrogin he is an enigmatic figure only by reason of his creator's indecision, like Stavrogin in being an unsatisfactory composite with empty places in his history and no continuity of character. (And like Iago and Stavrogin, Heathcliff has been made the object of much misdirected critical industry on the assumption that he is not merely a convenience.) There is nothing enigmatic about either Catherine, we note, and this points to the novelist's distribution of her interest.

There are various signs that the novelist intended to stress the aspect of her theme represented by the corruption of the child's native goodness by Society and to make this part of the explanation of Catherine's failure in life. She evidently had in mind the difficulties and dangers inevitable in civilizing children to enter the artificial world of class, organized religion, social intercourse and authoritarian family life. This is the point of Catherine's childhood journal that Lockwood reads, which gives a caricature of the torments suffered by children in the enforcement of the Puritan Sabbath, and another caricature is the account given by the boy Heathcliff of the parlour life of the broken-in Linton children as seen from the other side of the window by a Noble Savage whose natural good instincts have not been destroyed like theirs. More impressive is the beautifully rendered exemplary relation between the child Catherine and the adults as reported by Nelly in Chapter V. Her father's attempts to improve her, or tame her to an approved pattern,[9] resulted only in "a naughty delight to provoke him: she was never so happy as when we were all scolding her at once, and she defying us with her bold, saucy look, and her ready words; turning Joseph's religious curses into ridicule, baiting me, and doing just what her father hated most"—"Mr. Earnshaw did not understand jokes from his children," Nelly notes, "he had always been strict and grave with them."

> After behaving as badly as possible all day, she sometimes came fondling to make it up at night. "Nay, Cathy" the old man would say, "I cannot love thee; go, say thy prayers, child, and ask God's pardon. I doubt thy mother and I must rue that we ever reared thee!" That made her cry, at first; and then, being repulsed continually hardened her, and she laughed if I told her to say she was sorry for her faults, and beg to be forgiven. . . . It pleased the master rarely to see her gentle—saying "Why canst thou not always be a good lass, Cathy?" And she turned up her face to his, and laughed, and answered, Why cannot you always be a good man, father?"

We note that the child is allowed the last word—and a very telling rejoinder it is. Emily Brontë, the girl in the family most sympathetic to the black-sheep brother, was the most recalcitrant to the domestic training of her rigid aunt, to schooling, and to orthodox religion; she had plainly thought about the psychological effects of conventional disciplines and taken this opportunity to report adversely in the strongest terms a novelist can use—by showing their part in destroying the possibilities of a happy childhood and maturity.

But this originally naïve and commonplace subject—the Romantics' image of childhood in conflict with society—becomes something that in this novel is neither superficial nor theoretic because the interests of the responsible novelist gave it, as we have seen above, a new insight, and also a specific and informed sociological content. The theme is here very firmly rooted in time and place and richly documented: we cannot forget that Gimmerton and the neighbourhood are so bleak that the oats are always green there three weeks later than anywhere else, and that old Joseph's Puritan preachings accompany his "overlaying his large Bible with dirty bank-notes, the produce of the day's transactions" at market; and we have a thoroughly realistic account of the life indoors and outdoors at Wuthering Heights as well as at the gentleman's residence at the Grange. In fact, there would be some excuse for taking this, the pervasive and carefully maintained sociological theme which fleshes the skeleton, for the real novel. This novel, which could be extracted by cutting away the rest, was deliberately built, to advance a thesis, on the opposition between Wuthering Heights and Thrushcross Grange, two different cultures of which the latter inevitably supersedes the former. The point about dating this novel as ending in 1801 (instead of its being contemporary with the Brontës' own lives)—and much trouble was taken to keep the dates, time-scheme and externals such as legal data, accurate[10]— is to fix its happenings at a time when the old rough farming culture based on a naturally patriarchal family life, was to be challenged, tamed and routed by social and cultural changes that were to produce the Victorian class consciousness and "unnatural" ideal of gentility.[11]

The inspiration for this structure, based on a conflict between, roughly speaking, a wholesome primitive and natural unit of a healthy society and its very opposite, felt to be an unwholesome refinement of the parasitic "educated," comes from observation—in the Brontës' youth and county the old order visibly survived. But the clue to making such perceptions and sympathies into a novel was found, I suspect, in Scott, whose novels and poetry were immensely admired by Charlotte and Emily. His own sympathies were with the wild rough Border-farmers, not only because they represented a romantic past of balladry. He felt that civilization introduced there entailed losses more than gains, and a novel where—before, with characteristic lack of staying power, he divagated from a serious theme into tushery—he made some effort to express this, *The Black Dwarf,* has long been known as the source for surnames used in *Wuthering Heights.* Scott's Earnscliffe [= Eaglescliff] and Ellieslaw suggested Heathcliff[12] and Earnshaw no doubt, but more important is their suggesting, it seems to me, that Emily Brontë found part of her theme in that novel's contrast between a weak, corrupt, refined upper-class, and the old-style Border farmers' "natural" or socially primitive way of life in which feuds and violence were a recognized part of the code (though transacted for the most part strictly according to rule and tradition and quite compatible with good-humour and a generous humanity); there, the rich and great live in their castles, are treacherous, and come to grief, the rough Borderers, eking out subsistence farming by hunting, suffer drastic ups and downs with hardihood and survive; the setting is on the moors and hills, and an essential element in establishing the primitive social condition of the Borderers is the superstition and folk-lore believed in by them all. Now the Yorkshire moors with the hardy yeomen farmers of pre-Victorian times who had lived thereabouts and whose histories Tabby used to tell the Brontë children[13] in her broad dialect, must have seemed to them not essentially different from Scott's Border farmers. Emily and Charlotte were genuinely attached to their moorland country but Scott's example was what made it usable for them as literature and gave it rich associations, so it is natural that in her first attempt at a novel Emily should draw on even a poor fiction like *The Black Dwarf* to give meaning and purpose to her feelings about what was happening or had happened recently to the world she lived in. It is proof of her development out of her daydream world of the Gondals that she was thus interested in the real world and roused to the need to inquire into the true nature of the change, perhaps as a way to alert her own (Early Victorian) generation to what this was. From being a self-indulgent storytelling, *Wuthering Heights* thus became a responsible piece of work, and the writer thought herself into the positions, outlooks, sufferings and tragedies of the actors in these typical events as an *artist*.

But if we were to take the sociological novel as the real novel and relegate the Heathcliff-Catherine-Edgar relationship and the corresponding Cathy-Linton-Hareton one, as exciting but ex-centric dramatic episodes, we should be misconceiving the novel and slighting it, for it is surely these relationships and their working out that give all the meaning to the rest. For instance, though Cathy has in the second half to unlearn, very painfully, the assumptions of superiority on which she has been brought up at the Grange, this is only part of her schooling; it is only incidental to the process by which we see her transcend the psychological temptations and the impulses which would have made her repeat her mother's history; and this is not a question of sociology or social history but is timeless.

Another misconception for which the novelist gives little excuse is to attribute a mystique to the moor; the moor is not meaningful like Hawthorne's forests that surround the Puritan settlements in the wild, it is not even powerful over man's destiny like Egdon Heath. The moor is a way of pointing a distinction: to the child Cathy brought up in the gentleman's park at the Grange, the moor means freedom from restraint, and romantic Nature to which she longs to escape, and in which she delights, but to the people who live there of necessity it is something they have to wrest a living out of:

in the long run man lives by farming, and the farmhouse at the Heights is braced against the challenge the extreme conditions there represent (for instance, on our first sight of it we see that the architecture is determined by the violence of the winds). Lockwood (characteristically) demands that the farm should provide him with a guide home when, though snow threatened, he foolishly paid a call, and he thinks, as we at first do, that the refusal is brutal and wanton; but there is no guide to spare—the hands are needed to get in the sheep before the animals are snowed under and to see to the horses. Similarly, when Cathy in her thoughtlessness uses her new power over Hareton to get him to pull up the fruit-bushes to make her a flower-garden, old Joseph, who has worked all his life at the Heights and meant to die there, is so outraged that he gives notice rather than stay to witness such a sinful proceeding as to sacrifice food to flowers. Unattractive as Joseph usually is, his disinterested identification with the family's well-being is impressive and as so often he is the vehicle for expressing a truth to which we need to have our attention called: here, that where fertile soil is precious, flower-gardens are an unjustified self-indulgence. Another example (there are plenty) is Linton Heathcliff's selfishness, due like Cathy's to ignorance of the facts of life on such a farm: Zillah complains "he must always have sweets and dainties, and always milk, milk for ever—heeding naught how the rest of us are pinched in winter." The novelist knows that thrift as well as austerity is a necessary virtue in such a context, so that old Joseph's indignation when the feckless Isabella flings down the tray of porridge is wholly respectable: " 'yah desarve pining froo this tuh Churstmas, flinging t'precious gifts uh God under fooit i' yer flaysome rages!' "

The clearest light is thrown on the moor by Catherine's likening Heathcliff to "an arid wilderness of furze and whinstone" when trying to make the romantic Isabella understand the basic irreducibility of the nature of the man Isabella fancies she is in love with. But Catherine has also said to Nelly, in trying to explain her own "love" for Heathcliff, that it is like "the eternal rocks: a source of little visible delight, but necessary," in fact it is not love but a need of some fundamental kind that is quite separate from her normal love for Edgar Linton, a love which leads to a happily consummated marriage and the expectation of providing an heir.

The focus of the first half of the novel is most certainly Catherine, and it is her case that is the real moral centre of the book. This case is examined with wonderful subtlety and conveyed in a succession of brilliantly managed dramatic scenes with complete impersonality. Charlotte Brontë rightly defended her sister against allegations of abnormality by pointing out that, as well as what Charlotte justly describes as "the perverted passion and passionate perversity" of the first Catherine, and Heathcliff's "warped nature," Emily had created the wholesome, maternal Nelly Dean, Edgar Linton's touching devotion and tenderness, and the "grace and gaiety" of the younger Cathy— she might have instanced much more. And what precisely is this case, in which—and not in the sociological novel, which is more a matter of course in its age—lies the real originality of *Wuthering Heights*?

Notes

1.   Mr. Justice Vaisey, giving a legal opinion of the text "The Authorship of *Wuthering Heights*," *Brontë Society Transactions* 56 (1946), notes such a distinction in "diction, style and taste" between "the introductory portion" and the rest of the book, that he believed it to indicate two authors; which would give ground to an old theory or tradition that Emily worked from a manuscript of Branwell's at the start (joint composition being probably a practice of the Brontë children, and Emily and Branwell are said to have written practically undistinguishable minute hands). Writing at two different periods by Emily alone, and at the earlier under the influence of Branwell or in deliberate imitation of his style (as Lockwood) would, however, account for such a disparity.

2.   The speech (Chap. IX) in which Catherine explains to Nelly why she couldn't marry Heathcliff—on social grounds—belongs to the sociological *Wuthering Heights*. But even then she intends, she declares, to keep up her old (sisterly) relations with him, to help him get on in the world—"to rise" as she significantly puts it in purely social terms.

3.   Tabby had, Mrs. Gaskell reports, "known the 'bottom' or valley in those primitive days when the faeries frequented the margin of the 'beck' on moonlight nights, and has known folk who had seen them. But that was when there were no mills in the valley, and when all the wool-spinning was done by hand in the farm-houses round. 'It wur the factories as had driven 'em away,' she said."

4.   I am referring to the invaluable book, *The Image of Childhood*, by P. Coveney, though this does not in fact deal with *Wuthering Heights*.

5.   This very evident judgement of Nelly's on the gentility with which Catherine has been infected by her stay at Thrushcross Grange (lavishly annotated in the whole scene of her return home in Chap. VII) is clearly endorsed by the author, since it is based on values that are fundamental to the novel and in consonance with Emily's Wordsworthian sympathies. It is supplemented by another similar but even more radical judgement, put into old Joseph's mouth, the indispensable Joseph who survives the whole action to go on farming the Heights and who is made the vehicle of several central judgements, as well as of many disagreeable Calvinistic attitudes. Resenting the boy Linton Heathcliff's contempt for the staple food, porridge, made, like the oat-cake, from the home-grown oats, Joseph remembers the boy's fine-lady mother: "His mother were just soa—we wer almost too mucky tuh sow t'corn fur makking her breead." There are many related judgements in the novel. We may note here the near-caricature of Lockwood in the first three chapters as the town visitor continually exposing his ignorance of country life and farming.

6.   A regular Victorian theme, springing from the consciousness and resentment by creative artists of a new class snobbery and expressed in such widely different novels as *Alton Locke, North and South, Felix Holt, Dombey and Son, Great Expectations,* as well as *Wuthering Heights* which is earlier than all these.

7.   David Copperfield's Peggotty is the same type, registered through the nursling's eyes (she is supplemented, as he grows out of her, by his great-aunt Betsy Trotwood) and Dickens's testimony to such truths is important. It will be noticed that Peggotty has to mother not only David but also his permanently immature mother. Our nineteenth-century fiction and memoirs are full of such nurses (sometimes they are spinster aunts), bearing witness to the living reality (see, e.g., Lord Shaftesbury's nurse, the Strachey nurse, and the Darwin nurse in Gwen Raverat's autobiography *Period Piece*). Nelly Dean seems to have incurred a good deal of unjustified ill-will, and perverse misrepresentations in consequence, from Catherine's defend-

ers. That Peggotty and Miss Trotwood haven't (so far—or so far as I know) must be due less to Dickens's fairly unambiguous presentation of David's Dora and (but to a lesser degree) of David's mother, than to the fact that Doras are not now in esteem.

8. Hence Nelly's indignant rebuke to Hareton's father in Chap. IX takes the form of telling him: "Oh! I wonder his mother does not rise from her grave to see how you use him."

9. Significantly, because old Joseph "was relentless in worrying him about ruling his children rigidly," as religion required.

10. C. P. Sanger's *The Structure of "Wuthering Heights"* (a Hogarth Press pamphlet).

11. Other pre-Victorian novelists noted and resented the effects on children too. In the original preface to her children's classic *Holiday House* (1839), Catherine Sinclair wrote: "In these pages the author has endeavoured to paint that species of noisy, frolicsome, mischievous children, now almost extinct, wishing to preserve a sort of fabulous remembrance of days long past, when young people were like wild horses on the prairies, rather than like well-broken hacks on the road."

12. With the added force of Scott's dark and violent *Ravenswood* who both in name-pattern and type of hero suggests Heathcliff.

13. Mrs Gaskell says she told "of bygone days of the countryside; old ways of living, former inhabitants, decayed gentry who had melted away, and whose places knew them no more; family tragedies, and dark superstitious dooms; and in telling these things, without the least consciousness that there might ever be anything requiring to be softened down, would give at full length the bare and simple details." This is evidence of external, real life, sources for *Wuthering Heights* which cannot be dismissed.

Wuthering Heights

FRANK KERMODE*

When Lockwood first visits Wuthering Heights he notices, among other-wise irrelevant decorations carved above the door, the date *1500* and the name *Hareton Earnshaw*. It is quite clear that everybody read and reads this (I) as a sort of promise of something else to come. It is part of what is nowadays called a "hermeneutic code"; something that promises, and perhaps after some delay provides, explanation. There is, of course, likely to be some mea-sure of peripeteia or trick; you would be surprised if the explanation were not, in some way, surprising, or at any rate, at this stage unpredictable. And so it proves. The expectations aroused by these inscriptions are strictly *generic;* you must know things of this kind before you can entertain expectations of the sort I mention. Genre in this sense is what Leonard Meyer (writing of music) calls "an internalized probability system." Such a system could, but perhaps shouldn't, be thought of as constituting some sort of contract between reader and writer. Either way, the inscriptions can be seen as something other than simple elements in a series of one damned thing after another, or even of events relative to a story as such. They reduce the range of probabilities, reduce randomness, and are expected to recur. There will be "feedback." This may not extinguish all the informational possibilities in the original stimulus, which may be, and in this case is, obscurer than we thought, "higher," as the information theorists say, "in entropy." The narrative is more than merely a lengthy delay, after which a true descendant of Hareton Earnshaw reoccupies the ancestral house; though there is little delay before we hear about him, and can make a guess if we want.

When Hareton is first discussed, Nelly Dean rather oddly describes him as "the late Mrs. Linton's nephew." Why not "the late Mr. Earnshaw's son"? It is only in the previous sentence that we have first heard the name Linton, when the family of that name is mentioned as having previously occupied Thrushcross Grange. Perhaps we are to wonder how Mrs. Linton came to have a nephew named Earnshaw. At any rate, Nelly's obliquity thus serves to associate Hareton, in a hazy way, with the house on which his name is *not* carved, and with a family no longer in evidence. Only later do we discover

*Reprinted from F. Kermode *The Classic* (London: Faber and Faber, 1971), 119–30.

that he is in the direct Earnshaw line, in fact, as Nelly says, "the last of them." So begins the provision of information which both fulfils and qualifies the early "hermeneutic" promise; because, of course, Hareton, his inheritance restored, goes to live at the Grange. The two principal characters remaining at the end are Mr. and Mrs. Hareton Earnshaw. The other names, which have intruded on Earnshaw—Linton and Heathcliff—are extinct. In between there have been significant recursions to the original inscription—in Chapter XX Hareton cannot read it; in XXIV he can read the name but not the date.

We could say, I suppose, that this so far tells us nothing about *Wuthering Heights* that couldn't, with appropriate changes, be said of most novels. All of them contain the equivalent of such inscriptions; indeed all writing is a sort of inscription, cut memorably into the uncaused flux of event; and inscriptions of the kind I am talking about are interesting secondary clues about the nature of the writing in which they occur. They draw attention to the literariness of what we are reading, indicate that the story is a story, perhaps with beneficial effects on our normal powers of perception; above all they distinguish a *literary* system which has no constant relation to readers with interests and expectations altered by long passages of time. Or, to put it another way, Emily Brontë's contemporaries operated different probability systems from ours, and might well ignore whatever in a text did not comply with their generic expectations, dismissing the rest somehow—by skipping, by accusations of bad craftsmanship, inexperience, or the like. In short, their internalized probability systems survive them in altered and less stringent forms; we can read more of the text than they could, and of course read it differently. In fact, the only works we value enough to call classic are those which, and they demonstrate by surviving, are complex and indeterminate enough to allow us our necessary pluralities. That "Mene, Mene, Tekel, Upharsin" has now many interpretations. It is in the nature of works of art to be open, in so far as they are "good"; though it is in the nature of authors, and of readers, to close them.

The openness of *Wuthering Heights* might be somewhat more extensively illustrated by an inquiry into the passage describing Lockwood's bad night at the house, when, on his second visit, he was cut off from Thrushcross Grange by a storm. He is given an odd sort of bed in a bedroom-within-a-bedroom; Catherine Earnshaw slept in it and later Heathcliff would die in it. Both the bed and the lattice are subjects of very elaborate "play"; but I want rather to consider the inscriptions Lockwood examines before retiring. There is writing on the wall, or on the ledge by his bed: it "was nothing but a name repeated in all kinds of characters, large and small—*Catherine Earnshaw,* here and there varied to *Catherine Heathcliff,* and then again to *Catherine Linton.*" When he closes his eyes Lockwood is assailed by white letters "which started from the dark, as vivid as spectres—the air swarmed with Catherines." He has no idea whatever to whom these names belong, yet the expression "nothing but a name" seems to suggest that they all belong to one person. Waking from a doze he finds the name *Catherine Earnshaw* inscribed in a book his candle has scorched.

It is true that Lockwood has earlier met a Mrs. Heathcliff, and got into a tangle about who she was, taking first Heathcliff and then Hareton Earnshaw for her husband, as indeed, we discover she, in a different sense, had also done or was to do. For she had a merely apparent kinship relation with Heathcliff—bearing his name as the wife of his impotent son and having to tolerate his ironic claim to fatherhood—as a prelude to the restoration of her true name, Earnshaw; it is her mother's story reversed. But Lockwood was not told her first name. Soon he is to encounter a ghost called Catherine Linton; but if the scribbled names signify one person he and we are obviously going to have to wait to find out who it is. Soon we learn that Mrs. Heathcliff is Heathcliff's daughter-in-law, *née* Catherine Linton, and obviously not the ghost. Later it becomes evident that the scratcher must have been Catherine Earnshaw, later Linton, a girl long dead who might well have been Catherine Heathcliff, but wasn't.

When you have processed all the information you have been waiting for you see the point of the order of the scribbled names, as Lockwood gives them: *Catherine Earnshaw, Catherine Heathcliff, Catherine Linton.* Read from left to right they recapitulate Catherine Earnshaw's story; read from right to left, the story of her daughter, Catherine Linton. The names Catherine and Earnshaw begin and end the narrative. Of course some of the events needed to complete this pattern had not occurred when Lockwood slept in the little bedroom; indeed the marriage of Hareton and Catherine is still in the future when the novel ends. Still, this is an account of the movement of the book: away from Earnshaw and back, like the movement of the house itself. And all the movement must be *through* Heathcliff.

Charlotte Brontë remarks, from her own experience that the writer says more than he knows, and was emphatic that this was so with Emily. "Having formed these beings, she did not know what she had done." Of course this strikes us as no more than common sense; though Charlotte chooses to attribute it to Emily's ignorance of the world. A narrative is not a transcription of something pre-existent. And this is precisely the situation represented by Lockwood's play with the names he does not understand, his constituting, out of many scribbles, a rebus for the plot of the novel he's in. The situation indicates the kind of work we must do when a narrative opens itself to us, and contains information in excess of what generic probability requires.

Consider the names again; of course they reflect the isolation of the society under consideration, but still it is remarkable that in a story whose principal characters all marry there are effectively only three surnames, all of which each Catherine assumes. Furthermore, the Earnshaw family makes do with only three Christian names, Catherine, Hindley, Hareton. Heathcliff is a family name also, but parsimoniously, serving as both Christian name and surname; always lacking one or the other, he wears his name as an indication of his difference, and this persists after death since his tombstone is inscribed with the one word *Heathcliff*. Like Frances, briefly the wife of Hindley, he is simply a sort of interruption in the Earnshaw system.

Heathcliff is then as it were between names, as between families (he is the door through which Earnshaw passes into Linton, and out again to Earnshaw). He is often introduced, as if characteristically, standing outside, or entering, or leaving, a door. He is in and out of the Earnshaw family simultaneously; servant and child of the family (like Hareton whom he puts in the same position, he helps to indicate the archaic nature of the house's society, the lack of sharp social division, which is not characteristic of the Grange). His origins are equally betwixt and between: the gutter or the royal origin imagined for him by Nelly; prince or pauper, American or Lascar, child of God or devil. This betweenness persists, I think: Heathcliff, for instance, fluctuates between poverty and riches; also between virility and impotence. To Catherine he is between brother and lover; he slept with her as a child, and again in death, but not between latency and extinction. He has much force, yet fathers an exceptionally puny child. Domestic yet savage like the dogs, bleak yet full of fire like the house, he bestrides the great opposites: love and death (the necrophiliac confession), culture and nature ("half-civilized ferocity") in a posture that certainly cannot be explained by any generic formula ("Byronic" or "Gothic").

He stands also between a past and a future; when his force expires the old Earnshaw family moves into the future associated with the civilized Grange, where the insane authoritarianism of the Heights is a thing of the past, where there are cultivated distinctions between gentle and simple—a new world in the more civil south. It was the Grange that first separated Heathcliff from Catherine, so that Earnshaws might eventually live there. Of the children—Hareton, Cathy, and Linton—none physically resembles Heathcliff; the first two have Catherine's eyes (XXXIII) and the other is, as his first name implies, a Linton. Cathy's two cousin-marriages, constituting an endogamous route to the civilized exogamy of the south—are the consequence of Heathcliff's standing between Earnshaw and Linton, north and south; earlier he had involuntarily saved the life of the baby Hareton. His ghost and Catherine's, at the end, are of interest only to the superstitious, the indigenous now to be dispossessed by a more rational culture.

If we look, once more, at Lockwood's inscriptions, we may read them thus.

Earnshaws persist, but they must eventually do so within the Linton culture. Catherine burns up in her transit from left to right. The quasi-Earnshaw union of Heathcliff and Isabella leaves the younger Cathy an easier passage; she has only to get through Linton Heathcliff, who is replaced by Hareton Earnshaw. Hareton has suffered part of Heathcliff's fate, moved, as it were, from Earnshaw to Heathcliff, and replaced him as son-servant, as gratuitously cruel; but he is the last of the Earnshaws, and Cathy can both restore to him the house on which his name is carved, and take him on the now smooth path to Thrushcross Grange.

Novels, even this one, were read in houses more like the Grange than the Heights, as the emphasis on the ferocious piety of the Earnshaw library suggests. The order of the novel is a civilized order; it presupposes a reader in the midst of an educated family and habituated to novel reading; a reader, moreover, who believes in the possibility of effective ethical choices. And because this is the case, the author can allow herself to meet his proper expectations without imposing on the text or on him absolute generic control. She need not, that is, know all that she is saying. She can, in all manner of ways, invite the reader to collaborate, leave to him the supply of meaning where the text is indeterminate or discontinuous, where explanations are required to fill narrative lacunae.

Instances of this are provided by some of the dreams in the book. Lockwood's brief dream of the spectral letters is followed by another about an interminable sermon, which develops from hints about Joseph in Catherine's Bible. The purport of this dream is obscure. The preacher Jabes Branderham takes a hint from his text and expands the seven deadly sins into seventy times seven plus one. It is when he reaches the last section that Lockwood's patience runs out, and he protests, with his own allusion to the Bible: "He shall return no more to his house, neither shall his place know him any more." Dreams in stories are usually given a measure of oneiric ambiguity, but stay fairly close to the narrative line, or if not, convey information otherwise useful; but this one does not appear to do so, except in so far as that text may bear obscurely and incorrectly on the question of where Hareton will end up. It is, however, given a naturalistic explanation: the rapping of the preacher on the pulpit is a dream version of the rapping of the fir tree on the window.

Lockwood once more falls asleep, but dreams again, and "if possible, still more disagreeably than before." Once more he hears the fir-bough, and rises to silence it; he breaks the window and finds himself clutching the cold hand of a child who calls herself Catherine Linton.

He speaks of this as a dream, indeed he ascribes to it "the intense horror of nightmare," and the blood that runs down into the bedclothes may be explained by his having cut his hand as he broke the glass; but he does not say so, attributing it to his own cruelty in rubbing the child's wrist on the pane; and Heathcliff immediately makes it obvious that of the two choices the text has so far allowed us the more acceptable is that Lockwood was not dreaming at all.

So we cannot dismiss this dream as "Gothic" ornament or commentary, or even as the kind of dream Lockwood has just had, in which the same fir-bough produced a comically extended dream-explanation of its presence. There remain all manner of puzzles: why is the visitant a child and, if a child, why Catherine *Linton?* The explanation, that this name got into Lockwood's dream from a scribble in the Bible is one even he finds hard to accept. He hovers between an explanation involving "ghosts and goblins," and the simpler one of nightmare; though he has no more doubt than Heathcliff that "it"—the child—was trying to enter. For good measure he is greeted, on going downstairs, by a cat, a brindled cat, with its echo of Shakespearian witchcraft.

It seems plain, then, that the dream is not simply a transformation of the narrative, a commentary on another level, but an integral part of it. The Branderham dream is, in a sense, a trick, suggesting a measure of rationality in the earlier dream which we might want to transfer to the later experience, as Lockwood partly does. When we see that there is a considerable conflict in the clues as to how we should read the second tapping and relate it to the first we grow aware of further contrasts between the two, for the first is a comic treatment of 491 specific and resistible sins for which Lockwood is about to be punished by exile from his home, and the second is a more horrible spectral invasion of the womb-like or tomb-like room in which he is housed. There are doubtless many other observations to be made; it is not a question of deciding which is the single right reading, but of dealing, as reader, with a series of indeterminacies which the text will not resolve.

Nelly Dean refuses to listen to Catherine's dream, one of those which went through and through her "like wine through water"; and of those dreams we hear nothing save this account of their power. "We're dismal enough without conjuring up ghosts and visions to perplex us," says Nelly—another speaking silence in the text, for it is implied that we are here denied relevant information. But she herself suffers a dream or vision. After Heathcliff's return she finds herself at the signpost: engraved in its sandstone—with all the permanence that Hareton's name has on the house—are "Wuthering Heights" to the north, "Gimmerton" to the east, and "Thrushcross Grange" to the south. Soft south, harsh north, and the rough civility of the market town (something like that of Nelly herself) in between. As before, these inscriptions provoke a dream apparition, a vision of Hindley as a child. Fearing that he has come to harm, she rushes to the Heights and again sees the spectral child, but it turns out to be Hareton, Hindley's son. His appearance betwixt and between the Heights and the Grange was proleptic; now he is back at the Heights, a stone in his hand, threatening his old nurse, rejecting the Grange. And as Hindley turned into Hareton, so Hareton turns into Heathcliff, for the figure that appears in the doorway is Heathcliff.

This is very like a real dream in its transformations and displacements. It has no simple narrative function whatever, and an abridgement might leave it out. But the confusion of generations, and the double usurpation of Hindley by his son and Heathcliff, all three of them variants of the incivility of the Heights, gives a new relation to the agents, and qualifies our sense of all narrative explanations offered in the text. For it is worth remarking that no naturalistic explanation of Nelly's experience is offered; in this it is unlike the treatment of the later vision, when the little boy sees the ghost of Heathcliff and "a woman," a passage which is a preparation for further ambiguities in the ending. Dreams, visions, ghosts—the whole pneumatology of the book is only indeterminately related to the "natural" narrative. And this serves to muddle routine "single" readings, to confound explanation and expectation, and to make necessary a full recognition of the intrinsic plurality of the text.

Would it be reasonable to say this: that the mingling of generic opposites—daylight and dream narratives—creates a need, which we must supply, for something that will mediate between them? If so, we can go on to argue that the text in our response to it is a provision of such mediators, between life and death, the barbaric and the civilized, family and sexual relations. The principal instrument of mediation may well be Heathcliff: neither inside nor out, neither wholly master nor wholly servant, the husband who is no husband, the brother who is no brother, the father who abuses his changeling child, the cousin without kin. And that the chain of narrators serve to mediate between the barbarism of the story and the civility of the reader—making the text itself an intermediate term between archaic and modern—must surely have been pointed out.

What we must not forget, however, is that it is in the completion of the text by the reader that these adjustments are made; and each reader will make them differently. Plurality is here not a prescription but a fact. There is so much that is blurred and tentative, incapable of decisive explanation; however we set about our reading, with a sociological or a pneumatological, a cultural or a narrative code uppermost in our minds, we must fall into division and discrepancy; the doors of communication are sometimes locked, sometimes open, and Heathcliff may be astride the threshold, opening, closing, breaking. And it is surely evident that the possibilities of interpretation increase as time goes on. The constraints of a period culture dissolve, generic presumptions which concealed gaps disappear, and we now see that the book, as James thought novels should, truly "glories in a gap," a hermeneutic gap in which the reader's imagination must operate, so that he speaks continuously in the text. For these reasons the rebus—*Catherine Earnshaw, Catherine Heathcliff, Catherine Linton*—has exemplary significance. It is a riddle that the text answers only silently; for example it will neither urge nor forbid you to remember that it resembles the riddle of the Sphinx—what manner of person exists in these three forms?—to which the single acceptable and probable answer involves incest and ruin.

Wuthering Heights

Terry Eagleton*

I have said that *Wuthering Heights* remains unriven by the conflicts it releases, and it contrasts as such with those Charlotte works which are formally flawed by the strains and frictions of their "content." Charlotte's fiction sets out to reconcile thematically what I have crudely termed "Romance" and "realism" but sometimes displays severe structural disjunctions between the two; *Wuthering Heights* fastens thematically on a near-absolute antagonism between these modes but achieves, structurally and stylistically, an astonishing unity between them. Single incidents are inseparably high drama and domestic farce, figures like Catherine Earnshaw contradictory amalgams of the passionate and the pettish. There seems to me an ideological basis to this paradoxical contrast between the two sisters' works. Charlotte's novels, as I have suggested, are ideological in that they exploit fiction and fable to smooth the jagged edges of real conflict, and the evasions which that entails emerge as aesthetic unevennesses—as slanting, overemphasis, idealisation, structural dissonance. *Wuthering Heights,* on the other hand, confronts the tragic truth that the passion and society it presents are not fundamentally reconcilable—that there remains at the deepest level an ineradicable contradiction between them which refuses to be unlocked, which obtrudes itself as the very stuff and secret of experience. It is, then, precisely the imagination capable of confronting this tragic duality which has the power to produce the aesthetically superior work—which can synchronise in its internal structures the most shattering passion with the most rigorous realist control. The more authentic social and moral recognitions of the book, in other words, generate a finer artistic control; the unflinchingness with which the novel penetrates into fundamental contradictions is realised in a range of richer imaginative perceptions.

The primary contradiction I have in mind is the choice posed for Catherine between Heathcliff and Edgar Linton. That choice seems to me the pivotal event of the novel, the decisive catalyst of the tragedy; and if this is so, then the crux of *Wuthering Heights* must be conceded by even the most remorselessly mythological and mystical of critics to be a social one. In a crucial act of

*Reprinted from T. Eagleton, *Myths of Power: A Marxist Study of the Brontës* (London: Macmillan, 1975).

self-betrayal and bad faith, Catherine rejects Heathcliff as a suitor because he is socially inferior to Linton; and it is from this that the train of destruction follows. Heathcliff's own view of the option is not, of course, to be wholly credited: he is clearly wrong to think that Edgar "is scarcely a degree dearer [to Catherine] than her dog, or her horse." Linton lacks spirit, but he is, as Nelly says, kind, honourable and trustful, a loving husband to Catherine and utterly distraught at her loss. Even so, the perverse act of *mauvaise foi* by which Catherine trades her authentic selfhood for social privilege is rightly denounced by Heathcliff as spiritual suicide and murder:

> "*Why* did you betray your own heart, Cathy? I have not one word of comfort. You deserve this. You have killed yourself. Yes, you may kiss me, and cry; and ring out my kisses and tears: they'll blight you—they'll damn you. You loved me—then what *right* had you to leave me? What right—answer me—for the poor fancy you felt for Linton? Because misery and degradation, and death, and nothing that God or Satan could inflict would have parted us, *you,* of your own will, did it. I have not broken your heart—*you* have broken it; and in breaking it, you have broken mine." (xv)

Like Lucy Snowe, Catherine tries to lead two lives: she hopes to square authenticity with social convention, running in harness an ontological commitment to Heathcliff with a phenomenal relationship to Linton. "I *am* Heathcliff!" is dramatically arresting, but it is also a way of keeping the outcast at arm's length, evading the challenge he offers. If Catherine is Heathcliff—if identity rather than relationship is in question—then their estrangement is inconceivable, and Catherine can therefore turn to others without violating the timeless metaphysical idea Heathcliff embodies. She finds in him an integrity of being denied or diluted in routine social relations; but to preserve that ideal means reifying him to a Hegelian essence, sublimely untainted by empirical fact. Heathcliff, understandably, refuses to settle for this: he would rather enact his essence in existence by becoming Catherine's lover. He can, it seems, be endowed with impressive ontological status only at the price of being nullified as a person.

The uneasy alliance of social conformity and personal fulfilment for which Charlotte's novels works is not, then, feasible in the world of *Wuthering Heights;* Catherine's attempt to compromise unleashes the contradictions which will drive both her and Heathcliff to their deaths. One such contradiction lies in the relation between Heathcliff and the Earnshaw family. As a waif and orphan, Heathcliff is inserted into the close-knit family structure as an alien; he emerges from that ambivalent domain of darkness which is the "outside" of the tightly defined domestic system. That darkness is ambivalent because it is at once fearful and fertilising, as Heathcliff himself is both gift and threat. Earnshaw's first words about him make this clear: " 'See here, wife! I was never so beaten with anything in my life: but you must e'en take

it as a gift of God; though it's as dark almost as if it came from the devil'"
(iv). Stripped as he is of determinate social relations, of a given function within
the family, Heathcliff's presence is radically gratuitous; the arbitrary, unmoti-
vated event of his arrival at the Heights offers its inhabitants a chance to
transcend the constrictions of their self-enclosed social structure and gather
him in. Because Heathcliff's circumstances are so obscure he is available to be
accepted or rejected simply for himself, laying claim to no status other than a
human one. He is, of course, proletarian in appearance, but the obscurity of
his origins also frees him of any exact social role; as Nelly Dean muses later,
he might equally be a prince. He is ushered into the Heights for no good reason other than to be arbitrarily loved; and in this sense he is a touchstone of
others' responses, a liberating force for Cathy and a stumbling-block for others. Nelly hates him at first, unable to transcend her bigotry against the new
and non-related; she puts him on the landing like a dog, hoping he will be
gone by morning. Earnshaw pets and favours him, and in doing so creates
fresh inequalities in the family hierarchy which become the source of Hindley's hatred. As heir to the Heights, Hindley understandably feels his social
role subverted by this irrational, unpredictable intrusion.

Catherine, who does not expect to inherit, responds spontaneously to
Heathcliff's presence; and because this antagonises Hindley she becomes after
Earnshaw's death a spiritual orphan as Heathcliff is a literal one. Both are
allowed to run wild; both become the "outside" of the domestic structure.
Because his birth is unknown, Heathcliff is a purely atomised individual, free
of generational ties in a novel where genealogical relations are of crucial thematic and structural importance; and it is because he is an internal *émigré*
within the Heights that he can lay claim to a relationship of direct personal
equality with Catherine who, as the daughter of the family, is the least economically integral member. Heathcliff offers Catherine a friendship which
opens fresh possibilities of freedom within the internal system of the Heights;
in a situation where social determinants are insistent, freedom can mean only
a relative independence of given blood-ties, of the settled, evolving, predictable structures of kinship. Whereas in Charlotte's fiction the severing or
lapsing of such relations frees you for progress up the class-system, the freedom which Cathy achieves with Heathcliff takes her down that system, into
consorting with a "gypsy." Yet "down" is also "outside," just as gypsy signifies
"lower class" but also asocial vagrant, classless natural life-form. As the eternal rocks beneath the woods, Heathcliff is both lowly and natural, enjoying
the partial freedom from social pressures appropriate to those at the bottom
of the class-structure. In loving Heathcliff, Catherine is taken outside the
family and society into an opposing realm which can be adequately imaged
only as "Nature."

The loving equality between Catherine and Heathcliff stands, then, as a
paradigm of human possibilities which reach beyond, and might ideally

unlock, the tightly dominative system of the Heights. Yet at the same time Heathcliff's mere presence fiercely intensifies that system's harshness, twisting all the Earnshaw relationships into bitter antagonism. He unwittingly sharpens a violence endemic to the Heights—a violence which springs both from the hard exigencies imposed by its struggle with the land, and from its social exclusiveness as a self-consciously ancient, respectable family. The violence which Heathcliff unwittingly triggers is turned against him: he is cast out by Hindley, culturally deprived, reduced to the status of farm-labourer. What Hindley does, in fact, is to invert the potential freedom symbolised by Heathcliff into a parody of itself, into the non-freedom of neglect. Heathcliff is robbed of liberty in two antithetical ways: exploited as a servant on the one hand, allowed to run wild on the other; and this contradiction is appropriate to childhood, which is a time of relative freedom from convention and yet, paradoxically, a phase of authoritarian repression. In this sense there is freedom for Heathcliff neither within society nor outside it; his two conditions are inverted mirror-images of one another. It is a contradiction which encapsulates a crucial truth about bourgeois society. If there is no genuine liberty on its "inside"—Heathcliff is oppressed by work and the familial structure—neither is there more than a caricature of liberty on the "outside," since the release of running wild is merely a function of cultural impoverishment. The friendship of Heathcliff and Cathy crystallises under the pressures of economic and cultural violence, so that the freedom it seems to signify ("half-savage and hardy, and free") is always the other face of oppression, always exists in its shadow. With Heathcliff and Catherine, as in Charlotte's fiction, bitter social reality breeds Romantic escapism; but whereas Charlotte's novels try to trim the balance between them, *Wuthering Heights* shows a more dialectical interrelation at work. Romantic intensity is locked in combat with society, but cannot wholly transcend it; your freedom is bred and deformed in the shadow of your oppression, just as, in the adult Heathcliff, oppression is the logical consequence of the exploiter's "freedom."

Just as Hindley withdraws culture from Heathcliff as a mode of domination, so Heathcliff acquires culture as a weapon. He amasses a certain amount of cultural capital in his two years' absence in order to shackle others more effectively, buying up the expensive commodity of gentility in order punitively to re-enter the society from which he was punitively expelled. This is liberty of a kind, in contrast with his previous condition; but the novel is insistent on its ultimately illusory nature. In oppressing others the exploiter imprisons himself; the adult Heathcliff's systematic tormenting is fed by his victims' pain but also drains him of blood, impels and possesses him as an external force. His alienation from Catherine estranges him from himself to the point where his brutalities become tediously perfunctory gestures, the mechanical motions of a man who is already withdrawing himself from his own body. Heathcliff moves from being Hindley's victim to becoming, like Catherine, his own executioner.

Throughout *Wuthering Heights,* labour and culture, bondage and freedom, Nature and artifice appear at once as each other's dialectical negations and as subtly matched, mutually reflective. Culture—gentility—is the opposite of labour for young Heathcliff and Hareton; but it is also a crucial economic weapon, as well as a product of work itself. The delicate spiritless Lintons in their crimson-carpeted drawing-room are radically severed from the labour which sustains them; gentility grows from the production of others, detaches itself from that work (as the Grange is separate from the Heights), and then comes to dominate the labour on which it is parasitic. In doing so, it becomes a form of self-bondage; if work is servitude, so in a subtler sense is civilisation. To some extent, these polarities are held together in the yeoman-farming structure of the Heights. Here labour and culture, freedom and necessity, Nature and society are roughly complementary. The Earnshaws are gentlemen yet they work the land; they enjoy the freedom of being their own masters, but that freedom moves within the tough discipline of labour; and because the social unit of the Heights—the family—is both "natural"' (biological) and an economic system, it acts to some degree as a mediation between Nature and artifice, naturalising property relations and socialising blood-ties. Relationships in this isolated world are turbulently face-to-face, but they are also impersonally mediated through a working relation with Nature. This is not to share Mrs Q. D. Leavis's view of the Heights as "a wholesome primitive and natural unit of a healthy society";[1] there does not, for instance, seem much that is wholesome about Joseph. Joseph incarnates a grimness inherent in conditions of economic exigency, where relationships must be tightly ordered and are easily warped into violence. One of *Wuthering Heights'* more notable achievements is ruthlessly to de-mystify the Victorian notion of the family as a pious, pacific space within social conflict. Even so, the Heights does pin together contradictions which the entry of Heathcliff will break open. Heathcliff disturbs the Heights because he is simply superfluous: he has no defined place within its biological and economic system. (He may well be Catherine's illegitimate half-brother, just as he may well have passed his two-year absence in Tunbridge Wells.) The superfluity he embodies is that of a sheerly human demand for recognition; but since there is no space for such surplus within the terse economy of the Heights, it proves destructive rather than creative in effect, straining and overloading already taut relationships. Heathcliff catalyses an aggression intrinsic to Heights society; that sound blow Hindley hands out to Catherine on the evening of Heathcliff's first appearance is slight but significant evidence against the case that conflict starts only with Heathcliff's arrival.

The effect of Heathcliff is to explode those conflicts into antagonisms which finally rip the place apart. In particular, he marks the beginnings of that process whereby passion and personal intensity separate out from the social domain and offer an alternative commitment to it. For farming families like the Earnshaws, work and human relations are roughly coterminous: work is socialised, personal relations mediated through a context of labour. Heathcliff, however, is set to work meaninglessly, as a servant rather than a member of the family; and his fervent emotional life with Catherine is thus forced outside the working environment into the wild Nature of the heath, rather than Nature reclaimed and worked up into significant value in the social activity of labour. Heathcliff is stripped of culture in the sense of gentility, but the result is a paradoxical intensifying of his fertile imaginative liaison with Catherine. It is fitting, then, that their free, neglected wanderings lead them to their adventure at Thrushcross Grange. For if the Romantic childhood culture of Catherine and Heathcliff exists in a social limbo divorced from the minatory world of working relations, the same can be said in a different sense of the genteel culture of the Lintons, surviving as it does on the basis of material conditions it simultaneously conceals. As the children spy on the Linton family, that concealed brutality is unleashed in the shape of bulldogs brought to the defence of civility. The natural energy in which the Linton's culture is rooted bursts literally through to savage the "savages" who appear to threaten property. The underlying truth of violence, continuously visible at the Heights, is momentarily exposed; old Linton thinks the intruders are after his rents. Culture draws a veil over such brute force but also sharpens it: the more property you have, the more ruthlessly you need to defend it. Indeed, Heathcliff himself seems dimly aware of how cultivation exacerbates "natural" conflict, as we see in his scornful account of the Linton children's petulant squabbling; cultivation, by pampering and swaddling "natural" drives, at once represses serious physical violence and breeds a neurasthenic sensitivity which allows selfish impulse free rein. "Natural" aggression is nurtured both by an excess and an absence of culture—a paradox demonstrated by Catherine Earnshaw, who is at once wild and pettish, savage and spoilt. Nature and culture, then, are locked in a complex relation of antagonism and affinity: the Romantic fantasies of Heathcliff and Catherine, and the Romantic Linton drawing-room with its gold-bordered ceiling and shimmering chandelier, both bear the scars of the material conditions which produced them—scars visibly inscribed on Cathy's ankle. Yet to leave the matter there would be to draw a purely formal parallel. For what distinguishes the two forms of Romance is Heathcliff: his intense communion with Catherine is an uncompromising rejection of the Linton world.

The opposition, however, is not merely one between the values of personal relationship and those of conventional society. What prevents this is the curious impersonality of the relationship between Catherine and Heathcliff. Edgar Linton shows at his best a genuine capacity for tender, loving fidelity; but this thrives on obvious limits. The limits are those of the closed room into which the children peer—the glowing, sheltered space within which those close, immediate encounters which make for both tenderness and pettishness may be conducted. Linton is released from material pressures into such a civilised enclave; and in that sense his situation differs from that of the

Heights, where personal relations are more intimately entwined with a working context. The relationship of Heathcliff and Catherine, however, provides a third term. It really is a personal relationship, yet seems also to transcend the personal into some region beyond it. Indeed, there is a sense in which the unity the couple briefly achieve is narrowed and degutted by being described as "personal." In so far as "personal" suggests the liberal humanism of Edgar, with his concern (crudely despised by Heathcliff) for pity, charity and humanity, the word is clearly inapplicable to the fierce mutual tearings of Catherine and Heathcliff. Yet it is inadequate to the positive as well as the destructive aspects of their love. Their relationship is, we say, "ontological" or "metaphysical" because it opens out into the more-than-personal, enacts a style of being which is more than just the property of two individuals, which suggests in its impersonality something beyond a merely Romantic-individualist response to social oppression. Their relationship articulates a depth inexpressible in routine social practice, transcendent of available social languages. Its impersonality suggests both a savage depersonalising and a paradigmatic significance; and in neither sense is the relationship wholly within their conscious control. What Heathcliff offers Cathy is a non- or pre-social relationship, as the only authentic form of living in a world of exploitation and inequality, a world where one must refuse to measure oneself by the criteria of the class-structure and so must appear inevitably subversive. Whereas in Charlotte's novels the love-relationship takes you into society, in *Wuthering Heights* it drives you out of it. The love between Heathcliff and Catherine is an intuitive intimacy raised to cosmic status, by-passing the mediation of the "social"; and this, indeed, is both its strength and its limit. Its non-sociality is on the one hand a revolutionary refusal of the given language of social roles and values; and if the relationship is to remain unabsorbed by society it must therefore appear as natural rather than social, since Nature is the "outside" of society. On the other hand, the novel cannot realise the meaning of that revolutionary refusal in social terms; the most it can do is to *universalise* that meaning by intimating the mysteriously impersonal energies from which the relationship springs.

Catherine, of course, *is* absorbed: she enters the civilised world of the Lintons and leaves Heathcliff behind, to become a "wolfish, pitiless" man. To avoid incorporation means remaining as unreclaimed as the wild furze: there is no way in this novel of temporising between conformity and rebellion. But there is equally no way for the revolutionary depth of relationship between Heathcliff and Catherine to realise itself as a historical force; instead, it becomes an elusive dream of absolute value, an incomparably more powerful version of Charlotte's myth of lost origins. Catherine and Heathcliff seek to preserve the primordial moment of pre-social harmony, before the fall into history and oppression. But it won't do to see them merely as children eternally fixated in some Edenic infancy: we do not see them merely as children, and in any case to be "merely" a child is to endure the punitive pressures of an adult world. Moreover, it is none of Heathcliff's fault that the relationship remains "metaphysical": it is Catherine who consigns it to unfulfilment. Their love remains an unhistorical essence which fails to enter into concrete existence and can do so, ironically, only in death. Death indeed, as the ultimate outer limit of consciousness and society, is the locus of Catherine and Heathcliff's love, the horizon on which it moves. The absolutism of death is prefigured, echoed back, in the remorseless intensity with which their relationship is actually lived; yet their union can be achieved only in the act of abandoning the actual world.

Catherine and Heathcliff's love, then, is pushed to the periphery by society itself, projected into myth; yet the fact that it seems *inherently* convertible to myth spotlights the threshold of the novel's "possible consciousness." I take that phrase from Lukács and Goldmann to suggest those restrictions set on the consciousness of a historical period which only a transformation of real social relations could abolish—the point at which the most enterprising imagination presses against boundaries which signify not mere failures of personal perception but the limits of what can be historically said. The force Heathcliff symbolises can be truly realised only in some more than merely individualist form; *Wuthering Heights* has its roots not in that narrowed, simplified Romanticism which pits the lonely rebel against an anonymous order, but in that earlier, more authentic Romantic impulse which posits its own kind of "transindividual" order of value, its own totality, against the order which forces it into exile. Heathcliff may be Byronic, but not in the way Rochester is: the novel counterposes social convention not merely with contrasting personal life-styles but with an alternative world of meaning. Yet it is here that the limits of "possible consciousness" assert themselves: the offered totalities of Nature, myth and cosmic energy are forced to figure as social worlds unable to engage in more than idealist ways with the society they subject to judgement. The price of universality is to be fixed eternally at a point extrinsic to social life—fixed, indeed, at the moment of death, which both manifests a depth challengingly alien to the Lintons and withdraws the character from that conventional landscape into an isolated realm of his own.

Nature, in any case, is no true "outside" to society, since its conflicts are transposed into the social arena. In one sense the novel sharply contrasts Nature and society; in another sense it grasps civilised life as a higher distillation of ferocious natural appetite. Nature, then, is a thoroughly ambiguous category, inside and outside society simultaneously. At one level it represents the unsalvaged region beyond the pale of culture; at another level it signifies the all-pervasive reality of which culture itself is a particular outcropping. It is, indeed, this ambiguity which supplies the vital link between the childhood and adult phases of Heathcliff's career. Heathcliff the child is "natural" both because he is allowed to run wild and because he is reduced as Hindley's labourer to a mere physical instrument; Heathcliff the adult is "natural" man in a Hobbesian sense: an appetitive exploiter to whom no tie or tradition is sacred, a callous predator violently sundering the bonds of custom and piety. If the first kind of "naturalness" is anti-social in its estrangement from the norms of "civilised" life, the second involves the unsociality of one set at the centre of a world whose social relations are inhuman. Heathcliff moves from being natural in the sense of an anarchic outsider to adopting the behaviour natural to an insider in a viciously competitive society. Of course, to be natural in both senses is at a different level to be unnatural. From the viewpoint of culture, it is unnatural that a child should be degraded to a savage, and unnatural too that a man should behave in the obscene way Heathcliff does. But culture in this novel is as problematical at Nature. There are no cool Arnoldian touchstones by which to take the measure of natural degeneracy, since the dialectical vision of *Wuthering Heights* puts culture into question in the very act of exploring the "naturalness" which is its negation. Just as being natural involves being either completely outside or inside society, as roaming waif or manipulative landlord, so culture signifies either free-wheeling Romantic fantasy or that well-appointed Linton drawing-room. The adult Heathcliff is the focus of these contradictions: as he worms his way into the social structure he becomes progressively detached in spirit from all it holds dear. But *contradiction* is the essential emphasis. Heathcliff's schizophrenia is symptomatic of a world in which there can be no true dialectic between culture and Nature—a world in which culture is merely refuge from or reflex of material conditions, and so either too estranged from or entwined with those conditions to offer a viable alternative.

I take it that Heathcliff, up to the point at which Cathy rejects him, is in general an admirable character. His account of the Grange adventure, candid, satirical and self-aware as it is, might itself be enough to enforce this point; and we have in any case on the other side only the self-confessedly biased testimony of Nelly Dean. Even according to Nelly's grudging commentary, Heathcliff as a child is impressively patient and uncomplaining (although Nelly adds "sullen" out of spite), and the heart-rending cry he raises when old Earnshaw dies is difficult to square with her implication that he felt no gratitude to his benefactor. He bears Hindley's vindictive treatment well, and tries pathetically to keep culturally abreast of Catherine despite it. The novel says quite explicitly that Hindley's systematic degradation of Heathcliff "was enough to make a fiend of a saint"; and we should not therefore be surprised that what it does, more precisely, is to produce a pitiless capitalist landlord out of an oppressed child. Heathcliff the adult is in one sense an inversion, in another sense an organic outgrowth, of Heathcliff the child. Heathcliff the child was an isolated figure whose freedom from given genealogical ties offered, as I have argued, fresh possibilities of relationship; Heathcliff the adult is the atomic capitalist to whom relational bonds are nothing, whose individualism is now enslaving rather than liberating. The child knew the purely negative freedom of running wild; the adult, as a man vehemently pursuing ends progressively alien to him, knows only the delusory freedom of exploiting others. The point is that such freedom seems the only kind available in this society, once the relationship with Catherine has collapsed; the only mode of self-affirmation left to Heathcliff is that of oppression which, since it involves self-oppression, is no affirmation at all. Heathcliff is a self-tormentor, a man who is in hell because he can avenge himself on the system which has robbed him of his soul only by battling with it on its own hated terms. If as a child he was outside and inside that system simultaneously, wandering on the moors and working on the farm, he lives out a similar self-division as an adult, trapped in the grinding contradiction between a false social self and the true identity which lies with Catherine. The social self is false, not because Heathcliff is only apparently brutal—that he certainly is—but because it is contradictorily related to the authentic selfhood which is his passion for Catherine. He installs himself at the centre of conventional society, but with wholly negative and inimical intent; his social role is a calculated self-contradiction, created first to further, and then fiercely displace, his asocial passion for Catherine.

Heathcliff's social relation to both Heights and Grange is one of the most complex issues in the novel. Lockwood remarks that he looks too genteel for the Heights; and indeed, in so far as he represents the victory of capitalist property-dealing over the traditional yeoman economy of the Earnshaws, he is inevitably aligned with the world of the Grange. Heathcliff is a dynamic force which seeks to destroy the old yeoman settlement by dispossessing Hareton; yet he does this partly to revenge himself on the very Linton world whose weapons (property deals, arranged marriages) he deploys so efficiently. He does this, moreover, with a crude intensity which is a quality of the Heights world; his roughness and resilience link him culturally to Wuthering Heights, and he exploits those qualities to destroy both it and the Grange. He is, then, a force which springs out of the Heights yet subverts it, breaking beyond its constrictions into a new, voracious acquisitiveness. His capitalist brutality is an extension as well as a negation of the Heights world he knew as a child; and to that extent there is continuity between his childhood and adult protests against Grange values, if not against Grange weapons. Heathcliff is subjectively a Heights figure opposing the Grange, and objectively a Grange figure undermining the Heights; he focuses acutely the contradictions between the two worlds. His rise to power symbolises at once the triumph of the oppressed over capitalism and the triumph of capitalism over the oppressed.

He is, indeed, contradiction incarnate—both progressive and outdated, at once caricature of and traditionalist protest against the agrarian capitalist forces of Thrushcross Grange. He harnesses those forces to worst the Grange, to beat it at its own game; but in doing so he parodies that property-system, operates against the Lintons with an un–Linton-like explicitness and extremism. He behaves in this way because his "soul" belongs not to that world but to Catherine; and in that sense his true commitment is an "outdated" one, to a past, increasingly mythical realm of absolute personal value which capitalist social relations cancel. He embodies a passionate human protest against the marriage-market values of both Grange and Heights at the same time as he callously images those values in caricatured form. Heathcliff exacts vengeance from that society precisely by extravagantly enacting its twisted priorities, becoming a darkly satirical commentary on conventional mores. If he is in one sense a progressive historical force, he belongs in another sense to the superseded world of the Heights, so that his death and the closing-up of the house seem logically related. In the end Heathcliff is defeated and the Heights restored to its rightful owner; yet at the same time the trends he epitomises triumph in the form of the Grange, to which Hareton and young Catherine move away. Hareton wins and loses the Heights simultaneously; dispossessed by Heathcliff, he repossesses the place only to be in that act assimilated by Thrushcross Grange. And if Hareton both wins and loses, then Heathcliff himself is both ousted and victorious.

Quite who has in fact won in the end is a matter of critical contention. Mrs Leavis and Tom Winnifrith both see the old world as having yielded to the new, in contrast to T. K. Meier, who reads the conclusion as "the victory of tradition over innovation."[2] The critical contention reflects a real ambiguity in the novel. In one sense, the old values have triumphed over the disruptive usurper: Hareton has wrested back his birthright, and the qualities he symbolises, while preserving their authentic vigour, will be fertilised by the civilising grace which the Grange, in the form of young Catherine, can bring. Heathcliff's career appears from his perspective as a shattering but short-lived interlude, after which true balance may be slowly recovered. In a more obvious sense, however, the Grange has won: the Heights is shut up and Hareton will become the new squire. Heathcliff, then, has been the blunt instrument by which the remnants of the Earnshaw world have been transformed into a fully-fledged capitalist class—the historical medium whereby that world is at once annihilated and elevated to the Grange. Thrushcross values have entered into productive dialogue with rough material reality and, by virtue of this spiritual transfusion, ensured their continuing survival; the Grange comes to the Heights and gathers back to itself what the Heights can yield it. This is why it will not do to read the novel's conclusion as some neatly reciprocal symbolic alliance between the two universes, a symmetrical symbiosis of bourgeois realism and upper-class cultivation. Whatever unity the book finally establishes, it is certainly not symmetrical: in a victory for the progressive forces of agrarian capitalism, Hareton, last survivor of the traditional order, is smoothly incorporated into the Grange.

There is another significant reason why the "defeat" of Heathcliff cannot be read as the resilient recovery of a traditional world from the injuries it has suffered at his hands. As an extreme parody of capitalist activity, Heathcliff is also an untypical deviation from its norms; as a remorseless, crudely transparent revelation of the real historical character of the Grange, he stands askew to that reality in the very act of becoming its paradigm. It *is* true that Heathcliff, far from signifying some merely ephemeral intervention, is a type of the historically ascendant world of capital; but because he typifies it so "unnaturally" the novel can move beyond him, into the gracefully gradualistic settlement symbolised by the union of Hareton and young Catherine. Heathcliff is finally fought off, while the social values he incarnates can be prised loose from the self-parodic mould in which he cast them and slowly accommodated. His undisguised violence, like the absolutism of his love, come to seem features of a past more brutal but also more heroic than the present; if the decorous, muted milieu of the Grange will not easily accommodate such passionate intensities, neither will it so readily reveal the more unpleasant face of its social and economic power. The "defeat" of Heathcliff, then, is at once the transcending of such naked power and the collapse of that passionate protest against it which was the inner secret of Heathcliff's outrageous dealings.

We can now ask what these contradictions in the figure of Heathcliff actually amount to. It seems to me possible to decipher in the struggle between Heathcliff and the Grange an imaginatively transposed version of that contemporary conflict between bourgeoisie and landed gentry which I have argued is central to Charlotte's work. The relationship holds in no precise detail, since Heathcliff is not literally an industrial entrepreneur; but the double-edgedness of his relation with the Lintons, with its blend of antagonism and emulation, reproduces the complex structure of class-forces we found in Charlotte's fiction. Having mysteriously amassed capital outside agrarian society, Heathcliff forces his way into that society to expropriate the expropriators; and in this sense his machinations reflect the behaviour of a contemporary bourgeois class increasingly successful in its penetration of landed property. He belongs fully to neither Heights nor Grange, opposing them both; he embodies a force which at once destroys the traditional Earnshaw settlement and effectively confronts the power of the squirearchy. In his contradictory amalgam of "Heights" and "Grange," then, Heathcliff's career fleshes out a contemporary ideological dilemma which Charlotte also explores: the contradiction that the fortunes of the industrial bourgeoisie belong *economically* to an increasing extent with the landed gentry but that there can still exist between them, socially, culturally and personally, a profound hostility. If they are increasingly bound up objectively in a single power-bloc, there is still sharp subjective conflict between them. I take it that *Wuthering Heights,* like Charlotte's fiction, needs mythically to resolve this historical contradiction. If the exploitative adult Heathcliff belongs economically with the capitalist power of the Grange, he is culturally closer to the traditional world of the Heights; his contemptuous response to the Grange as a child, and later to Edgar, is of a piece with Joseph's scorn for the finicky Linton Heathcliff and the haughty young Catherine. If Heathcliff exploits Hareton culturally and economically, he nevertheless feels a certain rough-and-ready *rapport* with him. The contradiction Heathcliff embodies, then, is brought home in the fact that he combines Heights violence with Grange methods to gain power over both properties; and this means that while he is economically progressive he is culturally outdated. He represents a turbulent form of capitalist aggression which must historically be civilised—blended with spiritual values, as it will be in the case of his surrogate Hareton. The terms into which the novel casts this imperative are those of the need to refine, in the person of Hareton, the old yeoman class; but since Hareton's achievement of the Grange is an ironic consequence of Heathcliff's own activity, there is a sense in which it is the capitalist drive symbolised by Heathcliff which must submit to spiritual cultivation. It is worth recalling at this point the cultural affinities between the old yeoman and the new industrial classes touched on by David Wilson;[3] and F. M. L. Thompson comments that by the early 1830s a depleted yeomanry were often forced to sell their land either to a large landowner, or to a local tradesman who would put a tenant in.[4] On the other hand, as Mrs Gaskell notes, some landed yeomen turned to manufacture. Heathcliff the heartless capitalist and Hareton the lumpish yeoman thus have a real as well as an alliterative relation. In so far as Heathcliff symbolises the dispossessing bourgeoisie, he links hands with the large capitalist landowner Linton in common historical opposition to yeoman society; in so far as he himself has sprung from that society and turned to amassing capital outside it, still sharing its dour life-style, he joins spiritual forces with the uncouth Hareton against the pampered squirearchy.

In pitting himself against both yeomanry and large-scale agrarian capitalism, then, Heathcliff is an indirect symbol of the aggressive industrial bourgeoisie of Emily Brontë's own time, a social trend extrinsic to both classes but implicated in their fortunes. The contradiction of the *novel*, however, is that Heathcliff cannot represent at once an absolute metaphysical refusal of an inhuman society and a class which is intrinsically part of it. Heathcliff is both metaphysical hero, spiritually marooned from all material concern in his obsessional love for Catherine, and a skilful exploiter who cannily expropriates the wealth of others. It is a limit of the novel's "possible consciousness" that its absolute metaphysical protest can be socially articulated only in such terms—that its "outside" is in this sense an "inside." The industrial bourgeoisie is outside the farming world of both Earnshaws and Lintons; but it is no longer a *revolutionary* class, and so provides no sufficient social correlative for what Heathcliff "metaphysically" represents. He can thus be presented only as a conflictive unity of spiritual rejection and social integration; and this, indeed, is his personal tragedy. With this in mind, we can understand why what he did in that two years' absence has to remain mysterious. The actual facts of his return, as an ambitious *parvenu* armed with presumably non-agrarian wealth and bent on penetrating agrarian society, speak eloquently enough of the real situation of the contemporary bourgeoisie; but it is clear that such social realities offer no adequate symbolism for Heathcliff's unswerving drive, which transcends all social determinants and has its end in Catherine alone. The novel, then, can dramatise its "metaphysical" challenge to society only by refracting it through the distorting terms of existing social relations, while simultaneously, at a "deeper" level, isolating that challenge in a realm eternally divorced from the actual.

It seems clear that the novel's sympathies lie on balance with the Heights rather than the Grange. As Tom Winnifrith points out, the Heights is the more homely, egalitarian place; Lockwood's inability at the beginning of the book to work out its social relationships (is Hareton a servant or not?) marks a significant contrast with the Grange. (Lockwood is here a kind of surrogate reader: we too are forestalled from "reading off" the relationships at first glance, since they are historically moulded and so only historically intelligible.) The passing of the Heights, then, is regretted: it lingers on in the ghostly myth of Heathcliff and Catherine as an unbanishable intimation of a world of hungering absolution askew to the civilised present. Winnifrith declares himself puzzled by Mrs Leavis's point that the action of Hareton and Catherine in replacing the Heights' currant-bushes with flowers symbolises the victory of capitalist over yeoman, but Mrs Leavis is surely right: flowers are a form of "surplus value," redundant luxuries in the spare Heights world which can accommodate the superfluous neither in its horticulture nor in its social network. But though the novel mourns the death of Wuthering Heights, it invests deeply in the new life which struggles out of it. In so far as Heathcliff signifies a demonic capitalist drive, his defeat is obviously approved; in so far as his passing marks the demise of a lifeform rougher but also richer than the Grange, his death symbolises the fleeing of absolute value over the horizon of history into the sealed realm of myth. That death, however tragic, is essential: the future lies with a fusion rather than a confrontation of interests between gentry and bourgeoisie.

The novel's final settlement might seem to qualify what I have said earlier about its confronting of irreconcilable contradictions. *Wuthering Heights* does, after all, end on a note of tentative convergence between labour and culture, sinew and gentility. The culture which Catherine imparts to Hareton in teaching him to read promises equality rather than oppression, an unemasculating refinement of physical energy. But this is a consequence rather than a resolution of the novel's tragic action; it does nothing to dissolve the deadlock of Heathcliff's relationship with Catherine, as the language used to describe that cultural transfusion unconsciously suggests:

> "Con-*trary!*" said a voice as sweet as a silver bell—"That for the third time, you dunce! I'm not going to tell you again. Recollect or I'll pull your hair!"
>
> "Contrary, then," answered another, in deep but softened tones. "And now, kiss me, for minding so well."
>
> "No, read it over first correctly, without a single mistake." The male speaker began to read; he was a young man, respectably dressed and seated at a table, having a book before him. His handsome features glowed with pleasure, and his eyes kept impatiently wandering from the page to a small white hand over his shoulder, which recalled him by a smart slap on the cheek, whenever its

owner detected such signs of inattention. Its owner stood behind; her light, shining ringlets blending, at intervals, with his brown locks, as she bent to superintend his studies; and her face—it was lucky he could not see her face, or he would never have been so steady. I could; and I bit my lip in spite, at having thrown away the chance I might have had of doing something besides staring at its smiting beauty. (xxxii)

The aesthetic false moves of this are transparently dictated by ideological compromise. "Sweet as a silver bell," "glowed with pleasure," "shining ringlets," "smiting beauty": there is a coy, beaming, sentimental self-indulgence about the whole passage which belongs more to Lockwood than to Emily Brontë, although her voice has clearly been confiscated by his. It is Jane and Rochester in a different key; yet the difference is as marked as the parallel. The conclusion, while in a sense symbolically resolving the tragic disjunctions which precede it, moves at a level sufficiently distanced from those disjunctions to preserve their significance intact. It is true that *Wuthering Heights* finally reveals the limits of its "possible consciousness" by having recourse to a gradualist model of social change: the antinomies of passion and civility will be harmonised by the genetic fusion of both strains in the off-spring of Catherine and Hareton, effecting an equable interchange of Nature and culture, biology and education. But those possibilities of growth are exploratory and undeveloped, darkened by the shadow of the tragic action. If it is not exactly true to say that Hareton and Catherine play Fortinbras to Heathcliff's Hamlet, since what they symbolise emerges from, rather than merely imposes itself upon, the narrative, there is none the less a kernel of truth in that proposition. Hareton and Catherine are the products of their history, but they cannot negate it; the quarrel between their sedate future at Thrushcross Grange and the spectre of Heathcliff and Catherine on the hills lives on, in a way alien to Charlotte's reconciliatory imagination.

There is another reason why the ending of *Wuthering Heights* differs from the ideological integration which concludes Charlotte's novels. I have argued that those novels aim for a balance or fusion of "genteel" and bourgeois traits, enacting a growing convergence of interests between two powerful segments of a ruling social bloc. The union of Hareton and Catherine parallels this complex unity in obvious ways: the brash vigour of the petty-bourgeois yeoman is smoothed and sensitised by the cultivating grace of the squirearchy. But the crucial difference lies in the fact that the yeomanry of *Wuthering Heights* is no longer a significant class but a historically superannuated force. The transfusion of class-qualities in Charlotte's case rests on a real historical symbiosis; in *Wuthering Heights* that symbolic interchange has no such solid historical foundation. The world of the Heights is over, lingering on only in the figure of Hareton Earnshaw; and in that sense Hareton's marriage to Catherine signifies more at the level of symbolism than historical fact, as a salutary grafting of the values of a dying class on to a thriving, progressive one. If Hareton is thought of as a surrogate, symbolic Heathcliff, then the novel's ending suggests a rapprochement between gentry and capitalist akin to Charlotte's mythical resolutions; if he is taken literally, as a survivor of yeoman stock, then there can be no such historical balance of power. Literally, indeed, this is what finally happens: Hareton's social class is effectively swallowed up into the hegemony of the Grange. Symbolically, however, Hareton represents a Heathcliff-like robustness with which the Grange must come to terms. It is this tension between literal and symbolic meanings which makes the ending of *Wuthering Heights* considerably more complex than the conclusion of any Charlotte Brontë novel. Read symbolically, the ending of *Wuthering Heights* seems to echo the fusion of qualities found in Charlotte; but since the basis of that fusion is the absorption and effective disappearance of a class on which the novel places considerable value, Emily's conclusion is a good deal more subtly shaded than anything apparent in her sister's work.

Wuthering Heights has been alternately read as a social and a metaphysical novel—as a work rooted in a particular time and place, or as a novel preoccupied with the eternal grounds rather than the shifting conditions of human relationship. That critical conflict mirrors a crucial thematic dislocation in the novel itself. The social and metaphysical are indeed ripped rudely apart in the book: existences only feebly incarnate essences, the discourse of ethics makes little creative contact with that of ontology. So much is apparent in Heathcliff's scathing dismissal of Edgar Linton's compassion and moral concern: "and that insipid, paltry creature attending her from *duty* and *humanity! From pity* and *charity!* He might as well plant an oak in a flower-pot, and expect it to thrive, as imagine he can restore her to vigour in the soil of his shallow cares!" The novel's dialectical vision proves Heathcliff both right and wrong. There *is* something insipid about Linton, but his concern for Catherine is not in the least shallow; if his pity and charity are less fertile than Heathcliff's passion, they are also less destructive. But if ethical and ontological idioms fail to mesh, if social existence negates rather than realises spiritual essence, this is itself a profoundly social fact. The novel projects a condition in which the available social languages are too warped and constrictive to be the bearers of love, freedom and equality; and it follows that in such a condition those values can be sustained only in the realms of myth and metaphysics. It is a function of the metaphysical to preserve those possibilities which a society cancels, to act as its reservoir of unrealised value. This is the history of Heathcliff and Catherine—the history of a wedge driven between the actual and the possible which, by estranging the ideal from concrete existence, twists that existence into violence and despair. The actual is denatured to a mere husk of the ideal, the empty shell of some tormentingly inaccessible truth. It is an index of the dialectical vision of *Wuthering Heights* that it shows at once the terror and the necessity of that denaturing, as it shows both the splendour and the impotence of the ideal.

Notes

1.   Q. D. Leavis, *Lectures in America* (London: Chatto & Windus, 1960), 99.

2.   Chap. VIII, T. Meier, "*Wuthering Heights* and Violation of Class," *Transactions of the Brontë Society* 78 (1968): 233–36.

3.   D. Wilson, "Emily Brontë, First of the Moderns," *Modern Quarterly Miscellany* 1 (1947): 94–115.

4.   F. Thompson, *English Landed Society in the Nineteenth Century* (London: Routledge and Kegan Paul, 1963), 233.

WUTHERING HEIGHTS:
CRITICISM 1975–1995
◆

Decoding *Wuthering Heights*

GILLIAN FRITH

"The reader has the experience, in struggling to understand [*Wuthering Heights*], that a certain number of elements which present themselves for explanation can be reduced to order. This act of interpretation always leaves something over, something just at the edge of the circle of theoretical vision which that vision does not encompass . . . The text is over-rich" (J. Hillis Miller, *Fiction and Repetition*, 52). Hillis Miller's comment serves usefully to characterize the direction that *Wuthering Heights* criticism has taken in the past 20 years. As the previous section will have demonstrated, critics have long relinquished the quest to decipher a single meaning, a transcendental truth or organic whole in this novel. In the past 20 years, there has been a general acknowledgment that it is, precisely, the multiplicity and indeterminacy of its meaning that makes the novel irresistible. Critics have also long seen *Wuthering Heights* in terms of conflicting polarities: hell/heaven, calm/storm, fair/dark, Heights/Grange. Contemporary scholars have continued to examine the dualities and oppositions at work in the novel, but it is the instability of the text's apparent polarizations that now attracts most interest. Critics since 1975 have set out to "decode" Brontë's novel without fixing or delimiting its boundaries, and Miller's essay provides a serviceable and influential exposition of the perils and pleasures of this task.

What is exceptional about *Wuthering Heights*, Miller argues, is the way in which it simultaneously invites interpretation and resists it. The opening of the novel establishes the position of the reader: like Lockwood, the reader enters a vividly "real" yet confusingly strange world and is confronted with a mass of fascinating but bewildering information that he struggles to collate. Miller suggests that *Wuthering Heights* may be seen as an "uncanny" text, in Freud's sense of the word, because it seems constantly to be exposing "something which seems familiar and which one feels ought to have been kept secret" (69). Just as Lockwood moves from room to room until he reaches the inner, intimate space of Catherine's paneled bed, so is the reader drawn into a narrative structured like Chinese boxes—text within text. The reader is continually confronted with the sense that there is a hidden principle, a secret explanation, at the heart of the text and that its pieces can be assembled into a coherent pattern, "like the child's game in which a duck or a rabbit is magically drawn by tracing lines between numbered dots" (57). The problem is that not all of the dots are visible; the reader is easily led astray, confused by the missing links, and frustrated by the multiplication of narratives within narratives and the absence of a single reliable narrator. The act of interpretation is always incomplete; it always leaves something over, something unaccounted for, and it is precisely this dissatisfaction that impels the reader to read on.

The criticism of the past twenty years bears out Miller's argument that the best readings are those that best account for the heterogeneity of the text, and the analytical methods used have been equally diverse. Post-structuralism, feminism, deconstruction, and psychoanalysis have all made their mark on contemporary Brontë criticism. The influence of theorists such as Derrida, Althusser, Foucault, Lacan, Irigaray, and Bakhtin is evident in many recent essays. For the uninitiated reader the best starting-point is Patsy Stoneman's introduction to the Macmillan New Casebook on *Wuthering Heights* (1-23). Stoneman's essay takes the reader, with exemplary succinctness and lucidity, through the minefield of contemporary literary theory and shows how recent theoretical developments have produced new, interrogative readings of *Wuthering Heights,* "in which readers are not passive consumers but active participators in the construction of the text" (16). The St. Martin's Press edition of *Wuthering Heights,* edited by Linda H. Peterson, also includes illustrative essays on the novel written from the perspectives of psychoanalytic, feminist, deconstructive, Marxist, and cultural criticism together with helpful summaries of the distinguishing features of each approach. A useful, practical demonstration of the ways in which different strands within feminist theory may be deployed to produce very divergent readings of *Wuthering Heights* is found in *Feminist Readings/Feminists Reading* by Mills et al. It would be redundant to repeat these exercises here. In this essay, I want to demonstrate how contemporary critics, aided by recent theoretical developments, have produced new answers to old questions: what is Emily Brontë's place in the literary tradition? how does "the Grange" relate to "the Heights"? what is the status of Nelly Dean's narrative? what is the relationship between the stories of the two Catherines? who is Heathcliff?

As Miller comments, there do not seem to be enough names to go around in *Wuthering Heights.* The repetition and overlapping of given and family names indicates relationships of similarity and difference among the characters and seems to identify them as elements in a system rather than separate, unique individuals. To read the novel in terms of the permutation of names, Miller suggests, would lead to a focus on the network of kinship relations and the theme of reading. This is, broadly speaking, the direction that contemporary criticism has taken but often in different terms from those set out by Miller. The question of gender is notably absent from his essay, and the metaphor of penetration which he uses to identify the reader's dilemma seems pretty clearly to position the reader, and critic, as male:

The double guilt of Lockwood's narration as of any critic's discourse is the following. If he does not penetrate all the way to the innermost core of the story he tells, he keeps the story going, repeating itself interminably in its incompletion. This is like the guilt of the one who keeps a grave open, or like the guilt of a sexual failure. On the other hand, to pierce all the way in is to be guilty of the desecration of a grave, to be guilty, like Heathcliff when he opens Cathy's grave, of necrophilia. (70)

There can be no doubt that the most significant shift in *Wuthering Heights* criticism since 1975 has been the impact of feminism. There has been a dramatic proliferation of books and essays that take up the position of the woman reader or attempt to place Emily Brontë as, specifically, a woman writer. Feminist analyses of kinship relations and the theme of reading in *Wuthering Heights* draw on the picture mapped by contemporary feminist historians. The 1840s saw the consolidation of a social and ideological shift in which the woman's place in the family took on a new significance: she was confined to the "private sphere" of the home but, from within that safe space, she was to act as the guardian of morality, civilization, and culture. As Sandra Gilbert and Susan Gubar put it in their pioneering and influential book, *The Madwoman in the Attic, Wuthering Heights* may be seen as a Victorian woman's myth of origins: "the myth of how culture came about, and specifically of how nineteenth-century society occurred, the tale of where tea-tables, sofas, crinolines and parsonages like the one at Haworth came from" (257). Gilbert and Gubar identify *Wuthering Heights* as "a novel haunted by Milton's bogey" (253) and Emily Brontë as Milton's rebellious daughter. Her novel is a parodic, topsy-turvy retelling of *Paradise Lost* in which the central characters "fall" from hell into heaven. In analyzing this revisionary myth, Gilbert and Gubar draw on Levi-Strauss's distinction between "raw" and "cooked" cultures. Lockwood represents civilized man at his most "cooked" and literary. The Heights, with its uncarpeted floors and barely literate inhabitants, exemplifies the "raw"; the clothed, carpeted, cultured, elegant, ordered world of the Grange is thoroughly "cooked." For Lockwood, the fierce, antihierarchical world of Wuthering Heights is hell. But for Catherine and her creator, Gilbert and Gubar argue, the Heights is a paradise that nurtures female self-will and "diabolical" energy. The first half of *Wuthering Heights* traces Catherine's "fall" into the constraints of adult female sexuality, which is mythologized in the novel as a fall from "hell," her natural habitat, into the "heavenly gentility" of the Grange. Here, Catherine is cossetted into ladyhood: she is fed rich, alien food, learns to repress her own impulses, and loses her power.

Gilbert and Gubar's analysis of *Wuthering Heights* needs to be placed in the context of their overall argument in *The Madwoman in the Attic*. Gilbert and Gubar take up Harold Bloom's patrilineal theory of creativity as the product of an oedipal struggle between writer-father and writer-son and turn

it round to analyze nineteenth-century women's writing in terms of a constraining and debilitating "anxiety of authorship." Women in literature, they
argue, are doubly marginalized: as authors and as characters. Women have
been "framed" by the male literary tradition, which allows women only two
possible roles: passive angel or transgressive monster. Since creativity has traditionally been defined as a male gift and prerogative, linked to male physi-
cality and virility, for a woman to take up the pen is to identify with the monstrous transgressor. So, Gilbert and Gubar assert, women writers resort to
covert strategies to express their feelings of confinement and rage, and they
pursue this argument through a range of texts by nineteenth-century women
writers and poets. They identify, in each work, a surface, conformist text and
a covert, rebellious text in which certain motifs recur: the trope of the female
body as a prison, structural patternings of enclosure and escape, and the figure of the "alter ego," the monstrous figure or madwoman who acts as an
expression of the author's repressed rebelliousness.

While *The Madwoman in the Attic* is distinguished by the ambitious vir-
tuosity of its readings, it has been criticized on a number of counts. In the
hands of Gilbert and Gubar, any text becomes a feminist text: all of the writers discussed seem to tell the same story of rebellion and rage, of "every-
woman" dispossessed in patriarchal society. Their approach does not allow for
differences between women, of race, of class, or sexual orientation. It assumes
that literary texts "tell the truth" about female experience and that that experience has changed little over the past couple of centuries. And while Gilbert
and Gubar paint a powerful picture of the way women have fought back
against their exclusion from the literary tradition, they evade the question of
how, in the face of such constraints, women came to take up the pen at all.

Gilbert and Gubar draw occasionally, if haphazardly, on Freudian terminology in their analysis: they identify the wound to Catherine's foot, which
precipitates her entry into the Grange, as symbolic castration. In *Bearing the
Word*, Margaret Homans offers a much more systematically psychoanalytic
reading of *Wuthering Heights*. Like Gilbert and Gubar, she sees *Wuthering
Heights* as a revisionary, mythologizing text by a rebellious daughter, a woman
writer struggling against her exclusion from the dominant literary tradition.
But for Homans, the myth that Emily Brontë is revising is not female psy-
chosocial experience but literary exclusion itself: "the dominant myth of language that excludes the possibility of women writing" (68). Homans draws
on Lacanian psychoanalytic theory to argue that *Wuthering Heights* explores
the gendered nature of the "symbolic order" of language and culture and the
difficulties, for women, of entering that order. The choice of a male narrator,
Homans suggests, allows Brontë to write as a "son," to enter the kind of discourse in which nineteenth-century fiction had to be written, a discourse in
which the figurative is privileged over the literal. Literal meaning and actual
nature are identified with the figure of the mother, whose power must be
relinquished, or repressed, upon entry into the symbolic order. Lockwood's

narrative follows the pattern of a "son's language" in that it continuously avoids the literal or natural, finding substitutes in figurative language and symbolic landscapes. But within Lockwood's narrative there is a brief example of a "daughter's" writing: a fragment of Catherine Earnshaw's diary. Catherine abandons her writing for a "scamper on the moors," and this interruption, Homans argues, represents Catherine's choice for nature, the literal, and the unnamed mother. The problem is that a novel following Cathy's principles of writing would never be written: Cathy prefers being *in* nature to writing about it. This, Homans suggests, exemplifies Emily Brontë's own problem as a woman writer: she has to transform herself from wild girl to male author. Catherine I must die: "By having her represent a woman writer's allegiance to the literal and her refusal of figuration, and then by killing her, the text reasserts its own figure-making powers. Brontë probes the psychic and imaginative possibilities that the literal represents, yet in the end she identifies these possibilities as dangers within the only terms in which she can write, and she seals up her novel's defenses against them" (83). The story of the second Catherine represents the compromise that results when the daughter accepts her incorporation within the father's law, "an acceptance that makes her a safer model for the author's own practice" (82).

The question of women's relationship to language is also central to Regina Barreca's essay, "The Power of Excommunication: Sex and the Feminine Text in *Wuthering Heights*" (227-40). But Barreca's essay belongs to a later phase of feminism, more inclined to emphasize female agency than female victimization, while acknowledging the limitations of that agency. Homans sees women's access to language as a difficult process, involving inevitable loss; Barreca argues that "rather than forever locking women into silence by damning all their inscription as mimicry, we should look at the way words free rather than bind women" (235). In *Wuthering Heights,* Barreca contends, women take control of language: their storytelling, writing, and reading forms a "decipherable text of resistance" (235). Lockwood may be the nominal narrator, but he soon hands over to Nelly, whose narrative draws on "contraband" forms—folklore, the letter, the song, the ballad—to tell a tale constructed by women. When threatened by men, women reach for pen and paper, and the words of the two Catherines form a lively, disruptive commentary throughout the novel. The male characters, by contrast, "can barely articulate their simplest thoughts" (231). Heathcliff moves from pure gibberish to garbled inarticulacy; Hareton is incomprehensible until the second Catherine takes him in hand. Gilbert and Gubar state that Edgar Linton's power begins with words. He rules his house from his library: "his mastery is contained in books, wills, testaments, leases, titles, rent-rolls, documents, languages, all the paraphernalia by which patriarchal culture is transmitted from one generation to the next" (*The Madwoman in the Attic,* 281). Barreca, however, argues that Linton is the nominal owner rather than the true possessor of books: he shuts himself away among volumes that he never actually opens. Women's control over books is demonstrated when the ghostly Catherine pushes onto Lockwood the books that he had piled up in a pyramid against her. Just as women take control of language, Barreca argues, so do they take control of sex: it is the female characters who initiate sexual activity, who "speak their desire and act on it" (237).

A similar argument is made by Stevie Davies in her book *Emily Brontë*: "Women have always made language. They have handed it on from generation to generation, on behalf of the race" (9). Like Barreca, Davies emphasizes Brontë's debt to an oral tradition passed on primarily by women—lullaby, folktale, ballad, nursery story, gossip. Davies relates this to the importance of the *Muttersprache* through which most children are initiated into language. Up to the age of five, it is the mother who authorizes language and sets the pattern of communication. Davies sees *Wuthering Heights* as a defiant return to and assertion of the anarchic, primitive, uncensored, egotistic world of childhood. The novel's arena is "the authentic theatre of childhood" (43), in which even the supposed adults are children in disguise. The characters "teem with childhood animosities, allegiances and obsessions; they brawl, taunt, mock, manipulate, weep and play their indoor and outdoor orgiastic games" (44). But these are children with the lethal power to put into action their fantasies of vengeance and desire. Davies argues that the central structuring device and mode of address in *Wuthering Heights* is that of the quarrel. The Heights represents a space of saturnalian misrule where bad behavior is licensed and blood-kin are the authentic objects of desire.

For Davies, the dominant language in *Wuthering Heights* is that of "familial desire." She sees the story of the second generation as recapitulating and completing that of the first: the union of Catherine and Hareton is the mating of kin with kin, like with like. "In the marriage of Catherine II and Hareton, the family goes home to itself" (44). The incest theme in *Wuthering Heights* has been much discussed by twentieth-century critics, and Davies notes the Byronic influence here. Byron's obsession with forbidden love, particularly between brothers and sisters, may have provided Brontë with the idea of sibling love as an earthly alternative, a means of protesting against the power of the Almighty Father. But, Davies argues, there is no question of literal incest here. It is the passionate innocence of the relationship that matters: Brontë takes the reader into a premoral, presocial, prelapsarian world in which androgyny reigns and gender roles are not an issue. Drawing on the possibility that Brontë may have been left-handed, Davies identifies her vision as a "sinistral" one, a kind of "mirror-writing" in which the usual norms are reversed and the accepted boundaries and polarities capsize: "subject and object, self and other, observer and world, male and female, are not necessarily seen as *opposite* in the same way as 'normal' perception detects them to be" (15).

Like Gilbert and Gubar, Davies sees Milton as an important influence on Emily Brontë's work, but she reverses the terms. Brontë is not Milton's rebellious daughter but his legitimate daughter. Davies evokes an "enabling" Milton, whose revolutionary puritanism spurred and vindicated Brontë's own heretical version of radical protestantism. But if Brontë is Milton's legitimate daughter, she is not necessarily an obedient one: "she pockets what she chooses from the traditions of the fathers" (Davies, 22) and emphasizes likeness between the sexes rather than difference. *Wuthering Heights* is a novel that "answers back": "The novel is a sublime act of filial, literary and religious disobedience. It presents a child's-eye-view of Scripture, specifically, a girl-child's. The work mocks God and his angels; it derides the godly community. It reverses scriptural values, elevating mortal woman above God, and the creation above the Creator" (18).

Davies suggests that Emily Brontë was able to write as she did because she managed to escape the usual constraints upon Victorian women: she refused, in effect, to grow up. Davies notes that natural mothers are almost entirely absent from *Wuthering Heights,* where the controlling figures are that of foster mother, the kind father, and the devil daddy. She suggests that Brontë's particular circumstances—self-educated, living in the remote north, free from the taming influence of a natural mother—gave her a unique immunity from the sense of guilt that was both the burden and the incentive for Victorian womanhood. Davies's book is a very appealing one because it conjures up, with spirit and skill, a playful, powerful Emily Brontë, gleefully pilfering from her literary forebears. But it does so by detaching Emily Brontë from history, seeing her as "outside" the run of womanhood and the female literary tradition. Other contemporary critics have sought, in various ways, to place *Wuthering Heights* firmly within that history.

Joseph Boone, in *Tradition Counter Tradition* sees *Wuthering Heights* as a key text in a "counter-tradition" of novelists who wished to break loose of the formal constraints of the traditional marriage plot and to expose the conflicts within a system of conjugal love "that defined the sexes as complementary but unequal partners" (142). In these texts, the unease of marital discord is formally manifested through temporal and spatial dislocations, juxtaposition, the irresolution of narrative parts, and the unsettling repetition of characters and events. In *Wuthering Heights,* he argues, the constant and disorienting duplication of characters, gestures, and settings, and the repeating plots that uneasily mirror one another stand against the passionate bond between Catherine and Heathcliff, which is characterized by oneness, affinity, merging, and identification. The text keeps its possibilities in open suspension but continually affirms "the radical difference of a love based on likeness and equality" (156) as opposed to one based on conventional polarities.

In *Desire and Domestic Fiction*, Nancy Armstrong also positions Emily Brontë as a central figure in a major change in the representation of sexuality in fiction. Armstrong's book is an ambitious rewriting of the history presented by Ian Watt in *The Rise of the Novel* (1957). She argues that the development of the novel was associated with the rise of the domestic woman and her responsibility for all those practices that we associate with private life. Writing for and about the female introduced a new vocabulary for sexual relations: competing class interests were mapped onto the more containable, "apolitical" arena of the struggle between the sexes. Drawing on Michel Foucault, Armstrong suggests that power works through discourse "to create a subject ideally suited to inhabit a modern institutional culture" (190). She identifies a significant shift in the 1840s: in the fiction of that period, political resistance is gendered, neutralized, and reconceived as aberrant sexual desire.

Armstrong sees the Brontës as agents of history, who played a vital part in formulating modern notions of subjectivity and desire in a reaction against the kind of domestic fiction exemplified by Jane Austen. Austen's heroines, typically, marry as soon as they have identified their appropriate suitor and desire has been communicated. But the Brontës locate desire outside marriage, in an extrasocial dimension. Their heroines typically desire the one man whom society forbids them to marry, giving rise to the notion that social conventions are, in an essential way, opposed to individual desire. Armstrong rejects the conventional view that the fiction of the Brontës records a process of sublimation and sexual repression, to be decoded by the critic. It is rather, she says, that sexual repression obscures the fact of social oppression.

Armstrong points out that Victorian fiction often uncovers a sexual scandal as the source of disturbances that tear a family apart: Catherine and Heathcliff share a bond that violates the marriage law. When Catherine's ghost disturbs Lockwood's slumber, she compels him to seek out the history of sexual relations that reveals Catherine and Heathcliff as the secret cause of all the disruptive events in the novel. Catherine's invasion of Lockwood's room—grasping him with ice-cold hand—turns the room into something resembling a scene of rape. This, Armstrong argues, is material not to be domesticated by marriage: "it is definitely outside of culture" (180). Also, in *Wuthering Heights,* women's knowledge is given precedence over that of men in explaining social relationships. Lockwood's education and foreign travel qualify him to write the family history of the Earnshaws, but he cannot do so without the assistance of Nelly, who alone has the knowledge from gossip, local lore, and personal memory to make sense of the family relationships. "In the process of handing over such powers of motivation to the female, fiction does something to history . . . [it] requires another order of history that is no longer considered history at all. It is a tale told by a woman. It is a history of sexuality" (197).

The question of how far and in what way *Wuthering Heights* may be seen as a "tale told by a woman" has been much discussed. The naïveté and unreliability of Lockwood's narrative has long been established. In recent years, there has been considerable debate about the "reliability" of Nelly Dean as a narrator. In *The Madwoman in the Attic,* Gilbert and Gubar take issue with Q. D. Leavis's notion of Nelly as a "wholesome, maternal" figure. On the contrary, they argue, Nelly is "patriarchy's paradigmatic housekeeper, the man's woman who has traditionally been hired to keep men's houses in order by straightening out their parlors, their daughters, and their stories" (291). They see Nelly as "Milton's cook": most often seen preparing, carrying, and offering food, Nelly is the constraining nurturer who tells stories to make a "moral meal." Nelly, say Gilbert and Gubar, denies the demonic in life: she is the keeper of the house of heavenly gentility who "closes windows . . . and locks women into the common sitting-room" (292).

James Kavanagh, in his *Emily Brontë*, takes a somewhat similar view from a very different theoretical perspective. Like Stevie Davies, Kavanagh focuses on the idea of *Wuthering Heights* as a family romance. But Kavanagh sees the novel as representative rather than singular, and he perceives the family as an oppressive rather than liberating institution, in both socioeconomic and psychosexual terms. For Kavanagh, what is at stake in *Wuthering Heights* is the changing nature of family and class relations at a time of economic and social crisis, when the family was taking on a new ideological role as the source of stability in a world destabilized by the progress of capitalism. Kavanagh's rather eccentric and eclectic book invokes Marxist, feminist, and psychoanalytic theory to integrate the questions of gender and class. There is, he argues, a sadistic, infanticidal impulse at work in the novel, which he sees in terms of a battle between Heathcliff and Nelly. Initially, the two characters occupy a common position as household workers put in their place by different "masters." But as the narrative develops, they pull in different directions. Heathcliff is identified with libidinal desire and with the figure of the father, who "enters into a tempestuous, passionate and 'taboo' relationship with the daughter, and seeks to become 'master' over the son" (27). According to Kavanagh, Heathcliff represents the primitive father's phallic desire; Edgar Linton represents the upright father's patriarchal law. Catherine is "the daughter" torn between the two. Nelly directs Cathy "towards the 'adult,' sublimated sexuality that is congruent with submission to the father's Law— that is, to marriage with Edgar Linton" (46). Nelly is the female figure who controls the phallic tools of nature and culture and works to prohibit the consummation of the primal father's incestuous desire: she is "'the phallic mother'; the mother who situates herself in, and speaks for (in the voice of) the Father's Law" (39).

But, Kavanagh argues, Heathcliff is not simply a representative of subversive libidinal desire; he also enfigures the resentful vengeance of an oppressed class. Nelly, despite her lower-class origins, adheres to bourgeois values: moderate upward mobility within accepted class parameters. She acts as the intelligent agent of the Linton regime and the hidden enemy of Heathcliff and Catherine. But since Emily Brontë's project is to preserve some of Heathcliff's "difference" without dismantling the social order, the aims of Heathcliff and Nelly veer toward complementarity as the narrative progresses. Nelly becomes co-opted as Heathcliff's "intelligence agent" and is the appropriate figure to oversee the unification of the two families at the

Grange. Taboo, obsessive desire is exiled and replaced by tranquil domestic-
ity; an acceptable, socialized desire is given a civilized form under the
guardianship of the phallic mother. But, says Kavanagh, it is a precarious stability; the conclusion of the novel suggests that there is always a possibility
that the outlawed, repressed phallic desire will return.

Lyn Pykett, in her *Emily Brontë*, gives a much more positive account of
Nelly Dean. *Wuthering Heights,* Pykett points out, is a novel that straddles literary traditions and genres, containing elements of the Gothic, folk material,
and Victorian domestic fiction. While the movement of the novel is, broadly
speaking, from the Gothic in the direction of Victorian domestic realism,
Lockwood's narrative indicates to the reader from the start that the codes and
conventions of genteel fiction are not adequate to interpret life at the
Heights. Nelly's inner narrative blurs the boundaries between the genres:
legendary and potentially melodramatic material is "embedded in a matrix of
Yorkshire common sense" (100). Her unobtrusive, self-effacing narrative
might be seen as a "feminine disguise in which apparent passivity masks a
covert activity which is a narrative version of feminine influence working by
stealth" (101). While acknowledging that Nelly's history is one of progressive
co-optation to gentry values, Pykett observes that the narrative repeatedly
draws our attention to the material realities of Nelly's class position, which
keeps her at a distance from the families whose history she recounts: "Nelly
must, and does, *work*" (102). Her "common-sense" and emotional control
may be the product of her precarious position as a servant, and the limitations
in her point of view might be seen as "a means of placing the emotional
intensities of the central characters as the self-indulgent and self-referential
emotionalism of a leisured class" (102). Nelly is "perhaps, less the preserver of
Linton family law and order, than the preserver and advocate of an idea of the
family" (106), and it is over the definition of the family that she is in compe-
tition with Heathcliff. Nelly, Pykett suggests, is ultimately the survivor in
this battle: "an image of female resilience, resourcefulness and power" (107).

Pykett sees the key oppositions in Emily Brontë's writing as imprisonment and the yearning for release: "Emily Brontë's life and works vividly
demonstrate and explore the fact that cocoons can enmesh and stifle as well
as shelter and nurture, and that there is nothing more secure than a prison"
(7). She suggests that it was, paradoxically, by retreating within the limits of
domestic life that Brontë managed to explore and expand its boundaries: "by
retreating ever further into the 'dream-worlds' of her fictional creations she
was able to experiment with alternative visions of reality in which dominance,
power, and energy are not exclusively masculine qualities, and nor do they
necessarily prevail" (17). Pykett sees Emily Brontë as a dramatic writer who
experimented with a variety of alternative selves and whose elusiveness
derives from the fact that her work offers "a variety of voices and guises" (18).
It is this quality of "polyphony"—speaking with more than one voice—
which, Pykett suggests, distinguishes Nelly's narrative: Nelly's own declared

prejudices and apparent sympathies are subverted by the variety of voices and perspectives that her narrative actually contains.

Pykett takes the term "polyphony" from the work of the Marxist theorist Mikhail Bakhtin, the influence of whose work is evident in a number of contemporary essays on *Wuthering Heights*. Lynne Pearce's analysis of the novel in her book *Reading Dialogics* is an interesting recent example. Pearce comments that *Wuthering Heights* may seem to eschew dialogue in favor of polemic: "the protagonists rarely talk *to* one another or even pause to listen to what the other has to say. They prefer, instead, to rant and rave, to dismiss or ridicule their interlocutor's reply before it is even uttered" (121). But Pearce, like Pykett, argues that *Wuthering Heights* may be seen as a "polyphonic" novel in the sense that it offers a plurality of distinct voices and consciousnesses that are received by the reader as independent and autonomous. "Despite Nelly's repeated attempts to convince us of the moral depravity of her hero and heroine, generations of readers have sought to excuse and reclaim them by every means possible. If Nelly's narration does attempt to impose a monologizing frame on the novel, then never was monologism less successful" (126).

Pearce draws further on Bakhtin's terminology to argue that *Wuthering Heights* is not only a "polyglossic" novel, in that the characters speak with different accents and social registers, carefully graded in terms of education and class, but also "heteroglossic," in that they seem at times to be speaking different languages: the marriage of Hareton Earnshaw and the second Catherine may be seen as a "bilingual" union. But while the gradation of language and register is associated in the novel with power, "the power is not all on the side of those with the 'cultural capital' of genteel pronunciation" (127). The less articulate male characters, notably Heathcliff and Hareton, make their claim for power by making refined and polite speech look ridiculous. "A 'refined' use of language is associated with the feminine principle, to the extent that the men who share in its use (Lockwood, Edgar and Linton) are branded 'effeminate'. By making the Heights into a separate machochismic kingdom, with its own 'alternative' language and culture, Heathcliff, Hareton and Joseph succeed in temporarily undermining the authority of the educated English middle class, and install a new philistinism in its stead" (128). The register of this philistinism is the alternative authority of "bad language": the curse is their habitual mode of expression, used to establish power over the addressee. But, Pearce notes, its use is not confined to uneducated or renegade men. When Catherine moves to the Heights, she revels in matching their curses with her own: "A superior accent has no purchase here: linguistic superiority is established and sustained through a constant barrage of oath and invective" (129).

The question of how exactly we are to interpret the move to "polite society" at the end of *Wuthering Heights* has been much discussed by contemporary critics. It is generally accepted that the relationship between the stories of the two generations, the two Catherines, hinges on a progression from "nature" to "culture," but there is less agreement about how, and how favorably, "culture" is being represented in this novel. Miller, noting the proliferation in the text of characters learning to read, sees books as a paradoxical emblem of the reader's own experience. "Reading seems to be opposed to the wind on the moors, to death, and to sexual experience" (*Fiction and Repetition,* 46)—and yet, the reader's only access to the experience represented in *Wuthering Heights* is, precisely, through a book. James Kavanagh also sees the book as an ambivalent, multifaceted image linking cultural order and the control of language with sublimation and the control of desire: "if linguistic and cultural competence signifies repression, it also signifies a social power withheld from potentially troublesome classes, constantly kept on display and out of reach, somewhat like a shiny new gun" (*Emily Brontë,* 20). (Kavanagh likes guns; he makes much of Emily Brontë's relationship with her father's pistol.)

Many feminist critics have followed Gilbert and Gubar in seeing the conclusion of the novel as a qualified acceptance of the sway of culture: rebellious, passionate, mad Catherine is replaced by her more docile daughter, the ideal Victorian woman. The ghosts of Heathcliff and Catherine linger in the text to remind the reader of lost primordial possibilities, but the satanic, libidinal, and irrational have been exorcised from the real world. "It is now 1802; the Heights-hell has been converted into the Grange-heaven; and with patriarchal history redefined, renovated, restored, the nineteenth century can truly begin, complete with tea-parties, ministering angels, governesses, and parsonages" (*The Madwoman in the Attic,* 302). Margaret Homans says much the same thing, in psychoanalytic terms: "the first Cathy's story is about a girl's refusal to enter something very like the Lacanian symbolic order, while the second Cathy's story revises her mother's, by having the girl accept her entry into the father's law" (*Bearing the Word,* 68). Nancy Armstrong gives the argument a historical inflection: "as these recalcitrant elements are contained in and banished from the novel, one feels the text flattening; in giving its materials over to pure ideology, domestic fiction sticks the reader with a paler version of love, a narrower idea of sexuality" (*Desire and Domestic Fiction,* 201). Armstrong sees the second Catherine's education of Hareton as indicative of a political and literary shift: "Novels incorporated new political material and sexualized it in such a manner that only one resolution would do: a partitioned and hierarchical space under a woman's surveillance" (185).

Lyn Pykett also sees the relationship between the two halves of the novel in terms of literary history. She argues that, overtly, the novel moves progressively from the Gothic in the direction of Victorian realism. The second generation story, with its withdrawal into the private realm, rewrites the Gothic plot as domestic fiction. But, Pykett argues, the Gothic is not obliterated in the process: the reader's expectations are increasingly at odds with the literary genre and social world into which the novel has moved. The mixing of genres, the narrative dislocations, and the disruptions of chronology allow Brontë to have it both ways. The two genres work together to keep other versions of domestic life before the reader: the domestic space as prison, the family as the site of violence, struggle, and control. Pykett suggests also that Brontë's portrayal of the union between Catherine II and Hareton offers a revisionary portrayal of the domestic. Catherine's knowledge is empowering; Hareton is not simply a pale, emasculated version of Heathcliff but "a Heathcliff whose energies become enabling and operative, rather than repressive and restrictive" (119).

Pykett acknowledges, however, that Heathcliff himself remains to trouble the temporary equilibrium of the novel: "although he is displaced, Heathcliff is not expelled from the text. In Heathcliff's powerful fictional presence, and his persistence in the narrative in spirit form, the novel acknowledges both the force of libidinal desire and its continuing and inevitable challenge to the necessary repressions of civilisation" (119-20). Which brings us to the old question, the "hermeneutical riddle," which, in Terry Eagleton's words, "'haunts every page of *Wuthering Heights:* Who is Heathcliff? What is he? What does he want?'" (*Heathcliff and the Great Hunger,* 21).

For Gilbert and Gubar, Heathcliff is Cathy's rebellious alter ego, her "whip": "an alternative self or double for her, a complementary addition to her being who fleshes out all her lacks the way a bandage might staunch a wound. Thus in her union with him she becomes . . . a perfect androgyne" (*The Madwoman in the Attic,* 265). Noting that the hunger strike is the traditional tool of the powerless, Gilbert and Gubar observe that Heathcliff is locked up and starved while Catherine learns table manners. They suggest that Heathcliff preserves in his being the qualities that Catherine gradually loses: "despite his outward masculinity, Heathcliff is somehow female in his monstrosity" (293). The fact that he speaks gibberish "suggests the profound alienation of the physical/natural/female realm he represents from language, culture's tool and the glory of 'spirits Masculine'" (294).

This is a long way from Terry Eagleton, who in his *Myths of Power,* from which an extract was included in the previous section, identifies Heathcliff with the yeomanry. But for Eagleton, Heathcliff is also an index of the instability of the ideological project of *Wuthering Heights:* he is hero and villain, oppressor and oppressed, the embodiment of the novel's contradictions. James Kavanagh takes up Eagleton's argument to query his identification of Heathcliff with the yeomanry. For Kavanagh, Heathcliff represents both the phallic father's desire and the capitalist dynamic that threatens traditional family structures. He is, Kavanagh argues, both worker and capitalist, and Heathcliff images the relationship between the two that *is* capitalism: "figuring the anarchic movement of 'productive' capital, and the ironic potency of the worker catalysed by capital, he rages through the social universe, revolutionizing previous social relations, abolishing obsolescent property formations and building new ones, and, ultimately, destroying the ground from under himself" (*Emily Brontë,* 94).

Nancy Armstrong, however, contends that during the course of *Wuthering Heights* Heathcliff undergoes a transformation "that strips away the features of a Gypsy from Liverpool at the turn of the century and attributes all his behaviour to sexual desire" (*Desire and Domestic Fiction,* 4). She argues that the narrative works progressively to depoliticize Heathcliff: "Never mind that Heathcliff comes from the streets of Liverpool and that Brontë sets the date of his appearance in the novel around the time of the provincial hunger riots (1766). By the end of *Wuthering Heights* he has become a phantasm of unfulfilled sexual desire" (187).

Two recent "new historicist" essays make precisely the opposite point, arguing that Heathcliff's identification with Irishness is central to the novel. In *Outside the Pale*, the Marxist-feminist critic Elsie B. Michie places *Wuthering Heights* in the context of the Victorian fascination with stories of self-advancement. Such stories, she suggests, appealed to midcentury audiences because they suggest that everyone can overcome the limitations of their social position, but they tend to be articulated in a colonial context:

While the Victorian audience recognized that it was extremely difficult to redress social inequities at home, they could fantasize that the unlimited expansion of the empire made it easy to do so abroad. The colonial grounding of fantasies of upward mobility, however, also made visible what mid-Victorian audiences wished to deny: that the desire to elevate oneself in class implicitly involved a desire to dominate others. (46)

Michie argues that the stories of Rochester in *Jane Eyre* and Heathcliff in *Wuthering Heights* demonstrate how the fantasies of class elevation were grounded in a desire for domination that "could not be acknowledged when they were seen at work in places close to home such as Ireland, but could be allowed free rein when they were projected onto more exotic locales" (46-7). Michie draws extensively on Victorian ethnography and journalism to argue that when Heathcliff and Rochester are "down," they are associated with mid-nineteenth-century stereotypes of "the Irish" as volatile, savage, dark, and "simianized" in appearance. When they are "up," however, they are described as "oriental despots": princes, sultans, emirs, paynims, Grand Turks. Among Michie's wide range of examples of caricatures of the Irish is this satirical sketch from *Punch* in 1862:

A creature manifestly between the Gorilla and the Negro is to be met with in some of the lowest districts of London and Liverpool by adventurous explorers. It comes from Ireland, whence it has contrived to migrate; it belongs in fact to a tribe of Irish savages: the lowest species of the Irish yahoo. When conversing with its kind it talks a sort of gibberish. (48)

The applicability of this quotation to Heathcliff—found in Liverpool, speaking gibberish—is clear enough. But the quotation also demonstrates another of Michie's points: unease about indeterminate national difference gets overlaid by more exotic or explicitly racial stereotypes of otherness. Michie quotes a letter from Charles Kingsley in which he describes the Irish as "white chimpanzees": "if they were black, one would not feel it so much, but their skins, except where tanned by exposure, are as white as ours" (49). In a similar fashion, she argues, the traces of Irishness in Heathcliff are masked by references to him—as "dusky" and "black"—that draw on the discourse of racial difference.

Michie draws on Homi Bhabha's account of the way in which stereotypes of racial difference work to argue that Heathcliff functions in the novel as both "phobia" and "fetish," thereby opening up "the royal road to colonial fantasy" (62). When Nelly describes Heathcliff as a "regular black," she opens up a fantasy about him that can only be articulated in colonial imagery. Nelly sees Heathcliff as a potential prince: son of the emperor of China and an Indian queen, kidnapped by wicked sailors. Her use of oriental imagery constructs a fantasy scenario that maintains the social hierarchy but imagines a member of the servant class being able to attain dizzying class elevation. When Heathcliff returns home as a self-made man, he is characterized in terms that approximate to contemporary stereotypes of the "oriental despot": activated by blind passion and absolute ambition, acquiring power and wealth through conquest or appropriation, "assuming a semi-godlike status, taking the law into their own hands, and delighting in mastery almost to the point of torture" (64). Michie comments that such powerful and fantasizing responses to Heathcliff have often been replicated in critics' responses to *Wuthering Heights:* "a fantasy in which the 'dark other' functions as the fetish that when joined to its 'golden' half brings about completeness" (76). Identifying the way in which imperialist imagery imbues the novel "may help us recognize the moments when we as critics are likely to become caught up in stereotypical thinking about racial difference" (76).

Michie's moderate assertion is that there are unidentified traces of Irishness in the representation of Heathcliff and Rochester. In *Heathcliff and the Great Hunger* (1995), Terry Eagleton makes a much bolder claim. For Eagleton, Heathcliff *is* Ireland. "It is clear that this little Caliban has a nature on which nurture will never stick; and that is simply an English way of saying that he is quite possibly Irish" (3). Heathcliff dramatizes the hunger of the famine, the frustration and rebellion of the colonized. But "Heathcliff is oppressor and oppressed in one body, condensing in his own person the various stages of the Irish revolution" (19). As a child, he is an image of the famished immigrant or the rural proletariat chased out by the bourgeoisie. He becomes a landless laborer set to work in the Heights. He ends up "as a symbol of the constitutional nationalism of the Irish parliamentary party" (19). He enters the rural bourgeoisie and cheats smallholder Hindley out of his possession of his home. Finally, he "becomes a pitiless landlord" himself and sets about dispossessing the local landowner and taking over the Grange.

Eagleton admits, with disarming insouciance, that Heathcliff may be a
gypsy, a lascar, or another sort of alien; he is never identified as Irish, "and
even if he is the chronology is awry as far as the Famine goes. But in this essay
Heathcliff is Irish, and the chronology is not awry" (11). Eagleton's discussion
of Heathcliff comes in the context of a larger argument about Irish history.
Ireland, he says, has acted as England's unconscious: "the place where the
British were forced to betray their own principles, in a kind of negation or
inversion of their conscious beliefs" (9). Ireland is nature to England's culture
(although, as Eagleton comments, the terms can just as easily be reversed).
Thrushcross Grange "stands roughly speaking for culture—for nature worked
up, cultivated and thus concealed" (4). The Heights, by contrast, is a working
farm where the Earnshaws work their own soil. "Nature and *Wuthering
Heights* are names for [British] civility's sickening precariousness; for it too
had in its time to be wrested inch by inch from the soil, and is thus permanently capable of sliding back into it" (11).

Heathcliff and Catherine together represent a potential alternative to
both the Grange and the Heights, but the revolt fails for reasons that Eagleton explains partly in psychoanalytic terms:

> The Heathcliff-Catherine relationship is a classic case of the Lacanian "imagi-
> nary," an utter merging of identities in which the existence of each is wholly
> dependent on the existence of the other, to the exclusion of the world about
> them. But young Catherine must assume her allotted place in the symbolic
> order, leaving her anguished companion historically arrested in the imaginary
> register. Catherine and Heathcliff—an oppressed woman and an exploited farm
> labourer—have a chance, so it would seem, to inaugurate a form of relationship
> at odds with the instrumental economy of the Heights; but Catherine's rene-
> gacy prevents that relationship from entering upon material existence, just as it
> compels Heathcliff to run off, turn himself into a gentleman and appropriate
> the weapons of the ruling class in order to bring them low (18).

But, Eagleton comments, Heathcliff doesn't make too good a job of
turning himself into an English gentleman: "You can take Heathcliff out of
the Heights, but you can't take the Heights out of Heathcliff" (18). Heathcliff represents the rural revolution gone sour: he "is forced to nurture his idealism—his love for Catherine—in some quite separate inward sphere, in the
realms of myth, the imaginary and cherished childhood memory, while
behaving externally like any predatory English landlord; and this destructive
non-congruence of myth and reality has a long history in Ireland" (20).
Heathcliff is "forced to inflect his desire in terms which can only alienate it,"
and he dies, torn apart by that contradiction "of unappeasable longing" (20).
The revolutionary potential embodied in the partnership between Catherine
and Heathcliff is distanced into mythology; the Grange wins out over the
Heights, leaving behind only the lurking memory of "a bungled utopian

moment, a subjunctive mood which still haunts the hills and refuses to lie quiet in its grave" (21).

For Eagleton, *Wuthering Heights* encapsulates both a complex historical shift and an imagined anarchic eruption: nature threatens culture but the threat is ultimately fended off. Camille Paglia, in *Sexual Personae*, argues the opposite: the novel dramatizes a retreat through history back into nature. Paglia's provocative and flamboyant analysis emphasizes the incestuous and sadomasochistic impulses at work in *Wuthering Heights*. Like Stevie Davies, Paglia draws attention to Brontë's debt to Byron and sees the novel as a "family romance" full of tantrums and squabbles; "we witness or hear of whipping, slapping, thrashing, cuffing, wrenching, pinching, scratching, hair-pulling, gouging, kicking, trampling and the hanging of dogs" (449). But where Davies sees innocent children, Paglia sees sex and violence. Paglia suggests that the theme of incest is central to the Romantic consciousness, but while Shelley "swerves from the gross facts of primitive experience," Emily Brontë "completes the High Romantic quest for incest" (447). Incest may not be physically realized, but it is there, signaled by the "repetition of names or echoes of names: Heathcliff, Hindley, Hareton, Linton" (447) and represented in the "hermaphroditic doubling" of Heathcliff and Catherine. Their love, Paglia argues, may be called sexless, "mirrored self-love" (446), but Heathcliff and Catherine are engaged in a mad striving for an impossible union, in which they seek "sadomasochistic annihilation of their separate identities. Their desire to collapse into one another produces a giant spirit-body in the text, preventing other family members from attaining normal size" (448).

One of Paglia's central themes in *Sexual Personae* is the idea of "sexual metathesis," which she defines as "an artistic sex-change" in which the artist takes on a socially forbidden identity. Male Romantic poets hermaphroditize themselves "to seize the Delphic powers of feminine receptivity," but a female artist in this tradition, "sexually advantaged by birth, must extend her imperial reach in the other direction, toward the masculine" (454). In the process, Paglia argues, Emily Brontë revised the Romantic conception of nature, presenting it not as an inexhaustible well of fertility and renewal but as a stormy, destructive, masculine force, "*a nature without a mother*" (449). She illustrates this through analysis of Lockwood's dream, which, like Nancy Armstrong, she sees in terms of a rape, of both Lockwood and the reader. The books that Lockwood piles up are the barriers of rationalism, but "daemonic divination prevails" (453). But unlike Armstrong, Paglia emphasizes the violence of this scene. A child is tortured: "a man who would normally tenderly clasp or kiss a lady's hand tries to hack it off" (451). This scene, Paglia comments, "has a wonderful dream-logic. For example, the ghost's arm is a fir-bough because wild Catherine has been reabsorbed into nature . . . Lockwood therefore runs her wrist across jagged glass because he is *sawing a branch*" (452).

Like others before her, Paglia sees Heathcliff's identity as the central enigma posed by the novel: "*Wuthering Heights* goads the reader with questions: 'Is Mr. Heathcliff a man? If so, is he mad? And if not, is he a devil?' " (459). Paglia's answer is that Heathcliff "*is* a monster and not a man insofar as he is a woman transfigured into a hero" (459). Heathcliff, she argues, is Brontë's Byronic self-portrait: "a woman with a man's energy but without a man's potency" (455). Heathcliff is the means by which his creator fantasizes an escape from the constraints of her female body and sexual identity, but "she is in double relation to her hermaphrodite hero, in whom she is simultaneously present and absent" (459). Paglia suggests that the particular form of the narrative—its mediation through two limited narrators, the shifts of time and point of view—represents Brontë's "intercession between a real and fictive self" (459).

Like other critics, Paglia sees the second half of the novel as a "flattening" in which the text turns into a Victorian social novel and leaves its irrational Romanticism behind. But her answer to the question of *why* the novel suddenly reduces its time and scale is unique: "Emily Brontë's sexual metathesis into Heathcliff is inseparable from the incestuous-twin theme. Heathcliff is conceived as one end of an erotic polarity. If Brontë enters her novel as a man, then her feeling for the vanished Catherine is homosexual" (456).

Paglia's contention is that *Wuthering Heights* is not about brother-sister desire but about lesbian incest. She notes that the narrative lapses in energy after Catherine's death and says that she finds in many of Brontë's lyric poems a "delicate lesbian eroticism": "Brontë's poetry may reflect a premodern sexual state, inflamed but celibate" (456). The spirit that propels *Wuthering Heights,* Paglia argues, is the haunting memory of Brontë's eldest sister Maria, who died at the age of eight, but it is a Maria "erotically transformed": "in *Wuthering Heights,* Maria becomes the incestuous Romantic sister-spirit to Emily's male poetic genius" (457).

From the perspective of traditional literary scholarship, Eagleton and Paglia are both "taking liberties" with *Wuthering Heights.* But I think their essays may be seen as representative of a new freedom in literary criticism, which no longer sees it as the task of the critic simply to decode the text within its own terms. Eagleton and Paglia take Brontë's novel as a stimulus, a springboard for rethinking social and literary history in ways that are at once scholarly and inventive. Their adventurous readings testify to the elastic fascination offered by a text that "goads the reader with questions," hints tantalizingly at secrets to be discovered, dares the critic to attempt ever more ambitious readings. As long as literary criticism continues to ask new questions, *Wuthering Heights* will continue to invite, and elude, interpretation. In the words of Stevie Davies:

> It is this intransigent otherness which generations of readers have confronted with obsessive curiosity in *Wuthering Heights,* recognising there a language

which brings with it an aura of intense familiarity (as if it spoke of something we had once known and since forgotten) and a hoarding inwardness, impervious to the literary interpreter's immemorial desire to break codes and betray secrets. (*Emily Brontë*, 2)

Note

Page references in the text of this chapter are to the editions listed in the bibliography.

Selected Bibliography

Critical Anthologies

Allott, M., ed. *Emily Brontë: Wuthering Heights*. Casebook Series. Rev. ed. London: Macmillan, 1992.

————.*The Brontës: The Critical Heritage*. London: Routledge and Kegan Paul, 1974.

Barclay, J. *Emily Brontë Criticism: An Annotated Checklist*. Westport, Iowa: Meckler, 1980.

Bloom, H. *Emily Brontë: Wuthering Heights*. New York: Chelsea, 1987.

————. *Heathcliff.* New York: Chelsea, 1993.

Everitt, A., ed. *Wuthering Heights: An Anthology of Criticism*. London: Cass and Co., 1967.

Gregor, I., ed. *The Brontës: A Collection of Critical Essays*. Englewood Cliffs, N.J.: Prentice-Hall, 1970.

Letts, R. and W. Morris, eds. *A Wuthering Heights Handbook*. New York: Odyssey Press, 1961.

Moser, T., ed. *Wuthering Heights: Text, Sources and Criticism*. New York: Harcourt, Brace and World, 1962.

O'Neill, J., ed. *Critics on Charlotte and Emily Brontë*. London: Allen and Unwin, 1968.

Peterson, L., ed. *Wuthering Heights*. Case Studies in Contemporary Criticism Series. Boston: St. Martin's Press, 1992.

Petit, J-P., ed. *Emily Brontë: A Critical Anthology*. Harmondsworth: Penguin, 1973.

Sale, W. Jr, ed. *Wuthering Heights: An Authoritative Text with Essays in Criticism*. New York: Norton, 1963.

Stoneman, P., ed. *Wuthering Heights*. New Casebook Series. London: Macmillan, 1993.

Biography

Barker, J. *The Brontës*. London: Weidenfeld and Nicholson, 1994.

Blondel, E. *Emily Brontë: Experience spirituelle et création poétique*. Paris: Presses universitaires de France, 1955.

Chitham, E. *A Life of Emily Brontë*. Oxford: Basil Blackwell, 1987.

Frank, K. *A Chainless Soul: A Life of Emily Brontë*. Boston: Houghton Mifflin Co., 1990.

Gaskell, E. *The Life of Charlotte Brontë*. London: Smith, Elder and Co., 1857.

Gerin, W. *Emily Brontë*. Oxford: Clarendon Press, 1967.

Hewish, J., *Emily Brontë*. London: Macmillan, 1969.

Robinson, A. *Emily Brontë*. London: W. H. Allen, 1883.

Simpson, C., *Emily Brontë*. London: Country Life, 1929.

Spark, M., and D. Stanford. *Emily Brontë: Her Life and Work*. London: Owen, 1953.

Winnifrith, T. *The Brontës and Their Background*. London: Macmillan, 1973.

Poetry

Editions

Barker, J., ed. *The Brontës: Selected Poems*. London: Dent, 1985.

Chitham, E., and T. Winnifrith, eds. *Selected Brontë Poems*. Oxford: Basil Blackwell, 1984.

Davies, S., ed. *Poems by Charlotte, Emily Jane and Anne Brontë*. London: Folio Press, 1987.

Gezari, J., ed. *Emily Jane Brontë: The Complete Poems*. Harmondsworth: Penguin, 1992.

Hatfield, C., ed. *The Complete Poems of Emily Jane Brontë*. New York: Columbia University Press, 1941.

Lloyd Evans, B., ed. *The Poems of Emily Brontë*. London: Batsford, 1992.

Criticism

Davies, S. *Emily Brontë*. Hemel Hempstead: Harvester, 1988.

Donoghue, D. "Emily Brontë: The Latitude of Interpretation." In *The Interpretation of Narrative Theory and Practice,* ed. M. Bloomfield, 105–33. *Harvard English Studies I*. Cambridge, Mass.: Harvard University Press, 1970.

Grove, R. " 'It Would Not Do': Emily Brontë as Poet." In *The Art of Emily Brontë*, ed. A. Smith. 33–67. London: Vision Press, 1976.

Hardy, B. "The Lyricism of Emily Brontë." *The Art of Emily Brontë*, ed. A. Smith. 94–118. London: Vision Press, 1976.

Miles, R. "A Baby God: The Creative Dynamism of Emily Brontë's Poetry." in A. Smith, ed., *The Art of Emily Brontë*, 68–93. London: Vision Press, 1976.

Ratchford, F. *Gondal's Queen*. Austin: University of Texas Press, 1948.

Visick, M. *The Genesis of Wuthering Heights*. Hong Kong University Press, 1948.

Criticism 1848–1951

The best place to find contemporary reviews of *Wuthering Heights* is M. Allott, ed., *The Brontës: The Critical Heritage* (London: Routledge and Kegan Paul,

1974). There is a list of such reviews in T. Winnifrith, *The Brontës and their Background* (London: Macmillan, 1973). The following list of reviews, articles, and books on *Wuthering Heights* in the first hundred years after its publication is of necessity highly selective.

Arnold, M., "Haworth Churchyard" published in *Fraser's Magazine,* May, 1855, 327–30.

Cecil, D. *Early Victorian Novelists.* London: Constable, 1934.

Chase, R. "The Brontës or Myth Domesticated." In *Forms of Modern Fiction,* ed. W. Van O Connor, *102–19.* Minneapolis: University of Minnesota Press, 1948.

Chorley, H. Unsigned review of *Wuthering Heights* and *Agnes Grey. Athenaeum* 25 (December 1847): 1324–25.

Dallas, E. Unsigned review of *The Life of Charlotte Brontë. Blackwood's Magazine* (July 1857): 71–94.

Dobell, S. *"Currer Bell"* and *Wuthering Heights. Palladium* (September 1850): 161–75.

Ford, B. *Wuthering Heights. Scrutiny* 7 (1939): 375–89.

Kettle, A. *An Introduction to the English Novel.* London: Hutchinson, 1951.

Klingopulos, G. "The Novel as Dramatic Poem (11): *Wuthering Heights." Scrutiny* 14 (1946–7): 69–86.

Sanger, C. "The Structure of *Wuthering Heights." Hogarth Essays* 19. London: The Hogarth Press, 1926.

Schorer, M. "Fiction and the Matrix of Analogy." *Kenyon Review* 11 (1949): 539–60.

Swinburne, A. Review of Mary Robinson, *Emily Brontë. Athenaeum* 16 (June 1883): 62–3.

Traversi, D. *"Wuthering Heights* after a Hundred Years." *Dublin Review* 449 (1949): 154–68.

Ward, M. Preface to *Wuthering Heights.* London: Smith Elder, 1900.

Watson, M. *"Wuthering Heights* and the Critics." *The Trollopian* 3 (1948): 243–63.

Watson, M. "Tempest in the Soul: The Theme and Structure of *Wuthering Heights." Nineteenth Century Fiction* 4 (1949): 87–100.

Criticism 1951–75

Allott, M. "The Rejection of Heathcliff?" *Essays in Criticism* 8 (1958): 27–47.

Buckler, W. "Chapter VII of *Wuthering Heights:* A Key to Interpretation." *Nineteenth Century Fiction* 7 (1952): 51–55.

Buckley, V. "Passion and Control in *Wuthering Heights." Southern Review* 1 (1964): 5–23.

Craik, W. *The Brontë Novels.* London: Methuen, 1964.

Davies, C. "A Reading of *Wuthering Heights." Essays in Criticism* 19 (1969): 254–72.

Eagleton, T. *Myths of Power: A Marxist Study of the Brontës.* London: Macmillan, 1975.

Ewbank, I-S. *Their Proper Sphere: A Study of the Brontë Sisters as Early-Victorian Novelists.* London: Edward Arnold, 1966.

Hafley, J. "The Villain in *Wuthering Heights.*" *Nineteenth Century Fiction* 13 (1958–9): 199–215.

Hagan, J. "Control of Sympathy in *Wuthering Heights.*" *Nineteenth Century Fiction* 21 (1966–7): 305–23.

Kermode, F. *The Classic.* London: Faber and Faber, 1971.

Langman, F. H. "*Wuthering Heights.*" *Essays in Criticism* 15 (1965): 294–312.

Leavis, F. R. and Q. D. *Lectures in America.* London: Chatto and Windus, 1969.

McKibbon, R. "The Image of the Book in *Wuthering Heights.*" *Nineteenth Century Fiction* 15 (1960–1): 217–24.

Mathison, J. "Nelly Dean and the Power of *Wuthering Heights.*" *Nineteenth Century Fiction* 11 (1956–7): 106–29.

Miller, J. Hillis. *The Disappearance of God.* Cambridge, Mass.: Harvard University Press, 1963.

Moser, T. "What is the Matter with Emily Jane? Conflicting Impulses in *Wuthering Heights.*" *Nineteenth Century Fiction* 13 (1962–3): 1–19.

Thompson, W. "Infanticide and Sadism in *Wuthering Heights.*" *Proceedings of the Modern Language Association* 78 (1963): 69–74.

Van Ghent, D. "The Window Figure and the Two-Children Figure in *Wuthering Heights.*" *Nineteenth Century Fiction* 7 (1952): 189–97.

Criticism 1975–1995

Armstrong, N. *Desire and Domestic Fiction: A Political History of the Novel.* New York and Oxford: Oxford University Press, 1987.

Barreca, R. "The Power of Excommunication: Sex and the Feminine Text in Wuthering Heights." In *Sex and Death in Victorian Literature,* ed. R. Barreca, 227–40. Basingstoke: Macmillan, 1990.

Boone, J. A. *Tradition Counter Tradition: Love and the Form of Fiction.* Chicago and London: University of Chicago Press, 1987.

Brontë, E. *Wuthering Heights.* [includes 1847 text along with essays from five contemporary critical perspectives] Edited by L. H. Peterson. Boston: Bedford Books of St. Martin's Press, 1992.

Davies, S. *Emily Brontë.* Hemel Hempstead: Harvester Wheatsheaf, 1988.

Delamotte, E. C. *Perils of the Night: A Feminist Study of Nineteenth-Century Gothic.* New York and Oxford: Oxford University Press, 1990.

Eagleton, T. *Heathcliff and the Great Hunger: Studies in Irish Culture.* London and New York: Verso, 1995.

Gilbert, S. M. and S. Gubar. *The Madwoman in the Attic: The Woman Writer and the Nineteenth-Century Literary Imagination.* New Haven and London: Yale University Press, 1979.

Grove, R. *Emily Brontë's "Wuthering Heights."* South Melbourne: Sidney University Press, 1994.

Homans, M. *Bearing the Word: Language and Female Experience in Nineteenth-Century Women's Writing.* Chicago and London: Chicago University Press, 1986.

Kavanagh, J. H. *Emily Brontë*. Oxford: Basil Blackwell, 1985.

Knoepflmacher, U. C. *Emily Brontë: Wuthering Heights*. Cambridge: Cambridge University Press, 1989.

Matthews, J. T. "Framing in Wuthering Heights." *Texas Studies in Literature and Language* 27:1 (Spring 1985): 25–61.

Michie, E. B. *Outside the Pale: Cultural Exclusion, Gender Difference, and the Victorian Woman Writer*. Ithaca and London: Cornell University Press, 1993.

Miller, J. Hillis. *Fiction and Repetition: Seven English Novels*. Oxford: Basil Blackwell, 1982.

Mills, S.,et al. *Feminist Readings/Feminists Reading*. Hemel Hempstead: Harvester Wheatsheaf, 1989.

Paglia, C. *Sexual Personae: Art and Decadence from Nefertiti to Emily Dickinson*. London and New Haven: Yale University Press, 1990.

Pearce, L. *Reading Dialogics*. London: Edward Arnold, 1994.

Pykett, L. *Emily Brontë*. Basingstoke: Macmillan, 1989.

Index

♦

Allott, Miriam, 2, 115–16, 178, 198, 204
Angria, 2, 59
Armstrong, Nancy, 249–50, 254, 256, 259
Arnold, Matthew, 16–18, 89, 117, 178, 231
Athas, Daphne, 112
Auden, W. H., 77
Austen, Jane, 146, 161, 173, 250

Bakhtin, Mikhail, 244, 253
Balzac, Honoré de, 85
Barker, Juliet, 6–7, 48–51, 59, 115
Barreca, Regina, 247–48
Barthes, Roland, 89
Bellour, Raymond, 27
Bhabha, Homi, 257
Blackwood's magazine, 37, 120, 123
Blake, William, 145–46, 157, 173
Bloom, Harold, 245
Boone, Joseph, 249
Branwell, Elizabeth, 5, 6, 24, 30–31
Brontë, Anne, 5, 38, 44, 52–53; *Agnes Grey*,
    9, 33, 59, 77, 121; diary notes, 19,
    23–24, 49–50; poems, 2, 40, 47, 48,
    59, 77, 121; *Tenant of Wildfell Hall*, 16,
    34, 36, 38, 115
Brontë, Branwell, 2, 6, 17, 34, 36, 46,
    51–53, 59, 120–21, 124, 210, 214
Brontë, Charlotte, 5, 29, 39, 44, 64, 116,
    223, 234, 237–38; as critic of Emily's
    work, 7, 24–25, 36, 38, 47, 115; dis-
    covers Emily's poems, 6, 62, 77, 121;
    letters, 8, 9, 25

NOVELS

Jane Eyre, 16, 29, 33–34, 36, 85, 117,
    121–22, 124, 230, 256

Professor, The, 33–34, 121–22
Shirley, 42, 124
Villette, 26, 122, 224

poems, 2, 59, 77, 121
Brontë, Elizabeth, 5, 38–40, 44–46
Brontë, Emily: diary notes, 23–24, 48, 50;
    essays, 8, 11, 17, 26–27, 30–32

POEMS (LISTED BY FIRST LINE)

Ah! why, because the dazzling sun, 85,
    100–101
A little while, a little while, 85
All blue and bright, in glorious light,
    74–75
At such a time, in such a spot, 68–69,
    90
Aye, there it is! It wakes to-night, 23–24,
    41, 85–86
Cold in the earth, and the deep snow piled
    above thee, 78, 85, 106–107
Come, the wind may never again, 90
Come, walk with me, 90
Death, that struck when I was most confid-
    ing, 11, 81, 85, 95, 100
Enough of thought, philosopher, 10, 85,
    105
Fair sinks the summer evening now, 20
Fall, leaves, fall; die, flowers, away, 85, 90
Far away is the land of rest, 95
Geraldine, the moon is shining, 75
Heavy hangs the snowdrop, 39, 66–67, 77,
    85
How beautiful the earth is still, 85
How clear she shines! How quietly, 85,
    102–103

How do I love on summer nights, 29, 30, 41, 73
How still, how happy! Those are words, 80, 85
I am the only being whose doom, 9
I die; but when the grave shall press, 9
If grief for grief can touch thee, 85
I knew not 'twas so dire a crime, 76
I'm happiest when most away, 83, 90
In summer's mellow midnight, 82, 85
In the dungeon crypts idly did I stray, 85–86
In the earth, the earth, thou shalt be laid, 91
In the same place, when Nature wore, 67–68
I saw thee, child, one summer's day, 9, 43
I see around me tombstones grey, 23–24, 109
It is too late to call thee now, 105
May flowers are opening, 80
Mild the mist upon the hill, 21
No coward soul is mine, 6, 10, 79, 82, 86, 98, 105
O Dream, where art thou now?, 103
Often rebuked, yet always back returning, 85, 99
O God of heaven! the dream of horror, 9
On a sunny brae alone I lay, 45
O thy bright eyes must answer now, 44, 83, 85, 105
O wander not so far away!, 72
Sacred watcher, wave thy bells!, 72, 85
Shall Earth no more inspire thee, 82
Shed no tears o'er that tomb, 9
Silent is the House—all are laid asleep, 11, 45–46, 54, 65, 81, 86, 91–92
Sleep not, dream not; this bright day, 21
That wind, I used to hear it swelling, 9
The busy day has hurried by, 20
The evening passes fast away, 31, 73
The linnet in the rocky dells, 85, 90
The night is darkening round me, 77, 85, 93–94, 98
There let thy bleeding branch atone, 10
This summer wind, with thee and me, 71
Thou standest in the greenwood now, 70–71
Thy sun is near meridian height, 9, 21
Well hast thou spoken—and yet not taught, 11, 45, 85, 101
Were they shepherds, who sat all day, 10
When weary with the long day's care, 44, 82, 85
Yes, holy be thy resting-place, 74–75

Brontë, Maria (sister), 5, 38–39, 44–46, 260
Brontë, Maria (mother), 5–6, 38–39, 43–46
Brontë, Patrick, 5, 6, 31, 34–35, 38, 55–56, 120
Brontë Society, 118, 214, 239
Bunyan, John, 30
Byron, Lord George, 25, 37, 46, 110, 161, 167, 219, 230, 248, 259, 260

Carlyle, Thomas, 119–20
Cecil, Lord David, 17, 46–47, 118, 144–52, 177, 205
Chadwick, E. M., 59
Chase, Richard, 118
Chaworth, Mary, 37
childhood, 5, 12, 39, 40, 46, 65, 67, 83, 125, 207–10, 214–15, 230, 246–49
Chitham, Edward, 5, 6, 33–47, 51, 59
class relations in *Wuthering Heights,* 165, 169, 171–73, 211–14, 225–39, 250, 251–52, 253, 255–59
colonialism in *Wuthering Heights,* 256–59
Conrad, Joseph, 206
Constant, Benjamin, 28
Cowan Bridge School, 5, 43

Dallas, E. S., 114–15, 265
Davies, Stevie, 46–47, 49, 59, 109–12, 248–49, 251, 259, 260–61
deconstruction, 244
Dickens, Charles, 21, 144–48, 161–62, 165, 169, 173, 208–209, 214
Dickinson, Emily, 23, 78
Dingle, Herbert, 38, 48–49
Dobell, Sidney, 115
domestic realism in *Wuthering Heights,* 249–50, 252, 254, 260
Donoghue, Denis, 2, 60, 77–89
Dostoevsky, Fyodor, 210
Drew, Philip, 115

Eagleton, Terry, 178, 223–39, 255, 257–59, 260
Earle, John, 27
Edinburgh Review, 120
Eliot, George, 214
Eliot, T. S., 89, 125, 214
Emerson, Ralph Waldo, 55, 79

family relations in *Wuthering Heights,* 40, 224, 244–49, 251–52

feminism, 109–12, 178, 244, 245–52, 254–55
Fielding, Henry, 190
Foucault, Michel, 244, 250
Frank, Kathleen, 7, 55–58
Fraser's magazine, 37, 119–20, 123
French language and literature, 25, 27, 120, 122, 144
Freud, Sigmund, 177, 243, 246
Frith, Gill, 2, 242–61
Frost, Robert, 97

Gaskell, Elizabeth, 25, 28, 30–33, 47, 121, 145, 147, 214–15, 235
Gerin, Winifred, 7, 25, 32, 37, 47, 52–54
German language and literature, 6, 29, 37, 119, 121–22, 207
Gilbert, Sandra and Susan Gubar, 245–47, 250–51, 254, 255
Goethe, Johann, 120, 129
Gondal, 2, 5–6, 8, 20–21, 34, 37, 39–41, 48, 59, 62, 78, 84, 88, 90, 92–93
Gothic influences, 37, 41, 219–20, 252, 254–55
Greek language and literature, 6
Grove, Robin, 60

Hafley, James, 18, 178
Hardy, Barbara, 60, 90–108
Hardy, Thomas, 146–47, 212
Hatfield, C. W., 2, 59, 62, 73–74, 108
Haworth, 6, 20, 31, 35–36, 42, 53, 88, 121, 126, 128, 145, 161, 173, 177
Hawthorne, Nathaniel, 150, 212
Hazlitt, William, 84
Heaton family, 38
Heger family, 5–6, 24–25, 28, 30–32, 44, 52, 120–21
Hewish, John, 4–6, 19–32, 37, 47, 59
Hinkley, Laura, 63–64
Hobbes, Thomas, 230
Hoffmann, E. T. A., 25, 37–38, 121, 123–24, 129, 207
Hogg, James, 119, 207
Homans, Margaret, 246–47, 254
Howells, William Dean, 156
Hugo, Victor, 28, 122–23

incest, 177, 207, 219, 227, 248, 259–60
Ireland and the Irish, 34–35, 119, 256–58

James, Henry, 85, 204
Joyce, James, 93, 173

Kavanagh, James, 251–52, 254, 255
Keats, John, 84, 87–88, 95, 106
Kenner, Hugh, 89
Kermode, Frank, 2, 178, 216–22
Kettle, Arnold, 118, 161–73
Kingsley, Charles, 214, 257
Klingopulos, G. D., 170, 173, 205

Latin language and literature, 6
Law Hill School, 5, 19, 24, 34
Leavis, Queenie, 178, 205, 215, 233, 236, 239, 250
Lewes, G. H., 115
Liverpool, 132, 152, 160, 164, 256
Lytton, Lord Bulwer, 35

Marlowe, Christopher, 14–15, 18
Marxism, 230, 244, 251–52, 256
Mathison, Joan, 2, 177–97
Maurier, Daphne du, 17
Meier, T. K., 233, 239
Meyer, Leonard, 216
Michie, Elsie B., 256–57
Miles, Rosalind, 60
Miller, J. Hillis, 243–45, 254
Mills, Sara, 244
Milton, John, 84, 110–11, 245, 248–49, 251
Montegut, Emile, 116
More, Hannah, 119–20

Nerval, Walter de, 25
Newby, Thomas, 35, 121
Nicholls, Arthur, 23, 39
Nussey, Ellen, 31, 40, 42, 53, 201

Orientalism, 256–57

Paglia, Camille, 259–60
Pascal, Blaise, 116
Pearce, Lynne, 253
Peterson, Linda H., 244
Petyt, K. M., 36, 47
Plato, 41
polyphony, 252–53
post-structuralism, 244
Proust, Marcel, 89, 146

psychoanalysis, 244, 246–47, 251–52, 254, 258
Pykett, Lyn, 252–53, 254–55

Ratchford, Fanny, 8, 17, 60–61, 63, 75–76
Raverat, Gwen, 214
religion, 1, 5, 8–18, 21–23, 26, 29, 70, 80, 99–100, 149, 171
Robinson family of Thorp Green, 6, 51, 116
Robinson, Mary, 5, 35, 47, 116
Roe Head School, 5, 24
Roscoe, W., 116
Rossetti, Christina, 17
Rossetti, Dante Gabriel, 9
Rousseau, Jean-Jacques, 162
Royce, Josiah, 89

sadomasochism, 11, 259
Saintsbury, George, 116
Sand, George, 122–23
Sanger, C. P., 117, 132–43
Schiller, Friedrich von, 119
Scott, Sir Walter, 35, 37, 119, 125–29, 146, 211–12, 215
Shakespeare, William, 17–18, 37, 80, 84, 88, 122, 170, 178, 182, 206–10, 221, 237
Shelley, Percy Bysshe, 23, 37, 40–41, 45–46, 259
Shorter, Clement, 23, 32, 59
Sidgwick family, 19
Simpson, Charles, 5
Sinclair, May, 215
Skelton, Sir John, 116
Smith, George, 52–53, 60, 116
Sophocles, 178
Southey, Robert, 119, 129
Stephen, Sir Leslie, 116

Stoneman, Patsy, 2, 42, 244
Swinburne, A. C., 116

Taylor family, 24–25, 30–31
Tchekov, Anton, 204
Tennyson, Lord Alfred, 24, 29
Thackeray, William Makepeace, 144–45
Thompson, F. M. L., 235, 239
Tieck, Johan Ludwig, 120, 124, 129
Tolstoy, Leo, 209
Trollope, Anthony, 137, 145–46
Turgenev, Ivan, 122
Tuzet, Hélène, 83

uncanny, the, 13, 41, 44, 129, 156, 187, 204, 207, 220–22, 243

Visick, Mary, 31, 35, 40, 59, 60, 62–76

Wagner, Richard, 9
Ward, Mary, 116–17, 119–29
Watson, Melvin, 117–18, 151–60, 177
Watt, Ian, 249
Webb, Mary, 42
Weightman, William, 20, 30, 38, 51
Weil, Simone, 29
Wemyss Reid, Sir Thomas, 116
Wheelwright family, 29, 32
Whipple, E. W., 115
Williams, W. S., 52, 55
Wilson, David, 172–73, 235, 239
Wise, Thomas, 59
Wooler, Margaret, 24
Woolf, Virginia, 17–18, 116–17, 130–31, 173
Wordsworth, William, 37, 43–44, 46, 84, 106, 119, 207

Yeats, William Butler, 89